SHRINES, RELICS, AND SAINTS

A volume in the series

Medieval Societies, Religions, and Cultures
Edited by M. Cecilia Gaposchkin and Anne E. Lester

A list of titles in this series is available at cornellpress.cornell.edu.

SHRINES, RELICS, AND SAINTS

CHRISTIAN SANCTUARIES FROM LATE ANTIQUITY THROUGH THE MIDDLE AGES

André Vauchez
Translated by
Michael F. Cusato
Foreword by
M. Cecilia Gaposchkin and
Anne E. Lester

CORNELL UNIVERSITY PRESS
Ithaca and London

Original French-language edition, *Sanctuaires chrétiens d'Occident, IVe–XVIe siècle*, by André Vauchez, © Les Éditions du Cerf, 2021

English translation by Michael F. Cusato

Copyright © 2025 by Cornell University

All rights reserved. Except for brief quotations in a review, this book, or parts thereof, must not be reproduced in any form without permission in writing from the publisher. For information, address Cornell University Press, Sage House, 512 East State Street, Ithaca, New York 14850. Visit our website at cornellpress.cornell.edu.

First published 2025 by Cornell University Press

Library of Congress Cataloging-in-Publication Data

Names: Vauchez, André, author. | Cusato, Michael F., translator.
Title: Shrines, relics, and saints : Christian sanctuaries from late antiquity through the Middle Ages / André Vauchez, translated by Michael F. Cusato.
Other titles: Sanctuaires chrétiens d'Occident. English
Description: Ithaca [New York] : Cornell University Press, 2026. | Series: Medieval societies, religions, and cultures | Includes bibliographical references and index.
Identifiers: LCCN 2025016429 (print) | LCCN 2025016430 (ebook) | ISBN 9781501776700 (hardcover) | ISBN 9781501786211 (paperback) | ISBN 9781501785146 (pdf) | ISBN 9781501785153 (epub)
Subjects: LCSH: Christian shrines—Europe, Western—History—To 1500. | Christian pilgrims and pilgrimages—Europe, Western—History—To 1500. | Christian art and symbolism—Europe, Western. | Europe, Western—Church history—Middle Ages, 600–1500.
Classification: LCC BX2320.5.E85 V3813 2021 (print) | LCC BX2320.5.E85 (ebook)
LC record available at https://lccn.loc.gov/2025016429
LC ebook record available at https://lccn.loc.gov/2025016430

CONTENTS

Series Editors' Foreword vii
Translator's Note ix
Preface xi

Introduction: What Is a Sanctuary? 1

PART I: THE CHRISTIANIZATION OF PLACE AND THE SACRALIZATION OF CHRISTIANITY

1. Late Antiquity and the Early Middle Ages 17

PART II: THE SACRED AND ITS INTEGRATION INTO EUROPEAN SPACES

2. From the Middle Ages to the Renaissance 59

PART III: THE FUNCTIONS, LIFE, AND ROLE OF SANCTUARIES

3. Typologies: The Different Kinds of Sanctuaries 125

4. The Life of Sanctuaries 157

5. Capitalizing on the Sacred 207

Conclusion 245

Bibliography 251
Index 275

Series Editors' Foreword

We are delighted to bring André Vauchez's book *Sanctuaires chrétiens d'Occident, IVe–XVIe siècle* to an English-speaking audience. Vauchez is one of the foremost scholars of medieval saints, sanctity, heresy, and spirituality of his generation. Moreover, his numerous books and articles on the religious beliefs and practices of the medieval West have profoundly shaped Anglo-American scholarship. *Sainthood in the Later Middle Ages*, originally published in French as *La sainteté en Occident aux derniers siècles du Moyen Âge: D'après les procès de canonisation et les documents hagiographiques* in 1981, and translated into English in 1987, remains the fundamental touchstone for ongoing scholarship on sanctity and saint-making. Two additional monographs, *The Laity in the Middle Ages: Religious Beliefs and Devotional Practices* (1993; translated in 2010) and *Francis of Assisi: The Life and Afterlife of a Medieval Saint* (2009; translated in 2012), were likewise translated into English and exerted a shaping force on Anglo-American and international scholarship.

Vauchez's prolific studies of the laity and lay devotion helped scholars to grapple with the actions and ideas of laypeople in relation to the institutional Church and in affecting their own spiritual practices. Similarly, his immensely compelling biography of Francis of Assisi analyzed the founder of the Franciscan order in his local religious and social world in the early thirteenth century but then moved beyond this by asking readers to reflect on the life lived by the *man* through the lens of the afterlives of the saint spanning from the thirteenth to the twentieth centuries. He is quite simply one of the most important scholars of medieval religion, who brings his capacious intellect to all dimensions of medieval spiritual life. It is an honor for us to bring this, his most recent book, to an English reading audience in the Medieval Societies, Religions, and Cultures Series.

This book, about Christian sanctuaries from late antiquity through the Middle Ages and well beyond into the 1600s, is at once a broad synthesis and a work reflective of original scholarship. Taking as his starting point the cult of relics in the medieval world, Vauchez traces the role that the *locus sanctus* holds in relation to rituals and spiritual experiences. He focuses in particular on the dynamics of sacred space and how the space of the sanctuary—where holiness was located, contained, and accessible—provided the conceptual and physical locations of Christian spiritual practice and belief. Sanctuary itself is both a concept and a location that Vauchez traces over the long history of the Christian Church in the West, from the first shrine located at Golgotha and the site of the Holy Sepulcher that marked Christ's tomb, to the local shrines that dotted the early medieval world, through the rise of Marian devotion that would come to unite Christendom. The study is, in short, a *tour-de-force* of key sites and practices that defined medieval Christian belief from between 300 and 1600, a study simultaneously of sacred objects (relics and tombs) at the heart of the holy space, the miracles preformed at shrines, and pilgrimage as a practice that united Christians in the West. He demonstrates that sanctuaries were the fundamental spaces that brought the faithful together and created the living Christian community, which would in turn shape a sense of European Christian identity that was both inclusionary and exclusionary.

We are deeply grateful to André Vauchez for bringing this project to the series, and to Michael Cusato for his deft translation. Additionally, we thank Abigail Christesen for producing new and accurate versions of the maps, and for Pelia Werth for locating the images included in this version of the book.

M. Cecilia Gaposchkin and Anne E. Lester

Translator's Note

André Vauchez uses the term *sanctuaire/sanctuaires* to describe the subject of this book. The word itself can be rendered in English alternately as either "shrine" or "sanctuary." Because the word "shrine" has broader connotations in contemporary usage and can also refer to various "shrine churches"—that is to say, large parochial establishments, often in urban settings in the United States, that are centers of worship and administer the sacraments and the celebration of various popular devotional practices—the translator has opted to retain, in most cases, the word "sanctuary" to describe the various kinds of sacred spaces described throughout this volume. Moreover, this choice likewise reflects, etymologically, the sacred nature (*sanctus*) of these various sites. Finally, it should be noted that the entirety of the present translation has been thoroughly reviewed and nuanced by the editorial director at Cornell University Press, Mahinder Kingra, in accord with the stylistic preferences of the press.

Preface

                    This book emerges from two personal experiences. The first goes back to the years of my youth; and the second, to my journeys throughout Italy, where I lived for eighteen years.

    Beginning in 1947, I spent my summers in a small region in the Jura from where my father's family had come. Along with a good part of the population of the surrounding villages, I took part in the feast of Saint Sorlin, which was celebrated on the first Sunday of August. No need to bother looking for the name in the liturgical calendar! It is, in fact, nothing more than a local deformation of the name of Saint Saturnin, who had been martyred in Toulouse in the third century of the Christian era. I have no idea as to when or how his cult arrived in these central eastern mountains; nor would the people who came here on pilgrimage every year; nor probably even would their pastor. We gathered in the morning at the crossroads in Lieffenans, a little elevation rising above the Ain valley, and from there, we followed the path up Mount Saint-Sorlin, through the forest, to a chapel located at the very top, not far from the ruins of a castle destroyed at the end of the fifteenth century during the invasion of Franche-Comté by the troops of Louis XI. But before arriving there, we stopped for a moment in front of a statue of the Virgin Mary etched with silver lettering so that we could sing a song and recite a few prayers. We then entered the chapel where the priests celebrated Mass for the intentions of those present and for the prosperity of the inhabitants of the surrounding villages. At the entrance, there was a rather simple depiction, carved into stone, of the martyrdom of Saint "Sorlin" being dragged by a bull through the streets of a town. This was the creation of a hermit drawn up at the beginning of the nineteenth century who had lived there with his wife and a small community for a few years. In 1834, he had built a chapel upon the ruins of the first church, as well as a small adjacent building.

    After the Mass, someone rang the bell in the tower, and its tolling echoed throughout the whole valley. We next took out of our backpacks a meal that had been prepared beforehand, along with a nice bottle, and everyone exchanged the latest news about our families, the harvests, and the weather before dispersing in the afternoon and going back down the same path, while the younger ones wandered off into the woods. But was this really a sanctuary? The child (and then the adolescent) that I was never asked such a question. From these events, I especially retain the memory of an atmosphere that was both reflective and heartwarming.

A few years later, after completing my studies in history and undertaking some research, I discovered that the chapel of Saint-Sorlin—the goal of this annual pilgrimage—had been, over the centuries, the "mother church" of this region; that is, it was the place where its inhabitants had to go in order to be baptized and where they were then buried. There are many such churches throughout Italy: they are called *pievi*—a word that comes from the Latin *plebs* (the people). Once these had been abandoned, they often became shrines for popular religiosity. It seems that the same thing happened here in this remote corner of the Jura. Indeed, beginning around the end of the seventeenth century, the neighboring villages sent numerous petitions to the local authorities in order to obtain the right to have their own church and cemetery, while underscoring just how hard it was, during the winter, to haul their dead all the way up to Saint-Sorlin on paths that were covered with snow or ice. They ended up getting what they wanted: by the end of the French Revolution, all the surrounding churches possessed a bell tower and the full spectrum of parish rights. But the memory of the old mother church, stripped of its prerogatives and having fallen into ruins during the revolutionary period, had to survive in people's memories; it is probably this memory that explains the birth and persistence of the pilgrimage there up to the present. It only lacked relics. But in 1987, the remains of the hermit who had built the present chapel were brought to Saint-Sorlin, having been conveniently—in the Middle Ages, one would say "miraculously"—rediscovered in the Auvergne within a monastery. The bishop of Saint-Claude arranged for their translation, and a scholarly monk wrote and then published a biography of this saintly man. Only miracles were still lacking, but it does not appear that any have been forthcoming since then. And so it has remained ever since....[1]

---

1. René Charrier, *L'ermite de Saint-Sorlin, Joseph-Élie Simonin (1792–1856): Contribution à l'histoire religieuse du Jura et de la Congrégation du Saint-Esprit* (Langres: Éditions Dominique Guéniot, 2000).

Much later—but more decisively for me—was the second experience that I had in Italy during the years while I was director of the École Française de Rome (1995-2003). Having devoted myself, during the previous decades, to the history of sanctity in the Middle Ages, I had become aware of the fact that this notion had been incarnated in various places, many of which had afterward become sanctuaries frequented by pilgrims searching for healings and miracles. There have been important historical works on pilgrimages in the medieval and modern periods. However, they often had a monographic character or have been more interested in the pilgrims and their journeys than in the motivations that might have shaped their choice of going to this or that shrine. In Italy, I discovered particularly favorable ground for this kind of research in that various other historians were similarly interested in this same problematic, beginning with Sofia Boesch Gajano from the University of Rome III, whose studies concerning the impact of holiness upon places have very much influenced me. Moreover, without any pretense of being exhaustive, I will also mention here Giorgio Cracco, Giorgio Otranto, Roberto Rusconi, Anna Benvenuti, and, last but not least, the late Mario Sensi, who had both a lived experience of the area (having investigated for many years the sanctuaries of Umbria) and an exceptional knowledge of the archives of this region.

Starting in 1996, with these and many other colleagues from Italian universities and their teams of researchers (whom I cannot possibly list here given their number), we were able to unite our efforts and we laid down the foundations of a vast program of research on Christian shrines within Italy during the medieval and modern periods. The outcomes were as abundant as they were varied: an inventory of the relevant sanctuaries with a database (soon welcomed by an institute associated with the Ministry of Cultural Patrimony); various colloquia, the proceedings of which have all been published and that have allowed us to deepen and enrich the focus of our inquiry; and finally a series in which a dozen volumes on Christian shrines in different regions of Italy have already appeared.

This research has continued after the conclusion of the program in 2003, as several later publications attest, with respect to sanctuaries dedicated to Saint Michael and Saint Nicholas in both France and Italy. It was not long after this that these studies were coordinated with efforts being led by Catherine Vincent, professor of the History of the Middle Ages at the University of Paris-Nanterre, who had entered the fray with a worthy team undertaking similar inquiries into shrines in

France. This collaboration led to the creation of an International Association of Research on Sanctuaries, which has a bright future ahead of it. To all those whom I have named or mentioned, I wish to express my gratitude for what they have taught me, hoping that they will find in this volume an accounting, albeit premature, of at least something of the spirit of what has animated our common investigations. As to my readers, they will not be surprised, in light of this preface, by the importance that Italy holds, next to France, in this history of sanctuaries within a European perspective.

Introduction
What Is a Sanctuary?

The word "sanctuary" in the current use of the term is invested with meanings as varied as they are imprecise. The term can designate both a religious structure, like the Basilica of Our Lady of Lourdes, or a refuge for certain animals or even a protected zone for nuclear deterrence. Behind these rich and multiple meanings, one can, however, discern a few common themes, beginning with the notion of space: a sanctuary—any kind of sanctuary—is part of a delimited space inside of which are found objects or persons considered especially important and valuable in a given society. Such is the case with children, for example, which explains why schools in France are considered "sanctuaries." The notion of sanctuary evokes ideas of protection and of the sacred: it is a particular space that safeguards those found therein or those who enter them searching for protection or salvation.

The sanctuaries discussed in this volume correspond in large measure to this description. Fustel de Coulanges in *La Cité ancienne* (1864) and Émile Durkheim in *Formes élémentaires de la vie religieuese* (1912) both stressed that "the sacred" constitutes an essential dimension of religious reality insofar as one of the functions of religion is to conceive of, organize, and control space: in short, to ensure the ritualized administration of the territory founded on the distinction between the sacred and the secular.[1] But the sacred also includes other aspects as well. In 1917, Rudolf Otto published a foundational work in which he showed that the sacred presents itself under a form both frightening and fascinating.[2] The two aspects seem contradictory but are simultaneously present in what he calls "the numinous" (from the Latin word *numen*, which refers to the active power of the divinity), the experience that allows believers to be aware both of the existence of a reality beyond themselves and also of their own limits. Later, Mircea Eliade deepened the study of this idea by relating it to "hierophanies": those manifestations of the sacred at the root of the myths, rites, and symbols of countless cultures.[3] More recently still, the works of Julien Ries—taking a philosophical and anthropological approach—emphasized the sacred as the constitutive experience of the human, whereas Alphonse Dupront studied its forms and expressions in the history of Europe.[4] As even these few references make clear, the concept of the sacred is hardly a marginal question, even if it has only recently captured the attention of historians of Christianity.

This book explores the history of Christian sanctuaries from the end of antiquity through the Renaissance and early modern period. The Middle Ages will, of course, be at the very center of this study, but it would be somewhat artificial to limit the discussion to this period alone, for it was in late antiquity that the network of Christian shrines and holy sites was first established, and only in the middle of the sixteenth century did the nature of these sanctuaries appreciably change with the enactment of the decrees of the Council of Trent (1545–63). The Protestant Reformation constituted an important step in this

---

1. Fustel de Coulanges, *The Ancient City: A Study on the Religions, Laws and Institutions of Ancient Greece and Rome*, trans. Numa Denis (Garden City, NY: Doubleday, 1956); Émile Durkheim, *The Elementary Forms of the Religious Life: A Study in Religious Sociology*, trans. Joseph Ward Swain (London: G. Allen & Unwin, 1915).

2. Rudolf Otto, *The Idea of the Holy: An Inquiry into the Non-Rational Factor in the Idea of the Divine and Its Relation to the Rational*, trans. John W. Harvey (New York: Oxford University Press, 1958). Originally published in German as *Das Heilige* (Gotha: C. H. Beck, 1917).

3. Mircea Eliade, *The Sacred and the Profane: The Nature of Religion*, trans. Willard R. Trask (New York: Harcourt, Brace & World, 1959). Originally published in French as *Le sacré et le profane* (Paris: Gallimard, 1957).

4. Julien Ries, *Les Chemins du sacré dans l'histoire* (Paris: Éditions Aubier, 1992); and Alphonse Dupront, *Du sacré: Croisades et pèlerinage. Images et langages* (Paris: Gallimard, 1987). On the influence of the social and human sciences to the study of the sacred, see Françoise Paul-Lévy and Marion Segaud, *Anthropologie de l'espace* (Paris: Centre de création industrielle / Centre Georges Pompidou, 1984); Michel Carrier, *Penser le sacré: Les sciences humaines et l'invention du sacré* (Montreal: Liber, 2005); and Hans Joas, *Les pouvoirs du sacré* (Paris: Seuil, 2020).

process insofar as it challenged the very notions of sacred spaces and places. But in countries or regions that were steadfast in their Roman Catholicism, the real changes in this sphere occurred only at the end of the sixteenth or the beginning of the seventeenth centuries. This inquiry does not extend beyond the sixteenth century, although there are now several important studies of Christian sanctuaries in the modern period.[5]

In Search of a Definition

The Catholic Church did not precisely define what a sanctuary is until the twentieth century. The Concordat of 1929 between Italy and the Holy See first labeled certain major churches, such as Saint Peter's Basilica in Rome and the Basilica of Saint Francis of Assisi, as sanctuaries, granting them special status, recognized by both parties. And it was only in 1983 that canon law officially codified the meaning of a sanctuary: "The term sanctuary refers to a church or other sacred place to which the faithful, for a particular reason of piety, go in large numbers on pilgrimage with the approval of the local Ordinary."[6]

The ecclesiastical hierarchy had been interested in sanctuaries in previous centuries, as the following pages make clear, but had long refused to officially recognize the existence of what were essentially charismatic institutions, insofar as for them every church in which the Eucharist was celebrated on a consecrated altar constituted a sanctuary. Thus, pastoral visits of bishops in their dioceses rarely mentioned the existence of holy places and, in most regions, do not come to the attention of ecclesiastical authorities until the seventeenth century. By the

---

5. In French alone, these include: Dominique Julia, "Sanctuaires et lieux sacrés à l'époque moderne," in *Lieux sacrés, lieux de culte, sanctuaires*, ed. André Vauchez (Rome: École Française de Rome, 2000), 241-95 ; Dominique Julia, *Le voyage aux saints: Les pèlerinages dans l'Occident moderne (XVe–XVIIIe siècle)* (Paris: Seuil, 2016); Philippe Boutry, ed., *Reine au Mont-Auxois: Le culte et le pèlerinage de sainte Reine, des origines à nos jours* (Paris: Éditions du Cerf, 1997); Philippe Boutry and Dominique Julia, eds., *Pèlerins et pèlerinages dans l'Europe moderne (XVIe–XVIIIe siècle)* (Rome: École Française de Rome, 2000); Marie-Hélène Froeschlé-Chopard, *Itinéraires pèlerins de l'ancienne Provence* (Marseilles: La Thune, 2004); Nicolas Balzamo, *Les miracles dans la France du XVIe siècle* (Paris: Les Belles Lettres, 2014); and Nicolas Balzamo, "Image miraculeuse: Le mot, le concept et la chose," in *L'image miraculeuse dans le christianisme occidental: Moyen Age – Temps modernes*, ed. Nicolas Balzamo and Estelle Leutrat (Tours: Presses universitaires François Rabelais, 2020), 15-41.

6. *Codice di Diritto canonico* (Rome: Unione editori cattolici italiani, 1983), § 1230; Lamberto de Etcheverria, *Code de droit canonique annoté* (Paris: Éditions du Cerf; Bourges: Tardy, 1989), 669.

twentieth century, however, clerics were obliged to admit that, in addition to churches (places that had been consecrated through specific rituals and dedicated to liturgical worship), there also existed sanctuaries associated with holy figures and with places of pilgrimage where the laity deliberately went seeking a particular outcome. Moreover, the canonical definition cited above complements what might appear to be static in the term "sanctuary." As Dominique Julia has observed, this gives value to the "place-term" without accounting for the "going toward," and it says nothing explicitly about the extent to which visiting these sacred sites is closely associated with intercessory prayer, pilgrimage, and miracles.[7]

After Vatican II—which emphasized the Church as the people of God making their way forward in this world—a definition of sanctuary rooted in the "gathering of people" became possible as shown in the juridical definition of 1983. Sanctuaries did not exist without pilgrimage, and pilgrimage did not exist without piety—that is, the search for God or some form of transcendence—nor without the authorization of the local bishop. On this last point, the historian should remain cautious given that, since late antiquity, a number of sanctuaries had been created by the laity or by monks without any ecclesiastical authorities playing a role in their creation.

Drawing on historical and anthropological perspectives, a sanctuary can be defined as the spatial setting where the Invisible has been made manifest. It is distinguishable from churches and other religious buildings by

- the presence of one or several objects considered to be sacred that inspire a particular devotion (relics, a tomb, an *ymage* or icon);
- the memory of miracles that occurred there, attested to by the presence of votive offerings (ex-voto);
- an enthusiastic visitation, at least once a year, taking the form of pilgrimage that attracts a gathering of people, often from distant places outside of diocesan boundaries.

Sanctuaries are distinct from other religious edifices because they possess specific characteristics. Churches are consecrated through the

---

7. Julia, "Sanctuaires et lieux sacrés à l'époque moderne," 242–50.

rituals performed by the clergy, and in some circumstances, consecration can likewise be annulled by a liturgical ceremony—execration—that returns the monument to the realm of the profane.[8] Holy sites and sanctuaries, on the contrary, possess an intrinsic sacredness, as pilgrims who visit them hope to acquire special graces there. In practice, it is not easy to escape from the labyrinth of attempting to categorize religious edifices, since most Christian sanctuaries are simultaneously also places of worship. Moreover, the Catholic hierarchy confused matters at the end of the nineteenth century by granting the title of "sanctuary" or "basilica" to large churches that, for various reasons, they wanted to honor and bring to the attention of the faithful. And some parish churches and cathedrals have also served as shrines at given moments in their history, particularly when important relics were placed there to attract supplicant crowds.

Apart from this extended confusion over definitions, the study of the history of sanctuaries has been difficult owing to the sparsity of documentary sources. As Alain Guerreau has written: "It is essential to acknowledge the silence of medieval texts on spaces and objects that specifically had the function of structuring social space: churches, relics, cemeteries. These objects 'spoke for themselves,' so to speak, and did not give rise, except in the rarest of circumstances, to any abstract development."[9] Certainly, the role of the great shrines in the spiritual lives of the faithful is attested in the various accounts of voyages (to the Holy Land or to Rome, Santiago de Compostela, and Notre-Dame of Loreto), hagiographical texts—as, for example, the Lives of Saint Rainier († 1160) and Saint Bona († 1207) of Pisa or that of Blessed Facio of Cremona († 1272) in the twelfth and thirteenth centuries—as well as in the collections of miracles and in literary sources such as the *Canterbury Tales*, about the city and cathedral where the relics of Thomas à Becket († 1170) were venerated, or the autobiography of the English pilgrim Margery Kempe († ca. 1438), who made the rounds of the sanctuaries of Christendom at the beginning of the fifteenth century.[10] A number

---

8. Isabelle Saint-Martin, "Les églises sont des lieux consacrés plus que des lieux sacrés," *Le Monde de la Bible*, no. 233 (2020): 72–76.

9. Alain Guerreau, "Structure et évolution: Les représentations de l'espace dans le haut Moyen Age occidental," in *Uomo e spazio nell'Alto Medioevo* (Spoleto: CISAM, 2003), 91–115; Anna Benvenuti, "Il santuario: Definizioni, metodo di studio, significato storico," in *Andare per santuari*, ed. Giorgio Cracco and Paolo Cozzo (Aosta: Bertoncello, 2006).

10. Clarissa Atkinson, *Mystic and Pilgrim: The Book and the World of Margery Kempe* (Ithaca, NY: Cornell University Press, 1985).

of documents emanating from the papal chancery can help as well, as do testaments from the thirteenth and fourteenth centuries, depending on the region. But, on the whole, few written traces survive relating to the organization and function of local sanctuaries (which were the most numerous), and iconographical sources, however important, are not sufficient to fill in the gaps.

To understand the role of sanctuaries, it is important to take stock of their historical dimension and their often-lengthy existence. As Alphonse Dupront has written: "Sacred places . . . living, surviving, or memorialized speak about choices regarding their physical establishment, their centuries-old loyalties, their endurance, sometimes their stubbornness to endure . . . eminently stable establishments. Stability is a sacred force. A sacred force, just like the faithful succession of generations."[11] But a sanctuary is not only an island of focused sacrality, set within a particular landscape through a ritualizing process. It is also a space traversed by way of narrative, the collective memory of actors with particular aims. Language and writing played key roles in elaborating a sanctuary's founding legends, allowing for the reconstruction of the connection between the pilgrim and the saint venerated there, as well as the establishment of the place where that cult was sustained.

The difficulty encountered by the historian of Christianity in understanding the appearance of sanctuaries and following their evolution across time results from the diversity of terminology used over the centuries to refer to them. The word *sanctuarium* does not appear in the New Testament, and over the first three centuries of the Christian era, there is no particular term that designated the place where Christians gathered. Forced into hiding during times of persecution, Christian communities did not congregate in so-called churches but rather in homes or other locales where they could worship without running too many risks.[12] Since the beginning of the fourth century, when Constantine inaugurated a regime of tolerance with respect to the religion of the Christ, open-air religious structures began to proliferate. The most common type of sanctuary in this period was a simple commemorative monument called a *martyrium*.[13] The word *sanctuarium* appears in the

---

11. Dupront, *Du sacré*, 90–91.
12. Robert A. Markus, "How on Earth Could Places Become Holy? Origins of the Christian Ideas of Holy Places," *Journal of Early Christian Studies* 2 (1994): 257–70.
13. André Grabar, *Martyrium: Recherches sur le culte des reliques et l'art chrétien antique* (Paris: Collège de France, 1948).

Latin of Christians from the fourth century in the texts of late antiquity, and in particular in Jerome's Latin translation of the Bible, the Vulgate, where the word *sanctuarium* refers to the Temple of Jerusalem. By contrast, Gregory the Great († 604) used it to refer to the relics of saints, and soon the term served to designate a church's treasury and, more specifically, a treasury of relics, which popes, bishops, and some large abbeys began to establish. One of the most famous is the shrine known as the Sancta Sanctorum, a kind of private chapel for the Roman pontiff, located near Saint John Lateran, where the heads of the apostles Peter and Paul could be venerated, as could the *acheiropoiete* (not made by human hands) icon of Christ, said to have been painted by Saint Luke.[14] In the Carolingian period, different rulers likewise established treasuries of relics in their palace chapels, or in the churches or monasteries under their authority.

In time the term *sanctuarium* came to be applied to any structure that contained relics: tomb, altar, reliquary, or, within a church, that most sacred part of the building where the relics of the saints were kept. Starting in the tenth century, the word evolved to refer to the delimited area circumscribing church buildings, around which the faithful could process (in a ceremony known as the *circuitus ecclesiae*), and also to cemeteries that developed in the immediate vicinity of these holy places.[15] Finally, by extension, certain spaces considered sacred due to supernatural intervention, such as the grotto where Michael the Archangel appeared on Mount Gargano in Apulia, also came to be called sanctuaries. In such cases, sacredness was conferred on a place by way of the manifestation of a supernatural power, described in the texts of the period as a revelation.

Beginning in the fourteenth century, *sanctuarium* began to be used closer to the way it is now understood. For example, it was said that Saint Birgitta of Sweden († 1373) had made a long journey to the south of Italy to visit the sanctuaries of Saint Thomas the Apostle in Ortona,

---

14. Bruno Galland, *Les authentiques de reliques du Sancta Sanctorum* (Vatican City: Bibliotheca Apostolica Vaticana, 2004); Guido Cornini, "'Non est in toto sanctior orbe locus': Collecting Relics in Early Medieval Rome," in *Saints, Relics and Devotion in Medieval Europe*, ed. Martina Bagnoli, Holger A. Klein, C. Griffith Mann, and James Robinson (Cleveland: Cleveland Museum of Art, 2011), 69–78.

15. Michel Lauwers, "Sanctuaires, liturgie et rayonnement du sacré dans le bassin occidental de la Méditerranée," in *Les sanctuaires et leur rayonnement dans le monde méditerranéen, de l'antiquité à l'époque moderne*, ed. Juliette de la Genière, André Vauchez, and Jean Leclant (Paris: De Boccard, 2010), 359–72.

of Saint Matthew in Salerno, and of Saint Andrew in Amalfi. These were sites where particularly important relics—those of two apostles and an evangelist—were venerated. In French, this definition was not really used until the beginning in the seventeenth century and especially during the nineteenth century. Some ambiguity persists even in contemporary terminology since an important or prestigious church might be called a sanctuary today, even if it lacks its fundamental characteristics. This study restricts itself to the definition of sanctuary provided above, without overlooking the fact that this multidimensional notion has known a long and slow evolution and that its relation to pilgrimage—which appears to us today as central for differentiating a sanctuary from an ordinary church—came to be the norm only during the Middle Ages.

Sanctuaries before Christianity

From Prehistory to Greco-Roman Antiquity: The Gods and Their Temples

If the word "sanctuary" took on its current meaning only at the end of a long process, the phenomenon to which it refers—a space where the sacred is perceptible and accessible to human beings—is not a recent invention. Privileged sites of ritual assembly where people occasionally gathered in hopes of establishing direct contact with the sacred, such as the mysterious configurations at Stonehenge or Carnac, have always existed.[16] Other examples include the megalithic sanctuaries on the Islands of Malta or Sardinia, which date to 3500-2500 BCE and seem to have had been cultic in nature, and Mont Bégo in the Mercantour Massif, with its cave paintings and thousands of carved inscriptions, the meaning of which remains the subject of some conjecture.

The work of anthropologists and ethnologists on so-called traditional societies in Africa and the Americas is particularly helpful with respect to sanctuaries. Their research highlights the significance of the idea of territory in the conception of the sanctuary. For these scholars, a sanctuary is not merely a carefully delimited parcel of space, which in any event is rarely natural; rather it is a site that a group has made into a place of peace, a place that offers a sense of security. This is where the

---

16. Jean Guilaine, "Des pèlerinages dans la Préhistoire?," in *Les pèlerinages dans le monde: À travers le temps et l'espace*, ed. Jean Chelini and Henri Branthomme (Paris: Hachette Littératures, 2004), 13–20.

religious dimension is introduced, for in such cultures, no space is devoid of invisible powers. In these spaces are divinities—both the "spirits of places" and those of one's ancestors—whose behavior might be either beneficent or maleficent.[17] Thus the living seek out their protection (or impede them from doing harm) within the framework of what are virtually transactions, generally predicated on the exchange of care (from the divine realm) for offerings made by human actors. In these cultures, one of the essential functions of religion is the conceptualization and organization of space in order to assure its ritualized administration through practices such as perambulation—circular processions done periodically by the community within the space—so as to define and renew the limits of its territory.

In traditional societies, space was generally neither homogeneous nor neutral but differentiated qualitatively through symbolic association. A space was not merely a place that contained objects but a coherent matrix of collective images defining boundaries, chiefly (in antiquity) between, on the one hand, human space (*ager*) and, on the other, wild and uncultivated space (*saltus*).[18] The Italian anthropologist Ernesto De Martino defined this cognitive work as the "mythical reshaping of territory."[19] Indeed, all religions have a sacred space in which they locate the center of the world. In ancient Greece, temples often arose in a privileged place that linked a site—one often remarkable for its natural conditions and set aside within the landscape for religious purposes (the *temenos*)—with a structure (*hiéron*) in which divine power was exercised. These two elements together—the building *and* its sacred space—constituted the sanctuary, which carried the name of the divinity or the founding hero of the city worshiped there. In Greece, unlike in Egypt and most other kingdoms in the Middle East, temples were not served by a specialized clergy but run by the cities that founded them and cared for them. They were essential to the identity of the urban community and its civic space, even when the sanctuary

---

17. Jeanne-Françoise Vincent, Daniel Dory, and Raymond Verdier, eds., *La construction religieuse du territoire* (Paris: L'Harmattan, 1995).

18. Luce Pietri, "*Loca sancta*: La géographie de la sainteté dans l'hagiographie gauloise (IVe–Ve siècle)," in *Luoghi sacri e spazi della santità*, ed. Sofia Boesch Gajano and Lucetta Scaraffia (Turin: Rosenberg & Sellier, 1990), 23–36.

19. Ernesto De Martino, "Angoscia territoriale e riscatto culturale nel mito Achilpa delle origini," *Studi e materiali di storia e storia delle religioni* 23 (1951/52): 52–66.

predated the city that later made of it its *palladion*.²⁰ Those who visited these *palladia* underwent ritual purifications, in particular lustrations (ceremonial washings), which explains why a stream or spring was frequently found close by. A number of prohibitions had to be respected: one could not be born, die, or engage in sexual relations in or near the sanctuary for fear of angering the gods. These prohibitions functioned to give those who gathered there an awareness of their unity and strength in facing life's difficulties.²¹ The location's enduring stability, along with its associated memorial structure, ensured that the sanctuary's origins were remembered, as, for example, with the Erechtheion (Temple of Athena Polias) on the Acropolis. Certain shrines were also evidence of the spontaneous need to sacralize certain territories, such as frontier zones. Thus, cities were deliberately established where "the other manifested itself in the contact that was regularly maintained with it . . . to oppose each other, certainly, but to interpenetrate each other all the same."²²

In the Roman world, the sanctuary was likewise a defined space consecrated to a divinity, inviolable and served by an altar. The idea of its sacredness was predicated on the notion of a separation between immortals and mortals. That which pertained to the gods was *sacer*, a term that did not necessarily indicate a supernatural quality but rather designated a privileged status conferred in Rome by the Senate and magistrates, and then, as of the first century, by the emperor, placing the space under the protection of the gods. What was *sacer* was essentially that which belonged to the gods, as recognized by the city that offered sacrifices to them, through which mundane realities were made sacred.²³ In contrast, the Latin *sanctus* signifies the inviolable, the pure. *Sanctus* refers to something forbidden, the violation of which was severely punished, whether it concerned the walls of Rome itself,

---

20. Sandrine Agusta-Boularot, Sandrine Huber, and William van Andringa, eds., *Quand naissent les dieux: Fondation des sanctuaires antiques; motivations, agents, lieux* (Rome: École Française de Rome; Athens: École Française d'Athènes, 2017).

21. Olivier Picard, "Sanctuaire et prière dans la cité grecque classique," *Comptes rendus des séances de l'Académie des Inscriptions et Belles-Lettres* 160 (2016): 1529-37; Pierre Sineux, "La guérison dans les sanctuaires du monde grec antique: De Meiborn aux Edelstein, remarques historiographiques," *Anabases* 13 (2011): 11-25.

22. Jean-Pierre Vernant, *La mort dans les yeux* (Paris: Hachette, 1985), 17.

23. Pierre Gros and John Schied, "Sanctuaire, Grèce hellénistique et Rome antique," in *Encyclopedia universalis*, vol. 20 (Paris: Encyclopedia Universalis, 1986), 491-501; Manuel De Souza, *La question de la tripartition des catégories du droit divin dans l'Antiquité romaine* (Saint-Étienne: Presses universitaires de Saint-Étienne, 2004).

the *pomerium* (inside of which it was forbidden to bury the dead), or laws, or treaties, or the tribunes of the people, whom one could not lay hands against. Roman civil law defined *res sanctae* as places detached from the profane world by religious rites and protected by the fear of a "sanction" that would inevitably befall any transgressors. *Res sanctae* were in turn distinguished from *res religiosae*—burials and tombs—which belonged to the dead and their families, and also from *res sacrae*, those things publicly assigned to the gods the untouchable nature of which was guaranteed by the state. In Rome, as John Schied has shown, sacred space was neither divine nor human but rather a place placed under the protection of the gods and political power. The temple or sanctuary of a deity was a place of worship, often surrounded by a portico, a spring, baths, or even food for the sacrifices. Aside from these places of public worship were private cults and those tied to particular groups (confraternities, family groups, and the like) that developed in the places belonging to them. With the exception of a few empire-wide cults (the Capitoline Triad, the *Genius Augusti*), each city had its own gods. Their presence in strategic places represented the power of the city or the state and the extent of that power. As with the Greeks, sanctuaries could also be found on the periphery of cities or at the borders of their territory, as well as in sacred forests. Alongside the official state- or city-sanctioned religion was what could be called popular religiosity, often centered on streams, springs, and certain trees. But this phenomenon remains poorly known, having left few written or monumental traces.[24]

Pre-Rabbinic Judaism: One Singular Sacred Place, the Temple of Jerusalem

Starting with the Babylonian Exile and the return of the Israelites to their own land, Judaism was distinguished from the other religions of the ancient world by its monotheism—by the fact that its God, Yahweh, is singular and transcendent. God, for the Jews, is the Creator God, whereas for the Greeks and Romans the world was uncreated. In their eyes, the divinities that manifested themselves did not originate in the celestial beyond, but rather coexisted with nature. For Jews, on the

---

24. Giovanna Alvino and Terenzio Leggio, "Acque e culti salutari in Sabina," in *Usus veneratioque fontium: Fruizione e culto delle acque salutari nell'Italia romana*, ed. Lidio Gasparini (Tivoli: Tipigraf, 2006), 17–54.

contrary, omnipotence resides with the Creator. The world came from his hands, and although he formed the world, he is no longer present in it. No space is made sacred merely by nature. The idea of creation thus involved the de-enchantment of the world: even the places where God had revealed himself (such as Sinai, Hebron, or Mount Carmel associated with the memory of the prophet Elijah) do not contain his power. They are only places of memory.

The Temple of Jerusalem, built by Solomon around 950 BCE to house the tablets of the Law that manifested the presence of Yahweh among his people, is a special case. As God said, through the prophet Ezekiel: "And the nations shall know that I am the Lord the sanctifier of Israel, when my sanctuary shall be in the midst of them forever" (Ezek. 37:28). Leviticus provides a detailed description of how the priests worshiped God, a text that would come to influence Christian liturgy. Destroyed by Nebuchadnezzar in 586 BCE after he captured Jerusalem, the Temple was rebuilt between 521 and 515 following the return of the Hebrew people from Exile under the influence of Zerubbabel and Ezra.[25] Later, the Temple having been desecrated in 168 BCE by Antiochus Epiphanes, Herod the Great restored and sumptuously expanded it and had it encircled by powerful ramparts. In the second century BCE, the idea of Jerusalem as the center of the earth and the "umbilicus of the world" (following an expression from Ezekiel in Ezek. 38:12) first appears in apocalyptic literature. The first book of Enoch (26:1-2) attributed an eschatological role to "the holy mountain" of Zion, at the foot of which still flow the abundant waters from the spring of Siloah. The hills upon which Jerusalem was built included deep ravines, especially Gehenna, the place of the punishment of evildoers, and the valley of Jehoshaphat where the Last Judgment at the end of time was to take place.

Conquered by Pompey in 63 BCE, the Emperor Titus then set fire to the Temple of Jerusalem in 70 CE, and he carried off the sevenfold candelabra from the "Holy of Holies" to Rome. This definitive destruction spared only a part of the surrounding wall, known since then as the Wailing Wall. It was a terrible shock for Jews, who were expelled from Jerusalem, accelerating their dispersion throughout the Mediterranean and Eastern worlds. Although rabbinic exegesis stated that from

---

25. Mireille Hadas-Lebel, "Jérusalem cité terrestre et céleste," in *Solitudes sacrées et villes saintes*, ed. Catherine Marin and Anne-Marie Reijnen (Paris: Bayard, 2019), 211-28.

that point forward there would no longer be a sanctuary except in the New Jerusalem, whose coming was awaited, the Jewish people remained nonetheless attached to the symbolic importance of the Temple as a sign of the present and future of Israel, and also of the memory of Jerusalem, unique among earthly cities.

Part I

The Christianization of Place and the Sacralization of Christianity

Chapter 1

Late Antiquity and the Early Middle Ages

Christians against Sanctuaries?

Christianity did not share the same attachment as did Jews to the Temple, the imminent destruction of which Jesus had announced. But we should not overly exaggerate the contrast between the new religion and that which had preceded it. Jesus was an observant Jew; he freely preached in the Temple, especially during the last days of his earthly existence, and he sought to cleanse it by forcefully chasing out the merchants who were cluttering up its outer courtyard. In a diatribe against the Scribes and Pharisees, he reproached them to consider whether gold was more important than the Sanctuary, for "the one who swears by the Sanctuary swears an oath by the Sanctuary and by the One who dwells therein" (Matt. 23:13-22). However, the Temple was not an absolute for Christ: indeed, had he not said to the Samaritan woman that God was to be found neither on Mount Gerazim (the Temple in Samaria) nor in Jerusalem; rather, henceforth, one could worship him everywhere "in spirit and in truth" (John 4:23)?

In the Gospels, Jesus proclaims that it is in him alone that God will manifest his presence and no longer in the Temple of Jerusalem: His own body is the true sanctuary of God of which he says, in front of his dumbfounded auditors, that he will rebuild it in three days. On the other hand, after the Resurrection, in leaving behind him an empty tomb, henceforth, Christ had denied all legitimacy to the notion of sanctuary. There is nothing here to see nor to wait for after the Resurrection, as an angel points out while inviting the apostles to leave Jerusalem so as to meet up with Jesus in Galilee. Paul for his part, in the Letter to the Galatians (Gal. 4:24-26) explained to new converts that they should not attach themselves to the earthly Jerusalem (here, being compared to Hagar, who gave birth *in slavery*), while Christians are the sons and daughters of the Jerusalem on high (symbolized by Sarah, who was a *free woman*). Concerning this heavenly Jerusalem that, at the approach of the last days, will come down from heaven to earth "dressed like a bride who was adorned for her spouse," the author of the book of Revelation, attributed to Saint John, wrote significantly: "Of the sanctuary, I did not see anything within it; for it is the Lord, the master of all, who is its sanctuary, as well as that of the Lamb" (Rev. 21:24).

The religion of the day, Christianity, being centered on an expectation of the Parousia—that is, of the glorious return of the Son of God at the end of history—in its essence, saw itself, according to the words of Saint Augustine, as a "place-less" religion (*illocalis*) and without having any privileged spaces: the Church, the community of believers, is made up of people who are themselves like so many living stones and not sacred buildings. As Paul wrote to the Corinthians (1 Cor. 3:16-17): "Do you not know that you are the Temple of God and that the Spirit lives in you? If someone destroys the sanctuary of God, God will destroy that person because the sanctuary of God is holy and that sanctuary is you!" The Greek word is here translated as "sanctuary," and it refers to the most sacred part of the Temple, the Holy of Holies, thus underscoring that holiness is an attribute of hearts and minds and not of things. All in all, one can say that Christianity is an invitation to the sanctification of the world and not to its own sacralization.

Its novelty consisted, in fact, in applying the word "holy," in a positive sense, to persons judged to be close to God, whereas in Roman religion, this term referred one back to the notion of separation and prohibition. The sacred and the holy were distinct in principle in the new religion: the sacred, contrasted with the profane, separates, while holiness or sanctity is communion with God and human beings. There were not, therefore, holy places on the earth since, as Paul wrote, the faithful can "pray in every place, by lifting up their hands toward the heavens" (1 Tim. 2:8). Again, at the beginning of the fourth century, the bishop and historian Eusebius of Caesarea will assert that only Jews and pagans have sanctuaries, as distinct from Christians, and that Jerusalem itself is not the city of God. Henceforth, only the Church merited this name. Indeed, for the early Christians, the Lord was present whenever the faithful gathered for prayer in his name. The sacrifice of the Mass brings into being the consecrated bread and wine as the flesh and blood of Christ. But that did not necessitate a permanent presence in the same place any more than the idea of a "real presence" of the Son of God (apart from the assembly celebrating the Eucharistic sacrifice) would have been totally foreign to them.

After the conversion of Constantine, Christians showed their desire to put the time of persecutions behind them by making a place for themselves in the urban landscape. This desire to make their faith visible in space gets translated over the course of the fourth century through the construction of open-air places of worship.[1] These could appear, at first glance, similar to temples, but Christians rejected the seeming similarity by affirming that their churches had been sanctified by the blood of martyrs, and thus by human beings, rather than by the presence of statues or other idols of stone or bronze. Later, they would destroy pagan temples, beginning with that of Aphrodite in Jerusalem, which was located above the presumed tomb of Christ. Like the Jews in the Old Testament, the Church—the "New Israel"—tended to associate the gods of the pagans with demons. But these destructions were less numerous than later claimed, except with respect to the underground sanctuaries of Mithras, whose cult was the direct competitor of Christianity, and the Serapeum in Alexandria, destroyed by the Patriarch Theophilus and the monks of the city.[2] In 407, an imperial law ordered owners (*domini*) to destroy the pagan religious structures on their properties, but its implementation was slow and limited. In fact, ancient cultic structures eventually disappeared due to neglect. The majority of temples were closed and soon came to ruin by virtue of the imperial

---

1. Richard Krautheimer, *Rome: Profile of a City, 312–1308* (Princeton, NJ: Princeton University Press, 2000).

2. Francesco Gandolfo, "Luoghi dei santi e luoghi dei demoni: Il riuso dei templi nel Medioevo," in *Santi e demoni nell'Alto Medioevo occidentale* (Spoleto: CISAM, 1989), 883–923; Claire Sotinel, "La disparition des lieux de culte païens en Occident: Enjeux et méthodes," in *Hellénisme et christianisation*, ed. Michel Nancy and Éric Rebillard (Villeneuve d'Ascq: Septentrion, 2004), 35–60; Johannes Hahn, Stephen Emmel, and Ulrich Gotter, eds., *From Temple to Church: Destruction and Renewal of Local Cultic Topography in Late Antiquity* (Leiden: Brill, 2008).

legislation that deprived them of their resources. They were then demolished in order to harvest materials for building new churches or monasteries. Sometimes, the governing authority "secularized" them by transforming them into workshops, entrusted to corporations that gathered in the *cella* of the temple, or earmarking them for other uses like dwellings or places of business. Nevertheless, they took care to lop the heads off the statues of the gods and pagan emperors, since these were perceived as possessing a maleficent power. Self-standing sculptures therefore disappeared for more than five centuries in the West. In the countryside, the traditional sanctuaries were often destroyed by monks or zealous preachers like Saint Martin in Gaul, to put an end to the harmful influence of pagan "demons" and to demonstrate to the still-pagan populations the powerlessness of these divinities to protect their temples and idols.

In many regions, pagan sanctuaries were repurposed by Christians, especially those that were located on the heights or near the grottos where the cult of Saint Michael often replaced Mercury or other divinities. Thus, at the end of the fifth century, on Mount Gargano in Apulia, the archangel took over from a pagan divinity in a grotto already famous in antiquity for the curative powers of the waters that flowed along its walls.[3] Cases of such repurposing multiplied thereafter. When he settled in 529 on Montecassino, Saint Benedict took over the temple of Apollo located on the summit of the mountain; he had the woods that surrounded them and where "demonic" cults had been celebrated cut down, transformed the pagan temple into an oratory dedicated to Saint Martin, and undertook the construction of a basilica dedicated to Saint John. And although pagan temples had been a priori considered impure, Pope Gregory the Great († 604) recommended that missionaries who were departing to evangelize England transform them into churches, after destroying the idols therein, in order to reorient the habits ingrained among the local populations toward conversion. Later, churches were established in the *cella* of certain great temples; the most famous example is the Pantheon in Rome, which was rededicated to Saint Mary of the Martyrs in 609 by Pope Boniface I with the agreement of Emperor Phocas.

---

3. Giorgio Otranto and Carlo Carletti, *Il santuario di S. Michele Arcangelo sul Gargano, dalle origini al X secolo* (Bari: Edipuglia, 1990).

The Relics of the Saints: Epicenters of the Sacred

The *Martyria* and the Origins of the Cult of Relics

These hesitations between the destruction, maintenance, or repurposing of pagan temples are tied to the fact that Christians of late antiquity were rapidly creating new forms of sacredness within a religion that, in principle, prohibited sanctuaries. As the passage from the Acts of the Apostles regarding the stoning of Saint Stephen shows (Acts 7:55-60), early Christians considered that those among them who, impelled by faith, had been lifted above their sinful condition by following Christ up to his death were participating in a dynamic of sanctification that distinguished them from other people and also differentiated the places where their bones now lay. Thus, a new kind of Christian sanctuary began to appear in the fourth century: *martyria*.[4] These were defined by two inextricably linked elements: the place in which the holy person was entombed and the metamorphosis of this place into a sacred space through the consecration of the *virtus* of the martyrs—that is to say, the supernatural power that their fidelity to Christ had conferred upon them. These *martyria* were veritable trophies to the extent that they were built to celebrate the victory of the saints over their persecutors. In death, they had acquired for themselves merits with God, who rendered them visible posthumously through miraculous signs (*signa, miracula*). This new conception results from the Christian belief that God was both Other by his holiness and yet close to people through his grace active in creation.

The main phenomenon that resulted from this over the fourth and fifth centuries in the Christian world was the development of the cult of relics.[5] Relics are the bodily remains of martyrs and confessors that retained the strength, of supernatural origin, that had allowed them to stand firm in their defense of their faith in Christ or to lead an ascetic life in the desert. These remains were collected by local Christian communities, which kept them as a treasure until a public cult could be formed. The relics of the martyrs were, furthermore, considered incorruptible as the saint's sacrifice had conferred on them a particular status: that of the spiritual body that human beings possessed before

---

4. André Grabar, *Martyrium: Recherches sur le culte des reliques et l'art chrétien antique* (Paris: Collège de France, 1948).

5. Arnold Angenendt, *Heilige und Reliquien: Die Geschichte ihres Kultus vom frühen Christentum bis zur Gegenwart* (Munich: Beck, 1994); and Luigi Canetti, *Frammenti di eternità: Corpi e reliquie tra Antichità e Medioevo* (Rome: Viella, 2002).

original sin, as Saint Augustine underscores. The saint thus remained alive and active in his or her relics. The beneficent power emanating from them was capable of providing health, safety, and justice, manifesting in this world a foretaste of the fullness of life that these servants of God now enjoyed in the next world. The *virtus* subsisting in martyrs' precious remains resulted in essentially therapeutic miracles that believers attributed to their intercession.

Holy Bodies and Their Disarticulation

The most evocative example of this type of sanctuary is the tomb of Christ, the Holy Sepulcher in Jerusalem. In effect, it kept alive the memory of his body, which had resided herein for three days and had been impregnated with the power of his Resurrection, thus establishing a link between the earthly reality of the cadaver and eternal life. In the case of martyrs, rarely were entire bodies preserved; Christian communities therefore aspired to possess at least parts of them. The Church, concerned with defending the integrity of saintly bodies (as was the rule in Roman law), was opposed for a long time to their being parceled up. Pope Gregory the Great, around 600, refused to send to Constantinople relics of Saint Peter, as had been requested by the Empress Pulcheria. He also reminded the faithful and the clergy about the prohibition against touching the precious remains except with pieces of cloth, *brandea*, placed on the tomb or in the structure known as "the confession." But the Christian East did not share this opinion, and from the middle of the fifth century, the bishop and hagiographer Theodoret of Cyr had been able to affirm, without contradiction, that the *virtus* of relics—just like that of the Eucharistic body of Christ or of the True Cross—was not compromised or diminished by being divided up. This point of view had the support of the faithful and ended up being carried over to the West; from the sixth century on, there was a massive distribution of the fragments of relics. This would make possible a virtually infinite number of holy sites that had no direct relationship with the tombs of "the men and women of God," since, as Victricius, the bishop of Rouen, had written around 400 concerning relics, "where there is something, there is found everything" (ubi aliquid, ibi totu est).[6]

---

6. Victrix of Rouen, *De laude sanctorum*, ed. J. Mulders, in *Liber contra Arrianos; De laude sanctorum; Libellus emendationis; Epistulae; Commonitorium. Excerpta ex operibus s. Augustini;*

Equally, traces left in the soil by the blood of the martyrs and saints could produce miracles. According to the legend, the head of Saint Paul, after being severed, had bounced three times on the ground on the Via Ostiense, not far from Rome. Three springs had miraculously bubbled up with water believed to exhibit thaumaturgical properties, and a sanctuary called Saint Paul at the Three Fountains developed at this site of the martyrdom. In the hagiographical literature of the period, the perception of the holiness of a "person of God" is often associated with miraculous sensory phenomena, like the appearance of flashing lights around a tomb or the emanation of a pleasing characteristic scent—the so-called odor of sanctity—as well as extraordinary physical signs: the appearance of a spring, an abundant bloom outside a plant's normal season, snow falling everywhere except on the holy site or, conversely, appearing in the middle of August, as in the legend of the foundation of Santa Maria Maggiore in Rome, which is also known as Santa Maria delle Nevi (Our Lady of the Snows) as a result.[7]

A New Conception of Place: Saints and Their Sites

God as Present in Creation

In western Europe, from late antiquity until the end of the Middle Ages, the conceptualization of space marked a rupture with Greco-Roman antiquity. As Alain Guerreau has shown, under the influence of Christianity, which profoundly penetrated their worldview, the people of this time considered the world to be the result of an act of creation; from this perspective, reality was the relationship between heaven and earth, the Creator and his creatures.[8] These creatures were objects fixed in time and space, as opposed to God who was present everywhere and at every moment. The fundamental problem for mortals was thus their distance from a God who was wholly Other. To bridge this gap, a person could develop the spiritual dimension of their existence by, for example, entering into the monastic life—which only a small minority did—or by giving themselves over to the Church, the role of which was to reconcile human beings to God. Defined as the institution through

---

Altercatio legis inter Simonem Iudaeum et Theophilum christianum, Corpus Christianorum Series Latina 64 (Turnhout: Brepols, 1985).
   7. Edina Bozoky, *Miracle! Récits merveilleux des martyrs et des saints* (Paris: Vuibert, 2013).
   8. Alain Guerreau, "Structure et évolution: Les représentations de l'espace dans le haut Moyen Age occidental," in *Uomo e spazio nell'Alto Medioevo* (Spoleto: CISAM, 2003), 91–115.

which "the communion of saints" mentioned in the Credo was realized, the Church allowed believers still living in this world to benefit from the suffrages (merits and prayers) of the elect and to recommend to them the souls of the dead.

Among these last, major importance was accorded to the "very special dead" (as Peter Brown refers to them)—who were saints.[9] The sacred character of a holy place is derived from its association with a saint as a result of their holiness overflowing into this space and impregnating it for all time. Henceforth, the word *sanctus* would no longer refer, as it did in Roman religion, to the idea of a separation but, rather, to a relationship of closeness and connection between the martyr or the confessor and the Christian people. In this line of thinking, space was not perceived as being continuous and homogeneous. There were, on the one hand, places where ordinary, daily life ran its course and, on the other, certain special, sacralized spots, most notably holy sanctuaries where one benefited from a particular relationship to the world above: "the altar and its relics representing the absolute pole of local space."[10] Not until the Renaissance, with advances in mapmaking and the affirmation of the territorial nature of power exerted within well-defined boundaries, would the modern conception of space as being identical everywhere became predominant.

The Prestige of Asceticism: Holy Islands and Holy Mountains

Initially, individuals venerated by Christians were primarily martyrs whose holiness was both obviously recognizable and radiated in a beneficial way onto the place where their relics were venerated and, more broadly, over the community from where they had originated. But from the fourth century on, new forms of holiness appeared, like the eremitical or monastic life, that were soon seen as comparable to bloody martyrdoms that became rarer after the cessation of the persecutions carried out by the Roman Empire. This process is especially clear in the case of the Mediterranean island of Lérins. Saint Honoratus († 430) had founded a monastery there, where some ascetics were already living. He died in Arles, where he was archbishop, and was buried there in the cemetery of Alyscamps. Unable to arrange for his relics to be moved, the

---

9. Peter Brown, *The Cult of the Saints: Its Rise and Function in Latin Christianity* (Chicago: University of Chicago Press, 2014).

10. Guerreau, "Structure et évolution," 102.

FIGURE 1. Church and monastery of Lérins Abbey. Photo: Alberto Fernandez Fernandez via Wikimedia Commons (CC BY 2.5).

monks of Lérins extolled the holiness of the island in their writings, where a good part of Honoratus's religious life had unfolded. Already in 428, Eucherius of Lyons had written to the monks on the island, "The one who lived with you now has the joy of being indwelt by the Lord.... When one does not fear to live with you, one becomes oneself God's temple." After this, he praised these "deserted places to be illustrious by virtue of the withdrawal of pious men." Caesarius of Arles († 542) described Lérins as "a consecrated land" and "a holy island" (figure 1).[11] This latter expression is repeated, at the end of the sixth century, by Gregory of Tours, who attested to the existence of a pilgrimage to Lérins where the faithful took off their shoes once they had landed there, just as Moses had done in approaching the Burning Bush. After the murder of two of the abbey's monks by Saracens—Aygulf in the seventh century and Porcarius II in the eighth—later hagiographers underscored that the island had been further sanctified by the blood of the martyrs. But the discourse relative to Lérins is clear and unambiguous: if the island could be considered holy, it was because it had served over the centuries as a site of a collective experience of holiness, illustrated by the names of certain monks who had once lived there.

For the same reasons, a great devotion also began to surround "holy mountains" and "holy deserts"; in the Latin West, these referred to forests and mountainous regions that had been theaters of combat for saints against demons and the hostile forces of nature. In most religions, mountains play an important role as places where heaven and

---

11. Yann Codou and Michel Lauwers, eds., *Lérins: Une île sainte de l'Antiquité au Moyen Age* (Turnhout: Brepols, 2010).

earth, as well as human and divine beings, meet. Their height simulates the effect of transcendence, and so it is not by accident that mountains or hills have been privileged sites for theophanies. In the Bible, a whole religious vocabulary puts the emphasis on the idea that, to have access to God (or, at the very least, to approach him), it was necessary to ascend, often at the cost of a difficult climb. This is illustrated in medieval literature by the metaphor of the Ladder of Heaven, upon which a monk could hope to encounter God at the apex of their spiritual ascent.[12]

Moreover, by virtue of their natural beauty and by their floral and vegetal setting, these places sometimes constituted a kind of Eden-like landscape, the earthly anticipation of paradise, the contemplation of which raised souls up to God, according to the writings of certain hagiographers. These authors freely compared places of solitude such as Mount Athos or Mount Galesios in the Byzantine world or the high points of Italian eremitism—the Sila in Calabria or the forested elevation of Santa Serra—to the mountains of the Bible, from Mount Horeb to Mount Tabor. The tranquility of rocky areas and the forests that covered them made them an ideal environment for the practice of asceticism and the sanctification of anchorites or monks. Such spaces became sacred because some "man of God" had come there in search of direct contact with their Creator and conquered nature by disciplining their body; they thus acquired a power that made them a mediator between other human beings and God. The faithful who would later go to this intercessor's tomb did not travel there to adore nature but rather to witness the divine power being revealed there in order to actualize that power and change the course of their lives. This experience inspired the need to localize the sacred and to inscribe in that space an expression of their devotion in the form of a memorial or a sanctuary, where the charism of the servant of God could continue to manifest itself.

The figure of the saint inaugurated a new style of life, indifferent to possessions and the splendors of the world and turned entirely toward God—the veritable anticipation, *hic et nunc*, of the scriptural "new heavens" and "new earth." The places associated with them became ones where the harmony of creation could find itself restored, and their presence in specific settings was accompanied by the appearance of various

---

12. Christian Heck, *L'échelle celeste dans l'art du Moyen Age* (Paris: Flammarion, 1997).

manifestations of sacredness: a spring bursting forth, soon reputed for its curative properties; or the cessation of nature's violence (storms, droughts, various kinds of inclement weather). This ensemble of beliefs explains the long-lasting success of the model of the fourth-century Thebaid—a space of peace, populated by monks living in harmony with nature and animals—that had such an important place in the literature and art of the Middle Ages, in the Byzantine East and, from the fourteenth century onward, in Tuscany.[13] Medieval hagiographers celebrated the saint's role in civilizing the wilderness by eliminating its wild aspects, symbolized by the dragon, and rendering it livable and fraternal. Thus, "the saints—the intercessors necessary in every peregrination toward God and anchored in a stable manner in the countryside—constituted fundamental actors in the practical organization of space."[14] This would spur the concentration, around their tombs and the sanctuaries that housed them, of an immense energy of expectation and hope.

Loca Sanctorum

As Sophia Boesch Gajano has shown, holiness has "a tendency to create an effusive sacredness that radiates out from the body [of the saint] and flows into surrounding objects and places in concentric circles."[15] The birth of a sanctuary attracted pilgrims but also brought about settlement: A habitation was often organized around the holy site, which sometimes gave birth to a village or town. In an urban setting, the cult of martyrs had been the means for transforming Roman towns into networks of Christian holy places.[16] Indeed, the sacralizing of space occurred in connection with the cult of saints. Basilicas were often built on the peripheries of cities, in the necropolises where saints' remains had been interred. Nearby suburbs would take the name of the intercessor who was being venerated in the local sanctuary. In the fifth and

---

13. Alessandra Malquori, Manuela De Giorgi, and Laura Fenelli, eds., *Atlante delle Tebaidi e dei temi figurativi* (Florence: Centro Di, 2014).

14. Guerreau, "Structure et évolution," 103–07; *Construction de l'espace au Moyen Age: Pratiques et représentations*, Actes du 37ᵉ Congrès de la SHMES, 2006 (Paris: Publications de la Sorbonne, 2007).

15. Hippolyte Delehaye, "Loca sanctorum," *Analecta Bollandiana* 48 (1930): 5–64; Sofia Boesch Gajano and Marilena Modica, eds., *Miracoli: Dai segni alla storia* (Rome: Viella, 2015), 65.

16. Luce Pietri, *La ville de Tours du IVᵉ au VIᵉ siècle: Naissance d'une cité chrétienne* (Rome: École Française de Rome, 1983); Alba Maria Orselli, *Basileousa polis, Regia civitas: Studi sul Tardoantico Cristiano* (Spoleto: CISAM, 2015).

sixth centuries, these *martyria* took on the same functions as churches located within the city walls: namely, a liturgy held at a particular site, occasionally gathering the community of believers around the clergy. This was created through the celebration of processions connecting the center of the city with the peripheral zones where the tombs of the martyrs were located. During a saint's feast day, the celebration of their birth into heaven (*dies natalis*), the bishop would deliver a panegyric about the servant of God whose memory was being venerated, and he would invite the faithful to follow the saint's example and to have recourse to their intercession. Sometimes religious communities settled near the tombs, where they kept watch; as a site of pilgrimage, accommodations and markets developed around them as well. In a world where social organization was increasingly tied to the hierarchies of personal connections, sanctuaries, intended to gather pious people together, found favor because they were founded on holy remains and were ritually consecrated by an ecclesiastical authority. And from these sacred places emanated, throughout the Christian West, a reconstruction of space upon new foundations.[17]

Michel de Certeau has analyzed this dialectical relationship between these two notions:[18] place as a setting implying a certain stability versus space as "a convenient venue," that is, the intersection of elements that change by virtue of transformations produced by circumstances and outside influences. Sanctuaries are places associated with objects (body parts, tombs, grottos, churches), almost unchanging, that are intended to be seen or touched; the spaces laid out around them are made concrete by the actions of historical subjects. Between the two, their founding narratives or legends carry out the never-ending work of transforming mere places into "exalted places" that inspire people to want to visit them. Thus, the mythical or hagiographical accounts that were developed around the *loca sanctorum* constituted a culturally creative act; the saint, who in life was associated with journeys to various places and a constant change of settings, came to define in death a particular spiritual space that attracted the faithful. This process is illustrated by the appearance in the West of a *heteropia* (borrowing Michel Foucault's term) through which certain areas—in this instance, holy

---

17. Michel Lauwers and Laurent Ripart, "Représentations et gestions de l'espace dans l'Occident médiéval (V^e–XIIIe siècle)," in *Rome et l'État moderne européen*, ed. Jean-Philippe Genet (Rome: École Française de Rome, 2007), 115.
18. Michel de Certeau, *L'invention du quotidien*, vol. 1, *Arts de faire* (Paris: Gallimard, 1990), 222.

places and sanctuaries—accrued a particular status: physical spaces, holding within them a spiritual presence, and located on the *fringes* of society while at the same time playing an essential role *in* society. These privileged places were distinct from those that a saint had sacralized by their presence at a given moment of their existence, which the texts of the Middle Ages refer to as *loca sancta*. Thus, the monastery of Marmoutier, Saint Martin's customary dwelling place, or the church of Candes, where he drew his last breath, remained places of memory sanctified by his passage; but it was the monastery of Tours itself, where his precious remains were located, that constituted the center of his cult and the place to which pilgrims flocked. Significantly, Gregory of Tours placed emphasis less on the saints themselves than on the places where they were venerated and on the miracles that were produced there.[19]

Holy Bodies, Churches, and Reliquaries

How did this sacralizing of space get concretized through relics? If, in the Latin West—as distinct from the Greek East—one did not assume that the saint had always lived in the place where his body now reposed, one nevertheless believed that they were really present in the tomb that housed the relics, and that this presence could be accessed in order to respond to the petitions of believers, as well as to punish those who failed to respect the saints or who doubted their power. Thus, profanation, even if accidental, of the sanctuary demanded the severest punishment of the offenders, whether human or animal. Conversely, this space welcomed those who were being persecuted or fleeing; they could escape from their pursuers by virtue of the right of asylum, with which the sanctuary had been endowed. For their protection, the fragments of holy bodies were placed in reliquaries. Initially simple metal boxes, these became more and more ornate and elegantly crafted as the years progressed (figure 2). As Edina Bozoky has written, "To be worthy to receive such precious deposits, the reliquary had to be fashioned of noble metals and richly ornamented with precious stones, evoking the splendor of the heavenly Jerusalem and allowing

---

19. Luce Pietri, "Grégoire de Tours et la géographie du sacré," in *Grégoire de Tours et l'espace gaulois*, ed. Nancy Gauthier and Henri Galinié, supplement to the *Revue archéologique du Centre de la France* 13 (Tours: Association Grégoire 94, 1997), 11–114.

FIGURE 2. Arm reliquary, decorated with silver, gilded silver, niello, and gems, South Netherlandish, ca. 1230. The Metropolitan Museum of Art, The Cloisters Collection, 1947.

believers to imagine the Kingdom of Heaven where the souls of the saints already lived."[20]

In the hagiographical literature, which did not take long to develop in the West—it started with the *Vita Martini* of Sulpicius Severus in the late fourth century—the saint sometimes appeared to clerics or laypeople asking them to exhume their remains, while they still were lying under the earth, or requested a more honorable place of burial than the one they had originally been given. Generally, such interventions only reflected the perspective of the promotors of the saint's cult. But the ecclesiastical hierarchy could not remain indifferent for very long to such appeals organized by prominent monasteries or high-born laity. Beginning in the sixth century, bishops began intervening more and more in ceremonies that transformed chapels or churches into sanctuaries by means of the ritual exhumation and relocation of relics. This process of exhumation and relocation to a more prestigious reliquary or upon

---

20. Bozoky, *Miracle!*

an altar was called "deposition" or "translation."²¹ This liturgical action was in principle reserved to bishops, but in numerous cases, abbots took the initiative to do this on their own. In the hagiographical texts, these operations were justified by the use of dreams in which the saint would express their desire to have their remains recognized and honored.

On the occasion of these transfers of relics and the processions that accompanied them, numerous miracles were produced, demonstrating the power of the saint and bolstering the prestige of this sanctuary. In the Carolingian period, the deposition of relics progressively merged with the rite of dedicating churches.²² Relics preserved from one or several holy bodies were placed under the main altar by the bishop of the site, or even within the altar, inside a small hiding place called a sepulcher. The Church's desire to exert more control over sanctuaries appears clearly in 745, when the French episcopacy obtained from Pope Zachary the condemnation of a bishop of Gaul named Adalbert, who had distributed relics associated with his own body (toenails, fingernails, and hair, among other items) and built, in the countryside and close to springs, oratories that he claimed were as efficacious as the "sanctuaries of old." Moreover, he had had placed small crosses in nearby fields to demarcate sacred areas.²³ And in 813, a synod of the French Church prohibited the exhumation and translation of relics without the authorization of the local "prince" and a synod of bishops. But because of the anarchy that soon consumed western Europe after the Norman invasions, these rigorous regulations were rarely respected.

The Sanctification of the Cities

During the early Middle Ages, cities tended to be identified with the church where their patron saint reposed, whether a cathedral or

---

21. Martin Heinzelmann, *Translationsberichte und andere Quellen des Reliquienkultes* (Turnhout: Brepols, 1979); James H. Johnston and Paul A. Hayward, eds., *The Cult of Saints in Late Antiquity and the Early Middle Ages: Essays on the Contribution of Peter Brown* (Oxford: Oxford University Press, 2002).

22. Michel Zimmermann, "La consécration des églises de Cerdagne aux Xe et XIe siècles: Une territorialisation de la foi," *Études Roussillonnaises* 11 (2005): 65-85; Éric Palazzo, *L'espace rituel et le sacré dans le christianisme: La liturgie de l'autel portatif dans l'Antiquité et au Moyen Age* (Turnhout: Brepols, 2008); Giorgia Vocino, "Le traslazioni di reliquie in età carolingia: Uno studio comparativo," in *Del visibile credere*, ed. Davide Scotto (Florence: Olschki, 2011), 217-64.

23. Saint Boniface, *Epistolae selectae*, in *MGH* 59, 108-20, cited by Alain Dierkens and Anne Morelli, eds., *Topographie du sacré: L'emprise religieuse sur l'espace* (Brussels: Université de Bruxelles, 2008), 87-89.

a suburban monastery; sometimes the cities would even take on the saint's name (Saint-Quentin or Saint-Denis, for example), privileging those who, according to tradition, had evangelized the city or the region. These religious places, referred to by various terms—*basilica*, *monasterium*, *cella*, or *ecclesia*—were maintained and restored by the bishops. Indeed, one of their functions at this time was, precisely, to "raise up the bodies of the saints," that is, to accord them the honors due to them. Later, devotion toward the saint of the city would spread outward into the surrounding countryside with the creation of secondary places that in the absence of bodily relics used "relics of contact" (*brandea*)—pieces of cloth that had previously come into contact with an actual relic.

In the towns that had the good fortune to possess prestigious holy bodies, sacred spaces often extended beyond the structure where the relics rested. At Saint-Martin of Tours, this process went hand in hand with the development of the sanctuary, made increasingly more imposing through its architecture and setting, and soon endowed with a crypt for the use of pilgrims. In this period, the memorial itself tended to guarantee the holiness of the venerated saint, and various "Praises of the City" (*Laudes civitatis*)—of Auxerre, Milan, or Verona, for example—develop the idea that a city's true fortifications were, in fact, its sanctuaries, and the saints venerated there its best defenders.[24] Protected by its relics, the Christian city could become a holy city on the model of the perfect city, Jerusalem, and share in its glory. The birth and development of an ensemble of symbolic representations that inserted the new urban setting into the framework of the history of salvation would create a Christian memory for the city.

Where there was no local martyr, believers turned their veneration toward the tomb of a city's first bishop or bishops, called by God to play the role of protector—its official patron saint. A pillar of the Church, the patron saint offered to the city their intangible body, before which procession and prayer could unfold within the framework of the city.[25] But some bishops were more eminent than others in terms of the

---

24. Alba Maria Orselli, *L'immaginario religioso della città medievale* (Ravenna: Edizioni del girasole, 1985); Orselli, *Basileousa polis, Regia civitas*.

25. Jean-Charles Picard, *Évêques, saints et cités en Italie et en Gaule: Études d'archéologie et d'histoire* (Rome: École Française de Rome, 1998); Jean-Charles Picard, *Le souvenir des évêques: Sépultures, listes épiscopales et culte des évêques dans l'Italie du Nord, des origines au Xe siècle* (Rome: École Française de Rome, 1988); Christine Bousquet-Labouérie and Yossi Maurey, eds., *Espace sacré, mémoire sacrée: Le culte des évêques dans leurs villes (IVe–XXe siècle)* (Turnhout: Brepols, 2015), 352.

devotion they inspired. In Merovingian Gaul, the names of six or seven sanctuaries stand out, located in the cities that, it was claimed, had been evangelized by the disciples of the apostles, considered as the first bishops (figure 3). This is the case, for example, of Saturnin of Toulouse, Martial of Limoges, Denis of Paris, Irenaeus of Lyons, and the martyr Julian of Brioude in the Auvergne, who enjoyed a particular reputation as a thaumaturge.[26]

In the sixth century, Gregory of Tours lists approximately 150 sanctuaries (in present-day France), situated mostly in the southern half of the country. His historical and hagiographical writings essentially established the sacred geography of Gaul that emerged from both the irrepressible need of believers to localize the supernatural and the Church's desire to ensure that each town and each region had a specific place in the divine plan of the redemption of the world.[27] These new spaces of holiness were not merely devotional or spiritual insofar as the "religious" did not then constitute a category distinct from the political or the social; rather it encompassed all aspects of existence. As John Damascene wrote in the eighth century, "All places where the divine name is invoked, I venerate them and I adore them, not for their own nature but because they are receptacles of the divine energy, because God has chosen them to accomplish through them our salvation."[28]

Cities of God

The eighth century also witnessed the appearance of two simultaneous phenomena within Christianity: the assertion of the sacred character of certain cities or places that had played a particular role in holy history; and the birth of the pilgrimage as a meritorious religious practice.

---

26. Edina Bozoky, "La politique des reliques des premiers comtes de Flandres (fin du IXe siècle–fin du XIe siècle), in Edina Bozoky, *Le Moyen Age miraculeux: Études sur les légendes et les croyances médiévales* (Paris: Riveneuve, 2010), 42–61.

27. François Dolbeau, *Prophètes, apôtres et disciples dans la tradition chrétienne d'Occident* (Brussels: Société des Bollandistes, 2012); "Que sont devenus les apôtres de Jésus?," special issue, *Le Monde de la Bible*, no. 233 (2021); Charles Bonnet, "Les églises du haut Moyen Age d'après les recherches archéologiques," in Gauthier and Galinié, *Grégoire de Tours et l'espace gaulois*, 217–36.

28. John Damascene, in *PL* XCIV, col. 1353, cited by Edmond-René Labande, *Pauper et peregrinus: Problèmes, comportements et mentalités du pèlerin chrétien* (Turnhout: Brepols, 2004), 28.

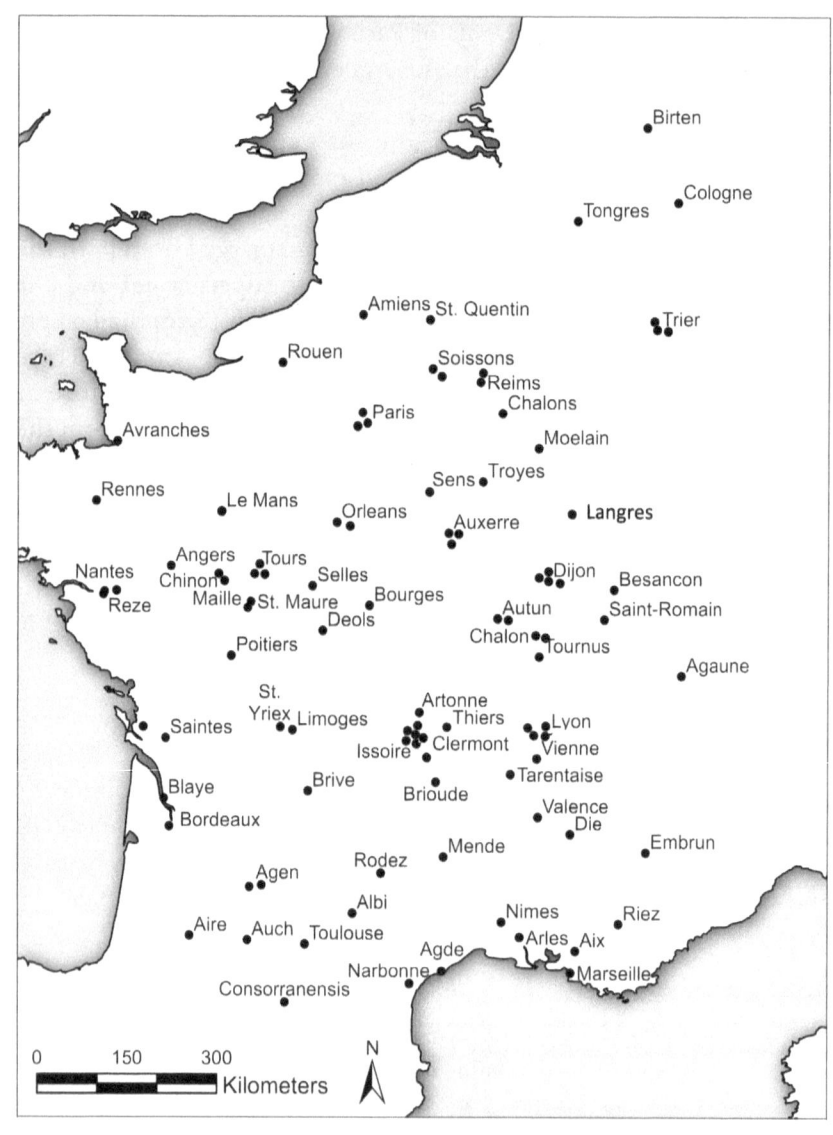

FIGURE 3. The principal sanctuaries of Gaul at the end of the fourth century. Credit: A. Christesen.

Jerusalem and the Origins of the "Holy Land"

From the first centuries, Christianity referred in its exegesis and liturgy to passages of the Old Testament that emphasized the sacred character of Jerusalem, connected to the presence within its walls of the Temple of Yahweh (Solomon's Temple). Moreover, other episodes of the Bible underscore the role of different privileged sites where God had revealed himself, such as during Jacob's vision in Bethel, where a modest memorial preserves the memory of the presence of Yahweh (Gen. 28:10-22), and his struggle with the angel at the stream of Jabbok in the Jordan Valley (Gen. 32:25-30). Similarly, the episode of the Burning Bush and of Moses's encounter with God on Mount Horeb contributed to making Mount Sinai a sacred place for Jews and later for the faithful of Christ.[29] Christianity would take over from Judaism the conviction that Jerusalem was "the naval of the world" (*omphalos* in Greek), while at the same time making the city its own by asserting that the Cross of Christ, the Tree of Life, had redeemed Adam's original sin in the very place where he had committed that sin and where Christ had been buried. Numerous iconographic depictions in the medieval and modern periods demonstrate the belief that the blood of the Redeemer had bathed the skull of the first human being, thus conferring upon Golgotha (and, more broadly, Jerusalem) a perfect center point in the history of salvation.

Beginning in the fourth century, a strong devotion developed among Christians toward the Holy Places in Palestine.[30] It is premature to speak of pilgrimages, rather than of voyages or sojourns made into these regions by bishops or abbots, as well as by certain devout people like the noble Egeria, who had come from Aquitaine to Palestine, or the spiritual followers of Saint Jerome, for whom understanding the Scriptures demanded visiting the Holy Land. But from the end of the fourth century, Bishop Cyril of Jerusalem († 386) had emphasized the unique character of the holy city by proclaiming in a homily: "That which others only hear about, we ourselves see it and we touch it."[31] By asserting that seeing Bethlehem and Calvary made Christian teaching

---

29. Peter Walker, *Holy City, Holy Places: Christian Attitudes to Jerusalem and the Holy Land in the Fourth Century* (Oxford: Clarendon Press, 1990).

30. Pierre Maraval, *Lieux saints et pèlerinages d'Orient: Histoire et géographie, des origines à la conquête arabe* (Paris: CNRS, 2011); see also Walker, *Holy City, Holy Places*.

31. Cyril of Jerusalem, *Catéchèses*, XIII, 22, ed. J. Bouvet (Namur: Éditions du Soleil Levant, 1962).

tangible, he placed Jerusalem and its diocese at the heart of the world. A few years later, Paulinus of Nola († 431) did not hide his desire to see and touch the places where Christ had been bodily present while he was alive, and he did not hesitate to write: "We went to adore at the place where the feet [of the Savior] stood."[32] In fact, it was especially important for the pious elite to have a concrete and edifying contact with biblical sites that God had imbued with spiritual power, from Mount Sinai to Golgotha.[33]

The Holy Sepulcher and the True Cross

The principal goal of pilgrims was the Holy Sepulcher where they could contemplate the empty tomb that memorialized both the death and resurrection of Christ. In 335, Constantine had a church built over it on the pattern of a basilica, extended by the Rotunda of the *Anastasis* (the Resurrection) above the grotto where Christ was entombed and was then raised up. According to Christian authors of the period, this was also the site of the Holy of Holies, the most sacred space in the ancient Temple of Solomon, thus coinciding with the birthplace of Adam, as well as with Mount Moriah, the place where Abraham had offered to sacrifice his son Isaac to God. The rest of the basilica was a vast *martyrium*, an essential element in the creation of a Christian Jerusalem, where this new Temple was intended to eradicate the memory of the earlier one.[34] The discovery of the True Cross by Constantine's mother, Helen, established Jerusalem as the holy city of Christ; and their shared devotion to his cross was the basis of a privileged link between the emperor and God. (The Orthodox Church has faithfully preserved this connection by venerating both Constantine and Helen as saints.)

The cross of Calvary, miraculously rediscovered during excavations on Golgotha that they had ordered, constituted a royal symbol because, according to the testimony of the Gospels, it was inscribed with the

---

32. Paulinus of Nola, *Epistulae*, XLIV, 14, ed. Wilhelm von Hartel (Vienna: Tempsky, 1894).

33. Bernhard Kötting, *Peregrinatio religiosa: Wallfahrt und Pilgerwesen in Antike und alter Kirche* (Münster: Verlag Regensberg, 1950); Ewa Wipszycka, "Les pèlerinages chrétiens dans l'Antiquité tardive: Problèmes de définitions et de repères temporels," *Byzantinoslavica* 56 (1995): 429–45.

34. Colin Morris, *The Sepulchre of Christ and the Medieval West: From the Beginning to 1600* (Oxford: Oxford University Press, 2005).

words, "Jesus of Nazareth, king of the Jews."[35] Responsible for the salvation of humanity, Christ was to become a model and an obligatory reference for Christian rulers. This explains the early and enduring devotion that surrounds the "True Cross" or the "Holy Cross," which would be stolen by the Persians when they conquered Palestine in 614 and then triumphantly returned to Jerusalem by Emperor Heraclius in 629. During the fourth and fifth centuries, churches were built on the presumed locations of the principal episodes in the final journey of Jesus and his disciples in Jerusalem. Thus, the Church of Sion was constructed on the spot where the apostles and the Virgin Mary stood on the evening of Easter and at Pentecost. Around the year 500, there were no fewer than eighteen Christian holy places in the city, connected to each other through a series of processions regulated by the liturgy.[36]

In the religious art of late antiquity and the Middle Ages, Jerusalem—"a city where everything together is one" (Ps. 122:3)—is often presented as an image of the Eternal City of God to which believers aspired to go. In illuminations found in missals and liturgical books, it appears as an ideal city, founded upon the holy mountains ("fundamenta eius in montibus sanctis," as the Psalmist has it), and whose principal memorials were organized on an orthogonal plan bounded by the principal axes of passage and by its twelve doors. It was also represented as a stronghold surrounded by walls, at the center of which could be found an image of Christ whose head was surrounded by a solar nimbus formed of five rays (figure 4).[37]

This iconography illustrates the assertion of the English monk the Venerable Bede († 735) in *De locis sanctis*—a Latin abridgment of a work with the same title by the Irish monk Saint Adomnán († 704), based on the Holy Land travels of a Frankish bishop, Arculf, around 670—that at the spot where the cross was planted, there was a pillar that did not cast any shadow at the summer solstice, for it was here that the center of the earth, the "naval of the world," was located.[38]

---

35. Anatole Frolow, *La relique de la Vraie Croix: Recherches sur le développement d'un culte* (Paris: Institut des études byzantines, 1961).

36. Bianca Kühnel, *From the Earthly to the Heavenly Jerusalem: Representations of the Holy City in Christian Art of the First Millenium* (Freiburg: Herder, 1987); see also Bianca Kühnel, Galit Noga-Banai, and Hanna Vorholt, eds., *Visual Constructs of Jerusalem* (Turnhout: Brepols, 2014).

37. André Vauchez, "Faire voir Jérusalem: Des imitations du Saint-Sépulcre aux 'Sacri Monti' italiens," *Comptes rendus des séances de l'Académie des Inscriptions et Belles-Lettres* 160 (2016): 1559–72.

38. The Venerable Bede, *Liber de locis sanctis*, ed. J. Fraipont, Corpus Christianorum Series Latina 175 (Turnhout: Brepols, 1965).

FIGURE 4. Bird's-eye representation of walled Jerusalem but with only a single monument in its midst: a column surmounted by a cross and a medallion of Christ = Helios. Twelfth century. Bayerische Staatsbibliothek, Munich, Glossarium Salomonis—Clm 13002, fol. 4v.

The Rome of Martyrs and Popes

Very few Christians in the West went off to Palestine in this period, and their number diminished even further after the conquest of Jerusalem by Muslim Arabs in 638. For them, the holy city par excellence was still Rome. This is where the Apostles Peter and Paul, whose martyrdom in 64 or 65 was commemorated by a common feast on June 29, were venerated. Saint Jerome had asserted that the fact of going "ad limina apostolorum" (literally: to the doorsteps of the apostles) was the equivalent—on the spiritual plane—of the journey to Jerusalem. Indeed, it was not the ancient monuments that attracted pilgrims to Rome but rather the basilicas of Saint Peter and Saint Paul, located respectively at the Vatican and on the road that led toward Ostia. To these sites were quickly added Santa Maria Maggiore, the Church of the Holy Apostles, which housed the relics of Saints Philip and James the Lesser, and the Basilica of San Lorenzo fuori le Mura (Saint Lawrence Outside the Walls), just beyond the city.[39] This significant change, as compared with antiquity, reflects the new dialectic as to the relationships between the spaces of the dead and the living that was established through the cult of the saints. The ancient city had removed the dead from the city by prohibiting them from being buried within the city proper (*pomerium*); the Christian city reinstated them through cults devoted to martyrs and the first bishops, and by granting to the faithful the right to be buried near places where their relics were found (*ad sanctos*, near the holy ones).[40] From the time of Damasus I (366-84), popes expended considerable effort to take care of these tombs and to allow visitors to go and pray there. Pope Damasus I's initiatives in the catacombs—which were originally only cemeteries like any other—and the inscriptions that he had had engraved into the marble express a conscious desire to give a material foundation to the cult of the saints and to frame it within a coherent vision of the primordial role of the Roman Church within Christianity. From the seventh century and especially the eighth, because of the chaos created by the Lombard invasions throughout central Italy, the popes ordered holy bodies to be transferred from necropolises located on the periphery to within the walls of Rome, which helped to accentuate the sacred character of the city (figure 5). This also allowed the papacy to donate relics to Christian rulers or to missionaries with the aim of increasing the authority and prestige of the Holy See.

In the medieval period, however, it was not only the tombs of martyrs that drew the clergy and faithful to Rome but also the hope for some contact with the pope, who was considered "the apostle" par excellence.[41] The Roman Church was in their eyes a direct continuation with the apostolic period, with which they associated themselves through the person of the pope as successor of Peter and holder of the power of the keys. Visitors were impressed by the size of the basilica of the Vatican, which unlike other churches was oriented toward the west,

---

39. Charles Pietri, *Roma christiana* (Rome: École Française de Rome, 1976).

40. Éric Rebillard, *Religion et sépulture: L'Église, les vivants et les morts dans l'Antiquité Tardive* (Paris: EHESS, 2003).

41. Debra J. Birch, *Pilgrimage to Rome in the Middle Ages: Continuity and Change* (Woodbridge: Boydell, 1998); Jean Guyon, "Le pèlerinage à Rome et dans l'Occident chrétien pendant l'Antiquité Tardive (IVe-VIIe siècle)," in *Les pèlerinages dans le monde: À travers le temps et l'espace*, ed. Jean Chélini and Henri Branthomme (Paris: Hachette Littératures, 2004), 21-42; Stéphane Baciocchi and Christophe Duhamelle, eds., *Reliques romaines: Invention et circulation des corps saints des catacombes à l'époque moderne* (Paris: École Française de Rome, 2016).

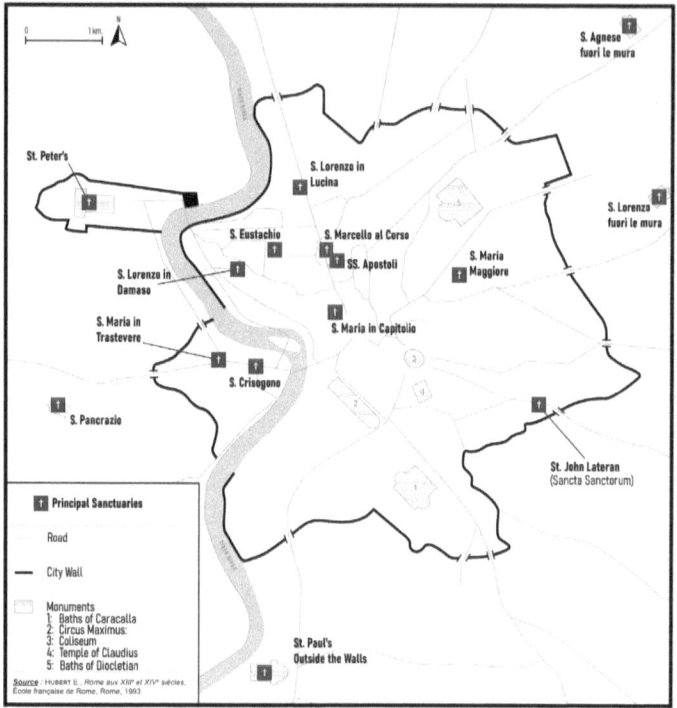

FIGURE 5. The principal sanctuaries of medieval Rome. Credit: A. Christesen.

its nave eighty-seven meters in length and its transept a hundred meters wide. It was built over a venerated cenotaph thought to be the tomb of Saint Peter, over which the basilica's altar and the Chapel of Confession was constructed; this was later surmounted by a baroque baldachin and a bronze casing (both designed by Bernini) enclosing the Chair of Saint Peter, a relic that celebrated his doctrinal magisterium and that of his successors, offered by Charles the Bald to Pope John VII in 876. Pilgrims also went to the basilica dedicated to Saint Sebastian on the Appian Way, which contained a commemorative monument called the Memoria Apostolorum (Monument of the Apostles), where the remains of Peter and Paul had for a time reposed.

Pilgrims coming to Rome also traveled to another basilica, founded by Constantine and Pope Sylvester I in 324: that of Saint John Lateran, which was the cathedral of the city and where the pope resided. There were many important relics there, such as a fragment of Jacob's Well, where Jesus had had his conversation with the Samaritan woman; the porphyry slab on which the soldiers had rolled dice for his tunic;

a column on top of which was mounted a bronze cock, which called to mind the denial of Peter; and the slab of the *mensura Christi* where the body of Christ had been placed and measured after his descent from the cross. Up to the eleventh century, Roman sanctuaries were especially frequented by visitors often recently converted to Christianity (like the English, the Frisians, and the Hungarians) who aspired to come there to drink from the streams of their faith.[42] After having sojourned in Rome, they often continued their journey toward the south, in the direction of Montecassino and especially toward the great Sanctuary of Monte Sant'Angelo on Mount Gargano on the Via dell'Angelo.

Constantinople: Holy City

During late antiquity, the East possessed very different types of sanctuaries, some of which attracted Christians from the West, as attested to in some voyagers' accounts. These include sites associated with the stylite ("pillar-dwelling") saints, Simeon († 459), venerated in Syria at Qal'at Se'man, and Daniel the Stylite († 493), revered at the site of his hermitage north of Constantinople, and the "Wondrous Mountain" near Antioch, where Simeon Stylites the Younger († 596/97) spent the last years of his life. The objects of these cults were the columns on which the ascetics dwelt (figure 6).

In Qal'at Se'man, this column was surrounded by a sacred octagonal space called a *mandra*, access to which was reserved to the emperor and to great ecclesiastical dignitaries.[43] It constituted the focal point of a single and completely covered cruciform building to which a sacred path led. The crossing of the threshold symbolized access to a sacred space separated from the world. The pilgrims eventually advanced into the great church that had been built close to the column of Saint Simeon, and where the altar, built over the relics, emphasized the preeminence of God over the saint. This sanctuary welcomed numerous visitors and pilgrims up to the time of the Arab conquest and even afterward. However, the relics of Simeon had been transported shortly

---

42. Julia Mary Howard Smith, "Care of Relics in Early Medieval Rome," in *Rome and Religion in the Medieval World: Studies in Honor of Thomas F. X. Noble*, ed. Valerie L. Garver and Owen Michael Phelan (Farnham: Ashgate, 2014), 179–205.

43. Jean-Pierre Sodini, "Saint Syméon: L'influence de Saint Syméon dans le culte et l'économie de l'Antiochène," in *Les sanctuaires et leur rayonnement dans le monde méditerranéen, de l'antiquité à l'époque moderne*, ed. Juliette de la Genière, André Vauchez, and Jean Leclant (Paris: De Boccard, 2010), 295–322.

FIGURE 6. Ex-voto plaque of Saint Simeon Stylites the Elder atop his column, ca. sixth–seventh centuries CE. From the treasury of the Church of Ma'aret in Noman in Syria and now in the collection of the Louvre Museum. Photo: Wikimedia Commons.

after his death into the neighboring city of Antioch, which made him its official protector. In the East, the devotion of the faithful also created considerable spaces for the Holy Saints of Palestine and the tombs of the ascetics of Syria and Egypt, in particular Saint Antony and the "Desert Fathers," as well as at the Monastery of Saint Catherine at the foot of Mount Sinai (figure 7).

After the Arab conquest of Jerusalem, Syria-Palestine, and Egypt in the seventh century, all of these sanctuaries declined, and Constantinople became for Eastern Christians the "second Jerusalem": a holy city dedicated to the worship of God and the saints of the Old and New Testaments.[44] For the Byzantine world, the imperial city was called to rule until the end of the world, as both the heir of Rome and, especially,

---

44. Alain Ducellier, "Une mythologie urbaine: Constantinople vue d'Occident au Moyen Age," *Mélanges de l'École Française de Rome–Moyen Âge* 96 (1984): 495–524.

FIGURE 7. Monastery of Saint Catherine, Mount Sinai, a major sanctuary for Christians from both East and West. Photo: Joonas Plaan via Wikimedia Commons (CC BY 2.0).

due to the protection of the Virgin Mary, the *Theotokos*, whose icon was attributed to Saint Luke and whose robe was kept and venerated in the Palace of Blachernae. Over the centuries, Byzantine emperors continued amassing in this place precious relics of the apostles, prophets, and saintly monks and bishops, and especially fragments of the True Cross, brought back from Jerusalem shortly before the fall of the city into the hands of the Muslims in 638. Around 530, Emperor Justinian built the Church of God's Holy Wisdom (Hagia Sophia)—the largest church in the Christian world—which, in his eyes, needed to rival the Temple of Solomon, or even surpass it by the beauty of its architecture and the richness of its mosaics.[45]

The preeminence of Constantinople was, however, contested even within the Byzantine Church by certain groups who asserted that the city risked becoming a "New Babylon" and being swallowed up by the nearby waves insofar as it wanted to see itself as the heir to imperial

---

45. Michel Kaplan, ed., *Le sacré et son inscription dans l'espace à Byzance et en Occident* (Paris: Publications de la Sorbonne, 2001).

Rome, whereas Jerusalem, even while captive, retained all of its prestige in their eyes since it was the place where the final episodes of the eschatological drama that had to precede the victorious return of Christ at the end of time were to be played out.[46] But this negative criticism remained negligible, and the sacral prestige of Constantinople held sway among Eastern and Russian Christians until the capture and pillaging of the city by the crusaders in 1204, which involved the dispersion of its treasury of relics throughout the whole western basin of the Mediterranean, up into France and the Netherlands.

Over the course of the early Middle Ages, the Eastern Church and the Roman Church diverged with regard to the cult of saints and the veneration of relics, which would never again have the same importance among Orthodox Christians as they would in the Latin Church. Bitter theological debates unfolded within the Byzantine Church about the nature of supernatural power. For example, did the sacred exist in the world in a "diffused" state within the relics of the saints and their images, or did it reside exclusively in the Eucharist? For the iconoclasts, the bread and wine consecrated on the altar were the true image of Christ, to the extent that it could only be consubstantial with his "prototype." In their eyes, the only bond existing between God and humans was the vertical one established on the altar through the Holy Spirit, agent of the sanctification of the "holy species." As for relics, they were certainly venerable, since for the saints, now being close to God in both body and spirit, their earthly remains no longer had anything but secondary value.[47] As a result, in the eighth century, the Isaurian emperors and their iconoclast clergy prohibited the placement of relics *inside* the altars but rather had them placed *beneath* the altars or in some other, less important places within churches. After the final victory of orthodoxy and the condemnation of iconoclasm, the Second Council of Nicaea (787) prohibited bishops from consecrating churches whose altars were devoid of relics, and they solemnly reestablished the cults around holy images or icons.[48] Nicaea had also asserted that the sanctuary, properly speaking, was the whole space located around the altar, behind the iconostasis (the wall of icons and religious paintings separating the nave from

---

46. Marie-Hélène Congourdeau, "Jérusalem et Constantinople dans la littérature apocalyptique," in Kaplan, *Le sacré et son inscription dans l'espace à Byzance et en Occident*, 125–36.

47. Marie-France Auzépy, "Les Isauriens et l'espace sacré: L'Église et les reliques," in Kaplan, *Le sacré et son inscription dans l'espace à Byzance et en Occident*, 13–24.

48. François Boespflug and Nicolas Lossky, eds., *Nicée II (787–1987)* (Paris: Éditions du Cerf, 1987).

the sanctuary), where the meeting between the human and divine took place at the moment of the consecration. Along these same lines, the vehicle of sacredness was the priest, not the saint, for the Church had to focus within itself all the manifestations of the relationship between human beings and God. In fact, as Gilbert Dagron has emphasized, the triumph of orthodoxy over iconoclasm was somewhat mixed "in that the former integrated a good part of its argumentation relative to the very status of the icon, holiness, and the miracle."[49]

The Latin West remained outside of this debate, which only marginally concerned it inasmuch as the images of the saints were even less numerous in sanctuaries and the cult of relics had taken on such a role that it was unimaginable to minimize their importance. Whereas Eastern Christian beliefs held that icons were inhabited by a supernatural presence that established a relationship between this world and the divine world above, in anticipation of the future glorification of the human person, the Latin West, since the time of Gregory the Great, accorded only a pedagogical role to images. The councils in the Carolingian period were therefore content to assert that there was no equivalency possible between a human "form" and a divine "prototype," which was of a wholly other nature, and that the holy image was not to become the object of adoration but of a simple veneration, for it did not have within itself any actual sacred character. By doing this, they did not define a doctrine of the image as much as they expressed their growing hostility to the Greek East and its religious practices, which had become foreign to them.

Tours and Saint-Martin

For the majority of Western Christians, however, Constantinople and even Rome were destinations too distant for easy travel, and so they restricted themselves mostly to regional or local sanctuaries. Even if Milan, Lyons, and Trier enjoyed a certain prestige as a result of the relics they possessed, the only holy site north of the Alps that benefited from a very broad influence during the Middle Ages was that of Saint-Martin in Tours. The presence of relics of "the apostle of the Gauls" helped to make Tours a holy city and the religious capital of the Frankish world. It was here that Clovis received the clothing and

---

49. Gilbert Dagron, "Vérité du miracle," in Scotto, *Del visibile credere*, 145.

insignia of consul (or *augustus*) sent by Emperor Anastasius II, which his successors would also don. The Frankish kings also preciously guarded Saint Martin's cloak (*capa*), which supposedly assured them of victory in battle. And when leading processions, the Frankish sovereigns inaugurated a sacred itinerary that would be later followed by numerous successors that went between the sepulchral Basilica of Saint-Martin (then located outside the city walls) and the cathedral dedicated to Saint Gatien. Toward the end of the sixth century, Gregory of Tours devoted four books to the *virtutes sancti Martini*, the 235 miracles accomplished by the bishop of Tours, whose sanctuary had been visited by Saint Columbanus and Saint Géry, as well as by King Dagobert and Saint Eloi.[50] Between the sixth and ninth centuries, Tours was really the city of Martin, and the numerous buildings that sprung up around the basilica housing his relics were considered a reflection of the power of the saint.[51] In his *Life of Saint Martin*, written around 800, Alcuin, counselor to Charlemagne, placed Tours among the cities of Christianity where the most important sanctuaries in the West could be found, a list that also included Rome, Milan (because of the relics of Saint Ambrose), Agaune in the Valais (where those of Saint Maurice and the martyrs of the Theban Legion were kept), Poitiers (with its memory of Saints Hilary and Radegonde), Paris (because of the abbeys of Saint-Germain and Saint-Denis), and Reims (through its association with Saint Rémy). But by 838, the only two places of pilgrimage recommended by the Carolingian clergy were Rome and Tours, confirmed in 938 by Pope Leo VIII when he stated, in a letter addressed to the abbot of Saint-Martin, that "no place of pilgrimage, except Saint Peter's in Rome, attracts as great a number of supplicants among all the different and faraway countries."[52]

Rural Sanctuaries and the Christianization of the Countryside

Between the fourth and eighth centuries, the Christianization of the countryside was one of the primary objectives of the Church, and it ended up transforming the beliefs and religious practices of rural

---

50. Pietri, *La ville de Tours du IVe au VIe siècle*.
51. Bruno Judic, "Le pèlerinage à Saint-Martin de Tours du VIIe au Xe siècle," in Chélini and Branthomme, *Les pèlerinages dans le monde*, 55–72.
52. Judic, "Le pèlerinage à Saint-Martin," 68.

inhabitants. This transformation did not happen in a day.[53] In ancient "paganism," the powers that revealed themselves in the world did not originate in the celestial beyond. Nature was everywhere impregnated with sacredness since it harbored forces that manifested themselves in privileged spaces like streams and springs, or around certain particularly venerable trees, like the Irminsul, a gigantic oak venerated by the Saxons that Charlemagne had cut down once he had subjugated their lands. It was thus necessary to convince the "pagans"—the Latin word *pagani* initially referred to peasants and then took on the meaning of "non-Christians"—that supernatural power resided not in things but in people, the saints, and in their relics. Once the phase of violent eradication of certain sanctuaries that marked the evangelization campaigns of Saint Martin in Touraine and Berry, or of Saint Columbanus on the borders of the Vosges, had passed, the transition between the two religious worlds took place most often quietly, as evidenced by the role played by the sacred springs where the name of a saint replaced that of a preexisting divinity. In this domain, there is a real continuity between the pagan sanctuaries like the one at the mouth of the Seine, with its numerous ex-voto, and the Christian water sanctuaries—streams and springs—to which the faithful ascribed therapeutic powers.

Emotional Communities and Enduring Solidarities

What made Christian sanctuaries so successful? Initially, it was the efficaciousness of the intercession of the saint that people came to implore, as well as the special ambiance that reigned there. The visitor or pilgrim approached the holy site with sadness, weighed down by their own sins and faults, and it was with fear that they crossed over the boundary (in Latin, *limina*) of this sacred space where a mysterious force resided. Having entered the church or grotto, the faithful were seized by the atmosphere of prayer and contemplation that reigned there, and they expressed their profound emotion by shedding tears and addressing petitions to the master of the place.[54] As they would often spend eight days there (a novena) and sometimes slept close to the tomb in the hope of being healed during the night by a vision of the saint, a kind of emotional

---

53. Hervé Inglebert, Sylvain Destephen, and Bruno Dumézil, eds., *Le problème de la christianisation du monde Antique* (Paris: Picard, 2010).
54. Barbara Rosenwein, *Emotional Communities in the Early Middle Ages* (Ithaca, NY: Cornell University Press, 2006).

community would sometimes form between the pilgrims who came there and those welcoming them as seen in collections of miracles.[55] Lasting bonds could afterward be established between the one healed and that sanctuary. These were translated into offerings, beginning with miraculously healed children who were then offered by their parents to the religious life (called oblates), as well as the creation of lasting connections between clerics and certain aristocratic families. This symbiosis between the sanctuary and its surroundings also involved the people in the countryside. Monks endeavored to nourish a devotion toward their patron saint among their dependents and their neighbors, while some of the devout and the healed put their energies to work in service to the religious community as "servants," testifying to their gratitude toward the holy ones of God who had healed or saved them. Thus, during the Middle Ages, sanctuaries were often poles around which collective identities grounded in the memory of the holy founder and his cult were formed.[56]

Grottos and Caverns: Rock Sanctuaries

The Role of Angels: Saint Michael between Heights and Depths

Parallel to this sacralizing of rural and forested spaces, another type of sanctuary developed in the Mediterranean world, from Palestine to Provence by way of southern and central Italy. They were sometimes called *theophanic*, as their origins were tied, in the foundation stories, to a divine manifestation, usually through an angel. In biblical texts, angels are presented as messengers who transmit the promises of God to humanity; in Christian liturgy, they were invoked as mediators between heaven and earth.[57] Between 490 and 492, Saint Michael the Archangel is said to have appeared on Mount Gargano, north of Apulia, at the entrance of an immense grotto, which was transformed into a Christian sanctuary during the sixth century (figure 8). This was not a given,

---

55. Albert Marignan, *Études sur la civilisation française*, vol. 2, *Le culte des saints sous les Mérovingiens* (Paris: Librairie Émile Bouillon, 1889); Cynthia Hahn, "Seeing and Believing: The Construction of Sanctity in Early-Medieval Saints' Shrines," *Speculum* 72 (1997): 1079–1106.

56. Philippe Faure, *Les Anges* (Paris: Éditions du Cerf, 1988).

57. Giorgio Otranto, "Le rayonnement du sanctuaire de saint Michel au mont Gargan en Italie du Sud, à l'époque médiévale," in de la Genière, Vauchez, and Leclant, *Les sanctuaires et leur rayonnement dans le monde méditerranéen*, 323–57; Armando Petrucci, "Aspetti del culto e del pellegrinaggio di S. Michele Arcangelo sul Monte Gargano," in *Pellegrinaggi e culto dei santi in Europa fino all prima Crociata* (Todi: Accademia tudertina, 1963), 145–80.

FIGURE 8. The grotto-sanctuary of Monte Sant'Angelo on Mount Gargano, Apulia, Italy. Photo: Paolo Monti via Wikimedia Commons/BEIC Foundation (CC BY-SA 4.0).

for the clergy held a certain antipathy toward such subterranean lairs where the cult of Mithras—for a long time the principal rival of Christianity—was celebrated. According to the founding legend, however, the manifestation of the archangel, which would have consecrated the grotto for Christian worship, overcame the doubts among the clergy, who thereafter sought to make of this fraught place an occasion for a meeting between God and human beings. To do so, they had recourse to a biblical reference, inscribing Jacob's words after his struggle with the angel in Genesis 28:17 onto the entrance of the sanctuary: "Oh how fearful is this place! It is nothing less than a house of God and the gateway to heaven!"

The origins of this cult were not indigenous: Saint Michael, mentioned in the Old Testament, was already venerated in the Byzantine East, and his cult did not take long to spread to Rome, where a basilica was built in his honor on the Via Flaminia. At the beginning of the seventh century, he was introduced into the Mausoleum of Hadrian (later called the Castel Sant'Angelo). An apparition of the archangel had appeared over it, putting an end to a plague there during an intercessory procession organized, according to tradition, by Pope Gregory the Great († 604). In fact, the cult of Saint Michael seems to have allowed the Church to Christianize both the heights (where one often found temples dedicated to Mercury or local divinities), as well as the depths of the earth, especially the darkened grottos considered to be the lair of demons.

Beginning in the fourth century, under the influence of Neoplatonism, however, this perspective changed. Certain doctors of the Church, like Gregory of Nyssa († 394), Christianized the myth of the cavern by seeing in it a metaphor of the obscurity in which the pagan world lived and of the illumination brought by the Christian faith to believers. Was not the Son of God born in Bethlehem in an underground cave (*spelunca*), which manifested its aptness for welcoming the Word of God and allowing itself to be illumined by him? And had not his body been placed, after the Passion, in a kind of grotto made into a tomb, the Holy Sepulcher, from which burst forth the light of the Resurrection? On the other hand, and in a more concrete fashion, pastoral necessities led bishops or monks to intervene and put an end to pagan cults, which were still surviving quietly in the shadows. This is what seems to have occurred at the grotto of the Tancia, in the Sabine Hills, according to the *Life* of Pope Sylvester († 335). The text attributes to him the deed of having chased away the dragon that had been living there, though in fact it was probably the goddess Vacuna, whose statue had been venerated there by locals. Over the following centuries, a cave-sanctuary developed in this grotto dedicated to Saint Michael; it later acquired a regional reputation, as witnessed by the dispute over its possession between the bishop of Sabina and the abbot of Farfa in the ninth century.[58]

Another sanctuary, very famous at the time, was Mons Aureus, in Olevano sul Tusciano (near Salerno) dedicated to the archangel in Italy. The Frankish monk Bernard, returning from his pilgrimage in the Holy Land, visited it around 870 before going on to Mont-Saint-Michel, and left a brief description of it:

> We arrived at Mons Aureus where there is a grotto [*crypta*] where are found seven altars and above which is a large forest. No one

---

58. Tessa Cannella, *Storia e leggenda del santuario di S. Michele al Monte Tancia* (Bari: Edipuglia, 2020).

could enter into this grotto because of its inky darkness that predominated there, except with lighted torches. The abbot of the place is the lord Valentine.[59]

Even today, the remains of these altars extend across the length of the deep grotto, the walls of which are covered with frescoes, which go back to the second half of the ninth century, devoted to the life of Christ and to the legend of Saint Peter.

Grottos and Wells: From the Gargano to the Purgatory of Saint Patrick

In fact, the exact nature of these sanctuaries is rather difficult to define due to the polyvalence of the word *crypta* in the texts of the period. This term can refer to both artificial excavations and natural grottos. Moreover, the difference between the two is further obscured because many of the grotto sanctuaries in central Italy were cavernous habitats from the Etruscan period, if not earlier, carved out of volcanic tuff or limestone that had later been enlarged and transformed into chapels or oratories. Almost all of them contained an altar and a basin for the waters running down the cave walls (*stilla*), which were said to have therapeutic properties for humans and livestock, as well as a holy image painted on the wall behind the altar.

One of the most remarkable examples is the underground church of Sutri, north of Rome (figure 9). Located near a Roman amphitheater, it replaced a *mithraeum* and was dedicated, during the Middle Ages, to Saint Michael the Archangel, as the frescoes on its walls, depicting the legend of Gargano and pilgrims journeying toward the holy mountain, illustrate. In the modern era, it became a Marian shrine and took on the name of Madonna del Parto (Our Lady of Childbirth).

Influenced by the grotto sanctuary of Gargano dedicated to Saint Michael, the Church oversaw the construction of grottos elsewhere. (This practice would recur at the end of the nineteenth century with the grotto in Lourdes, reproduced around the world.) In Rome, Pope Boniface V (619–25) created an oratory in the form of a crypt, dedicated to the archangel, on top of the Castel Sant'Angelo. And in the account

---

59. *Das "Itinerarium Bernardi monachi": Edition, Übersetzung, Kommentar*, ed. Josef Ackermann (Hannover: Verlag Hahnsche Buchhandlung, 2010), 154; Jean-René Gaborit and François Avril, "L'*Itinerarium Bernardi monachi*' et les pèlerinages d'Italie du Sud pendant le Haut Moyen Age," *Mélanges de l'École Française de Rome* 79 (1967): 259–98.

FIGURE 9. Fresco of the Nativity in the Church of the Madonna del Parto, Sutri, Italy. Photo by André Vauchez.

of the origins of the Abbey of Mont-Saint-Michel (*Revelatio ecclesiae sancti Michaelis*, composed at the beginning of the ninth century), the author reports that in 709, the bishop of Avranches, Aubert, built at the foot of the mountain an edifice that "was not constructed upward in the air with an elegant roofing but had a circular shape similar to a grotto capable of receiving over a hundred people."[60] Its prelate then sent monks to the sanctuary of Saint Michael of Gargano to bring back relics, including a piece of marble upon which the archangel was said to have placed his foot.

Sanctuaries of this type did not disappear after the year 1000, as the success of the pilgrimage to the Purgatory of Saint Patrick in Ireland attests. Indeed, at the end of the twelfth century, the *Treatise on the Purgatory of Saint Patrick* began to spread throughout all of Christianity; its author was a layman, Henry of Saltrey, who later became a Cistercian monk. In it, he recounts the story of a knight named Owein who,

---

60. *Revelatio ecclesiae sancti Michaelis*, transcription by Pierre Bouet and Olivier Desbordes of ms. Avranches, Bibliothèque municipal, 211, fol. 180v–89, in *Culte et pèlerinages à Saint Michel en Occident: Les trois monts dédiés à l'archange*, ed. Pierre Bouet, Giorgio Otranto, and André Vauchez (Rome: École Française de Rome, 2003), 19.

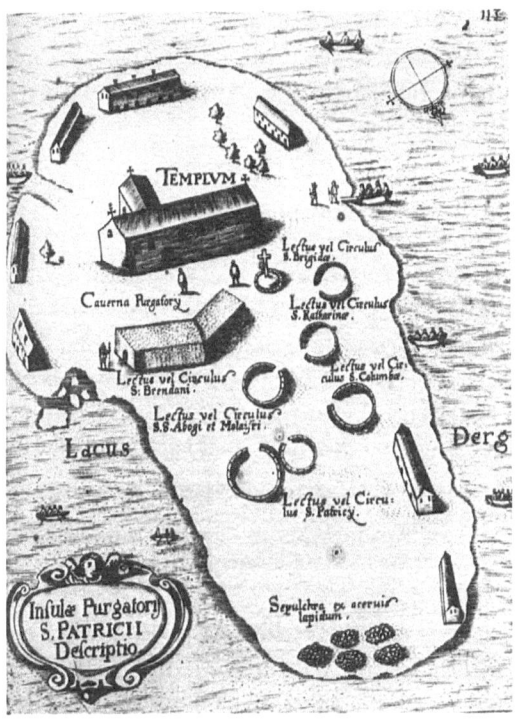

FIGURE 10. Map of the Isle of Saint Patrick's Purgatory (Lough Derg), with the entrance to the cave marked as "Caverna Purgatory." From Thomas Carve, *Lyra sive Anacephalaeosis Hibernica* (Sulzbach, 1666).

after having descended underground through a deep shaft, succeeded in entering purgatory at the end of a fifteenth day of penitential fasting, and after having suffered terrible demonic assaults. Concluding his otherworldly journey, Owein was assured that his sins had been forgiven and that he would be spared the pains of purgatory after death. The work enjoyed great success and was translated into the majority of the vernacular languages of Europe. Influenced by this account, a sanctuary and a pilgrimage developed around a well, located on the island of Lough Derg (Red Lake), in County Donegal, that allowed the living to have access to the world of the dead (figure 10). This site attracted innumerable visitors—women were admitted after 1323—and not only the laity. Around 1375, Saint Catherine of Siena had to write a letter to a Carthusian of Rome to soothe his feelings, who was furious that his prior had forbidden him to go there on pilgrimage.[61] This site ended up being banned in 1497 by Pope Alexander VI, perhaps because it allowed those who went there to be exempted from the punishments of purgatory without any need to resort to papal indulgences.

Eremitical Sanctuaries

In rural regions, numerous shrines mark eremitical foundations that developed in the West beginning in the sixth century and often led to the creation of sanctuaries, like that of Suppentona (Castel Sant'Elia, in Roman Tuscia, not far from Mount Soratte), associated with the memory of its founder, the monk Anastasius of Suppentona († 570), mentioned by Gregory the Great in his *Dialogues*.[62] The same work discusses Saint Benedict, who had spent some time in the Sacro Speco, near Subiaco, a cave that became a sanctuary following a miracle, before his departure for Montecassino. The spread of eremitism has been an important factor in the sacralizing of space, especially in the mountainous and wooded regions in the east of France where the "Fathers of the Jura"—Saint Romanus/Romain, Saint Lupicinus/Lupicin, and Saint Eugendus/Oyend—had settled at the beginning of the sixth century. They were at the origin of an abbey (renamed after Saint Claude in the thirteenth century) that became a place of pilgrimage very much frequented throughout the Middle Ages. For these "men of God," the forest was the equivalent of the Egyptian desert for Saint Antony.

Hermits are usually men—more rarely women—who choose solitude in order to do penance. They settle in natural sites located outside towns and routes of communication but not, however, too far from them. Dead to the world, they can devote themselves to prayer and the struggle against sin, while at the same time embracing asceticism. They have only a grotto or hut to shelter them, eat strictly vegetarian food, patch together clothing, display an abundant growth of hair, similar to that of John the Baptist, and exhibit some amiable rapport with animals: such is the prototype of the hermit in medieval iconography and literature.[63] The *vitae* of these anchorites are filled with episodes of them

---

61. Catherine of Siena, Letter 201, in *Le Lettere di Santa Caterina da Siena*, ed. Niccolò Tommaseo (Florence: Giunti Barbera, 1866), 76–77.

62. Gregory the Great, *Dialogues*, I, 8, 2, ed. Adalbert De Vogüé (Paris: Éditions du Cerf, 1980).

63. Liz Herbert McAvoy, *Anchoritic Traditions of Medieval Europe* (Woodbridge: Boydell, 2010); Florent Pouvreau, *Du poil et de la bête: Iconographie de corps sauvage en Occident à la fin du Moyen Age (XIIIe–XVIe siècle)* (Paris: Éditions du CTHS, 2015).

pushing back against a threatening landowner trying to put an end to the "wild" settlement of their domain by a man (or woman) of God, of welcoming and caring for animals, or of stopping a king engaged in hunting. Given its rigor, this life was definitely a dangerous one, but those who succeeded in finding a balance in this kind of life soon drew the attention of inhabitants of the surrounding regions, who came to them as mediators between the world below and the supernatural.

In life, these anchorites were said to have purged the wilderness of its demons (serpents, bears, or dragons, depending on the case) and often brought forth streams of clear spring water. They later took possession of a part of this land by constructing a cell and an oratory. Upon the death of the hermit (who was sometimes joined by a few companions), their holiness would confer an aura of sacredness over the places where they had lived. Frequently, a sanctuary was then established where their memory was venerated and where followers could implore their intercession in the face of the difficulties of existence (figure 11).[64] Later, the ecclesiastical authorities completed the sacralizing of the place by blessing the perimeter of the hermitage and consecrating a chapel or a church that housed their tomb. These liturgical ceremonies helped the new sanctuary gain formal juridical status through ecclesiastical legislation, which granted it a title, patrimony, and the benefit of the right of asylum. Quite often, this privileged place became a refuge for fugitives or women hoping to escape from violent husbands or aggressors.

The history of Saint-Gilles in the Gard (in Languedoc) provides an interesting example of a sanctuary of eremitical origin. The hermit lived on this site in the eighth century, or at the beginning of the ninth. His *vita*, highly legendary, was edited in the tenth century. A great abbey developed around his tomb; it belonged to Cluny between 1066 and 1132, when it was freed from Cluny's jurisdiction. Conveniently located near a port, where one could embark for Rome and the Holy Land, and on the routes that led to Compostela through Arles, the monastery underwent great expansion and was closely tied to the papacy at the time of the Gregorian Reform. The relics of Saint Gilles drew crowds of pilgrims, who came especially from German- and Slavic-speaking lands, most notably Poland. Between 1120 and 1124, its monks wrote a *Book of Miracles*, which was completed before 1160.[65] Considered a very

---

64. Charles Mériaux, *Gallia irradiata: Saints et sanctuaires dans le nord de la Gaule du Haut Moyen Age* (Stuttgart: Franz Steiner Verlag, 2006).

65. Marcel Girault and Pierre-Gilles Girault, *Visages de pèlerins au Moyen Age: Les pèlerinages européens dans l'art et l'épopée* (La-Pire-qui-Vire: Zodiaque, 2001).

FIGURE 11. The eremetical sanctuary of San Colombano, Trambileno, Italy. According to legend, the Irish monastic Columbanus († 615) slew a dragon that lived in one of the caves in the walls of the gorge near the monastery he founded at Bobbio. From 753 to 1782, the cave served as a hermitage. The present church was built in 1319. Photo: Wikimedia Commons (CC BY-SA 3.0).

powerful intercessor—he had a revelation of a sin that Charlemagne never confessed and obtained a pardon for him from God, allowing the emperor to enter paradise—Gilles is often invoked as a last resort by characters in medieval epics. In 1116, the monks there undertook the construction of a vast edifice, one of the masterpieces of Romanesque art in Languedoc, sumptuously decorated and provided with an ambulatory to facilitate the circulation of pilgrims inside the church. The reliquary of this hermit is described in minute detail in the twelfth-century *Iter pro peregrinis ad Compostellam* (*Guide for the Pilgrim to Compostela*), whose author asserts that "Saint Gilles, famous throughout all the countries in the world, must be venerated, worthily honored by all and by all loved, invoked, and petitioned."[66]

---

66. *Le Guide du pèlerin de Saint-Jacques de Compostelle*, ed. Jeanne Vielliard (Mâcon: Protat Frères, 1963), 38–39.

Part II

The Sacred and Its Integration into European Spaces

CHAPTER 2

From the Middle Ages to the Renaissance

Bridging Heaven and Earth: The Phenomenon of Relics in Europe

Beginning in the Carolingian period, a tendency to amass large numbers of relics appeared, which resulted in the creation of actual treasuries in a few privileged areas, designated as *sanctuaria*. From the fifth century, the popes had set an example by creating in Rome, next to the Lateran Palace, a vast reliquary chapel on the model of the Treasury of the Temple in Jerusalem. In the ninth century, it contained both precious objects—relics, jewels, sacred vessels, and illuminated liturgical books—as well as stones originally from Palestine, which is not surprising since, in the neighboring Basilica di Santa Croce in Gerusalemme, soil from Golgotha, along with a fragment of the True Cross, were venerated at the same time. Decorated with frescoes commissioned by the popes at the beginning of the ninth century, this edifice was enlarged and enriched with new relics by Nicholas III in 1277, when it took on the name the Holy of Holies (Sancta Sanctorum), the same name as the most sacred part of the Temple of Jerusalem, where the Ark of the Covenant was found.[1]

---

1. Bruno Galland, *Les authentiques de reliques du Sancta Sanctorum* (Vatican City: Biblioteca Apostolica Vaticana, 2004); Guido Cornini, "*'Non est in toto sanctior orbe locus*': Collecting Relics

The *Great Plundering* of Holy Bodies: Ninth and Tenth Centuries

Parallel to this development, certain abbeys in the northern half of France that were associated closely with imperial power created or enriched their preexisting sacred treasures, notably the Abbey of Saint-Riquier (originally called Centula, it boasted the stone upon which Christ was seated during the multiplication of loaves), Saint-Denis in Paris, and the Abbey of Saint-Médard de Soissons. The latter was still being reconstructed when, in 841, Abbot Hilduin installed Saint Sebastian's relics, which he had had brought from Rome, in the presence of Emperor Charles the Bald. They were placed in the crypt next to those of Saint Médard and other saints, such as the Roman martyr Tiburtius. However, the influence of this sanctuary declined after its pillaging and partial destruction by the Normans at the beginning of the tenth century. At Saint-Denis, tradition held that Charlemagne had offered to the abbey, upon his return from pilgrimage in Jerusalem, a few particularly precious relics—a nail from the Crucifixion and a fragment of the Crown of Thorns—to be added to those of the Parisian martyrs Denis, Rusticus, and Eleutherius that it already possessed.

During the waves of the Norman, Hungarian, and "Saracen" invasions that pummeled western Europe in the first half of the tenth century, many sanctuaries were destroyed and their relics dispersed throughout all of Christendom. An illustration of this forced migration of relics is the transfer of the remains of Saint Philbert († 665) from the island of Noirmoutier (in the Bay of Biscay) to the Abbey of Grandlieu near Nantes in 836, then to Cunault in Touraine, then into the Poitou and the Allier, before finally ending up in Tournus in Burgundy, where at the start of the eleventh century they were at the center of one of the earliest monuments of Romanesque architecture in France. This climate of chaos favored a process that the Italian historian Eugenio Dupré Theseider has called "the great plundering of holy bodies."[2] It was accompanied by a systematic pillaging of the Roman catacombs—where, it was believed, a number of martyrs were buried—through the

---

in Early Medieval Rome," in *Saints, Relics, and Devotion in Medieval Europe*, ed. Martina Bagnoli, Holger A. Klein, C. Griffith Mann, and James Robinson (Cleveland: Cleveland Museum of Art, 2011), 69–78.

2. Eugenio Dupré Theseider, "La grande rapina dei corpi santi dell'Italia al tempo di Ottone," in *Festschrift Percy Ernst Schramm: Zu Seinem Siebzigsten Geburtstag von Schülern und Freunden Zugeeignet*, ed. Peter Classen, Percy Ernst Schramm, and Peter Scheibert, vol. 1 (Wiesbaden: Franz Steiner, 1964), 420–32.

initiative of bishops and abbots in northwestern Europe, aided by local intermediaries. The importance of relics during this period, including politically, is made clear by the critical role they played during the first half of the eleventh century, during the Peace of God movement, in which public oaths were made on holy bodies from the surrounding region that were brought to the sites where Peace assemblies were held.

From Churches of Wood to Churches of Stone

The passage from the *Chronicle* of the Cluniac monk Raoul Glaber about the "white mantle of churches" dotting the landscape of Christianity is often quoted when discussing the first decades of the eleventh century. It is, in fact, a twofold phenomenon, both quantitative—the incontestable multiplication of the number of sanctuaries—and qualitative to the extent that this numerical increase was accompanied by a "monumentalization" of these structures, where stone often replaced wood. Parallel to this, as Dominique Iogna-Prat has demonstrated, the word *ecclesia* (church) imposed itself in the same period to refer to the places of worship, by way of a metonymy between its "content"—the Church as a community of believers—and the "container," that is, the building itself that housed their celebrations.[3] The ecclesiastical authors of the tenth and eleventh centuries multiplied the references to the places and structures in which, according to the Bible, God had revealed himself: Noah's Ark, the Tabernacle of Moses, and the Temple of Solomon in Jerusalem. In the liturgy, the ritual of the consecration or dedication of churches (*ordo ad consecrandam ecclesiam*) expanded considerably, to such an extent that this ceremony, accompanied by several bishops, came to last almost five hours and was likened to a baptism. The texts that were read or sung on this occasion developed the idea of a relationship between the earthly Church and the heavenly Jerusalem that will be revealed at the end of time, as described in the book of Revelation (Rev. 21:2-11), the church of stone being the reflection of this heavenly Church and of its splendor. As the place where the faithful gather, it prefigures the holy city, and the bond between the two is assured by

---

3. Charles Bonnet, "Les églises du haut Moyen Age d'après les recherches archéologiques," in *Grégoire de Tours et l'espace gaulois*, ed. Nancy Gauthier and Henri Galinié, supplement to the *Revue archéologique du Centre de la France* 13 (Tours: Association Grégoire 94, 1997), 217-36; John Crook, *The Architectural Setting of the Cult of Saints in the Early Christian West, ca. 300–1200* (Oxford: Clarendon Press, 2000); Dominique Iogna-Prat, *La Maison-Dieu: Une histoire monumentale de l'Église au Moyen Age (v. 800–v. 1200)* (Paris: Seuil, 2006).

FIGURE 12. The Majesty of Saint Foy, Conques, Aveyron. Photo: ZiYouXun Lu via Wikimedia Commons (CC BY-SA 3.0).

the presence of Christ on the altar at the moment of the Eucharistic sacrifice, as well as by the relics of the saints.

In the principal sanctuaries, starting in the ninth century, a special place was made for these relics. In the Germanic empire, *Westbau* (west buildings), often dedicated to Saint Michael the Archangel, were developed to house them, such as at the Abbey of Corvey in Saxony, around 880; in Burgundy or central-west France, they were called "Galilees," or porch-towers, as in Fleury around the year 1000. Meanwhile, pilgrims' spaces in churches began to be differentiated from the choir reserved for religious and clergy. Through works of art commissioned by bishops or monks, especially the frescos that adorned their churches, large crucifixes, and statues of the Virgin, the Christian imagination took root in the sacred space and imposed itself there in a stable and enduring manner. The Invisible then took on human form with the rebirth of freestanding sculptures and the appearance of statues of the saints in majesty, male and female, like that of Saint Foy in Conques, covered with gold and gems (figure 12). Finally, the Western Church recognized the sacred character of the images of Christ, the Virgin, and the saints, whose power it would then extol over the following centuries.

This evolution, however, inspired some hostile reactions. For example, the cleric Bernard d'Angers († 1059), in his prologue to the miracles of Saint Foy, very clearly expresses the revulsion that the first view of the saint's statue stirred in him—he does not hesitate to compare it to an idol—until the miracles that occurred at the sanctuary of Conques made him change his opinion. In Arras, in 1022, the uneasy laity—soon characterized by the clergy as heretics—protested that, citing Saint Paul, "the God who made the world and everything within it does not live in temples made by human hands" (Acts 17:24) and that the Church is a gathering of believers before being an edifice of stone.[4] But thereafter, it became a minority opinion, contradicted by the fever of religious building projects, from simple village churches up to abbeys and cathedrals that gripped the imagination of all Western Christianity.

The Religious Control of Space

This evolution went hand in hand with the sacralizing of certain spaces outside the church. Between the ninth and eleventh centuries, the parish cemetery, reserved exclusively for the burial of the faithful, became a reality in the West.[5] Instead of being buried in the open field or in necropolises, as was often the case before then, the remains of the dead were henceforth gathered into cemeteries near the parish church, which then became objects of consecration. In the course of this ceremony, the clergy sprinkled holy water in the enclosure, while lit candles were placed along its boundaries at the four cardinal points. These liturgical actions were intended to give the cemetery the specific characteristics of a religious site, withdrawing this space from the sphere of the profane to reserve it for God and the use of baptized believers, at least in the ideal. (In reality, however, the situation was often quite different, and cemeteries remained very busy places for a long time.) The ritual concluded with an appeal for divine protection to guard the bodies of the dead from demonic attacks until the Last Judgment and with prayers that they might find rest in the otherworld and not come

---

4. Robert I. Moore, *Hérétiques: Résistances et répression dans l'Occident médiéval* (Paris: Belin, 2017), 84–96. First published in English as *The War on Heresy: Faith and Power in Medieval Europe* (Cambridge, MA: Harvard University Press, 2012).

5. Cécile Treffort, *L'Église carolingienne et la mort: Christianisme, rites funéraires et pratiques commémoratives* (Lyons: Presses universitaires de Lyon, 1996); Cécile Treffort, "Consécrations de cimetières et contrôle épiscopal des lieux d'inhumation," in *Le sacré et son inscription dans l'espace à Byzance et en Occident*, ed. Michel Kaplan (Paris: Publications de la Sorbonne, 2001), 285–99; Michel Lauwers, *Naissance des cimetières: Lieux sacrés et terre des morts dans l'Occident médiéval* (Paris: Aubier, 2005).

back to bother the living through unexpected appearances. Burial in "Christian ground" was, in principle, denied to the excommunicated, to heretics, and of course to Jews. With the consecrated cemetery, the process of leading Christians, dead or living, toward salvation finally reached its end.

From the middle of the eleventh century, with the so-called Gregorian Reform—taken from the name of Pope Gregory VII (1073-85), who was its chief promotor—with this "great conversion of Christian society to the earthly world," according to Jacques Le Goff's formulation, the Church endeavored to give an increased visibility to the divine among human beings by incarnating it in tangible forms.[6] In the eyes of the clergy, everything that had been transformed by way of liturgical action, in the context of a consecration ceremony, was henceforth sacred. Through appropriate rituals, spiritual realities are inscribed in places or physical objects are made sacred. Parallel to this bridging of space between the earthly and the heavenly, the territorial structures of the Church were made more precise and the boundaries of dioceses and parishes began to be defined in a clearer fashion.[7] Sacred places—which in Roman law belonged to no one (*res nullius*)—also came to be considered the property of the Church and not of lay or individual authorities, due to their explicitly religious purpose. Bishops and monks then vigorously demanded from the laity the restitution of the altars that represented and commemorated the redemptive sacrifice of Christ due to their sacred character.

The Imprint of Monasticism

Monks and Space

The considerable increase in the number of sanctuaries throughout Western Christianity, starting around the end of the tenth century, must also be seen in the context of another important phenomenon in the religious domain: the evolution of the sacrament of penance between the ninth and the eleventh centuries. Pilgrimage, which had not been favored by ecclesiastical authorities during the Carolingian period, now became an expiatory practice—and prescribed as such by

---

6. Jacques Le Goff, *Héros du Moyen Âge, le Saint et le Roi* (Paris: Gallimard, 2004), 1281.

7. Florian Mazel, *L'évêque et le territoire: L'invention médiévale de l'espace (V^e–XIIIe siècle)* (Paris: Seuil, 2016).

bishops—especially for serious sins of a public nature, committed by laypeople who, by this fact, found themselves excluded from the community of believers.[8] Some eleventh-century texts, like the "Vision of Narni" contained in the *Life of Pope Leo IX* († 1054), even expressed the conviction that the dead undertook penance for their sins while on earth by posthumously traveling in groups from one sanctuary to another. Asked by someone who had known him in life, a revenant declared: "We are sinful souls; we do not yet merit the joys of the kingdom of heaven and, for our penance, we travel tirelessly to the holy sites. We have arrived today from Marmoutier, the Monastery of Saint-Martin, and we are heading toward the Abbey of Mary, the Blessed Mother of God, in Farfa."[9] (The great Monastery of Saint Mary of Farfa, located in the Sabine Hills, northeast of Rome, was founded after a Marian vision. Both it and Saint-Martin were important monastic sanctuaries, famous for the tenor of their religious observances.)

This evolution went hand in hand with the growing influence of Benedictine monasticism—which was founded on the prestige of the kind of life prescribed by the Rule of Saint Benedict and henceforth became the most prolific expression of monasticism in the West—and the way in which it organized and marked out space. In many texts during the early feudal age, the word "place" (*locus*, implying "holy" [*sanctus*] or "dedicated to God" [*Deo dicatus*]), refers to a religious establishment. Abbeys tended to become the structuring pillars of the territory over which they exercised a spiritual and sometimes temporal control. They played an important role in the process of *encellulement* (to use Robert Fossier's term) or enclosure, which characterized Western society, especially in the rural world, between the tenth and twelfth centuries. Whatever its configuration and spiritual influence, the monastery—which had often developed around the tomb of a saint, male or female—already comprised by itself a sacred space, isolated within a given territory and removed from the profane world. As a general rule, it included a cloister—the earthly anticipation of paradise—and, for the monks, the desire for God erased in some way the distance separating the present from the future Parousia (the Second Coming). Indeed, the monastery was in an ambiguous situation: those who made profession

---

8. Cyrille Vogel, *Le pécheur et la pénitence au Moyen Age* (Paris: Éditions du Cerf, 1969).

9. André Vauchez, "Pèlerinages posthumes et purgation des péchés: La vision de Narni (milieu du XIe siècle)," in *Mediterraneo, Mezzogiorno, Europa: Studi in onore di Cosimo Damiano Fonseca*, ed. Giancarlo Andenna and Hubert Houben, vol. 2 (Bari: Adda, 2004), 1081–90.

there removed themselves from the world, as Saint Bernard firmly reminded some of his monks who had wanted to leave on pilgrimage to the Holy Land, and yet they were not entirely indifferent to the world for whose salvation they prayed.

This dialectical relationship between flight from the world and action upon it is translated in a concrete way in the behaviors of religious communities. The monk inhabits a space and renders it sacred through his way of life, whereas the abbey manifests the divine presence in the midst of humanity by demonstrating what a world returned to order would be, in contrast with the prevailing disorder in society. The religious history of the Middle Ages has not taken into account sufficiently the role played by the numerous monastic or canonical establishments that appeared and crisscrossed the Christian world between the tenth and twelfth centuries. While there is no reason to idealize them, for not all were "citadels of prayer" or even edifying communities, a number of them did constitute "micro-sanctuaries" dedicated to their founding saints, whose cults attracted local laity and, in particular, those living on their lands. In this era, when a majority of faithful only received the sacrament of penance as they were approaching death and rarely took communion, there was little hope among the worldly for access to salvation unless it was through the intercession of one or several saints. This belief led to a constant influx of donations of lands and money, offered not (as is too commonly assumed) to the Church but to the patron saints of the religious communities to which the donors felt themselves connected.

Monks and Sanctuaries: From Holy Sites to Territories

At the same time, the monks asserted specific forms of control over space.[10] Religious orders arrogated to themselves the right to create sacred spaces, carved out from the surrounding territories and their preexisting historical heritage, as Cluny and the *Ordo cluniacensis* in the eleventh and twelfth centuries clearly shows.[11] This practice was ratified by Pope Urban II during his journey to France between 1095 and 1098,

---

10. Barbara Rosenwein, *Negotiating Space: Power, Restraint and Privileges of Immunity in Early Medieval Europe* (Ithaca, NY: Cornell University Press, 1999); Laura Gaffuri, "Luoghi di culto e santuari del Medioevo occidentale: Bibliografia ragionata," in *Lieux sacrés, lieux de culte, sanctuaires*, ed. André Vauchez (Rome: École Française de Rome, 2000), 176–86.

11. Didier Méhu, *Paix et communauté autour de l'abbaye de Cluny (X^e–XIe siècle)* (Lyons: Presses universitaires de Lyon, 2001).

when he consecrated the church of Cluny III, as well as five cemeteries, which accentuated the Church's desire to sacralize funerary spaces.[12] In some cases, the monks' possession of important relics was the starting point for the construction of a territorial entity: such is the case for the Abbey of Montecassino that, in the eleventh and twelfth centuries, created a veritable monastic state in Campania, which documents of the time called the "Land of Saint Benedict," around the holy mountain where the relics of the father of Western monasticism reposed. Similarly, in the Byzantine world in the same period, a collection of monasteries formed around Mount Athos, on a peninsula jutting out into the Aegean Sea, constituting, even today, a largely autonomous entity within the Greek state.

In this context, the Black Monks (as the Benedictines were called, after the color of their habits) frequently transformed their monasteries into sanctuaries. At Sainte-Foy in Conques, five books of miracles were composed between 1020 and 1050, devoted to the miracles that their heavenly protectoress, Saint Foy, accomplished. In disputes with neighboring lords, the monks would process their reliquary-statues throughout the countryside to assert their rights over certain lands that were being denied to or taken from them.[13]

At Fleury in Saint-Benoît-sur-Loire, during the reconstruction of the abbey in the eleventh century, Abbot Gauzlin—eager to appropriately honor Saint Benedict's relics in the monastery's possession—oversaw the installation of the new structure's splendid marble flooring in the nave, with plaques and tiles of porphyry based on Roman models like those found in the basilicas of Saint Peter and Saint John Lateran. In the thirteenth century, Benedict's remains, which had been found in the abbey's crypt, were placed in a magnificent reliquary of gold and silver. The abbey's entire apse constituted a veritable monumental reliquary with its historiated capitals devoted to the miracles of Saint Benedict, which can also be found on the lintels of the side portals.

The monks of Stavelot, in present-day Belgium, staged spectacular ceremonies, such as the one in 1104 in which their abbot excommunicated the lords who had usurped property belonging to the abbey by

---

12. Elisabeth Zadora-Rio, "Lieux d'inhumation et espaces consacrés: Le voyage d'Urbain II en France (août 1095–août 1096)," in Vauchez, *Lieux sacrés, lieux de culte, sanctuaires*, 197–213.

13. Louis Brouillet, ed., *Liber miraculorum Sanctae fidis* (Paris: Alphonse Picard et Fils, 1897); Dominique Barthélemy, *Chevaliers et miracles: La violence et le sacré dans la société féodale* (Paris: Armand Colin, 2004).

hurling vehement curses against them: "Let them be cursed in their house, cursed in their fields, cursed in every place where they will stop and walk, sit and rest; cursed while eating, cursed while drinking; cursed be their food and cursed their drink. . . . May the land rise up and cover them while living, like Dathan and Abiram; and may they go down into hell while still alive!"[14]

Others, like those at Saint-Martial in Limoges at the beginning of the eleventh century, threw themselves into a policy of promoting their patron saint, presented by Adhémar of Chabannes as a disciple of Saint Peter. The monks devoted themselves to diffusing the miracles accomplished through the relics they possessed, for both prestige and economic motives, because the pilgrims who came to the abbey to venerate them never failed to make donations and offerings.[15]

These monastic sanctuaries were frequently in competition with each other. For example, the monks of Montecassino engaged in a long polemic during the twelfth century with those of Fleury, who claimed to possess the relics of Saint Benedict, whereas Montecassino's monks asserted that they were still to be found in their abbey in Italy. In other cases, the monasteries were the principal beneficiaries of *furta sacra* (sacred thefts) carried out in the eastern Mediterranean by sailors and the merchants of the great cities, like those of Bari in southern Italy, who in 1087 brought back the relics of Saint Nicholas of Myra (in present-day Turkey), for which the great Monastery of Saint-Nicholas of Bari was built, becoming an often-visited pilgrimage destination, remaining so up until today.[16]

Certain monastic establishments and congregations, however, appear to have remained for a long time indifferent to demonstrations of popular devotion toward the relics of the saints, because doing so risked disturbing the regularity of religious life. Thus, the Abbey of Cluny—the greatest religious edifice in Christianity at the start of the twelfth century—never became a sanctuary, despite housing numerous

---

14. Philippe George, "*Maledictio adversus ecclesiae Dei persecutores*: À propos d'un ouvrage récent," *Revue belge de philologie et d'histoire* 73 (1995): 1013–14.

15. Richard Landes, *The Peace of God: Social Violence and Religious Response in France around the Year 1000* (Ithaca, NY: Cornell University Press, 1992); Éliane Vergnolle, ed., *Saint-Martial de Limoges: Millénaire de l'abbaye romane (1018–2018)*, Bulletin monumental 178 (1978) (Paris: Société française d'archéologie, 2020).

16. Patrick J. Geary, *Furta sacra: Thefts of Relics in the Central Middle Ages* (Princeton, NJ: Princeton University Press, 1978); Giorgio Cioffari and Angela Laghezza, eds., *Alle origini dell'Europa: Il culto di San Nicola tra Oriente e Occidente, Italia-Francia* (Bari: Nicolaus Studi Storici, 2011).

relics. Moreover, its first great abbots, Odo and Hugh, who were considered saints, were interred more than a hundred kilometers away in Souvigny, in the Bourbonnais. New orders of eremitical inspiration, like the Camaldolese or the Chartreux, exhibited the same indifference to the relics of their founders. Saint Bruno is not buried at the Monastery of the Grande Chartreuse he founded in southeastern France but in a church in Calabria; and the tomb of Saint Romuald is not found at Camaldoli but at Fonte Avellana. At Grandmont, a successor of Stephen of Muret († 1124) even forbade the relics of this saint to effect any miracles so that the religious of this order—who wished to be poor and austere—would not be disturbed in their devotions by an onslaught of pilgrims.[17] It was not that these monks refused to create sacred spaces; rather, like the Cistercians who settled out in the countryside, they wanted them to be devoid of people and villages in order to fully give themselves over to holy solitude. As Georges Duby has noted:

> The Cistercian abbey would have preferred to remain free of the responsibilities of funerary functions, leaving the care of the dead to others. . . . No longer were there miraculous sarcophagi nor, subsequently, pilgrims; that is, no more spectacle. If ostentation and liturgical theater were reduced, along with the splendor of the divine office, this did not impede the accumulation and collection of relics. It is important to distinguish between periods: after the beginnings of the order and the strict observance of its early years, this primitive rigor, as in other domains, also gradually loosened up.[18]

Indeed, in the thirteenth century, subsequent generations would show themselves to be less finicky on this point than the founders and the reformers, and even the most austere religious orders ended up soliciting dispensations from the papacy in order to welcome pilgrims of both genders into their monasteries.

Sanctuaries of Christ and the Apostles

References to the holy apostles were nothing new in Christianity, and there had existed for a long time, throughout all of Christianity,

---

17. Pierre-André Sigal, "Les miracles de saint Étienne de Muret († 1124) au XIIe siècle," *Études héraultaises* (1992): 47.
18. Georges Duby, *L'art cistercien* (Paris: Flammarion, 2017), 75.

sanctuaries dedicated to Saint Peter on the model of the basilica that Constantine had built in Rome to honor him, or to other companions of Christ. When, for example, laypeople in Burgundy donated lands or serfs to Cluny in the eleventh century, the charters of donation did not mention any monks or abbots but rather Saint Peter, patron of the abbey, as the beneficiary of their generosity, as if he were a living person. But after the eleventh century, a new form of spirituality appeared in the West, one marked by a desire to return to the apostolic life, a way of living that took its inspiration from the first Christian community of Jerusalem, as described in the Acts of the Apostles. This evolution in piety was accompanied by a rediscovery of the humanity of Christ and his role as protagonist in the history of salvation. Henceforth, the faithful would have to follow the footsteps of Jesus and his disciples, as witnessed by the launching of the crusades and the growth of a few great sanctuaries, starting with the Holy Sepulcher in Jerusalem, which it was said had been consecrated by Christ himself.

The *furta sacra* at the expense of the churches of the East came to favor a cult of fleshly relics of Christ, the incarnate God, especially those of his Passion: the Holy Blood of Mantua at the Abbey of Fécamp in the eleventh century; the Holy Grail of Glastonbury—the vessel in which Joseph of Arimathea had collected the blood of Christ on the cross—in the twelfth century; the column of the Flagellation venerated in the Church of Saint Praxedes in Rome; holy nails from the Cross, thorns from the Crown of Thorns, and so on. At the Abbey of the Saint-Sauveur in Charroux, starting at the end of the eleventh century, a cult formed that was dedicated to the Holy Prepuce or Foreskin (in Latin, the *sancta virtus*) of Christ, which was kept in a reliquary. The popular success of this particular devotion was probably not unrelated to the monks' construction, from 1096 forward, of a new church whose plan took its inspiration from that of the Holy Sepulcher.

In the Shadow of the Holy Sepulcher and the True Cross

At the beginning of the tenth century, the West had resumed contact with Jerusalem, and large pilgrimages led by bishops or abbots from France and Germany brought thousands of members of the clergy and laity to the Holy Land, where they had the opportunity to rediscover the historical reality of Christ and his companions. Returning to the West, some of them had octagonal churches built on the model of the Holy

Sepulcher.[19] There were at least sixty-five of them in western Europe, the oldest of which is Santo Stefano, a collection of seven churches and oratories called "Jerusalem" that were built in Bologna beginning in the eighth century and dedicated to the first bishop of the city, Saint Petronius. The movement accelerated after the year 1000.[20] Among these replicas of the Holy Sepulcher were the abbeys of Saint-Benignus in Dijon and of Fruttuaria in the Piedmont during the years 1010–30, and the churches of Neuvy-Saint-Sépulcre in Berry in 1043; San Sepulcro in Tuscany, constructed at the initiative of the Camaldolese; and in Paderborn in Westphalia, which the Bishop Meinwerk constructed in 1036, reproducing the exact measurements of the Church of Jerusalem. These were clearly intended as substitutes for the Holy Sepulcher, as an inscription attests on a similar edifice in Piacenza from 1055 made by two believers for their fellow citizens: "so that in seeing it, in remembering the Lord who suffered and was buried for us, they might meditate, renounce their sins, and do penance."[21]

Upon his return from crusade around 1100, Peter the Hermit erected a sanctuary, Neufmoustier, at the gates of Huy-sur-Meuse, dedicated to the Holy Sepulcher and to Saint John the Baptist, having obtained from the patriarch of Jerusalem relics and a privilege allowing pilgrims unable to go to the Holy Land to fulfill their vow there.[22] The catalogue of the treasury of relics in this sanctuary mirrors all the steps of a pilgrimage to the Holy Land. In addition to various relics related to Christ, there are also relics from the Gospels, such as the five loaves and two fish from the multiplication of loaves (Luke 9:13); soil from the precise spot of the Ascension on the Mount of Olives; as well as a few fragments of the Holy Cross. (Peter the Hermit was known as "the first preacher of the Holy Cross.") The catalogue of Neufmoustier's treasury also includes a number of relics connected to Mary—some of the Virgin's clothing, pieces of her tomb and of the sheltering tree during the flight into Egypt, hair and flowers related to her visit with Elizabeth

---

19. Colin Morris, *The Sepulchre of Christ and the Medieval West: From the Beginning to 1600* (Oxford: Oxford University Press, 2005).

20. Geneviève Bresc-Bautier, "Les imitations du Saint-Sépulcre de Jérusalem (IXe–XVe siècle): Archéologie d'une dévotion," *Revue d'histoire de la spiritualité* 50 (1974): 319–42; Geneviève Bresc-Bautier, "Partir, prier, donner: Les églises fondées en souvenir du pèlerinage en Terre Sainte (X^e–XIe siècle), in *Il Cammino di Gerusalemme*, ed. Maria Stella Calò Mariani (Bari: Adda, 2002), 565–89.

21. Pietro Maria Campi, *Dell'istoria ecclesiastica di Piacenza*, ed. Pietro Maria Campi [the younger], 1 (Piacenza, 1651), no. lxxxix, 513–14.

22. Philippe George, *Reliques: Se connecter à l'au-delà* (Paris: CNRS, 2018), 329.

FIGURE 13. Reliquary Cross, ca. 1150–75, Mosan Workshop, Meuse (Belgium); champlevé and cloisonné enamel on gilded copper. Walters Art Gallery, Baltimore (CC Zero).

(Luke 1:39–45)—all of which allowed Philippe George to write that the Abbey of Neufmoustier was really "part of the Holy Land in the region of the Meuse."[23]

Parallel to this, numerous churches in this period were dedicated to the Holy Cross, considered since the time of Constantine to be the symbol of the divine victory over adversarial forces. In the twelfth century, relic-crosses (which incorporated fragments of the True Cross) proliferated in the West, thanks to the canons of the Holy Sepulcher and the military orders who were seeking to keep the fervor for the Holy Land and its liberation alive among the faithful (figure 13).[24] Some churches

---

23. Philippe George, "Le trésor de reliques du Neufmoustier près de Huy (XIIe–XVIIIe siècle): Une part de Terre Sainte en pays mosan," *Bulletin de la Commission royale d'Histoire* 169 (2003): 35. On these references to the Holy Sepulcher in the urban onomastics in the West, see Jacques Heers, "Bourgs et faubourgs en Occident: Pèlerinages et dévotion au Saint-Sépulcre," in *Jérusalem, Rome, Constantinople: L'image et le mythe de la ville au Moyen Age*, ed. Daniel Poirrion (Paris: Presses universitaires de Paris-Sorbonne, 1986), 205–15.

24. Anatole Frolow, *La relique de la Vraie Croix: Recherches sur le développement d'un culte* (Paris: Institut français des études byzantines, 1961); Marie-Madeleine Gauthier, *Les routes de*

possessing such relics, like the Iglesia de la Vera Cruz (Church of the True Cross) in Segovia, became esteemed sanctuaries.

The new interest in the humanity of Jesus was attested to by the success that the *Volto Santo* (Holy Face) of Lucca—a large wooden crucifix where the sufferings of Christ on the cross were depicted with a realism that did not efface his majesty, and which French pilgrims called *le Saint Voult*—enjoyed at this time. Legend had it that the cross had been fashioned by Nicodemus just after the Passion and that it had arrived in Italy from the Holy Land at the end of the eighth century in a small boat that ran aground on the beach at Luni, not far from Lucca.[25] This devotion was approved by Pope Paschal II at the start of the twelfth century, and pilgrims from all over Christianity flocked to the Tuscan city to visit the Cathedral of Saint-Martin, where a chapel had been consecrated to him. The sacred character of this relic was affirmed again at the end of the thirteenth century by Dante in the *Divine Comedy*.[26] In Vendôme, in the same period, believers began to venerate the Holy Teardrop that Christ was said to have shed upon learning of the death of Lazarus. It had been offered, in 1040, to the Abbey of the Trinity by its founder, Count Geoffroy Martel, upon his return from Constantinople, though it is not known how he might have procured it. And from the twelfth century, numerous sanctuaries claimed to have the Holy Shroud. If the most famous one found today in Turin only appeared in documentation in the middle of the fourteenth century, several other places—Aix-la-Chapelle, Compiègne, Besançon, the Cistercian Abbey of Cadouin in Périgord, and the church of the Augustinians in Carcassonne—claimed the privilege of possessing it as well.[27] In this context, the Holy Land acquired an unprecedented centrality in the religious life of Christians, many of whom aspired to go there either on pilgrimage or, after 1095, as part of a crusade. For them, Palestine was not only one place among others; it was the common homeland, a country that God had given them as a heritage and that it was necessary, at all costs, to take back from the "infidels" who wrongfully held it.

---

la foi: Reliques et reliquaires de Jérusalem à Compostelle (Fribourg im Breisgau: Bibliothèque des arts, 1983), 140–48; Franco Cardini, *Gerusalemme d'oro, di rame, di luce: Pellegrini, crociati, sognatori d'Oriente fra XI e XV secolo* (Milan: Il Saggiatore, 1991).

25. Gabriella Rossetti, *Santa Croce e Santo Volto: Contributi allo studio dell'origine e della fortuna del culto del Salvatore (secoli IX–XV)* (Pisa: ETS, 2003); Andreas Meyer, ed., *Il Volto Santo in Europa: Culto e immagini del Crocifisso nel Medioevo* (Lucca: Istituto Storico Lucchese, 2005).

26. Dante Alighieri, *Inferno*, XXI, 48.

27. Adeline Rucquoi, *Mille fois à Compostelle: Pèlerins au Moyen Age* (Paris: Les Belles Lettres, 2014); Xosé Luís Barreiro-Rivas, "Mille anni di pellegrinaggio a Santiago," in *Del visibile credere*, ed. Davide Scotto (Florence: Olschki, 2011), 573–90.

Sanctuaries of the Apostles: Santiago de Compostela

The most spectacular expression of this desire to reconnect with the Apostolic Age was the extraordinary popularity of the sanctuary of Santiago de Compostela. Since the seventh century, in such texts as the *Breviarium Apostolorum* and the *De ortu et obitu patrum*, each country had been assigned to one of the apostles for conversion, and Spain had been given to Saint James the Greater, brother of Saint John and one of the sons of Zebedee. At the end of the eighth century, the Spanish monk Beatus of Liébana picked up and diffused this assertion in his writings; in 829, James's tomb was rediscovered, near Iria in Galicia, in a place called Compostela ("field of the star"). This account conflicted with the well-established tradition according to which Saint James had been beheaded in Jerusalem by order of King Herod Agrippa. However, the Carolingian hagiographer Ado of Vienne and especially Usuard, a monk at Saint-Germain-des-Prés, whose martyrology was going to become authoritative throughout all of Christianity over the course of the subsequent centuries, resolved the contradiction by asserting that while James did indeed die in Jerusalem between 41 and 44, his remains had been transported to Spain across the sea, a theme that was developed at the same time in a narrative dedicated to the *Translation of Saint James*. Accounts attest to the presence of pilgrims coming from lands north of the Pyrenees to Compostela around the middle of the tenth century, and their numbers grew considerably thereafter. The promotors of his cult claimed its superiority over that of other saints by emphasizing that in Europe, outside of Rome, only Spain had been evangelized by an apostle, the first of the twelve to suffer martyrdom.

The first sanctuary there, built by Bishop Theodemir of Iria and King Alfonso II of Asturias, was destroyed by the forces of ibn Abi ʿĀmir "al-Mansūr" (the Victorious) in 997; but after the year 1000, the apostle's cult, supported by the network of Cluniac monasteries, experienced tremendous growth north of the Pyrenees. Toward the middle of the twelfth century, the archbishop, Diego Gelmírez († ca. 1140), commissioned an imposing basilica in Compostela to house the tomb of Saint James, which soon became one of the most visited places of pilgrimage in Christianity. To have the privilege of crossing over the threshold of this immense church constituted for pilgrims a kind of anticipation of the beatific vision of God in the hereafter (figure 14).

FIGURE 14. Portico of Glory, Santiago de Compostela.

At the same time, the prelate commissioned the composition of an imposing work, the *Liber sancti Jacobi* or *Codex Calixtinus*, a vast compilation intended to disseminate the (highly legendary) history of the sanctuary.[28] Only twenty-two miracles are mentioned therein, but the author underscores that he could have strung together more of them and that Saint James had many other powers, in particular the protection for those who invoked him during their struggles in life and the intervention on the side of Christians battling against Muslims in the context of the Reconquista. He was thus characterized as *matamoros* (Saint James the Moor-Slayer) in Spain and "noble baron" in the French epics that present him as the protector of Charlemagne and his descendants. The *Liber* also underscores the primacy of Compostela with respect to other sanctuaries, given that it contained the tomb of an apostle furthest from his original country. Sensitive to this argument,

---

28. *Liber Sancti Jacobi Codex Calixtinus*, ed. Klaus Herbers and Manuel Santos Noia (Santiago de Compostela: Xunta de Galicia, 1998).

pilgrims subsequently tended to visit, after Compostela, the satellite sanctuaries of Padrón, where the boat transporting the apostle (or his remains, depending on the version of the story) landed after its long, seafaring journey, and Saint Mary of the Finisterre (*de finibus Terrae*), which marked out the extreme western edge of the known world.[29]

Compostela's influence was so great that, in the twelfth century, numerous substitute sanctuaries were dedicated to Saint James throughout Christianity, like that of Saint James de Podio (or Poggio) near Pisa, founded around 1200 by a pious laywoman, Saint Bona († 1207), who had gone on pilgrimage nine times to Compostela and died at the beginning of her final voyage. Pilgrims who could not travel to Spain gladly visited these substitutes in the hope of acquiring indulgences there. Saint James's popularity was maintained over the centuries by the archbishops and the cathedral chapter of Compostela, which was frequently solicited to provide relics of the apostle for other churches. Thus, a fragment of his head could be found in Pistoia in Tuscany after the middle of the twelfth century, even though Arras and Aire-sur-la-Lys already shared it! The Abbey of Saint-Sernin in Toulouse, an important stop for pilgrims on the way to Compostela, claimed to have James's body, donated by Charlemagne, and at the beginning of the fourteenth century, the Countess Mahaut d'Artois offered one of his bones to the hospital Saint-Jacques in Paris, which housed and cared for pilgrims departing for Galicia. Earlier, in the twelfth century, the Abbey of Reading in England had received from the Empress Mathilda an arm of Saint James, famous for the numerous healings it produced there; but the Abbey of Saint-Denis likewise claimed to possess the arm of the apostle, which defended the kingdom of France against her enemies, whereas Liège claimed to have yet another.

It was similar for the other apostles of Christ whose cults developed between the twelfth and thirteenth centuries.[30] In 1080, for example, the relics of Saint Matthew were discovered in Salerno, which Pope Gregory VII then transferred to the new cathedral being built there. In the middle of the thirteenth century, a pontifical legate, Peter of Capua, brought back to Italy Saint Andrew's relics, taken from the Church of Patras in Greece, and placed them in the Cathedral of Amalfi in Campania, where they remained until the end of the twentieth century. And in

---

29. André Vauchez, *Religion et société dans l'Occident médiéval* (Turin: Bottega d'Erasmo, 1980), 188–89 and 197.

30. Émile Mâle, *Les saints compagnons du Christ* (Paris: Hartmann, 1959).

Benevento, numerous pilgrims came to venerate the relics of Saint Bartholomew, after their transfer in the ninth century. Devotion also was given to mythical figures like Saint Amadour, supposedly a servant of the Holy Family and connected to the Virgin Mary at her sanctuary in Rocamadour. His body, discovered intact in 1166, received visitations by numerous pilgrims and several rulers, among whom were Henry II Plantagenet and Saint Louis IX.

But Saint James surpassed them all in popularity. Indeed, he was depicted in iconography and accounts of visions as the one who led the souls of the dead up to the gates of paradise, sometimes accompanied by the Virgin Mary. This reputation is perhaps tied to the fact that, in the Letter of James (although not written by this James) found in the New Testament, he is associated with extreme unction, the anointing of the sick with oil in the moments preceding death.[31] Through this end-of-life role, he entered into the Christian imagination at the conclusion of a process of "folklorizing," which has been studied by the historian and anthropologist Luigi Maria Lombardi Satriani.[32] At Modica in Sicily, for example, believers held that, after death, the soul had to make a pilgrimage to Santiago de Compostela to be purified and, from there, undergo a long and fatiguing journey through the Milky Way, called the *Viollu de San Jabiccu*, at the end of which the apostle was waiting to lead it into paradise. This posthumous peregrination could, however, be avoided by accomplishing a pilgrimage to a small local church dedicated to Saint James during the night between July 24 and 25 and undertaking an extremely stringent fasting and clothing ritual while reciting nine *Paters* and nine *Aves* in honor of the apostle.

Mary Magdalene: From Vézelay to Saint-Maximin

This period also saw the rediscovery of the importance of female saints who had lived in Jesus's orbit, such as Martha, patroness of Tarascon, and especially Mary Magdalene. The latter had, in fact, enjoyed great popularity throughout the West beginning in the eleventh century. This gospel figure had certainly had a place in the liturgical calendars

---

31. Rosanna Bianco, *La conchiglia e il bordone: I viaggi di San Giacomo nella Puglia medievale* (Perugia: Edizioni Compostellane, 2017), 280; Xavier Barral i Altet, *Compostelle: Le grand chemin* (Paris: Gallimard, 1999).

32. Luigi Maria Lombardi Satriani and Mariano Meligrana, *Il Ponte di S. Giacomo: L'ideologia della morte nella società contadina del Sud* (Palermo: Rizzoli, 1982).

at least since the seventh century, as much in the East as in the Latin Church. But the success of her cult follows on the fusion—created by Gregory the Great at the beginning of the sixth century in a famous sermon, later taken up in the tenth century by Abbot Odo of Cluny—of three female figures mentioned in the Gospels: Mary of Bethany, who received Christ in her home with her sister Martha and brother Lazarus; the public sinner who, during the meal in the House of Simon, ceaselessly pours out her tears over Jesus's feet as a sign of her repentance; and Mary Magdalene who followed him during the greater part of his ministry and was present on Good Friday at the foot of the cross with his mother, before being the first person to receive the announcement of his Resurrection.[33] A symbol of conversion, Mary Magdalene constituted an attractive model for lay penitents and women who aspired to lead a religious life while still remaining in the world.[34] No relic of the saint was known in the West up to this point, but in the middle of the eleventh century, the Abbot Geoffroy of Vézelay claimed to have discovered her remains in the crypt of his abbey, where they would have been brought from Provence in the ninth century and immediately hidden away in order to protect them from thieves. The hagiographical tradition about the life of Mary Magdalene puts the emphasis on the last part of her life, after she had withdrawn into solitude. But Geoffroy composed a new *Life* that recounted how the holy woman, after Pentecost, had come to Provence in a boat with a disciple of Christ, Saint Maximin, and had participated in the evangelization of the region before dying in the grotto of Sainte-Baume. This "apostolic" *Life* possessed real originality, at a time when the ecclesiastical hierarchy did not hesitate in taking measures to forbid laypeople—especially women—from preaching in public. As a result, she enjoyed a lively success among the faithful, inspiring paintings and sculptures until the end of the Middle Ages.

The cult of Mary Magdalene conferred great prestige upon Vézelay, which became a stop for German pilgrims on their way to Compostela. And the great abbey built there in her honor during the first half of the twelfth century, one of the chief monuments of French Romanesque art, hosted assemblies of peace in this period, and the "Eternal Hill"

---

33. Victor Saxer, *Le dossier vézelien de Marie-Madeleine: Invention et translation des reliques en 1265–1267* (Brussels: Société des Bollandistes, 1975).

34. Katherine L. Jansen, *The Making of the Magdalen: Preaching and Popular Devotion in the Later Middle Ages* (Princeton, NJ: Princeton University Press, 2000).

FIGURE 15. Vézelay Abbey (Basilica of Sainte-Marie-Madeleine), Yonne, Burgundy. Photo: Dietrich Krieger via Wikimedia Commons (CC BY-SA 3.0).

dominated by the abbey assumed precedence in the sacred geography of Burgundy and France (figure 15). This is why Saint Bernard chose Vézelay as the place from which to preach the Second Crusade in 1147. Later, the importance of the abbey and its sanctuary declined, especially after the moment when, in 1279, an apparition of Mary Magdalene led Charles of Salerno, count of Provence and the son of Charles I of Anjou, to discover the saint's relics in a sarcophagus in the Dominican convent of Saint-Maximin in Sainte-Baume.

Pope Boniface VIII, who was dependent upon the support of the house of Anjou, struck a decisive blow to the claims of Vézelay by asserting in a 1295 papal bull that the relics at Saint-Maximin were the only authentic ones. That same year, Charles of Salerno, having become Charles II, king of Naples, entrusted to the Dominicans the grotto of Sainte-Baume, where Mary Magdalene is said to have retired. Both places became important pilgrimage sites, as the *Livre des Miracles de sainte Marie-Madeleine* (*Book of the Miracles of Saint Mary Magdalene*) by the hagiographer Gobi, prior of Saint-Maximin (1304–28), attests.[35] At the end of the fourteenth century, the Liège chronicler Jean d'Outremeuse, citing the Dominican cleric Bernardo Gui († 1331), affirms

---

35. Marie-Hélène Froeschlé-Chopard, *Itinéraires pèlerins de l'ancienne Provence* (Marseilles: La Thune, 2004); Jacqueline Sclafer, ed., *Miracles de sainte Marie Madeleine* (Paris: CNRS, 1996).

the discovery of her remains in Sainte-Baume, ascribing to it a miracle: "From the very holy tongue of Mary Magdalene, which still remained in her head and throat, issued a root with a little branch like fennel and it pointed outward in length. The admiring witnesses saw all of this with their own eyes."[36] He then notes that, according to this testimony, the root and branch, which had healing properties, were cut into several pieces and then kept in different places, "like so many relics."

Cathedrals and Sanctuaries

Processions and Pilgrimages

Cathedrals were among the most important edifices of Christian worship. Numerous examples were built (or rebuilt) during the Middle Ages, and even today, they are the pride of many European towns and cities. They may resemble sanctuaries, to the extent that they translate human time into cosmic time by way of liturgical ceremonies, but in the majority of cases, this terminology does not hold up to scrutiny. The misunderstanding may arise from the ambivalence of the French word *pèlerinage* (pilgrimage), which in French can refer to rather different realities. Whereas French has only one general term describing any pious peregrination, German for example possesses two: *Wallfahrt*, which designates a trip of a limited duration toward a religious building; and *Pilgerfahrt*, which characterizes a journey over a longer period of time. The first of these two forms of religious mobility finds its equivalence in a procession that departs from a church—generally speaking, a cathedral—and returns there, after having completed, on a specific date, a lengthy perambulation through the city, punctuated by "stations" near various religious sites, following an itinerary determined by a liturgical ritual. The second, the pilgrimage proper, consists of a journey, a kind of religious wandering, that can last several weeks, months, or years, and the aim of which is to reach one or several sanctuaries and to accomplish various devotions there, to give thanks for favors obtained, or to ask for new ones.

This second type was a matter of personal initiative and belonged, in most cases, to the sphere of "voluntary religion": indeed, in Christianity, pilgrimage has never constituted an obligatory practice, and at certain times in history, the faithful were sometimes even discouraged

---

36. Jean d'Outremeuse, *Ly Myreur des histors*, cited by George, *Reliques*, 402.

from undertaking one. The pilgrim favored the holy place (or places) that they had to reach at the terminus of an individual or collective journey.[37] In reality, any clear-cut distinction between processions and pilgrimages must be put into perspective according to their particular historical or religious contexts. For example, at Notre-Dame in Tournai (in present-day Belgium), a procession on September 14 to honor a relic of the True Cross kept in the cathedral would annually attract pilgrims come from all over Flanders and, especially, from Ghent; they would march around the city in cortège early in the morning before reaching the mother church.[38] This case is certainly not unique, but as a general rule, parish churches and cathedrals tended to be places of ordinary salvation (Masses, sacraments, funerals) while sanctuaries were sites of salvation in its extraordinary forms (the pilgrimage, the miracle, the ex-voto).

The Cathedral: Church of the Bishops and of the Chapter

The cathedral was, first and foremost, the church of the bishop of the diocese and of the clerics who surrounded him, and this function continued between late antiquity and the Carolingian era.[39] Specialists in the archaeology of these periods prefer to speak of a cathedral *group*, rather than a cathedral. The exemplary excavations by Charles Bonnet at Saint Peter's cathedral in Geneva reveals the complexity of this complex web of structures comprising an episcopal church (or sometimes two, one for winter and one for summer), a parish church, a baptistery, a bell tower, and an audience hall, while saints' relics were venerated in martyrial basilicas dispersed throughout urban and extra-urban spaces. During the early Middle Ages, the various elements of a cathedral group tended to be built closer together and blended with each other, in parallel with the strengthening power of the bishops who, during the Carolingian and Ottonian periods, became high dignitaries of the imperial or royal Church and often a powerful temporal lord. From

---

37. André Vauchez, "Un eroe medievale: Il santo pellegrino nell'agiografia italiana," in *San Pellegrino tra mito e storia: I luoghi di culto in Europa*, ed. Adelaide Trezzini (Rome: Gangemi, 2009), 33–42.

38. Catherine Vincent and Jacques Pycke, eds., *Cathédrale et pèlerinage aux époques médiévales et modernes* (Louvain-la-Neuve: Collège Érasme / Universiteitsbibliothek, 2010).

39. André Vauchez, "Les cathedrales," in *Les Lieux de mémoire*, vol. 3, *La France*, pt. 2, *Traditions*, ed. Pierre Nora (Paris: Gallimard, 1993), 94–127.

that time on, the cathedral would be, above all, a center of ecclesiastical power and liturgical life.

Up to the eleventh century, bishops were rarely buried in cathedrals, but this practice soon evolved, and crypts were then built to house the remains of prelates, certain of whom—especially the earliest—were considered saints and thus attracted cults.[40] In Naples, for example, the relics of Saint Januarius were transferred in the tenth century from the catacomb where they had been laid with those of other bishops over to the cathedral in the heart of the city. It makes sense to place this evolution in the role of the *ecclesia maior* (this designation is used even today at the cathedral in Marseilles, known as Saint Mary Major or Cathedral of the Major), in relation to the assertion of a diocese's awareness of its cultural importance. The cathedral was, in fact, not only the principal church of a city but also that of the diocese, the dispersed population of which was often more numerous than at the main site, at a time when episcopal power was appreciably fortifying its territorial jurisdiction. A sign of this prestige, the liturgical ceremony dedicating a cathedral took on unprecedented grandeur at this time, and its annual commemoration became the occasion for parish clergy to come and offer donations, both financially and in-kind, to the bishop and chapter; among the fees was a tax called the *cathedraticum*.

"Sanctuarization" in Decline

During the tenth and eleventh centuries, during the significant growth in the cult of relics and pilgrimages, the cathedrals did not, with rare exceptions, find themselves in a particularly advantageous position from this point of view. Their purpose was not to attract crowds, outside a few grand liturgical celebrations; and, above all, they appeared to the faithful as the prerogative of the high clergy. In principle, it was the prerogative of the bishop; in fact, from the beginning of the twelfth century, it was the cathedral chapter that reigned supreme there and actually directed both the organization of divine worship and the construction or improvement of the edifice. In France during this period, a number of cathedrals were devoid of prestigious relics, with the

---

40. Jean-Charles Picard, *Évêques, saints et cités en Italie et en Gaule: Études d'archéologie et d'histoire* (Rome: École Française de Rome, 1998); and Jean-Charles Picard, *Le souvenir des évêques: Sépultures, listes épiscopales et culte des évêques dans l'Italie du Nord, des origines au Xe siècle)* (Rome: École Française de Rome, 1988).

exception of Chartres, to which Charles the Bald had given the Tunic of the Virgin Mary (the *Sancta Camisa*), and of Le Puy, famous for its statue of the Black Madonna.

Most cathedrals were dedicated to Mary, but she was exalted above all as symbol of the Church, as demonstrated by the eleventh-century central portal of the Cathedral of Senlis. Sometimes, however, clever propaganda on the part of the clergy made it known that miracles attributed to the Mother of God had occurred in some of these churches. In Arras, the principal site of a new diocese created at the end of the eleventh century, the cathedral acquired a certain prestige with the "Miracle of the Ardents" (the "Healing of the Burning Poisoning") in 1092, which inspired the birth of a pilgrimage famous for healing sick people struck down by ergotism (grain fungus poisoning), called *Mal des Ardents* or "the fire of Saint Antony." The Holy Candle given by the Virgin Mary to two jugglers and endowed with great therapeutic power was venerated there.[41] In Paris, in 1129, the city was also struck by an ergotism epidemic, and about a hundred people were cured at Notre-Dame cathedral, where the reliquaries of Saint Geneviève and Saint Marcel had been brought from neighboring monasteries, indicating that the cathedral did not possess many relics of its own. In 1130, an "Altar of the Ardents" was consecrated there to celebrate the memory of the previous year, and the sick came there to implore the Virgin Mary. But in the middle of the thirteenth century, a papal legate ordered the eviction of pilgrims from the towers of the cathedral where they were stationing themselves overnight in the hopes of a cure; after this, attendance at the altar declined.[42] After the reconstruction of Notre-Dame of Paris by Bishop Maurice of Sully, beginning in 1163, a whole series of relics enclosed in a reliquary called the "Notre-Dame reliquary" were given to the cathedral by Philip Augustus in 1186. And in 1331, a large wooden statue of the Virgin Mary, placed outside the choir, soon became a place of pilgrimage as a result of a few miracles.[43] But these were not enough to make it into a sanctuary.

---

41. Alessandra Foscati, *"Ignis sacer": Una storia culturale del fuoco sacro dell'Antichità al Settecento* (Florence: SISMEL, 2013).

42. Gabriela Signori, "La bienheureuse polysémie: Miracles et pèlerinages de la Vierge (X^e-XIIe siècle)," in *Marie: Le culte de la Vierge dans la société médiévale*, ed. Dominique Iogna-Prat, Daniel Russo, and Éric Palazzo (Paris: Beauchesne, 1996), 591-617.

43. Mireille Vincent-Cassy, 'Pèlerinages et processions à la fin du Moyen Age: L'exemple parisien," in Vincent and Pycke, *Cathédrale et pèlerinage*, 21-39.

FIGURE 16. Reliquary (early thirteenth century) of Saint Thomas à Becket, decorated with Limoges enamel and depicting his murder. Musée de Cluny via Wikimedia Commons.

In Italy, the introduction into some cathedrals of Marian images deemed miraculous, often said to "come from across the sea" in a mysterious manner, sometimes helped attract crowds. In general, these were icons in the Byzantine style attributed to Saint Luke, increasingly numerous after the capture of Constantinople by the crusaders in 1204. Elsewhere, tragic events added a sacred charge to a cathedral, such as at Canterbury after the assassination in 1170 and canonization in 1173 of Saint Thomas à Becket (figure 16). At Hereford, the holy bishop Thomas de Cantilupe († 1282), persecuted by his archbishop, John Peckham, was interred in the cathedral where numerous stunning miracles were produced.

In sites lacking important relics, the chapters invested in "modern" holiness, as evidenced in the Cathedral of Tréguier, which embraced the monumental tomb of Saint Yves († 1303, canonized in 1347); or that of Vannes, where the remains of Saint Vincent Ferrer († 1419) reposed. But these cults retained a local character, such as the one that surrounded the memory of the bishop of Angers, Jean Michel, in the fifteenth century; a surge of miracles temporarily transformed these churches into sanctuaries, though this devotion never became deeply rooted.[44] It was the same in Italy where, in spite of the popular fervor that initially surrounded the tombs of some lay saints, like Saint Homobonus († 1197) in Cremona or the Blessed Rigo (Henry of Bolzano, † 1315) in Treviso, their cathedrals did not end up attracting crowds of pilgrims. Among the rare exceptions to this trend are Naples, thanks to the Chapel of Saint Januarius, which housed the relics of the patron of the city, and Saint-Omer, which became an oft-visited pilgrimage site, beginning in the thirteenth century, because of the statue of Our Lady of Miracles there.

Certain bishops, however, endeavored to stimulate the zeal of their flocks for fragments of saintly bodies kept in their cathedrals by granting indulgences to those who would come to venerate them. In Angers, in 1293, the diocesan synod deplored the fact that, "among the cathedral churches of this province, this church dedicated to Saint Maurice is the least venerated of all, as it appears from every indication since we do not notice any great influx of pilgrims as is seen elsewhere, whereas here reposes the bodies of several saints."[45] In Bordeaux, Archbishop Bertrand de Got, after becoming Pope Clement V in 1305, showered indulgences on his former cathedral, Saint-Andrew, which was in competition in the same town with the important sanctuary of Saint-Severinus, though his considerable efforts failed to increase its power of attraction. Similarly, the Cathedral of Saint-Étienne of Toulouse, even though it claimed to possess an arm of its patron saint, was for a long time relatively poor in relics when compared to Saint-Sernin, also in Toulouse, which prided itself on possessing a piece of the True Cross, the body of Saint James, relics of the Saints Sylvius, Hilary, Honoratus, and Papulus, as well as of five apostles, and many other precious treasures.[46]

---

44. Jean-Michel Matz, "Les miracles de l'évêque Jean Michel et le culte des saints dans le Diocèse d'Angers, v. 1370-v.1560" (PhD thesis, Université de Paris-Nanterre, 1993); and Jean-Michel Matz, "Les miracles de l'évêque Jean Michel," in *Mirakel im Mittelalter*, ed. Martin Heinzelmann, Klaus Herbers, and Dieter Bauer (Stuttgart: Steiner, 2002), 377-98.

45. *Decretorum Ecclesiae Gallicanae Libri, VII*, ed. Laurent Bouchel (Paris: Mural, 1609).

46. Sophie Brouquet and Michelle Fournié, "Le saint des saints: Le trésor de Saint-Sernin de Toulouse," in *Corps saints et reliques dans le Midi*. ed. Michelle Fournié, Daniel Le Blévec, and Catherine Vincent, Cahiers de Fanjeaux 53 (Toulouse: Privat, 2018), 205-64.

If it is indisputable that the prestige of urban cathedrals increased during the later centuries of the Middle Ages, it is more due to their appropriation by lay authorities and, especially, by royal power, as in Paris where Charles V became the first French king to visit Notre-Dame annually on pilgrimage. But his example was not really followed, and Notre-Dame does not figure in the itineraries of processions of supplication or thanksgiving that ended at the Abbey of Saint-Denis and were numerous in the capital during the fifteenth century. Nor were many cathedrals found on the lists of sanctuaries where those sentenced to go on pilgrimage as a penance by lay or ecclesiastical courts were dispatched. In France and present-day Belgium, the only ones that appeared on them were the cathedrals of Paris, Chartres, and Le Puy. Furthermore, from the fourteenth century on, the growing distance taken by the cathedral clergy with respect to demonstrations of popular religiosity was translated into the construction of rood screens and monumental barriers to the choirs that separated the faithful from the reliquaries that held the remains of saints, which they were forbidden to touch. In cathedrals that also functioned as sanctuaries, this activity continued to decline, becoming wholly marginal in the modern era, while reinforcing their role as places of memory of the religious and political history of the city and the diocese.

Leaving Jerusalem Behind?

The Transfer of Sacredness from the East to the West

During the eleventh and twelfth centuries, Latin Christianity, as we have seen, enriched itself with numerous relics of evangelical and apostolic figures, from Saint James and Saint Mary Magdalene to the Three Kings, whose remains were conserved first of all in Milan, then transported in 1164 by the Emperor Frederick Barbarossa to the Cathedral of Cologne, where they attracted large numbers of pilgrims all throughout the Middle Ages. But it was especially with the Fourth Crusade, marked out by the seizure and pillaging of Constantinople by the crusaders in 1204 and by the creation of the Latin Empire of the East, that a stream of prestigious relics—at least 3,600 (of not insignificant value) according to the documents of the period—flowed into the churches of the West.

The fact that the Greeks were considered to be schismatic Christians because they did not recognize the authority of the pope and followed liturgical practices different from those of the Western Church legitimized this massive transfer of holy remains in the eyes of Latins. Over the course of the twelfth and thirteenth centuries, clergy, crusaders, and merchants brought back to the West large numbers of corporeal relics of the Virgin Mary (milk, hair, fingernails) and the apostles, some of which led to the creation of new sanctuaries or increased the prestige of the old. The example of Soissons is particularly interesting in this regard. In 1205, the cathedral of this town received from its bishop, Nivelon de Quierzy (1176-1207)—a close friend of the Emperor Baldwin I and the Latin patriarch of Constantinople—two batches of prestigious remains taken from the chapel of the imperial palace of Pharos. The first, sent from the East, contained a fragment of the skull of Saint Mark, the head of Saint Stephen, and the finger that the Apostle Thomas had placed into the wounds of Christ.[47] The second, brought back by the prelate himself in 1205 upon his return to France as papal legate, contained the heads of Saint John the Baptist, Saint Thomas, and the Apostle Thaddeus, the skull of Saint Blaise, the walking stick of Moses, and two pieces of the Holy Cross. Soissons's Benedictine convent of Notre-Dame was given a veil of the Virgin Mary, while the prior of the Monastery of Saint-Jean-des-Vignes received an arm of Saint John. Later, Nivelon would establish a liturgical feast for the Translation of Saint Thomas, celebrated every year and marked by a procession beginning and ending at the cathedral after a perambulation around the city. In the years after these events, a canon of the Cathedral of Soissons wrote up a treatise with the title *De terra Iherosolimitana et quomodo ab urbi Constantinopolitana ad hanc ecclesiam allate sunt reliquie* (On the Land of Jerusalem and How the Relics Were Brought from the City of Constantinople to Our Church). These relics conferred a considerable luster to Soissons's cathedral, which until that time had only possessed the remains of a few Gallic saints from Christianity's early centuries, such as Anséric, Léger, Vaast of Arras, and notably Crépin and Crépinien, two brother-martyrs who evangelized the city and founded its first cathedral. But thanks to this providential wave of prestigious holy remains, Soissons could now rival the Holy Land itself.

---

47. M. Cecilia Gaposchkin, "Nivelon of Quierzy, the Cathedral of Soissons and the Relics of 1205: Liturgy and Devotion in the Aftermath of the Fourth Crusade," *Speculum* 95 (2020): 1087-1129.

Similarly, in Champagne, several churches shared a trove of precious relics sent from the Byzantine East in 1204 by the bishop of Troyes, Granier de Traînel. Among them were those of Saint Helena (no relation to the mother of Constantine, but often confused with her), and they attracted pilgrims who hoped to be delivered from their strong sexual urges by kissing the ring that the saint wore on her finger. The Cathedral of Langres, for its part, was honored with the head of Saint Mammès, a child-martyr from Caesarea in the third century, under whose patronage the church was now placed.[48]

Thus did the Christians of the West, at the end of their frenzied quest for biblical and evangelical artifacts, use—without guilt—the abundant resources of the East, transferring them back to the places from which they had come, especially France. The fact that they had been able to procure them was proof, in their eyes, that they enjoyed God's favor and were being rewarded for the zeal with which they reconquered and defended the Holy Land. Indeed, after 1250, Latin Christians had no more cause to be envious of the East, now that Christ, the Virgin Mary, and the saints had chosen to reside among them, as illustrated by the creation of a bishopric of Bethlehem in France itself, near Clamecy in the Nièvre, after Muslim forces under Saladin had captured the city of Christ's birth. After the repeated failures of the crusades, public opinion began to wonder if God had not abandoned the Holy Land to its fate and whether it might not be in vain to endeavor at such cost to reconquer it. Even Pope Innocent III (1198–1216), who greatly expanded the scope of the crusades, spoke with a certain condescension about "poor" (*misera*) earthly Jerusalem, contrasting it with the triumphal image of the heavenly Jerusalem, which the Church considered itself to be participating in here below.

France: The New Holy Land

This perspective makes clear the significance of Sainte-Chapelle, built by Louis IX to house the Crown of Thorns of Christ that had been purchased, at a hefty price, from the Venetians, who had held it as a pledge from the Latin emperor of Constantinople, Baldwin II. The precious

---

48. Laurent Durnecker, 'Tête de l'Église diocésaine et chef du saint patron: Le pèlerinage à Saint-Mammès de Langres à la fin du Moyen Age," in Vincent and Pycke, *Cathédrale et pèlerinage*, 145–59.

FIGURE 17. Louis IX depositing the Crown of Thorns in the Sainte-Chapelle. Detail from a miniature by the Master of Cardinal de Bourbon in the *Vie et miracles de monseigneur saint Louis*, 1480s. Bibliothèque nationale de France, MS Français 2829, fol. 17r.

relic arrived in France in August 1238.[49] The king went out to receive it at the frontier of the royal domain and brought it ostentatiously back to Paris. To house it, he had a magnificent chapel built, right next to the Royal Palace on the Île de la Cité, served initially by his own priests and chaplains, then by a chapter of canons whom he chose and financed (figure 17).

In the following years, twenty-one Byzantine reliquaries were added to its collection, containing relics mostly associated with the Passion of Christ: a fragment of the True Cross, a small quantity of the "Blood of Our Savior," a fragment of stone from the Holy Sepulcher, iron from the Holy Lance, a "triumphal cross" carried into battle by Byzantine emperors, the purple cloak with which Jesus was draped in derision by the soldiers, the rod that they placed in his hands as a kind of scepter,

---

49. Jean-Michel Leniaud and Françoise Perrot, *La Sainte-Chapelle* (Paris: Éditions du Patrimoine, 2016).

a piece of the Shroud, and the tunic that he wore when he washed and dried the feet of the apostles.[50]

By gathering together all of these relics within a single sanctuary, Saint Louis not only wanted to demonstrate his profound and very sincere devotion to the Passion of Christ. He also intended to make Paris into a New Jerusalem. In 1240, the archbishop of Sens, Gautier Cornut, a close advisor to the king, composed a special liturgy for Sainte-Chapelle, in which he developed the idea that it was God himself who had chosen to transfer the commemoration of his Passion to France through a special cult devoted to the Cross and the Crown of Thorns:

> Just as the Lord Jesus Christ chose the Promised Land to make known the mysteries of the Redemption, so we see too that he has especially chosen our Gaul for an even greater veneration of the triumph of his Passion.... Today, the King of Mercy grants to Gaul his own crown, as a testimony to and acclamation of the whole world and even the demons. The transfigured city of Paris becomes the training school of Gaul and, from the literal meaning, God moved it onto the spiritual plane. Noble Louis, king of the Franks: to you are now subject the diadems of former kings![51]

This text clearly exalts the providential role of France, elevated to the rank of "New Israel," the holy nation and chosen people, well illustrating the end of the Christian universalism incarnated up to that time in the papacy and empire. Significantly, its author refers to the Passion of Christ rather than to the Church of the Holy Sepulcher, which is not even mentioned. Nostalgia for the lost Holy Places, of course, remained in the depths of believers' hearts, but they were no more than a place of memory and a part of sacred history. Henceforth, it was Paris—and after it, every city in the West—that would be called to become a New Jerusalem; that is to say, a perfect city governed by evangelical precepts,

---

50. Chiara Mercuri, *Saint Louis et la couronne d'épines: Histoire d'une relique à la Sainte-Chapelle* (Paris: Riveneuve, 2011); M. Cecilia Gaposchkin, "Between Historical Narration and Liturgical Celebrations: Gautier Cornut and the Reception of the Crown of Thorns in France," *Revue Mabillon*, n.s., 30 (2019): 91–145.

51. *Historia translationis Sanctae Coronae Spineae*, § 9, ed. in Gaposchkin, "Between Historical Narration and Liturgical Celebrations," 125; trans. in Mercuri, *Saint Louis et la couronne d'épines*, 108–10; see also Christine Hediger, ed., *La Sainte-Chapelle de Paris: Royaume de France ou Jérusalem celeste?* (Turnhout: Brepols, 2007).

like the one that Savonarola would seek to create in Florence at the end of the fifteenth century.

Latin Christianity was not only capable of importing and housing the sacred objects of the East. It also had the ability to create new ones itself that were connected directly to the evangelical model. With the assassination of Thomas à Becket in 1170 in his cathedral in Canterbury, Christianity had at its disposal a "new martyr," immediately canonized and celebrated throughout all of Europe. And Francis of Assisi († 1226), the imitation of the poor and crucified Jesus was pushed to the point of a virtual identification; and soon the Order of Friars Minor readily presented their founder as a "second Christ" (*alter Christus*). For them, Umbria and Tuscany, where Francis's life had unfolded, became a new "seraphic" Holy Land that was spread out between the "New Bethlehem" of Assisi and Greccio and the "New Golgotha" of La Verna—the holy mountain where "the Poverello" had received the stigmata, often presented in spiritual texts of the period as a western Calvary. At the end of the thirteenth century, the Franciscan Peter of John Olivi wrote an entire treatise to justify the fact that the pilgrimage to the sanctuary of Portiuncula, which was the cradle of his order, deserved to be given a plenary indulgence "just like the Holy Sepulcher." All of these signs move in the same direction: from this point forward, the West considered itself the center of the Christian world, whereas the East saw itself relegated to the level of an increasingly distant memory.

Miracles and Eucharistic Sanctuaries

Around the middle of the thirteenth century, female spiritual groups associated with certain Cistercian monasteries or Dominican convents in Brabant and Flanders witnessed a great expansion of devotion toward the body and blood of Christ. The most illustrious example of this current was that of Juliana of Liège (also called Juliana of Mont-Cornillon, † 1258), a Beguine turned religious. She had a series of visions in which Christ deplored the absence of a feast celebrated by all the faithful in honor of the Eucharist, which he had instituted at the moment of the Last Supper on the eve of his Passion. In response to Christ's lament, the bishop of Liège, Robert de Thourotte, in 1246 introduced into his diocese the feast of Corpus Christi (la Fête-Dieu), which Pope Urban IV, the former archdeacon of Liège, extended to the universal Church through a papal bull, *Transiturus*, in 1264, in which he characterized it as a "feast instituted by God." The Dominican order immediately adhered to this liturgical initiative with the support of Hugh of Saint-Cher and of Thomas Aquinas, who wrote the hymn *Tantum ergo sacramentum* sung on this occasion.

But the Adoration of the Blessed Sacrament did not become widespread in Christianity until the fourteenth century, after the insertion of the *Transiturus* bull into the canonical collection established by Pope Clement V and edited by his successor, John XXII, in 1317. It is from this moment that word of "the miracle of Bolsena" began circulating through the efforts of the bishop of Orvieto, Beltrano Monaldeschi (1328-45). In 1263, a priest from Prague, who had gone to Rome and doubted the real presence of Christ in the Eucharist, celebrated Mass at Bolsena. During the elevation, he witnessed blood flowing abundantly from the chalice, so much so that the corporal and altar linens were stained with it. To house the precious relics, the prelate had the Sienese goldsmith Ugolino di Vieri craft a sumptuous, enameled reliquary in 1337/38, which contained the blood-stained corporal and was placed in the Cathedral of Orvieto. A large chapel dedicated to the *Corpus Domini* (Body of the Lord) was then built there, its walls covered with frescoes depicting Eucharistic or thaumaturgical miracles obtained by means of a consecrated Host. Pope Clement VI granted important indulgences to those who went there on pilgrimage, especially on the Feast of Corpus Christi and participated in the procession that unfolded in the streets of Orvieto—and still takes place there to this day. This solemn worship rendered to the Blessed Sacrament apparently aimed at shifting the piety of the faithful away from the relics of saints and toward the sacrament of the altar, through the recognition of the supernatural power of the holy species of bread and wine consecrated by the ministry of the priest.

With this miracle, and many others of the same type that ensued through the end of the Middle Ages, the distant Calvary of Christ (Golgotha) was transported onto the altars of the churches in the West, and Eucharistic relics supplemented, in the piety of Christians, the few drops of the blood of the Savior brought back from the East that were already being venerated in Mantua, Bruges, and Fécamp. The papal initiative was taken up throughout all of Christendom. In 1306, for example, the bishop of Autun, Bartholomew Bradareyre, recognized a Eucharistic miracle in the collegial church of Marigny-sur-Ouche in Burgundy: after a drop of consecrated wine fell from the chalice into an earthen pot, the face of a man—immediately considered to be that of

Christ—appeared at the base of the vessel. The bishop had it placed in a silver reliquary and granted an indulgence of forty days to those who came to venerate it in the church.[52]

Later, numerous miracles associated with sacred Hosts occurred in which, for example, the Eucharistic bread would start to bleed after having been sliced with a knife by a Jew. One of the most famous took place at Billettes in Paris in 1290. Philip the Fair purchased the house where the miracle occurred and created a cloister and a church there, which soon became a popular pilgrimage site. The same scenario occurred in Amsterdam in 1345, followed there, too, by the creation of a commemorative sanctuary in 1360 and a subsequent pilgrimage to this *Heilige Stede* (Holy Place). In Brussels in 1370, Jews supposedly stole and hid a sacred Host; when they stabbed it, blood flowed out of it. News of this miracle spread quickly, and the relic was carried into the Church of Saint-Catherine, where it became the object of a lively devotion. Following a Eucharistic miracle, the pope in 1435 granted one hundred days of indulgence to those who would go on pilgrimage to the site where it took place.[53] But none of these sanctuaries associated with antisemitism acquired any great renown beyond the city or region where they were founded.

Over the course of the fifteenth century, however, new Eucharistic sanctuaries appeared in northern Europe, similar in origin to the miracle of Bolsena (figure 18). The most celebrated in this period was the miracle of the Holy Blood of Wilsnack in Brandenburg.[54] In 1383, after the destruction of a village and the burning of its church by a plundering lord, the pastor found in its ruins three Hosts that had taken on the color of blood. The bishop of Havelberg went to the site, and when he consecrated the Hosts, blood issued from one of them. Once word spread, numerous pilgrims rushed to the site—as many as one hundred thousand in 1475—among whom were Scandinavian and English pilgrims. Urban VI granted to those who went there an indulgence, which was confirmed by Eugenius IV in 1447. The Hohenzollerns, to whom the Emperor Sigismund had given Brandenburg, constructed a great sanctuary there. Certain theologians, like Jan Hus and Heinrich Tocke,

---

52. Jacques Madignier, *Diocèse d'Autun*, Fasti Ecclesiae Gallicanae 12 (Turnhout: Brepols, 2010).

53. Miri Rubin, *Corpus Christi: The Eucharist in Late Medieval Culture* (Cambridge: Cambridge University Press, 1991).

54. Caroline Walker Bynum, *Wonderful Blood: Theology and Practice in Late Medieval Northern Germany and Beyond* (Philadelphia: University of Pennsylvania Press, 2007).

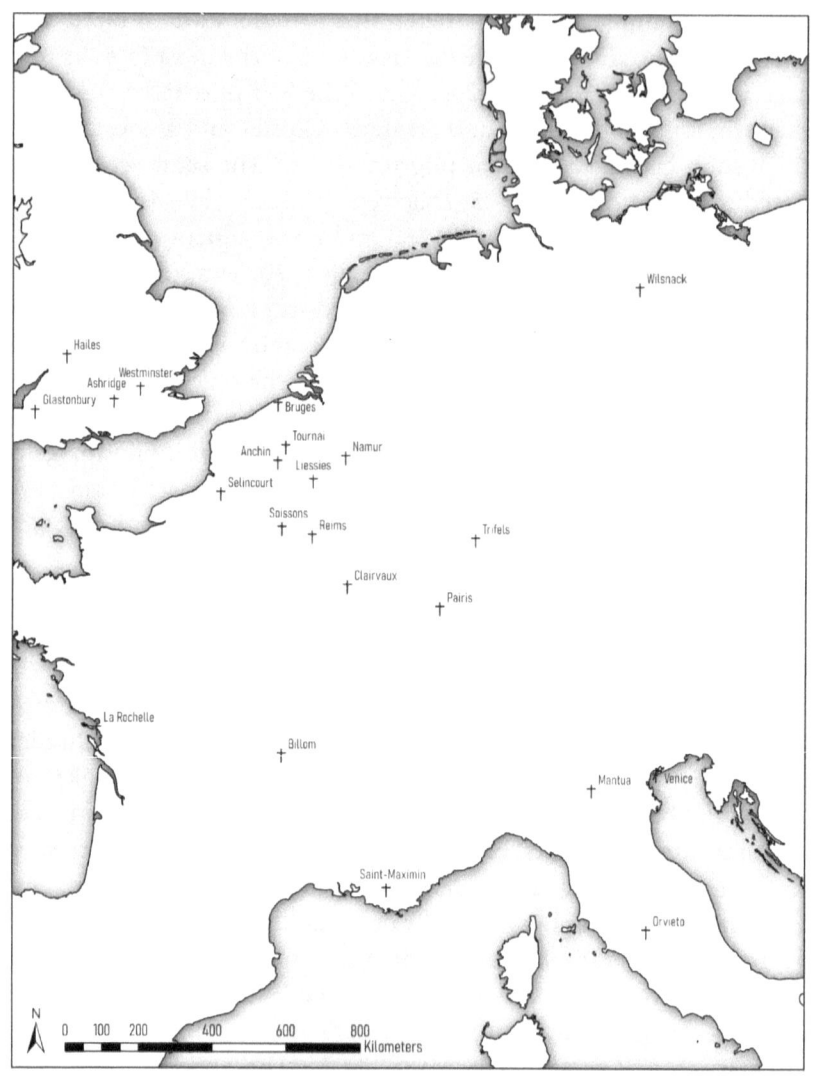

FIGURE 18. Holy Blood Sanctuaries in the Christian West, thirteenth–fifteenth centuries. Credit: A. Christesen.

the canon of Magdeburg, however, voiced serious reservations on this subject, emphasizing that the brown color of the Hosts could simply have been the result of their being exposed to the fire that burned down the church. Around 1445, an inquiry was opened by the local bishop with negative results. But the minister general of the Franciscans, Mathias Döring, supported the thesis of the authenticity of the miracle and, after the papal legate, Nicholas of Cusa, prohibited the cult in 1451, his decision was annulled a little later by Pope Nicholas V. Not until the Protestant Reformation in 1553 would the miraculous Hosts be destroyed and the pilgrimage to Wilsnack suppressed.

Less famous but no less interesting is the sanctuary of Bois-Seigneur-Isaac, near Ophain in Brabantian Wallonia. In the twelfth century, a crusading lord by the name of Isaac, freed from his captivity in the Holy Land, made a vow to the Virgin and had built on his own lands a chapel housing a Marian statue. In 1405, the village pastor came to celebrate the Mass, as he did every week, but when he opened the corporal, he discovered a morsel of the Host that immediately started to bleed.[55] The faithful of the area rushed there, and several healings immediately took place. After an inquiry, the archbishop of Cambrai, the theologian and cardinal Pierre d'Ailly, acknowledged the miracle in 1413 and authorized the sponsoring of a pilgrimage blessed with a forty-day indulgence. Processions around the church began the following year, and on this occasion, the preacher Nicholas Serrurier, of the order of the Hermits of Saint Augustine, spoke of the chapel as being a "Renewed Jerusalem, rightly so-called because of the miraculous Holy Blood and of the renewal in this place of the signs of the Passion of Christ." The same year, a recluse settled near this place, now called Jerusalem, and in 1417, a canoness of Nivelles offered an annuity to the miraculous chapel, referring to it in the act of donation as a "New Jerusalem." Beginning in 1418, the chapel became a priory entrusted to the canons regular of Windesheim, then an abbey that was recognized in 1431 by Pope Martin V. A reliquary cross containing the Host and corporal was made in 1555.

The reference to "New Jerusalem" to designate a Eucharistic sanctuary is a significant fact and effectively conveys the period's religious

---

55. François Baix, "Bois-Seigneur-Isaac," in *Dictionnaire d'histoire et de géographie ecclésiastiques IX* (Turnhout: Brepols, 1937), 547–73; Véronique Hazebrouck-Souche, *Spiritualité, sainteté et patriotisme: Glorification du Brabant dans l'oeuvre hagiographique de Jean Gielemans (1427–1487)* (Turnhout: Brepols, 2007).

aspirations. Taking the notion of transubstantiation literally, the faithful were disposed to believe that Christ could manifest himself to them *de visu* (visually) through the holy species of bread and wine, in order to accomplish miracles. This conviction was shared both by simple believers as by souls enamored by the pursuit of spiritual perfection, like the English visionary pilgrim Margery Kempe, who went to Wilsnack in 1431 to "venerate the Precious Blood of our Lord Jesus Christ that miraculously originated from the sacrament of the altar."[56]

Sanctuaries with Images

Beginning in the twelfth century, some sanctuaries began to be viewed as different from ordinary churches through their décor and their internal structure. This distinction was sometimes realized through the chancel, the space between the nave (where the laity were confined) and the choir or chevet (reserved for the clergy and centered around the altar). But the widespread use of stained-glass windows and large wall frescoes attenuated this contrast. As Jérôme Baschet has clearly shown, the sanctuary became a place of colors where the fluctuation of light spread out over the faithful, drawing them upward from the earthly sphere toward a heavenly world.[57] These believers were often welcomed by and drawn to *ymages* (icons) of saints, like the statue of the Apostle James at the entrance to the Basilica of Compostela. To enter into the church was already to penetrate the City of God through depictions of various episodes of sacred history that pilgrims associated with biblical and Christian temporality. By progressing into the nave, they would discover pictorial cycles and sometimes stained-glass windows that retraced the different episodes in the lives of Christ and Mary, and evoking the glory of the saints in the afterlife.

Ymages of the Saints: Importance and Influence

But soon the décor of some religious edifices no longer referred only to the fundamental sites of Christianity, like the Grotto of the Nativity in

---

56. *Le Livre de Margery Kempe: Une aventurière de la foi au Moyen Age*, trans. Louise Madignier (Paris: Éditions du Cerf, 1989), 336.
57. Jérôme Baschet, *Lieux sacrés, lieux d'images: Les fresques de Bominaco (Abruzzes, 1263). Thèmes, parcours, fonctions* (Rome: École Française de Rome, 1992); Michele Bacci, *Lo spazio dell'anima: Vita di una Chiesa medievale* (Bari: Laterza, 2005); Alphonse Dupront, *L'image de religion dans l'Occident chrétien* (Paris: Gallimard, 2015).

Bethlehem or the Mount of Olives in Jerusalem. Beginning in the thirteenth century, major episodes in the lives of the most recent saints—like the assassination of Saint Thomas à Becket in Canterbury Cathedral in 1170, with whom the theme of martyrdom was revived once again—would begin to be depicted. This evolution is particularly marked in the great sanctuaries of the mendicant orders, such as the Upper Basilica of Saint Francis of Assisi where pilgrims stood in the presence of the founder of the Friars Minor through the evocation of the principal steps of his earthly existence and of his glorification by the Church; the altar, meanwhile, lost at the back of the choir, hardly attracts attention. In Italy, beginning around the middle of the twelfth century, the tomb of the saint whose relics were being venerated—a monumental *arca* of sculpted marble by the greatest artists of the period—was often placed in the middle of the nave or in an easily accessible side aisle, as at San Domenico in Bologna, for the founder of the Friars Preacher in 1267, or at San'Eustorgio (Eustorgius I) in Milan, for the Dominican inquisitor Saint Peter Martyr, killed by heretics and immediately canonized by Pope Innocent IV in 1253. In Padua, the tomb of Saint Anthony was a veritable mausoleum located right in the middle of the church, around which candles and ex-votos placed by pilgrims accumulated.

During the last centuries of the Middle Ages, the walls of numerous sanctuaries were completely covered with paintings, so much so that, today, the name of the saint they were intended to honor is illegible. As the intercessors to whom the faithful appealed quickly evolved due to changing expectations and passing fads, their images were superimposed, one upon the other, with a surprising casualness. In the sanctuary of Santa Maria di Pietrarossa near Trevi in Umbria, the walls of the church feature myriad frescoes from the fourteenth and fifteenth centuries, around fifty of which depict the Virgin Mary, twenty-five the effigies of various saints, and a few with scenes from the Passion of Christ or the Trinity. One isolated fresco shows Joachim, the father of the Virgin Mary, expelled from the Temple and struck by God with sterility for his lack of faith—a scene rather rarely represented in the art of the period. Its presence here is probably explained by the particular specialization of this sanctuary, which had the reputation of curing men of sexual impotence and women of sterility.[58]

---

58. Mario Sensi, "Santuari del perdono e santuari eremitici 'à répit': Esempi umbro-marchigiani," in Vauchez, *Lieux sacrés, lieux de culte, sanctuaires*, 228–32. For the Alpine regions, see Simone Baiocco, Marie-Claude Morand, and Sylvie Aballéa, eds., *Des saints et des*

FIGURE 19. Painting by Hans Memling (ca. 1470/75) of Saint Veronica holding the veil (often called "the Veronica") with which she wiped Christ's face during the ascent to Calvary, imprinting the Holy Face on it. National Gallery of Art, Samuel H. Kress Collection.

To See God with One's Own Eyes: The Roman Veronica

In a general sense, at this time, emphasis was placed on the centrality of visions, which responded to a very strong need to see God, conferring upon the image a function of historicity (figure 19). Thus does Dante, in the *Divine Comedy* (*Paradiso* XXXI, 102–8), evoke a pilgrim he met in Rome:

> Just as one
> who, from Croatia perhaps, has come
> to visit our Veronica—one whose
> old hunger is not satisfied, who, as long
> as it is shown, repeats these words in thought:
> "O my Lord Jesus Christ, true God, was then
> Your face like the image I see now?"[59]

---

hommes: L'image des saints dans les Alpes occidentales au Moyen Age. Catalogue (Milan: Officina Libraria, 2013).

59. Dante, *The Divine Comedy, Paradiso*, trans. Allen Mandelbaum, Digital Dante, https://digitaldante.columbia.edu/dante/divine-comedy/paradiso/paradiso-31/. On the Roman

This aspiration to "see the mystery," so characteristic of the last centuries of the Middle Ages, as Roland Recht has shown, concerns, first and foremost, Eucharistic devotion, since the simple fact of looking with devotion upon the consecrated Host of the priest, during the Mass or during a procession, was commonly believed to have salutary power.[60]

This devotion then soon extended to relics and holy images, realities that were often equivalent: the former, encased within reliquaries and surrounded by crystals or magnifying glasses to enhance their viewing, tended to become works of art intended to strike the eye, while certain particularly prestigious images were treated as relics and surrounded by the same kind of veneration. In the eyes of clerics and especially theologians, all holy images were the same, and there was no place for attributing special sacredness to one or another. But it was not the same for the faithful, who held that some *did* possess a miraculous power, either by reason of their ancientness (such as the eleven known representations of the Virgin Mary attributed to Saint Luke) or because of a miracle that occurred in connection to them. From the fourteenth century on, the ecclesiastical hierarchy began to favorably welcome their requests by granting indulgences, as Pope John XXII did in 1318, for example, to those who would come to Santa Maria Maggiore in Rome to venerate the image of the Virgin known under the title *Salus Populi Romani* (Salvation of the Roman People), and to pray before it.[61]

In the last centuries of the Middle Ages, relics lost to such holy images the monopoly they had previously possessed, a development that would go hand in hand with the rise in requests for miracles made at a distance. This evolution occurred at different rates around Western Europe. It was already well advanced in Italy around 1500, but north and west of the Alps, the importance of relics must still have been considerable at the time of the Protestant Reformation, which explains why John Calvin devoted a whole treatise to demonstrating their idolizing character and calling for their destruction.

Veronica and its cult, see Ewa Kuryluk, *Veronica and Her Cloth: History, Symbolism, and Structure of a True Image* (Oxford: Blackwell, 1991).

60. Roland Recht, *Le croire et le voir: L'art des cathédrales (XIIe–XVe siècles)* (Paris: Gallimard, 1999).

61. Gerhard Wolf, *Salus populi romani: Die Geschichte römischer Kultbilder im Mittelalter* (Weinheim: Wiley-VCH Verlag, 1990).

The Marian Invasion (1300–1700)

The Growth of Miraculous Images

The cult of the Virgin Mary in the West dates to the beginning of the fourth century, as the existence of numerous churches dedicated to her in late antiquity and the early Middle Ages attests. In Rome, two of the principal basilicas of the city—Santa Maria in Trastevere and Santa Maria Maggiore—were consecrated to her in the fourth and fifth centuries respectively; and she would be venerated throughout the Middle Ages with icons of Byzantine origin, called *Hodegetria*, featuring the Virgin showing the way with her right hand, that is, to the Infant Christ, whom she is holding in her left arm, and attributed to the evangelist Luke (figure 20).

Later, however, most sanctuaries were placed under the patronage of saints whose relics they possessed. But those of the Virgin were very rare, limited to fragments of her cord or her blouse, as was the case in Chartres since the ninth century, or even to a few drops of her milk kept in a precious reliquary, as the one found in the treasury of the Abbey of Oignies in Wallonia. Therefore, there are hardly any traces of Marian pilgrimages within the territory of France prior to the year 1000, except the one that developed at the Cathedral of Reims after 924, at least according to the chronicler Flodoard of Reims († 966). But the dedication

Figure 20. The Madonna of Siponto, Manfredonia Cathedral, Apulia, a Byzantine-style *Hodegetria* (Greek: "She who shows the way") icon traditionally attributed to Saint Luke the Evangelist. Photo: Wikimedia Commons.

of cathedrals to "Notre Dame" clearly prevailed from the twelfth century on, and miracles began to be produced through her intercession in some of them. The survival of no fewer than thirty collections of miracles attributed to the Virgin, most often written by canons at the request of their bishops, attests to the growth of Marian devotion in this period. In 1128, the monastic chronicler Sigebert de Gembloux mentions the existence of seven large Marian sanctuaries in northern France: Arras, Cambrai, Chartres, Paris, Soissons, Lagny, and Fontaine. But, as Gabriela Signori has shown, with the exception of the last two, which are rather obscure, the collections that were drawn up there are, more than anything else, the expression of a rivalry between different cathedrals whose ecclesiastical authorities were looking for financing for their construction (or reconstruction) projects.[62]

True pilgrimage sanctuaries under the patronage of the Virgin only begin to appear in the second half of the twelfth century. One of the earliest such sanctuaries known is that of Walsingham in Norfolk, England.[63] A noble widow named Richeldis claimed she had been led in a dream by Mary to Nazareth, where she showed the widow the site of the Annunciation and ordered her to take measurements in order to re-create in England the house where the Holy Family had lived. Once she came to, the widow appealed to carpenters, who constructed on her property a replica of the Holy House, which was later replaced by a stone building. From the middle of the twelfth century, this novel sanctuary, curated by Augustinian monks, soon became the object of a popular devotion, and in the thirteenth century, every English person was encouraged to go there at least once in their lifetime. Henry II went there on pilgrimage in 1226 and, after him, nearly every English king, up to and including Henry VIII, did the same.

In France at this time, the two great Marian shrines were Notre-Dame du Puy and, especially, Rocamadour, which experienced tremendous growth from the 1160s.[64] A statue of the Black Madonna, believed to date back to the time of Christ, was venerated there, as was Roland's sword, Durendal, which connected this holy place to the Charlemagne cycle. According to the *Book of Miracles*, written in 1172 by a monk

---

62. Signori, "La bienheureuse polysémie."
63. Dominic James and Gary Waller, eds., *Walsingham in Literature and Culture from the Middle Ages to Modernity* (Aldershot: Routledge, 2010).
64. Jean Rocacher, *Rocamadour et son pèlerinage*, vol. 1 (Toulouse: Association les Amis de Rocamadour, 1979).

FIGURE 21. The Virgin of Monserrat, a Black Madonna statue in the Byzantine style venerated at the abbatial Monastery of Santa Maria de Montserrat. Photo: Jose Luis Filpo Cabana via Wikimedia Commons (CC BY 3.0).

who collected 127 miracles that had taken place at the sanctuary, Rocamadour's clientele was, at that time, mainly male and aristocratic.[65] Beginning in the twelfth century, at Montserrat in Catalonia, another Byzantine-style statue of the Black Madonna began to produce miracles and attract numerous pilgrims, in particular women who were unable to have children (figure 21).

The Growth of Apparition Sanctuaries

The last centuries of the Middle Ages and the early modern era witnessed a veritable explosion of Marian devotion and the appearance of a large number of new sanctuaries, great and small, associated either

---

65. Edmond Albe and Jean Rocacher, eds., *Les miracles de Notre-Dame de Rocamadour au XIIe siècle* (Toulouse: Le Pérégrinateur, 2007).

with "mariophanies"—that is, apparitions of Mary—or with the miraculous discovery of images depicting her. "Apparitions" were visible interventions of a person from the hereafter—Christ, Mary, demons, angels, saints, or the dead—whose appearance could not be explained through the normal course of nature; most often, they were apparitions of the Virgin Mary.[66]

In Italy, there are around 2,500 holy sites dedicated to the Madonna, out of the 3,500 sanctuaries whose existence is recorded for the period between roughly 1300 and 1700.[67] In Burgundy, the number of pilgrimages to Marian sanctuaries, more or less unchanging until the end of the thirteenth century, increased considerably to such a point that they represented more than a quarter of the total number of journeys around the year 1500. In Alsace and in Bavaria, around half of the sanctuaries that appeared between 1350 and 1525 were placed under the patronage of the Virgin. It is not easy to explain this massive phenomenon, which had various origins. The main one is obviously the growth of Marian devotion in the West: after Saint Bernard and the Cistercian monks, who had exalted the power of the Virgin's intercession, the mendicant orders presented her to the faithful in their preaching as a useful recourse in their daily lives, and they developed her cult wherever they settled.

In Rome, for example, beginning in the 1250s, the Franciscans transformed the old Church of Aracoeli, on the north summit of the Capitoline Hill—a place where, in a tradition later appropriated by Jacques de Voragine in the *Golden Legend*, the Emperor Augustus had a vision about the birth of Jesus—into a Marian sanctuary. During the thirteenth century, numerous collections of miracles of the Virgin were composed in the vernacular, like that of Gautier de Coincy or the *Cantigas de Santa Maria* of King Alfonso X "el Sabio," which spread the conviction that God could not refuse anything to Mary and, consequently, to anyone asking for her mercy. Furthermore, over the course of the thirteenth and fourteenth centuries, a very clear feminization of religious experience was occurring, as evidenced by the multiplication of Beguines and female penitents, tertiaries, and recluses—all of which allowed the men

---

66. Sylvie Barnay, *Le ciel sur la terre: Les apparitions de la Vierge au Moyen Age* (Paris: Éditions du Cerf, 1999).

67. Ada Campione, "Il Censimento dei santuari cristiani d'Italia: Ierofanie e luoghi di culto," in *Ierofanie e luoghi di culto*, ed. Luca Avellis (Bari: Edipuglia, 2016), 115-42; Martina Caroli, "Tipologia di santuari in Emilia Romagna," in *Santuari locali e religiosità popolare nelle diocesi di "Ravennatensia,"* ed. Maurizio Tagliaferri (Imola: Bologna University Press, 2003), 33-60.

of this time to discover the importance of female religious mediations and, especially, that of the Mother of God. Mary was a unique figure who contained within herself numerous potentialities and could take on a thousand faces: she was most often depicted with her son, but in visions and apparitions, she was generally alone. Bathed in divine light, she was both candelabra bearing the light of the Incarnate Word and transparent window through which one could see God. Mediatrix between God and humanity, she was considered to be the refuge of sinners and the suffering, who did not hesitate to resort in great numbers to her intercession and to beg from her consolations in their trials.[68]

Mary was a saint without relics. This allowed those who dwelled out in the countryside—people who were generally bereft of such things or had been despoiled of such by neighboring towns—to venerate her wherever she revealed herself. The extension of her cult is tied to the diffusion of her representations. As Jérôme Baschet has shown, these were not all, *stricto sensu*, miraculous, but they were active images that had the power to "create places" associated, for example, with an apparition of the Virgin and thus became sanctuaries after the fact. When these extraordinary phenomena occurred in a shrine, the image of the saint would confer on this place an additional sacred significance and a social visibility that contributed to the splendor of the ecclesial institution.[69] By way of synodal statutes, the ecclesiastical authorities encouraged the development of the Marian cult, far more commendable than the false relics of saints that had, at that time, become a scourge and that unscrupulous questers used to extort alms from the faithful by relying upon phony letters of indulgence. The extraordinary success of the Marian shrines between the fourteenth and seventeenth centuries really results from a confluence of the aspirations of popular piety—whose antiestablishment tendencies the Marian apparitions sometimes reinforced—and those of the ecclesiastical hierarchy, concerned to put a little order into the tangle of these devotions and to purify them by aligning them with the figure of the Mother of God.

---

68. Anna Maria Migdal, *Regina Coeli: Les images mariales et le culte des reliques. Entre Orient et Occident au Moyen Age* (Turnhout: Brepols, 2017).

69. Jérôme Baschet and Pierre-Olivier Dittmar, eds., *Les images dans l'Occident médiéval* (Turnhout: Brepols, 2015); Nicolas Balzamo, "Image miraculeuse: Le mot, le concept et la chose," in *L'image miraculeuse dans le christianisme occidental: Moyen Age – Temps modernes*, ed. Nicolas Balzamo and Estelle Leutrat (Tours: Presses universitaires François Rabelais, 2020), 15–41; and Jean-Marie Sansterre, *Les images sacrées en Occident au Moyen Age: Histoire, attitudes, croyances. Recherches sur le témoignage des textes* (Madrid: AKAL, 2021).

According to their founding legends, these Marian sanctuaries had their origin either in an apparition of the Virgin in the form of an iconic representation (that is, in the form of a visual image) or in the fortuitous discovery of a representation of the Madonna (whether it be a statue, a painting, or a long-forgotten fresco). For example, in 1485, near Trevi in Umbria, a fresco depicting the Virgin began to shed tears of blood. To commemorate the event, the inhabitants of the area inaugurated an annual procession; then, a pilgrimage church was built there, known as the Madonna delle Lacrime (Our Lady of Tears), which became a local sanctuary.[70] The incontestability of the sanctity of the Mother of God made it difficult to challenge the visions that simple believers claimed to have received, more so because they were sometimes accompanied by extraordinary phenomena, according to the testimonials: haloes of light, climatic oddities like snow falling in the middle of summer, or the appearance of out-of-season fruits and flowers. And lending credence to the vision, the seer was often also favored with a miraculous healing, as a result of the Virgin laying her hands on the dreamer, especially if they were sick or handicapped. The mere fact of her appearance in a given place meant this site and the surrounding territory were immediately graced with an aura of sacredness that had to be acknowledged and respected by all.

At the end of this long process of development and consolidation, therefore, miraculous *ymages* of Mary seemingly appeared everywhere in the West and were adorned with well-defined attributes. Although the few theologians who did become interested in these phenomena reminded people that "no image has any power in itself," the faithful did not pay much attention to these reservations and thought rather that Christ could not refuse anything to his Mother, just as the miracle that he performed on her pleading at the wedding feast of Cana had already demonstrated.

---

70. Mario Sensi, "Monti sacri, transfert di sacralità e santuari *ad instar*," in *Tra monti sacri, "sacri monti" e santuari: Il caso Veneto*, ed. Antonio Diano and Lionelli Puppi (Monselice: Il Poligrafo, 2004), 39–72; Maria Stella Calò Mariani, "Icone e statue: Lignee medievali nei santuari marini della Puglia," in *Santuari cristiani d'Italia: Committenze e fruizione tra Medioevo e età moderna*, ed. Mario Tosti (Rome: École Française de Rome, 2003), 3–44.

FIGURE 22. Apparition of the Virgin Mary, the Madonna dell'Ulivo, to a child in a field of olive trees. Anonymous fresco, Church of San Francesco, Leonessa, Lazio, ca. 1409.

The Virgin Mary: Saint for the Laity and the Reformed Religious Orders

As Giorgio Cracco has shown, the growth of Marian shrines in the fourteenth and fifteenth centuries must be contextualized within the crisis of ecclesiastical institutions that seems to have impelled numerous congregants to distance themselves from a secular clergy that was less than edifying and from monastics whose laxity eroded their luster.[71] In light of this, the laity took the initiative and invested in the cult of Mary, as the movement of the Bianchi demonstrates. Penitents who wandered around Italy in 1399 in an eschatological climate, the Bianchi were marked by a great devotion to the Madonna dell'Ulivo (Our Lady of the Olive Tree), whose images, reputed to be miraculous, were being painted on the exterior and interior walls of churches and public buildings, as well as on city gates (figure 22).[72]

---

71. Giorgio Cracco, "La grande stagione dei santuari mariani (XIVᵉ–XVIᵉ siècle)," in *I santuari d'Italia: Bilancio del censimento e proposte interpretative*, ed. André Vauchez (Rome: École Française de Rome, 2007), 17–44.

72. Amleto Spicciani, ed., *La devozione dei Bianchi nel 1399: Il miracolo del Crocifisso di Borgo a Buggiano* (Pisa: ETS, 1998).

In Italy, most of the first-generation Marian shrines were built thanks to the laity—by various communes or lords—often in the middle of nowhere: on a hilltop, in a forest, or near a body of water. Numerous foundation legends describe the fruitless efforts of the parish clergy to seize the holy *ymages* that were the object of popular veneration and to transfer them into parish churches. But very quickly and mysteriously, these icons somehow returned to the place where they had been miraculously discovered, whereupon the ecclesiastical authorities generally wound up authorizing the construction of a chapel on the site. This widespread phenomenon expressed an undeniable tension between two different conceptions of the sanctuary: that of the people, who intended to remain faithful to the apparition site, and that of the secular clergy, who wanted to integrate the new sacredness into the framework of parish life. Urban and rural sanctuaries dedicated to Mary were soon so numerous and influential in central Italy that, according to Richard Trexler, the period between the end of the fourteenth and beginning of the sixteenth centuries witnessed a "Mariological Renaissance."[73] But this description of a triumphant Mariology, of popular origin, can be extended to many other regions of Western Christianity, from Spain to the Rhine Valley, Flanders, and the Brabant.

Generally, at the origin of these new sanctuaries were humble people—children or adolescents, shepherds and shepherdesses, farm workers, and a whole panoply of poor, sick, or handicapped persons—whom ethnologists studying these phenomena refer to as "unwitting mediators." Indeed, it was through their mediation that messages from Mary were transmitted to particular communities, usually the first beneficiaries of her apparitions. Another characteristic of these sanctuaries was that they were no longer defined by the presence of relics. Foundation legends held that at the origin of the devotional site was the *ymage* of the Virgin: a pictorial depiction, a statue miraculously brought to shore from across the sea, or one discovered in a tree or underground by a laborer. Shepherds and peasants thus "invented" images of the Virgin, much as bishops, from the time of Saint Ambrose at the end of the fourth century, had "invented" (i.e., discovered) holy bodies and placed them in their churches.

Sometimes the Marian apparition was accompanied by an explicit request for a cult, as the account of the origins of the great Marian

---

73. Richard Trexler, "Florentine Religious Experience: The Sacred Image," *Studies in the Renaissance* 19 (1972): 7–41.

sanctuary of the Madonna della Quercia (Our Lady of the Oak) near Viterbo makes clear. Here, in 1467, Mary revealed herself in the middle of the fields to shepherds who were carrying out the seasonal migration of their flocks between the Maremme and the Apennines. After this event, an image of the Virgin was placed in a chapel built specifically to protect it, with the agreement of the bishop of Viterbo. As plague raged throughout the region, the faithful implored the intercession of this new Madonna, and the epidemic immediately ceased. The sanctuary then became famous in central Italy for its therapeutic powers, and the number of ex-votos preserved there also mention cures of malaria, which ran rampant at that time.[74] The majority of paintings that the founding legends present as the inspiration for devotion were described as being "ancient" images. Most often, this meant that the icons were *à la grècque*, that is, in the Byzantine style, inspired by images of the Virgin that, according to legend, were painted by Luke the Evangelist just prior to her Assumption.

Typical of this is the founding of the Sanctuary of the Beata Vergine delle Grazie (Sanctuary of the Blessed Virgin of Graces) near Mantua, on the plain of the Po Valley. In 1389, it was a small rural church that housed an icon depicting the Virgin with Child. Local pilgrims experienced miracles there, and at the beginning of the fifteenth century, the oratory was given to the Friars Minor who had established a small convent and church there between 1399 and 1407. The growth of this sanctuary, however, is especially linked to the strategy of the Franciscan Observants who typically settled in places that were isolated but not located too far from towns. With the help of the duke of Mantua, Francesco Gonzaga—who wanted to assert his legitimacy and increase his prestige among the faithful by creating a dynastic sanctuary—the friars were able to considerably expand it with four cloisters and a vast house for elite guests and pilgrims. Miracles multiplied, and the friars established, at the beginning of the sixteenth century, an extraordinary collection of relics and, especially, of ex-votos of every kind—including a preserved crocodile (a traditional Christian symbol of evil) suspended from the church's ceiling—comprising a kind of *Wunderkammer* (cabinet of curiosities) that attracted distant visitors.[75] Many of these new

---

74. Attilio Carosi and Gianfranco Ciprini, *Gli ex-voto del santuario della Madonna della Quercia di Viterbo: Immagini e testimonianze di fede* (Rome: Cassa di Risparmio di Viterbo, 1993).

75. Catherine Mayeur-Jaouen, "Crocodiles et saints du Nil: Du talisman au miracle," *Revue de l'histoire des religions* 217 (2000): 733–50.

Marian sanctuaries were dedicated not simply to the Virgin Mary, but to one of the joyful or sorrowful "mysteries" of her earthly life: the Annunciation, the Assumption, the fainting at the foot of the Cross (Madonna dello Spasimo), and events catalogued under various other titles, like Saint Mary of the Angels, Our Lady of Grace, and Saint Mary of Good Help, among others.

Not all Marian sanctuaries that appeared in this period were the result of a mariophany. The hermitage of Notre-Dame des Anges (Our Lady of Angels), located in the rocky terrain of Mimet in the diocese of Aix-en-Provence, on the outskirts of Marseilles, is one example.[76] According to its founding legend, which dates from the end of the fifteenth or beginning of the sixteenth century, it was established around 1220 by Friar Jean, a Franciscan hermit (or at least influenced by Franciscanism) who was soon joined by a companion with whom he transformed a natural grotto into a small church. This establishment is first mentioned in official documents in 1405–8, when the hermitage had already become a sanctuary frequently visited by locals. A testament from 1408 affirms this; in it, a layperson donates a wax candle to each of the four sanctuaries that were most highly esteemed by the citizens of Marseilles: Notre-Dame des Anges, Notre-Dame de la Garde, Notre-Dame de la Consolation in Aix-la-Provence, and Notre-Dame de Moustiers. But the people of Aix were no less devoted to Notre-Dame des Anges, as their numerous donations and wills benefiting the sanctuary attest. Four thousand people participated in a feast-day pilgrimage there in the middle of the fifteenth century, and René of Anjou (count of Provence and the former king of Naples) went there himself in 1472. Later, the hermitage was transformed into an oratory, and in 1526, the confraternity that managed its material needs constructed a hostel next to the hermitage for the exclusive use of people from Aix-en-Provence.

Images of Mary at the Origin of the New Urban Sanctuaries

Another factor that favored the blossoming of so many new places of worship dedicated to the Virgin at the end of the Middle Ages and the beginning of the modern era was the spread of the plague and its recurring outbreaks that, each time, decimated populations, especially

---

76. Noël Coulet, "L'ermitage de Notre-Dame des Anges de sa fondation (XIIIe siècle?) à l'installation des oratoriens," *Provence historique* 68 (2018): 401–20.

the elderly and the very young. To put an end to this scourge, the faithful considered it was necessary to repent of their sins and return to God.[77] In this context of crisis, chapels were built on a simple square design—sometimes in a single day!—and dedicated to Saint Sebastian, Saint Roch, or more often, to Mary, who was considered the most efficacious protectoress against disease. The initiative could be taken by individuals—at Norcia in Umbria, for example, a rich and prominent citizen had a *tempietto* (little temple) built in 1354 in honor of the Virgin—or by public authorities. Most often, these votive sanctuaries were raised not within the town but outside it, in the immediate proximity of the city gates, as in Todi, with its lovely Church of Santa Maria della Consolazione.[78]

During the fourteenth and fifteenth centuries, under the impetus of the spread of Marian devotion, depictions of Mary became numerous in cities. Some of them became focal points within existing churches that, because of the flow of visitors they attracted due to their healing properties, were transformed into sanctuaries. Others were located in houses or at the intersections of streets where oratories in her honor were built. As a result, at the end of the fourteenth century, Florentines preferred to practice their devotion at sites that belonged to neither parishes nor monasteries.[79] This was the case, to cite only one example, with the little Chapel of Santa Maria delle Grazie on the Rubaconte bridge, "made on the model of Christ's tomb," in imitation of the Holy Sepulcher. This private oratory had been created around 1370 by a rich merchant, Iacopo di Caroccio Alberti, so that prayers could be said for him and his family. Remodeled after his death around 1395, it housed a fresco depicting the Madonna seated on a throne, a crown on her head, and carrying a Child in the process of blessing, with a few angels around them. This painting became the object of worship among local penitents and recluses but, at the end of the century, after a series of miracles, its reputation extended to the whole city. A banker, Francesco

---

77. Klaus Schreiner, *Maria Jungfrau, Mutter, Herrscherin* (Vienna: Hanser, 1994); Christine M. Boeckl, *Images of Plague and Pestilence: Iconography and Iconology* (Kirksville, MO: Truman State University Press, 2000); and Mario Sensi, "Santuari, culti e riti 'ad repellendam pestem' tra Medioevo e Età Moderna," in *Luoghi sacri e spazi della santità*, ed. Sofia Boesch-Gajano and Lucetta Scaraffia (Turin: Rosenberg & Sellier, 1990), 381–96.

78. Erik Thunø and Gerhard Wolf, eds., *The Miraculous Image in the Middle Ages and Renaissance* (Rome: L'Erma di Bretschneider, 2004).

79. Michele Bacci, *"Pro remedio animae": Immagini e pratiche devozionali in Italia centrale (secoli XIII–XIV)* (Pisa: ETS, 2000).

di Marco Datini, then made a donation to what he called the Chapel of the Bridge. No trace of any kind of authorization on the part of the bishop has been found, and these activities seem to have been carried out completely outside the ecclesiastical framework, insofar as bridges, like city gates, were uniquely under the jurisdiction of the civil authority. Such "micro-sanctuaries" often operated in the shadows and could disappear from notice as quickly as they had appeared, but they testify to the extraordinary vitality of the Marian cult in this period.

Another example of a predominantly iconic Marian sanctuary is the Beautiful Virgin of Regensburg. In 1519—two years after the beginning of the Church's struggle with Martin Luther—the mayor of the city decided to have the houses of Jews razed, expelled them from the city, and had built in the piazza a church dedicated to the Virgin Mary. During the demolition work, a worker fell from the top of the structure onto a pile of rubble. When he came to, he declared that Mary had saved his life by supporting him during his fall. News of the miracle did not take long to spread, and a chapel made of wood, then in stone, was constructed on this site. A statue depicting a Virgin with Child, attributed to Hans Leinbergers, was placed outside. During the week after Pentecost in 1520, worshipers near the statue suddenly started to fall to the ground as if struck by lightning. Seeing this, others endeavored to do the same: some extended themselves in the form of a cross; others fell down while crying out and shaking, drool oozing out of their mouths. They would later say that the Virgin Mary had appeared to them, struck them down, and spoke to them; or they claimed that they had seen the souls of their father, their mother, their brother delivered from purgatory. Others were tormented because they despaired of ever obtaining pardons for their sins. Still others started to prophesy and spur others to conversion by speaking about the divine wrath that even the Virgin Mary could not restrain. And some bragged about having come from heaven on behalf of the Mother of God. People were also seen dancing around the statue while crying out (figure 23).[80]

However, it was after the installation of Albrecht Altdorfer's famous painting, the *Schöne Maria* (Beautiful Mary), painted circa 1519 and disseminated by means of numerous engravings throughout all of Germany, that the sanctuary began to grow and attracted innumerable pilgrims; 10,172 plaques made of lead and 2,430 made of silver bearing

---

80. Gerlinde Stahl, "Die Wallfahrt zur 'Schönen Maria' in Regensburg," *Beiträge zur Geschichte des Bistums Regensburg* 2 (1968): 69–70.

FIGURE 23. Pilgrims at the Church of the Beautiful Virgin at Regensburg. Woodcut by Michael Ostendorfer (ca. 1519). Photo: Wikimedia Commons.

her image were sold on site in 1519, before declining rapidly after 1523. This episode is particularly interesting to the extent that it affirms the role played during the Renaissance by works of art in the genesis of the sanctuaries.

Between 1652 and 1672, the Jesuit Wilhelm Gumppenberg authored and published the *Atlas Marianus*, in which he recounts the history of a hundred sanctuaries dedicated to miraculous Virgins and lists some 1,200 Marian images that were objects of devotion in Europe and the Americas. All were associated with a miracle demonstrating their extraordinary character.[81] By doing so, Gumppenberg aimed at proving the existence of the sacred world, dominated by the figure of Mary, who provided a privileged channel to the supernatural through her

---

81. Nicolas Balzamo and Olivier Christin, eds., *L'Atlas Marianus de Wilhelm Gumppenberg: Édition et traduction* (Neuchâtel: Éditions Alphil / Presses universitaires suisses, 2015).

miracles and her consoling manifestations that attested to her solicitude for sinful humanity. These little islets of sacredness, connected to each other through the imagery of the religious realms, mapped out a new spiritual Christianity, founded on the figure of the Virgin, mediator between heaven and earth, in order to encourage the faithful to persevere in their devotion and lead them toward the hoped-for goal: the Kingdom of God.

Latin Europe: The New Holy Land

Notre-Dame of Loreto

At the end of the Middle Ages, one Italian sanctuary in particular saw its influence expand throughout all of Christianity: Notre-Dame of Loreto, not far from the shores of the Adriatic and the port of Recanati.[82] In the thirteenth century, texts began to mention the presence of a chapel in Loreto dedicated to the Virgin Mary, located on a hill dominating the coastal plain. It was still only a local sanctuary housing a statue of the Virgin Mary made of cedar. The brick-and-masonry building was unique in lacking a foundation, as if seemingly placed on the ground. This was perhaps the reason why it was easy to believe that this was, in fact, the house of the Holy Family that had been transported by ship from Nazareth to the West before the fall of Acre, the last Christian stronghold in the Holy Land, in 1291. Over the course of the fourteenth century, miracles proliferated here, and indulgences were granted to those who pilgrimaged there on the feast of the Nativity of Mary (September 8) by Popes Gregory XI and Urban VI. The reputation of the Madonna of Loreto increased in the second half of the fifteenth century thanks to the effectiveness of her intercession against the plague. Beginning in the 1460s, the legend grew that the Santa Casa (Holy House) had been carried by angels from the Holy Land to Loreto through the air (figure 24). In addition to the wooden statue of Mary, another painting attributed to Saint Luke, depicting the Virgin at the moment of the Annunciation, was also venerated there.

The papacy—which had claimed Mary as its protector, characterizing her as mother and guide to the faithful—exalted this sanctuary

---

82. Ferdinando Citterio and Lucciano Vaccaro, eds., *Loreto crocevia religioso tra Italia, Europa e Oriente* (Brescia: Morcelliana, 1997); Dominique Julia, "Sanctuaires et lieux sacrés à l'époque moderne," in Vauchez, *Lieux sacrés, lieux de culte, sanctuaires*, 241–95; and Yves-Marie Bercé, *Lorette aux XVIe et XVIIe siècles* (Paris: Presses universitaires Paris-Sorbonne, 2011).

FIGURE 24. *The Translation of the Holy House of Loreto*, attributed to the Italian Saturnino Gatti (ca. 1490). Angels bear the Casa Santa across the Adriatic Sea from Dalmatia, where legend has it that it first settled in 1291, to Loreto. The Metropolitan Museum of Art, Gwynne Andrews Fund, 1973.

by showering it with indulgences. This followed the Council of Basel's proclamation of 1439 that belief in the Immaculate Conception of Mary, widely debated, was consistent with Christian faith. In 1470, Pope Paul II undertook the construction of a large basilica in Loreto dedicated to Mary the Liberator and placed the little town and its sanctuary under the protection of the Roman Church. Paul II was the first pope to promote the shrine on an international level, and pilgrims rushed there from everywhere in Christendom. King Louis XI, a fervent devotee of Loreto, made provisions for a resident chaplain to serve as a caretaker—a role still active today—and to pray to the Virgin on behalf of France and its king. Finally, in 1520, Leo X placed Notre-Dame of Loreto on the same level as Jerusalem, Rome, and Santiago de Compostela by granting a plenary indulgence to believers who went there on pilgrimage. In less than two centuries, Loreto had become the most important Marian sanctuary of Christianity and a veritable sanctuary-city, even if its urban development remained quite modest. By the end of the fifteenth century, the legend of the Holy House's flight from Nazareth had become widely accepted, and from that time on, the sacralization of western European space was no longer simply a matter of the translation of relics from East to West, as in preceding centuries. For the first time, this transfer had come directly from the Holy Land through supernatural intervention, rendering any detour by way of the East superfluous.

Sacred Mountains

Besides the affirmation of Loreto within Christianity, the principal novelty of the Renaissance was the appearance of large sanctuaries established in mountainous regions. These sacred mountains were particularly numerous in Italy but could also be found later in Germany and Poland, in the sixteenth and seventeenth centuries.[83] Their founders were looking to reproduce in the European wilderness the eminence of Mount Zion and the sacred topography of Jerusalem—"a city set upon a hill," according to the Psalmist. Their growth is tied to the decline of pilgrimages to the Holy Land, which had become dangerous since the fall of Acre. In the second half of the fifteenth century, it became practically impossible for Christians to go to the East, due to the almost permanent state of war with the Ottomans and the violence they perpetrated against Christians, such as the massacre of more than eight hundred inhabitants of Otranto in 1480. This troubled context explains the inscription above the portal to the Sacro Monte (Sacred Mountain) of Varallo in Piedmont—"in order that one might see Jerusalem, who has not been able to go there on pilgrimage"—attesting to the intention of its promoters to create a substitute sanctuary.

The idea had come to Italian Franciscans, who had lived in the Holy Land for a long time, to reconstitute in the West the natural landscape and architectural framework of the Incarnation (with the grotto of Bethlehem and the house in Nazareth) and of the Passion of Christ by creating replicas of the site in Jerusalem, its monuments, and the principal events in the life of the Savior in the countryside. More than merely an imitation, this project was a veritable transfer in space and time of the sacredness of the Holy Land. As the historian Dominique Julia sees it, this represented a major shift in the history of Christian pilgrimage: "Jerusalem, land of the promise and figure of the earthly Jerusalem during the time before the return of Christ, had ceased to be the *medium mundi* [center of the world] that it had been up until then."[84]

---

83. Luigi Zanzi, *Sacri monti e dintorni: Studi sulla cultura religiosa e artistica della Controriforma* (Milan: Jaca Book, 2005); Dorino Tuniz, ed., *I Sacri Monti: Itinerari ascetici Cristiani*, Archivio italiano per la storia della pietà 28 (Rome: Edizioni di storia e letteratura, 2015); Norman Housley, "Holy Land or Holy Lands? Palestine and the Catholic West in the Late Middle Ages and Renaissance," in *The Holy Land, Holy Lands and Christian History*, ed. R. N. Swanson (Oxford: Ecclesiastical History Society, 2000), 228-49.

84. Dominique Julia, "Continuités et ruptures dans la vie des pèlerinages, de la Réforme à la Révolution française," in Scotto, *Del visibile credere*, 3-39.

The journey of pilgrims to these sanctuaries was marked out by a succession of enclosed chapels and edicules (small shrines), often plain on the outside but with interiors that depicted the principal episodes of the life of Jesus with terra cotta sculptures and frescoes painted in lively colors, intended to allow the faithful to contemplate each scene in all its fullness and immerse themselves in the episode being represented.[85] The itinerary generally followed the verses of the Credo, so as to confront the visitor with each of the principal mysteries of the Christian faith, rendered more concrete by their insertion into the appropriate places (Mount of Olives, Kedron Valley, House of Anna, *Scala Santa*, Golgotha, the Upper Room of the Cenacle where the apostles and Virgin Mary gathered for Pentecost, and so on). At Varallo, these edifices are spread about over two areas: one includes chapels scattered along a slope covered with vegetation; the other, located on a six-hundred-meter-high plateau overlooking the valley, is an urban setting designed like a Renaissance city, with streets and piazzas that re-create the most important palaces and monuments of Jerusalem at the time of Christ (figure 25). Thanks to this "virtual reality," the pilgrim could believe that they were both seeing and touching the holy city, facilitating an imaginative interiorizing of the different sites and allowing them to retrace the steps of the Passion, as if in a comic strip or film.

Similarly, in Tuscany, there is another equally extraordinary sacred mountain: San Vivaldo at Montaione, in the diocese of Volterra.[86] It was initiated by a Franciscan Observant, Tommaso of Florence, who, upon his return from the Holy Land at the end of the fifteenth century, decided to create a "New Jerusalem" on a wooded hill where, in the thirteenth century, the saintly hermit Vivaldo Stricchi had lived. There was already a convent on the site (built between 1486 and 1499) when construction of the sanctuary began in 1500. The work was completed thanks to the enthusiasm of the local population and with the financial support of a few wealthy families of the Florentine aristocracy. The first wave of constructions, which comprised six chapels and numerous

---

85. André Vauchez, "Faire voir Jérusalem: Des imitations du Saint-Sépulcre aux 'Sacri Monti' italiens," *Comptes-rendus des séances de l'Académie des Inscriptions et Belles-Lettres* 160 (2016): 1559–72.

86. Sergio Gensini, ed., *La "Gerusalemme" di San Vivaldo e i Sacri Monti in Europa* (Pisa: Pacini, 1989); Rita Mazzei, "La Madonna degli Italiani: I santuari mariani d'Italia," in *Storia sociale e culturale d'Italia*, vol. 6, *La cultura folklorica*, ed. Franco Cardini (Florence: Bramante, 1988), 161–233; Riccardo Pacciani and Guido Vannini, *La Gerusalemme de San Vivaldo in Valdesa* (Montaione: Titivillus, 1998).

FIGURE 25. Sacro Monte in Varallo, Piedmont. Photo: iStock/fotoember.

other "evangelical sites" on a more modest scale, was probably finished in 1516, since that is when Pope Leo X (a Medici) granted important indulgences—seven years for each chapel visited—to those who went on pilgrimage to the new sanctuary. Later, other buildings devoted to the life of the Virgin Mary were added, bringing the number of chapels and oratories to thirty-four, all decorated with art from the Della Robbia workshops in Florence. These buildings were positioned according to a plan inspired by the topography and mapping of Jerusalem. More than just reproducing the principal monuments of the city at the time of Christ, San Vivaldo was a vast "set" meant to direct the attention of pilgrims to the principal episodes of the history of salvation, from the sin of Adam up to the Resurrection of Christ and the Pentecost.

Thus, in spite of the decline of pilgrimages to the Holy Land, Jerusalem had never been more present in the conscience of Latin Christians. But it was a dreamed-up Jerusalem, largely imaginary—even mythical—that these sacred mountains put within the reach of the faithful of the West. It was a place between heaven and earth, a city of origins with the memory of Abraham ready to sacrifice his only son on Mount Moriah, and the city of the end times where, according to the Apocalypse, the Antichrist will appear and definitively be defeated, prompting the glorious return of Christ. This Jerusalem of the mind was therefore an ideal city, no longer pulled between the misery of the "Jerusalem here below," subject to the happenstances of history, and the heavenly Jerusalem, the future city of the angels and the elect; rather, it anticipates the latter's arrival through a demonstration of beauty and harmony. In short, this Jerusalem was a true city-sanctuary, a place of sacred memory where the divine energies penetrated the earthly world and where humans could experience an encounter with the supernatural, both awesome and beneficent.

The introduction of the concept of sacred mountains marked the beginning of a new era with regard to pilgrimage: the Church favored them because they allowed the faithful to avoid the dangerous overseas passage and to benefit from the grace associated with the journey, but without having to go far from home. Furthermore, these were travels that families with children could undertake, which explains the instructional dimension that was very much present on the routes among the memorials. This trend equally reflects the influence of the *Devotio Moderna* movement, which discouraged exterior expressions of piety and instead put the emphasis on the inner pilgrimage—to seek out the Jerusalem within—through which the faithful believer journeyed toward Jesus, after having meditated upon his life and sufferings.[87] And finally, the appearance of these mountain sanctuaries manifested the need for the dramatization of religious life and the aspiration to create ideal cities that characterized the Renaissance and that blossomed, after the Council of Trent (1545–63), in Baroque art.

Rome: The Latin New Jerusalem?

During the final centuries of the Middle Ages, however, Rome remained for Christians of the West the place where more graces could be obtained for salvation than elsewhere. The long-lasting fascination with the Eternal City in the minds of the faithful can be precisely identified in the accounts of pilgrims and writers in this period. For example, the chronicler from Liège, Jean d'Outremeuse († 1400), in his vernacular work titled *Ly Myreur des Histors* (The Mirror of Histories), reproduces both a version of the *Mirabilia Urbis Romae*—a kind of guide

---

87. Dominique Julia, *Les voyages des saints: Les pèlerinages dans l'Occident moderne (XVe–XVIIIe siècle)* (Paris: Seuil, 2016).

to the principal monuments in the city—and a small work dedicated to the "Indulgences of the Churches of Rome," a list of sacred sites and information about which indulgences could be gained by visiting them.[88] This text enumerates no fewer than 472 holy sites, while underscoring the importance of the seven principal ones that had to be visited in order to obtain the jubilee (or plenary) indulgence. Saint Peter's Basilica was obviously the first, and the simple act of climbing the twenty-nine steps to the courtyard was worth an indulgence of seven years. Inside the basilica were eighty chapel altars that, when visited, conferred twenty-eight years of grace. Near the altar of Saints Simon and Jude are both the rope Judas used to hang himself and a Shroud of Christ, and according to Jean d'Outremeuse's *Myreur* (I, 74), anyone who had held the latter was assured of never becoming leprous or epileptic and would escape the fires of hell. In all, the pilgrim who made the rounds of this basilica could acquire twenty-eight thousand years of indulgences—a number that was doubled during Easter and on the occasion of the feasts of Saints Peter and Paul (June 29).

Saint John Lateran possessed no fewer than 114 relics, and the description in the *Myreur* of its contents becomes particularly detailed when addressing the pontifical treasury, the Sancta Sanctorum, located near the basilica.[89] D'Outremeuse lists the presence of the Ark of the Covenant, seven candelabras from the Jerusalem Temple, the Tablets of the Law, the staffs of Moses and Aaron, the swaddling clothes and cradle of Christ, the hair shirt of Saint John the Baptist (made from "camel's hair"), and many other objects related to the episodes of Christian history and the lives of its holy martyrs and confessors.

The pilgrim was then led toward Santa Maria Maggiore and its famous *ymage* of Mary and the infant Jesus, *Salus Populi Romani* (purportedly created by Saint Luke), which had been there since 590, when it had been carried in procession by Gregory the Great to put an end to a plague (figure 26). They then went on to Saint Paul Outside the Walls (the *Myreur* does not mention any relics here) and the Basilica di Santa Croce in Gerusalemme and Saint Sebastian ad Catacumbas (at the Catacombs), both at the beginning of the Appian Way. D'Outremeuse does not make any explicit mention of Rome's catacombs, but

---

88. Jean d'Outremeuse, *Ly Myrors des histors*, vol. 1, ed. Adolphe Borgnet (Brussels: Nabu Press, 2012), 74–84; Nine Robijntje Miedema, *Die Römischen Kirchen im Spätmittelalter nach den "Indulgentiae Ecclesiarum Urbis Romae"* (Tübingen: De Gruyter, 2001).

89. Galland, *Les authentiques de reliques du Sancta Sanctorum*.

FIGURE 26. *Salus Populi Romani*. Photo: Wikimedia Commons (CC0 1.0).

there is a suggestive reference to them in his entry about the cemetery of Pope Calixtus. Thanks to a new invention, the printing press, the itemization of relics and sanctuaries contained in this little book would enjoy widespread dissemination starting in the years 1470-80, shaping the imagination of pilgrims for a long time thereafter.

After the final dissolution of the Council of Basel in 1449 and the fall of Constantinople to the Ottoman Empire in 1453, Rome no longer had any rival in the Christian world, and it did not take long for the papacy to assert its claims over the city. Paul II (1464-71) and Sixtus IV (1471-84) beautified the city, and Julius II (1503-13) undertook to make it a New Jerusalem in Latin lands—both earthly and celestial—by rebuilding, from the ground up, Saint Peter's Basilica, as well as the pontifical palaces, and by having them decorated by the greatest artists and architects of the age, including Raphael, Donato Bramante, and Michelangelo. In so doing, the papacy intended to remind Christendom that its focal point was the tomb of the "Prince of the Apostles" and that Rome was the religious capital of the world, which extended itself toward the Americas and Asia. The splendor of the Saint Peter's design was necessary to illustrate the apocalyptic vision of the "holy city," the celestial Jerusalem come down from heaven, by means of a monumental achievement without precedent. The Augustinian orator Giles of Viterbo († 1532) was not alone in praising "the eternal temple of the New Law" that comprised the new Saint Peter's on the banks of the Tiber, the "new Jordan," and the "Holy Latin Jerusalem," realizing at last what had long been concealed by the "Synagogue" and whose destiny was to be the "bride of Christ."[90]

A few years later, these grandiose dreams collapsed under the blows of the duke of Bourbon's mercenaries, who set fire to the city and its churches in 1527. Luther, in his 1545 treatise, *Against the Papacy in Rome, Founded by the Devil* (followed by later Protestant polemicists), hurled invectives against Rome that were widely disseminated through the printing press and engravings. From this point, the traditional image of Rome as the Holy City would be opposed by the countries aligned with the Protestant Reformation, which cast the city as the New Babylon, corrupt, the mother of all vices, and seat of the Whore of Babylon mentioned in the book of Revelation, if not as the Antichrist himself. But for Christians who stayed faithful to the Roman Church, the city would remain—had to remain—the city of forgiveness.[91]

---

90. André Vauchez and Andrea Giardina, eds., *Rome, l'idée et le mythe, des origines à nos jours* (Paris: Fayard, 1999).

91. Nicole Lemaître, "Rome, cité de l'éternel pardon," in *Solitudes sacrées et villes saintes*, ed. Catherine Marin and Anne Marie Reijnen (Paris: Bayard, 2019), 229–49.

Part III

The Functions, Life, and Role of Sanctuaries

CHAPTER 3

Typologies
The Different Kinds of Sanctuaries

In the medieval West, different types of sanctuaries existed, each of which can be distinguished on the basis of several criteria.

According to the Nature of the Object Venerated

Sanctuaries are defined first of all by the presence of one or several sacred objects that can attract a large number of the faithful. These include such items as the column of the Flagellation at the Basilica of Saint Praxedes (Santa Prassede) in Rome; jugs from the wedding feast in Cana, which Count Roger of San Severino had placed in the Church of Santa Maria di Casaluce near Naples upon his return from the Holy Land in 1282; or, more generally, the miraculously preserved walking staff of a saintly pilgrim.[1] By themselves, these objects did not have any sacred power; they only obtained this status when a certain number of laity and clergy came to venerate them.

---

1. Genoveffa Palumbo, "Oggetti e devozioni nel Napoletano: Il sanctuario di Casaluce, le anfore, la Madonna, la scattola, il dragone," in *Santuari cristiani d'Italia: Committenze e fruizione tra Medioevo e età moderna*, ed. Mario Tosti (Rome: École Française de Rome, 2003), 109–24.

The majority of medieval sanctuaries, however, were above all associated with relics. These are known as sanctuaries *ad corpus* (in proximity to a body) and could refer to the presence of a whole body, only fragments (a head, bones, vertebrae, and the like), or even simple pieces of cloth called in Latin texts of the period *ex brandea*, which had been in contact with a saint's remains. A sanctuary could not lack for relics, and if they were not in a church's collection, they had to be invented or fabricated, with their thaumaturgical power confirmed by writing up its origins in a *vita* of the saint in question.

Other sanctuaries can be characterized as hierophanic (or, alternately, epiphanic). They are connected to a particular manifestation of God (theophany), of the Virgin Mary (mariophany), or of an image that stirred within the seer an intangible perception.[2] In these cases, vision is primary, as seeing creates a physical relationship between human and divine figures. But in order for the memory of this transitory vision to be maintained, it had to be described and fixed in texts explicating its meaning: these are the founding legends that imparted a sacredness to the place where the vision had occurred and then been integrated into its history. Such manifestations also required visible signs of the founding event so that a cult might develop. At Mont-Saint-Michel, for example, this was the mark imprinted into the rock by Saint Michael's foot, which was also the case for the sanctuary of Mount Gargano. In several churches dedicated to Saint Michael and in different reliquaries, the presence of a "footprint of the angel" is mentioned; this was a piece of stone that bore the imprint of the archangel, on the model of the "footprint of Christ" from the Mount of Olives, set into a silver foot that was venerated at Westminster Abbey. Other hierophanies included supernatural phenomena like the stigmatization of Saint Francis of Assisi, following his vision of a seraph at La Verna, a mountainous site that later became the seat of an important sanctuary.[3] Through such an apparition, often authenticated by a miracle, a sacred quality was passed on to the place where it had occurred and to the surrounding area.

A third category is the "iconic" sanctuary, associated with the presence of an *ymage* that could produce miracles. In principle, the holy image was simply a complement or a kind of conductor that drew its

---

2. Luca Avellis, ed., *Ierofanie e luoghi di culto* (Bari: Edipuglia, 2016).

3. Gábor Klaniczay, "Da Verna a San Giovanni Rotondo: La ierofania nelle esperienze dei stigmatizzati," in Avellis, *Ierofanie e luoghi di culto*, 197–215.

power from a relic's sacred character. Between the tenth and twelfth centuries, cultic statues were especially significant because they were capable of being carried in procession, like the Majesty of Saint Foy in Conques or the Black Virgin of Rocamadour. For the Church, the image constituted a legitimate form of mediation between the here-below and the beyond, the visible and the Invisible, and for this reason, images participated in the sacral universe. Near their tombs, the effigies of saints manifested their presence and served as a passageway to their thaumaturgical power.[4]

Miraculous Images

Starting in the twelfth century, certain *ymages* of Christ, the Virgin Mary, and the saints were considered miraculous in and of themselves and could become, at any given moment, focal points within a certain church or chapel. From that time, these statues and paintings were no longer simple effigies but reflections of heavenly beings that could manifest their presence through visible signs—the shedding of tears or blood, gestures, marks—and miracles.[5] There were also icons that seemed to behave like living persons—that had the ability to act or react in the context of a particular relationship with an individual or group—which has led scholars to speak about the "power of images," if not their "performance."[6] But this phenomenon must be placed in the context of the search for a more "sensual" rapport with the divine on the part of believers. In Déols, in the former Duchy of Berry, for example, men-at-arms in the service of King Henry II of England sacked

---

4. Jean-Marie Sansterre, "Variation d'une légende et genèse d'un culte entre la Jérusalem des origines et l'Occident: Quelques jalons de l'histoire de Véronique et de la Véronica jusqu'à la fin du XIIIe siècle," in *Passages: Déplacements des hommes, circulation des textes et identités dans l'Occident médiéval*, ed. Joëlle Ducos and Patrick Henriet (Toulouse: Presses universitaires du Midi, 2013), 217–31; Jean-Marie Sansterre, "La substitution des images aux reliques et des limites dans la diffusion de la *virtus* des saints (espace français, fin XIIIe–XVIe siècle), *Analecta Bollandiana* 126 (2018): 61–106; Jean-Marie Sansterre, *Les images sacrées en Occident au Moyen Age: Histoire, attitudes, croyances. Recherches sur le témoignage des textes* (Madrid: AKAL, 2021).
5. Thomas Golsenne, "Les images qui marchent: Performance et anthropologie des objets figuratifs," in *Les images dans l'Occident médiéval*, ed. Jérôme Baschet and Pierre-Olivier Dittmar (Turnhout: Brepols, 2015), 79–136.
6. David Freedberg, *The Power of Images* (Chicago: University of Chicago Press, 1991); Erik Thunø, "The Miraculous Image and the Centralized Church: Santa Maria della Consolazione in Todi," in *The Miraculous Image in the Middle Ages and Renaissance*, ed. Erik Thunø and Gerhard Wolf (Rome: L'Erma di Bretschneider, 2004), 29–56; Jean-Claude Schmitt, *Le corps des images: Essai sur la culture visuelle du Moyen Age* (Paris: Gallimard, 2002).

the village in 1187.⁷ The inhabitants ran and took refuge in front of the entrance to the abbey and petitioned the Virgin Mary, whose statue was above the portico. The soldiers, having invaded the piazza, mocked these poor people, and one of the soldiers, while cursing, threw a rock against the statue and broke off the arm of the infant Jesus she held in her arms. The arm fell upon the ground, and a drop of blood emerged from the broken stone, while the impious soldier fell to the ground, as if struck by lightning. The next day, the crowd returned and saw the Virgin move, tearing the two edges of the veil covering her breast to expose her chest. According to the *Book of the Miracles of Saint Mary of Déols*, composed by the monk Agnellus a few years later, this inspired a great wave of devotion in the region, and monks recorded numerous miracles that had taken place in the church. In the thirteenth century, comparable accounts are also found in the *Cantigas de Santa Maria* of King Alfonso X "el Sabio" about a church in Foggia in Apulia, where similar events took place.⁸

Calling miraculous the images around which such phenomena took place could make it seem as if the sculpture or painting in question possessed supernatural power. Because of their mimetic nature, they actually appeared to contemporaries as potentially dynamic, and the miracle was considered the actualization of the *virtus* (power) that was already latent in them. However, the sacred character that was attributed to them did not issue directly from them but rather from their miraculous origin and from the effect they produced within the faithful. These images, the presence of which often transformed churches into sanctuaries, struck people's minds either through their presumed antiquity—images said to be *acheiropoiete*, that is, not made by human hands, such as the portraits of the Virgin Mary attributed to Saint Luke—or through their unusual appearance (the Black Madonnas, of which there are 450 known examples, 300 of them in France), or through the appearance of particular physical signs (icons that bled, cried, or moved).⁹ Their sacredness was tied

---

7. Jean Hubert, "Le miracle de Déols et la trêve conclue en 1187 entre les rois de France et d'Angleterre," *Bibliothèque de l'Ecole des Chartes* 96 (1935): 285–300.

8. Alfonso X "El Sabio," *Cantigas de Santa Maria*, ed. Walter Mettmann, vol. 2 (Coimbra [Madrid]: Por ordem da Universidade, 1961), 106–7.

9. Michele Bacci, *Il pennello dell'evangelista: Storia delle immagini sacre attribuite a S. Luca* (Pisa: ETS, 1998); Sophie Cassagnes-Brouquet, *Culture, artiste et société dans la France médiévale* (Orphys: Gap, 2000), 35–49; Lalla Groppo and Oliviero Gerardi, eds., *Nigra sum: Culti, santuari e immagini delle Madonne nere d'Europa* (Turin: Atlas, 2012).

less to the subject represented than to their supernatural properties and miraculous effects, which did not take long to manifest and prompted the advent of a devotion with which a whole community could identify. In Rome, for example, the late antique painting of the Virgin of Santa Maria Maggiore, the *Salus Populi Romani* (Salvation of the Roman People), constituted the glue of the city's faithful, especially in times of grave crisis.

During the last centuries of the Middle Ages, these miraculous Marian images were the most common of these kinds of images.[10] What mattered to the faithful was less the person of Mary herself than the place where she had chosen to reveal her healing powers. In Florence, the first of these miraculous Madonnas was housed in the Church of Orsanmichele in 1292; but she was supplanted at the start of the fourteenth century by the Sanctuary of Santa Maria in the Florentine commune of Impruneta, which itself gave way in the hearts of Florence's citizens, after 1348, to the Madonna of the Annunciation in the Church of the Servants of Mary (that is, the Servites), which had proved its efficaciousness as a recourse against the plague and toward which the Medici showed particular favor. The earlier devotions did not disappear but, after having attracted large crowds from disparate places, the sanctuaries where they had developed often limited their influence to a neighborhood or social group, thanks to the actions taken by confraternities. The identification of a community with the image it claimed for itself was both a strength and a weakness: it certainly assured the continued devotion of individuals and social groups toward the image, but it also limited its reach by localizing the devotion to a specific place. Followers of the Virgin of one sanctuary had nothing to do with one that was being honored in a neighboring town or city. Only the great religious orders and the papacy were able to transcend these particularities, as shown by the Veil of Veronica, the Virgin of Loreto, or the stigmatization of Saint Francis of Assisi, which contributed to standardizing these devotions for all of Christianity.

---

10. Sylvie Barnay, *Le ciel sur la terre: Les apparitions de la Vierge au Moyen Age* (Paris: Éditions du Cerf, 1999); Martina Caroli, "Tipologia di santuari in Emilia Romagna," in *Santuari locali e religiosità popolare nelle diocesi di "Ravennatensia,"* ed. Maurizio Tagliaferri (Imola: Bologna University Press, 2003), 33-60; and Jean Wirth, *L'image à la fin du Moyen Age* (Paris: Éditions du Cerf, 2011).

According to Their Influence

In the past, as today, there were throughout Christendom sanctuaries with an influence that can be characterized as international, where pilgrims flocked from all over the West: the Holy Sepulcher in Jerusalem, Saint Peter's and the other major basilicas in Rome, Saint-Martin in Tours, the grotto-sanctuary of Saint Michael on Mount Gargano, Santiago de Compostela, and Saint-Gilles in the Gard from the eleventh century, Santa Maria degli Angeli and the Basilica of Saint Francis in Assisi in the thirteenth century, and after the fourteenth century, Saint-Antoine de Viennois and Notre-Dame of Loreto in central Italy. But this list is somewhat arbitrary since the comparative analysis of sanctuaries is difficult to measure, lacking statistical data, and the intensity of their attraction has varied over time. According to research by Marcel and Pierre-Gilles Girault on twelfth- and thirteenth-century literary texts in French, Saint-Gilles and Santiago de Compostela were the most visited shrines by Western Christians before 1180; between 1180 and 1200, Compostela clearly surpassed Saint-Gilles, followed by Jerusalem and Rome; between 1200 and 1250, the pilgrimage to the Holy Land would have had more importance than that of Compostela, far ahead of Rome (which held its own), whereas Saint-Gilles saw a marked decline after the crusade against the Albigensians.[11] Evaluations become more difficult after this period as sanctuaries became more numerous. According to a study of 470 mentions of pilgrimages that appear in testaments from the town of Foligno in Umbria, between 1428 and 1550 nearly half (47.5 percent) had as their goal the sanctuary of Saint Michael on Mount Gargano, followed by Notre-Dame of Loreto (19 percent), Rome (14 percent) and Santa Maria degli Angeli in Assisi (8.5 percent).[12] Much more work of this kind still needs to be done in order to prove the attraction of various sanctuaries by region and period, and to identify significant trends.

Major Sanctuaries and Replica Sanctuaries

More effective, from a historical perspective, is the distinction made between a certain number of major sanctuaries—which can be referred to as

---

11. Marcel Girault and Pierre-Gilles Girault, *Visages et pèlerins au Moyen Age: Les pèlerinages européens dans l'art et l'épopée* (La-Pierre-qui-Vire: Zodiaque, 2001).

12. Mario Sensi, *Santuari e pellegrini lungo le "vie dell'angelo": Storie sommerse del culto micaelico* (Rome: Istituto Storico Italiano per il Medioevo, 2014).

models—and other, more modest shrines called *ad instar* in Latin: replica sanctuaries or "look-alike-sanctuaries," which aimed to reproduce the models in different geographical areas. Among the most ancient examples in this category is the Basilica di Santa Croce in Gerusalemme in Rome, an imitation of the Holy Sepulcher in Jerusalem, or again the Church of San Pietro outside Spoleto, in Umbria, founded in the fifth century on the model of the Vatican's great basilica and where the iron rust from Saint Peter's chains was venerated. More than mere substitutes, these were really extensions of the major sanctuary they replicated. Whatever structural form they took, the cloning of the model sanctuaries rested on the conviction that the sacredness of the originals was so considerable that they could be extended to other places of remembrance, which adopted the name and certain characteristic elements of the original in their architectural plan. For this reason, these replicas allowed pilgrims to be connected to a great sanctuary where they would otherwise not have the opportunity to visit and to benefit from similar graces. Indeed, at the end of the Middle Ages, the papacy often granted the same indulgences to pilgrims for visiting these sanctuaries as to those who went to Jerusalem, making them particularly attractive in the eyes of believers.

The most famous case is that of the Holy Sepulcher that, as previously noted, was the object of numerous imitations since the early Middle Ages, beginning with the great complex of Santo Stefano in Bologna, where an ensemble of seven churches called Jerusalem was built around an octagonal church, on the model of the Holy Sepulcher, between the ninth and twelfth centuries.[13] There was no single architectural model, but these extensions comprised, in general, a structure on a symmetrical plan (polygonal or circular), referencing the Rotunda of the *Anastasis* that sits atop the Holy Sepulcher, followed sometimes by a longitudinal main body. In the thirteenth century, these sanctuaries were often associated with the military orders, like the Templars or Hospitalers, that had particular connections with the Holy Land. This explains why similar churches could be found in London or Paris, as well as in Lanleff in lower Brittany.

At the end of the fifteenth century, a wealthy Genoese merchant family, the Adornos, built a "church of Jerusalem" in Bruges as a kind of memorial, after having gone on pilgrimage to the Holy Land. In these replica churches, some of the ceremonies celebrated in them were

---

13. Colin Morris, *The Sepulchre of Christ and the Medieval West: From the Beginning to 1600* (Oxford: Oxford University Press, 2005).

inspired by the liturgical customs of the Holy Sepulcher in Jerusalem, like that of the "Holy Fire" that rained from heaven during the night of Holy Saturday and was apportioned miraculously to the lamps hanging over the tomb of Christ. In the liturgy, the patriarch of Jerusalem would then take a candle and transmit the light to the bishops and others surrounding him.[14] At the Cathedral of Florence, for example, a ceremonial fire (which became known as *Scoppio del Carro*) was lit on Holy Saturday by striking together three flints taken from the Holy Sepulcher that were, according to tradition, given by the Crusader Godfrey of Bouillon to a Tuscan knight, Pazzo de' Pazzi.

In central and northern Italy, a large number of cavern sanctuaries were dedicated to Saint Michael the Archangel (in Italian, Sant'Angelo or Sant'Arcangelo). They tended to imitate the grotto of Mount Gargano, where, as previously discussed, an important sanctuary dedicated to Saint Michael had developed, between the middle of the fifth century and the Carolingian period.[15] Later on, its cult would soon spread among the Lombards, then the Franks. In 709, Bishop Aubert of Avranches (in Normandy) sent emissaries to Mount Gargano who brought back relics of the archangel. The prelate then had them placed on a rocky isle washed by the sea, Mont Tombe, known ever since as Mont-Saint-Michel. Later still, an abbey, entrusted in 965 to Benedictine monks, was created there and the sanctuary became one of the most frequented places of pilgrimage within France and western Europe until modern times. In 963, the first mention of Saint-Michel d'Aiguilhe in Le Puy-en-Velay appeared.[16] In 983, an important monastery, Saint-Michel de la Cluse (the Sacra di San Michele) was built in the Piedmont Alps at the summit of a mountain looking out over the valley of Suse, through which one gained access to France, halfway between the sanctuary of Gargano and that of the Mont-Saint-Michel.[17] It became, in turn, an

---

14. Benjamin Z. Kedar, "Le miracle du feu de Jérusalem: Des origines à la suppression papale," in *De la Bourgogne à l'Orient: Mélanges offerts à Monsieur le Doyen Jean Richard*, ed. Jacques Meissonnier (Dijon: Jacques Meissonnier, 2020), 519–25.

15. Giorgio Otranto, "Le rayonnement du sanctuaire de saint Michel au mont Gargan en Italie du Sud, à l'époque médiévale," in *Les sanctuaires et leur rayonnement dans le monde méditerranéen, de l'antiquité à l'époque moderne*, ed. Juliette de la Genière, André Vauchez, and Jean Leclant (Paris: De Boccard, 2010), 323–57; Sensi, *Santuari e pellegrini lungo le "vie dell'angelo."*

16. Pierre Bouet, Giorgio Otranto, and André Vauchez, eds., *Culte et pèlerinages à Saint-Michel en Occident: Les trois monts dédiés à l'Archange* (Rome: École Française de Rome, 2003).

17. Giampiero Casiraghi and Giuseppe Sergi, eds., *Pellegrinaggi e santuari di S. Michele nell'Occidente medievale* (Bari: Edipuglia 2009); Giuseppe Sergi, *L'arcangelo sulli Alpi: Origini, cultura e caratteri dell'abbazia medievale di S. Michele della Chiusa* (Bari: Edipuglia, 2011).

imitation sanctuary of a cult devoted to the archangel and served as a "bridge sanctuary," a stopover for pilgrims who were going to Apulia. Around 1170, in the *contado* (outskirts) of Siena, the Sienese knight Galgano († 1181) abandoned a worldly life after a vision of the archangel Saint Michael, who ordered Galgano to follow him. Having traversed a cavern, they came upon a hill, Mount Siepi, where "he saw the Virgin Mary and the twelve apostles seated in a round house." The archangel ordered him to settle here and lead an eremitical life; Galgano built a round church on this site where, at the beginning of the thirteenth century, the Cistercian Abbey of San Galgano would be constructed.[18]

During the last centuries of the Middle Ages, the number of imitation sanctuaries continued to grow, within the broader context of the hierarchization of sacred places, which was taking place within the Latin Church through the granting of indulgences in varying degrees. They often played an increasing role as symbols of political identity in the process of being affirmed. As Véronique Hazebrouck-Souche has shown for the Brabant, and Philippe Martin has done for the Lorraine, the fifteenth and sixteenth centuries witnessed the affirmation of a desire for the communitarian appropriation of the sacral resources of a region, through which the divine plan had been etched into the topography. From the *Beata terra Brabantia* (*Blessed Land of Brabant*), in which Jean Gielemans exalted the region for its saints and miraculous sanctuaries, to the *Bavaria sancta* (*Holy Bavaria*) by the Jesuit Mattäus Rader, the perspective is the same: to establish a new geography of the sacred, focused on northwestern Europe and on some privileged regional areas at the intersection of the local and the universal.[19]

Local Sanctuaries

The major sanctuaries and their different imitators—famous for the lavishness of their monumental decorations and the abundance of

---

18. *Leggenda di Santo Galgano confessore*, ed. Franco Cardini (Siena: Cantagalli, 1982), 73-76 and 102-4.

19. Véronique Hazebrouck-Souche, *Spiritualité, sainteté et patriotisme: Glorification du Brabant dans l'oeuvre hagiographique de Jean Gielemans (1427-1487)* (Turnhout: Brepols, 2007); Philippe Martin, *Les chemins du sacré: Paroisses, processions, pèlerinages en Lorraine du XVIe au XIXe siècle* (Metz: Éditions Serpenoise, 1995); Philippe Martin, "Sanctuaires-mères et pèlerinages-relais," in *Identités pèlerines*, ed. Catherine Vincent (Rouen: Publications de l'Université de Rouen, 2004), 107-22; Stanislava Kuzmova, Anna Marinkovic, and Trpimir Vedrik, eds., *Cuius Patrocinio Tota Gaudet Regio: Saints' Cults and the Dynamics of Regional Cohesion* (Zagreb: Hagiotheca, 2014).

sources relating to them—have captured the attention of historians to the exclusion of other sanctuaries. But, in reality, the majority of holy places in the West were local sanctuaries, connected to particular communities or groups of villages. Unfortunately, they have not left many traces, and the surviving documentary record about them rarely goes back before the fifteenth or sixteenth centuries. To study them, there are only a few collections of miracles and accounts of the translation of relics, and in most cases, only a simple mention in a testament or in the acts of a pastoral visitation in the modern era. But this need not diminish historical interest in them, for these sanctuaries are undoubtedly the most representative of the mindset and religious life of the period.

Without being exhaustive about the roles these sanctuaries played in their communities, their thaumaturgical function was fundamental. The faithful went to a sanctuary in order to petition an intercessor, who could be either a universal saint—rarely the patron saint of a parish church—or a saint who specialized in healing particular kinds of illnesses or infirmities. As Marie-Hélène Froeschlé-Chopard has noted, "This thaumaturgical function was tied to the utilizing of terms provided by the Church in the context of a symbolic occupation of space, and the choice of intercessors is located at the intersection of the symbols of evangelization and local needs." Her research on Provence, and that of Alain Guerreau on the Mâconnais in Burgundy, demonstrates that it was almost always traditional saints, sometimes very ancient ones—martyrs, first bishops of dioceses, monks and hermits from distant centuries—whose protective function was affirmed and made, on the occasion of their feast day, the object of an annual pilgrimage. (In France, this was called a *romérage* or *romiage*, a word derived from the term *romiaux*, which refers to pilgrims destined for Rome.)[20] The churches or chapels that were dedicated to them preserved the memory—real or mythical—of the earliest Christianization of the area and of a few great universal saints. For saints who were venerated in several places, the site that had the longest association with them was the most honored. Through them, the village community could venerate its own history; the local sanctuary "is the cosmic place, outside of time, of the

---

20. Alain Guerreau, "Les pèlerinages du Mâconnais: Une structure d'organisation symbolique de l'espace," *Ethnologie française* 12 (1982): 7–30; Marie-Hélène Froeschlé-Chopard, *Itinéraires pèlerins de l'ancienne Provence* (Marseilles: La Thune, 2004).

divine presence, that roots a community of inhabitants, as well as its ancestors and its children, in the divine action."[21]

These micro-sanctuaries sometimes played a role in delimiting the territory of a rural or urban community. This function was already present in ancient religions, but it persisted under a Christianized form during the Middle Ages and up to the modern era. These edifices were often located in proximity to a waterway that served as a boundary between two groups of people. Generally of a modest size, they responded to the natural need of populations to mark out their lands by using sacred sites. For example, the ancient sanctuary of Santa Maria di Plestia was located on the frontier between the cities of Foligno in Umbria and Camerino in the Marches, which disputed its possession.[22] Or in Spello, near Foligno, according to the communal statutes of 1360, a delegation of representatives from the city had to go every year, on the feast of Santa Caterina di Rapecchiano, to the convent of Santa Caterina, occupied by reformed Franciscans (the Clareni) and located on the periphery of the *contado*, "as much out of devotion toward the saint who is held in great esteem among us, as for the recognition and the maintaining of the boundaries with the territory of Foligno." After having made an inspection of the "frontier," which separated Spello from Foligno, the municipal magistrates shared a festive meal with the religious—at the expense of the convent—before going back home.[23]

These border sanctuaries also answered the need for "free zones" within which to carry out essential economic exchanges between neighboring populations, as well as an "exchange of women," making exogamous unions possible. Indeed, the Latin word *confinium* designates both the border and the neighborhood or proximity; and so the frontier creates communication as much as separation. The feasts that were held there once or twice a year were occasions—rather rare the rest of the time—for social gatherings between individuals and families living in different villages, making it possible to bring together, around a shared cult, people who were separated by frontiers that were invisible

---

21. Marie-Hélène Froeschlé-Chopard, *Espace et sacré en Provence (XVIe–XIXe siècle): Cultes, images, confréries* (Paris: Éditions du Cerf, 1994), 153.

22. Mario Sensi, "Santuari terapeutici di frontiera nella montagna folignate," *Bollettino Storico della Città di Foligno* 4 (1980): 87–120; Andrea Tilatti, ed., *Santuari di confine: Una tipologia?* (Gorizia: Edizioni della Laguna, 2008), 294.

23. Sensi, "Santuari terapeutici di frontiera nella montagna folignate"; and Luciano Giacché, "Comunità locali e santuari di confine in Valnerina," in Tosti, *Santuari cristiani d'Italia*, 323–35.

but very real in their minds. The day chosen for the gathering was the feast of the sanctuary's patron saint. In addition to the religious ceremonies and festive practices, fairs were often held that could last two or three weeks or, indeed, for a whole grazing season, as was the case at Santa Maria di Plestia.

Local sanctuaries appear to have taken on a growing importance during the last centuries of the Middle Ages, especially those—more and more numerous from the fourteenth century—that were dedicated to the Virgin Mary, as Francis Rapp has shown for Alsace, Nicole Lemaître for the Rouergue, and Pierrette Paravy for the Dauphiné. As Catherine Vincent has noted: "These sites, having remained up until then unknown, now come out of the shadows thanks to a mention in a chronicle, cloth-selling accounts, or urban registers, or even in a testament in which the author asks his heirs to go on pilgrimage to them in his name."[24] This development did not only involve the laity, as is made clear by the places of pilgrimages frequented by the twenty-nine canons of Tournai Cathedral in Wallonia. Around the middle of the fourteenth century, they had not only gone to a few well-known French sanctuaries, but they also made time in their devotions to visit holy places in Flanders and the Brabant, often dedicated to the Virgin, about which little is known except their names.[25]

According to Their Functions

The numerous sanctuaries of medieval Christianity did not all have the same functions. Contemporaries deliberately went to one sanctuary over another, fully aware of this.

The Devotional Sanctuaries

Certain major sanctuaries were visited by pilgrims who were seeking not a miraculous cure but rather a human and religious experience. At the Holy Sepulcher, where there were no relics to see or to touch, people

---

24. Catherine Vincent, "Pour un inventaire des sanctuaires et lieux de pèlerinages français," in *Hagiographie et culte des saints dans la France méridionale (XIIIe–XVe siècles)*, Cahiers de Fanjeaux 37 (Toulouse: Privat, 2002), 267–81.

25. Jacques Pycke, "Étude sur les pèlerinages des chanoines de Tournai pendant une vingtaine d'années post-1450," in *Horae Tornacenses, 1171–1971: Recueil d'Études d'Histoire publiées à l'Occasion du VIIIe Centenaire de la Consécration de la Cathédrale de Tournai*, ed. Nicolas Huyghebaert (Tournai: Archives de la Cathédrale, 1971), 110–30.

went to venerate the dead and resurrected Christ. For these pilgrims, the important thing was to find the place where Jesus had suffered his Passion for the salvation of humanity and to obtain absolution for their sins in the hope of being raised up one day in his stead. Similarly, at Saint Peter's in Rome, visitation was tied to the devotion of the faithful toward the Prince of the Apostles, considered the gatekeeper of heaven. In approaching the tomb of Peter, visitors pleaded for him to grant them and their deceased loved ones eternal life. This did not prevent them from eventually procuring pieces of cloth that had been in contact with his relics—quite the contrary! Pilgrims also often brought back vials containing a little oil from the lamps of the Vatican basilica, rust from the iron chains of the apostle, and from the end of the Middle Ages, Agnus Dei—a protective wax medallion embossed with an image of the Lamb of God on one side and the saint on the other, blessed by the pope.[26] Some pilgrims benefited from their journey to Rome by also visiting other sanctuaries famous for their miracles, like those of Saint Sebastian Outside the Walls on the Appian Way or of the healing saints Cosmas and Damian near the Forum.

Seemingly, it was the same for pilgrims to Santiago de Compostela. Certainly, the apostle had an incontestable thaumaturgical power, as the collection of miracles that appear in the *Book of Saint James* attests, as do the iconographical depictions of the Miracle of the Hanged Man—a legend about a pilgrim who was unjustly hanged for theft by an innkeeper but propped up by Saint James until he could be rescued—that can be seen even today in numerous churches and chapels throughout Europe. But people went to his tomb essentially to place themselves under the protection of a saint who had been, along with his brother John, Jesus's closest friend and the first martyr of the Church, after having brought—according to the legend—the Christian faith into the West, starting in Spain.

The Sanctuaries of Pardon: Holy Years and Jubilees

Beginning in the eleventh century, certain sanctuaries began to be assigned as penances by the clergy to lay penitents, who were required to travel to them in order to obtain absolution for their sins and were granted full and rightful reintegration into the Church upon their

---

26. Debra J. Birch, *Pilgrimage to Rome in the Middle Ages: Continuity and Change* (Woodbridge: Boydell, 1998).

return. To go on pilgrimage to the Holy Land or to Santiago de Compostela was thus presented to the faithful as the surest means of escaping eternal damnation. Moreover, with the ascendency of the power of Rome in the wake of the Gregorian Reform, the remission of particularly serious sins—the murder of a priest or the willful burning of a church—was reserved to the pope, which led repentant offenders to go to Rome for absolution. From the thirteenth century, the expiatory pilgrimage acquired the status of a punitive penalty imposed by the Inquisition or even by secular tribunals, particularly in the large towns of Flanders and the Rhine Valley. It was a kind of temporary banishment that punished religious offenders, as well as those who attacked people or property and were sentenced by lay justice. This form of pilgrimage persisted until at the end of the Middle Ages, sending onto the roads of Europe numerous people who were considered, rightly or wrongly, bad apples.

Most of the time, however, pilgrims traveled voluntarily to sanctuaries to obtain pardon for their sins in the hope of eternal salvation.[27] Beginning in the thirteenth century, there was a steady inflation in the realm of indulgences. The plenary indulgence was up to that time reserved to laity who left on crusade to the Holy Land or Spain, having vowed to do so. But after 1250, it was said that Pope Innocent III had granted a plenary indulgence to Francis of Assisi and to all who went to the little Chapel of the Portiuncula dedicated to Santa Maria degli Angeli (Saint Mary of the Angels), where "the Poverello" had embarked on a religious life and where he also died (figure 27). In fact, no such papal document has ever been recovered, and it is unlikely that it ever existed in this form.[28] But, as the Friars Minor in their preaching certified its authenticity, this juridical lacuna did not stop pilgrims from coming in large numbers to Assisi on October 4, the saint's principal feast day. It was also on this occasion, in 1291, that the mystic Angela da Foligno had her first vision of Saint Francis, after which she led a life of penance, until her death, within the ambit of the Franciscan Third Order.

---

27. Mario Sensi, "Santuari del perdono e santuari eremitici 'à répit': Esempi umbro-marchigiani," in *Lieux sacrés, lieux de culte, sanctuaires*, ed. André Vauchez (Rome: École Française de Rome, 2000), 228–32; Maria Giusuppina Muzzarelli, *Penitenze nel Medioevo: Uomini e modelli a confronto* (Bologna: Pàtron, 1994); Henri-Jacques Stiker, *Religions et Handicap: Interdit, péché, symbole. Une analyse anthropologique* (Paris: Hermann, 2017).

28. Stefano Brufani and Enrico Menestò, eds., *Il Perdono di Assisi e le indulgenze plenarie* (Assisi: CISAM, 2017).

FIGURE 27. The Portiuncula, located within the Basilica of Santa Maria degli Angeli in Assisi, Italy. Photograph by Fczarnowski via Wikimedia Commons (CC BY-SA 4.0).

In 1294, Pope Celestine V—an aged hermit who had been persuaded to leave his grotto in the Abruzzi to become the Roman pontiff, but who resigned after just a few months—granted a plenary indulgence to all who attended his coronation at the Basilica of Santa Maria di Collemaggio in Aquila, as well as to pilgrims who traveled there on the anniversary of this event. His successor, Boniface VIII, suppressed this privilege—known as the *Perdonanza Celestiniana* (the Celestine Pardon) after 1295 as it was judged to be exorbitant, but the faithful did not heed this action and continued to flock there each year on August 29 to his tomb, where one could gain "the pardon of the good pope Celestine." Probably struck by these manifestations of popular fervor and by the hopes that these demonstrations revealed among Christians, Boniface VIII had the idea to have the Roman Church benefit from the enthusiasm of all the pilgrims who aspired to have their sins forgiven. Thus, at the start of the year 1300, he proclaimed a Jubilee year, during which all those who undertook the journey to Rome and devoutly made there the rounds of the basilicas of Saint Peter and Saint Paul within fifteen days (thirty for citizens of Rome) would obtain a plenary indulgence for their sins.[29] His call prompted an influx of pilgrims to Rome, resulting

---

29. Arsenio Frugoni, *Il Giubileo de Bonifacio VIII* (Bari: Laterza, 1999); and Agostino Paravicini Bagliani, *Boniface VIII: Un pape hérétique* (Paris: Payot, 2003).

in a deadly jostling on the single bridge connecting the Campus Martius, where most visitors entered the city, to the Vatican, by way of the Via del Pellegrino, which Dante mentions in his *Divine Comedy*.[30] For the papacy, the jubilee has, since that time, been a means for exalting the universal dimension of its authority and the central role of the Holy See in the Church.

The granting of the jubilee indulgence to pilgrims coming to Rome was, at first, going to be done once per century, but Clement VI, in 1349, reduced the time between two jubilees to fifty years. Later, some of his successors reduced it to thirty-three years and even, from the middle of the fifteenth century, to twenty years, so that each generation might benefit from this privilege.[31] The number of basilicas to visit increased to three in 1350 with the addition of Saint John Lateran, then to four with Santa Maria Maggiore—and eventually to seven churches (the *Sette chiese*) in the modern era. The jubilee years were, on the whole, a considerable success—even during the Great Schism—and contributed to Rome's reputation among Latin Christians as the city of pardon above all others.

Sanctuaries of "Recourse" and Sanctuaries of "Respite"

Most of the sanctuaries in Western Christianity, were, however, placed under the rubric of *recourse*, in the wider meaning of the term. According to the definition proposed by Dominique Julia, "recourse is a contract between the one who prays and the saint, where the role of the institutional clergy has only a small part to play and which responds to specific requests."[32] Many of them were polyvalent, inasmuch as the faithful visited them both in search of a healing of their maladies and those of their children or livestock, as well as the remission of their sins. Indeed, in the unified conception of the human being that was prevalent in this period, physical or psychic sufferings and moral evil were closely connected: it was the whole person that was in need of attention

---

30. Dante, *Paradiso*, XVIII, 32; see the collection of papers on this theme in Étienne Hubert and Odile Redon, eds., "Rome des Jubilés," special issue, *Médiévales*, no. 40 (2001).

31. André Vauchez, "Les jubilés romains des XIVe et XVe siècles," in *Le Grand Pardon de Chaumont et les Pardons dans la vie religieuse (XIVe–XXIe siècles)*, ed. Patrick Corbet, François Petrazoller, and Vincent Tabbagh (Dijon: Le Pythagore, 2011), 47–53; Lucetta Scaraffia, *Il Giubileo* (Bologna: Il Mulino, 1999).

32. Dominique Julia, "Sanctuaires et lieux sacrés à l'époque moderne," in Vauchez, *Lieux sacrés, lieux de culte, sanctuaires*, 294.

and care. Thus, at Mount Gargano, pilgrims, once having arrived at the grotto of Saint Michael, washed their eyes and their extremities with the waters that ran through the courtyard and pooled into a basin. After having prayed to the archangel to grant their pleas, they descended the holy mountain while tossing over their shoulders the stones they had carried with them on their backs or around their necks, symbolizing both the evils and the faults from which they wished to be delivered. Similar practices were documented not long ago during the annual pilgrimage to the Sanctuary of the Most Holy Trinity in Vallepietra in Italy, an ancient sanctuary on the top of a mountain above Subiaco, where a medieval fresco depicting the Trinity under the form of Christ with three crowned heads was venerated.[33]

In some cases, the faithful had recourse to specialized "prophylactic" or healing saints when they or their livestock were struck by grave illnesses or epidemics, and it was necessary to travel to their sanctuaries to solicit their intercession. Alain Guerreau's study of the Mâconnais, which encompassed around fifty local sanctuaries, shows that pilgrims had to journey an average of twenty to thirty kilometers from their homes in order to visit a church or chapel corresponding to the evil from which one hoped to be freed. Among these micro-sanctuaries, some were known for the healing of illnesses, while others were visited specifically by women to cure infertility.[34] These networks of therapeutic sites seem to have been very old, and it is difficult to know exactly when they were established. In the Perche-Gouët, Alban Bensa has found that fifty-eight healer-saints were invoked at various sites reputed to be miraculous: here again, specialization prevailed. Pilgrims had recourse to Saint Blaise for maladies of the throat, to Saint Évroul for illnesses of the skin, to Saint Gilles for convulsions, to Saint Mathurin in cases of madness, to Saint Marculf against scrofula . . . and to the Virgin Mary for gynecological diseases. These traditional saints were familiar figures to the peasants of the region and shared common attributes: Saint Antony with his pig, Saint Fiacre with a spade, Saint Gilles and Saint Blaise surrounded by wild animals—all of which undoubtedly contribute to explaining the lasting success of these cults.[35]

---

33. Paola Elisabetta Simeoni, "Santuari fra antropologia e storia: Il culto alla Santissima Trinità di Vallepietra," in *Lazio*, ed. Sofia Boesch Gajano, Santuari d'Italia 1 (Rome: De Luca, 2010), 104–17.

34. Guerreau, "Les pèlerinages du Mâconnais."

35. Alban Bensa, *Les Saints guérisseurs du Perche-Gouët: Espace symbolique du bocage* (Paris: Institut d'ethnologie, 1978), 222f.

The popular devotion surrounding these saints did not bring the laity into conflict with their clergy. Rather, they considered sanctuaries as places where communication with heaven was simpler and more direct than at their village church, and the cults around these intercessors responded to their hopes because they were positioned at the intersection of Christian mythology and the liturgy. Indeed, in the eyes of the laity, the saints assured the regularity and efficacy of the nurturing mechanisms of their nature, and through the grace they lavished upon humanity, they were able to maintain the health of their followers—that is, in the final analysis, their ability to work. The places where they were petitioned were "sacred landmarks" that delineated a territory by suffusing it, here and there, with beneficent forces. The visitation of these sites varied less according to the liturgical calendar than by the rhythm of agricultural work. Indeed, out in the fields, peasant life conditioned the terms of access to the sanctuaries: the pilgrimages that marked out the year generally took place outside of the harvest season, as if the symbolic work of the saints then came to take over the real work of the peasants and even to reinforce its efficacy. These religious celebrations were often associated with economic activities, since most of the feasts were accompanied or followed by fairs. As Alban Bensa writes, "The circulation of goods corresponds to a circulation of heavenly graces, within the context of a mixture of economic and symbolic transactions placed under the banner of bargaining, and in the context of a relationship of familiarity with the healing saints who broaden the ordinary social relationships between individuals."[36]

In the fourteenth century, a new religious practice developed in piecemeal fashion throughout the West: sanctuaries of respite. According to teachings of Saint Augustine that were ratified by the Church, when an infant was stillborn or died shortly after birth without having been baptized, it would remain forever excluded from the beatific vision of God, its soul consigned to limbo, an ill-defined and unrewarding place in the afterlife. In such cases, the parents sometimes brought their seemingly lifeless child to sanctuaries said to be "of respite" (that is, for the removal of a serious harm) in the hope that any movement or breath, interpreted as a sign of temporary survival, would allow the sacrament to be administered in order that the child could achieve

---

36. Bensa, *Les Saints guérisseurs du Perche-Gouët*, 230.

eternal salvation.[37] These holy places were most often administered by hermit-healers, but in the fifteenth century, bishops anxious to control the sites entrusted their care to religious orders, as at Notre-Dame de Beauvoir (near Moustiers-Sainte-Marie in Provence), a sanctuary that was operated by the Servites from 1483 until its suppression by the bishop of Riez in 1670.[38] The recourse to this practice was, in fact, discouraged by the Council of Trent and finally prohibited by the Church in the eighteenth century, although in the most remote regions, it disappeared only gradually. In any case, it testifies to the importance to parents of the salvation of their infant children: they did not appeal to a saint for the life of their child but to assure them a blessed eternity.

Water Sanctuaries: Sacred Streams and Springs

Among sanctuaries of recourse, it is necessary to accord a special place to those associated with a stream or spring. There may be no element as rich with symbolism as water, closely tied to the birth and preservation of life. In its purity and clarity, it washes away stains and rejuvenates beings and things.[39]

In the Judeo-Christian tradition, however, water can evoke death as well as life: both the destructive Flood and the spring that Moses brought forth from the rock in the desert to quench the thirst of the Hebrews (Num. 20:1-11), or the "living water" Christ offered to the Samaritan woman during their meeting at Jacob's well (John 4:5-15).[40] Different from light, water does not constitute an element tied to the divinity; in the Gospels, it is known for its forceful nature and heaving, as in the episode of the storm calmed by Christ on the Lake of Tiberias (John 21:1-9). Christian liturgy picked up on this aspect of its nature in multiple ways, and its ambivalence toward water is perhaps best illustrated by the ritual of baptism by immersion, which prevailed up to the sixth or seventh centuries, in which the convert was plunged into the baptismal pool. "The waters receive him like a tomb," says Basil

---

37. Jacques Gélis, *Les enfants des limbes: Mort-nés et parents dans l'Europe chrétienne* (Paris: Louis Audibert Éditions, 2006); and Sensi, "Santuari del perdono e santuari eremitici 'à répit.'"
38. Froeschlé-Chopard, *Itinéraires pèlerins de l'ancienne Provence*.
39. Gaston Bachelard, *L'eau et les rêves: Essai sur l'imagination de la matière* (Paris: Jose Corti, 1942).
40. Francesca Cocchini, "Eau," in *Dictionnaire encyclopédique du christianisme ancien*, vol. 1 (Paris: Éditions du Cerf, 1990), 735-37.

of Caesarea, "and restores to that person a new life in Christ after having been washed of their stains."[41]

Early in its history, Christianity came into conflict with the religious practices of the Roman world connected to the worship of water divinities. Saint Augustine in his sermons stigmatized the behavior of some believers who adhered to pagan ways: "If you see someone casting lots, either at springs or trees, draw that person vigorously away from so great a sin and tell him or her that whoever commits this crime will lose the grace of baptism."[42] In the sixth century, Caesarius of Arles wrote to deplore "this unfortunate custom that has remained up to the present day a pagan rite," by virtue of which, during the festivities of Saint John the Baptist, some of the faithful plunged into springs, ponds, and rivers during the night before the feast and during the earliest hours of the morning, "whereby this sacrilegious bathing loses souls and kills bodies."[43] Ordinances of the early Middle Ages—the penitentials and even certain Carolingian capitularies—repeated these condemnations in almost identical terms up to the beginning of the eleventh century.[44] As time moved on, however, this rigor seems to have become attenuated, and there can be found a certain continuity between pagan and Christian water sanctuaries. For example, at the spring of Clitunno in Umbria, an ancient *tempietto* erected in the Roman period to honor the river god Clitumnus was rededicated to the cult of Saint Michael and survives to the present day. The clergy often took an interest, for the benefit of the new religion, in places that in the eyes of rural populations were imbued with sacred power. In the Middle Ages, there were countless springs with therapeutic properties considered by laypeople to be sacred, and the Church found nothing wrong with any of them.

The integration of the sacredness of water into Christianity is made through the cult of saints.[45] In the foundation legends of many sanctuaries, these are often streams deemed miraculous at their origin: Saint

---

41. Basil of Caesarea, "Treatise on the Holy Spirit," in *Patrologiae Cursus Completus, Series Graeca*, ed. J.-P. Migne, vol. 32 (Paris: Migne, 1857), cols. 129-30.

42. Augustine, "Sermon CCLXV," § 5, in *Patrologiae Cursus Completus, Series Latina*, ed. J.-P. Migne, vol. 39 (Paris, Migne, 1863), cols. 39-40.

43. Caesarius of Arles, "Sermon CCLXXVII," in *Sermons au peuple*, ed. Marie-José Delage, vol. 2 (Paris: Éditions du Cerf, 1978), 178-79.

44. Cyrille Vogel, *Le pécheur et la pénitence au Moyen Age* (Paris: Éditions du Cerf, 1969), 89; Jean Hubert, "Sources sacrées et sources saintes," *Comptes rendus des séances de l'Académie des Inscriptions et Belles-Lettres* 111 (1967): 567-73.

45. Brigitte Caulier, *L'eau et le sacré: Les cultes thérapeutiques autour des fontaines en France du Moyen Age à nos jours* (Paris: Beauchesne, 1990).

Martin, like a new Moses, called forth one such stream by striking the ground with his staff, and several female saints seem to have accomplished the same miracle with spindles. When a martyred saint—or his or her corpse—had been thrown by their executioners into a well, its waters were later found to be endowed with a healing power, the *virtus* of the servant of God having been transmitted into the natural element. At Arles-sur-Tech in Roussillon, for example, the holy tomb containing the relics of the Roman martyrs Abdon and Sennen was venerated into the nineteenth century, and the water that flowed out of the sarcophagus possessed therapeutic powers; multiple cases of this phenomenon exist.[46] In fact, conflicts between the ecclesiastical authorities and the faithful around streams and springs deemed miraculous were rather rare before the fifteenth century, and for most of this time, the clergy seems to have been resigned to a Christianization linked to the name of the intercessor, whether angel or saint, invoked in such places. Beside them, chapels were built where *ymages*—icons, frescos, sculptures of wood or stone—of the figure who assured the relationship between the sacredness of the place and the Christian religion were venerated. Often, the saint's statue was immersed in the waters on their feast day, which had the effect of reactivating the power of both statue and spring or stream.

Symbolic of the spiritual purification and healing from the perspective of baptism, water possessed its own curative powers without the need for any special ritual or the blessing by a priest. A person could go to a sacred stream or spring any time—even if its efficacy was reported to be greater on the feast day of the saint to which it was dedicated—and to remain there as long as they chose. In Sardinia, for example, the anticipated healing could only take place if the population of a village, which traveled as a group to the sanctuary, celebrated a novena by residing in special dwellings, called *cumbessias* (small cabins), located around the holy site and its spring.[47] But most often, a simple journey of a day or night was sufficient to accomplish the ablutions and to obtain the desired effect.[48]

---

46. Pierre Saintyves, *Le folklore des eaux dans la région des Pyrénées: Enquête religieuse* (Paris: Société d'ethnographie de Paris, 1935), 10.

47. Maria Giuseppina Meloni, "Il fenomeno santuariale in Sardegna," in *I santuari cristiani d'Italia*, ed. André Vauchez (Rome: École Française de Rome, 2007), 203-15.

48. Giovanna Alvino and Terenzio Leggio, "Acque e culti salutari in Sabina," in *Usus veneratioque fontium: Fruizione e culto delle acque salutari nell'Italia romana*, ed. Lidio Gasparini (Tivoli: Tipigraf, 2006), 17-54.

Cults around sacred springs and miraculous streams have existed throughout Europe in the medieval and modern periods, but they take on specific traits in the Mediterranean region, where they are frequently associated with grottos, mountains, or hills. The coexistence of these elements in the same place can be found, for example, at Saint-Gilles in the Gard where, according to the legend, the holy hermit Gilles drank from a spring that afterward became miraculous; or, especially at Sainte-Baume, near Aix-en-Provence, site of the spring created by Mary Magdalene, according to the legend, from the tears of her repentance, which flowed in the grotto where she reputedly lived.[49] But it is in Italy where this phenomenon can best be studied and takes on its most characteristic aspects. Consulting the database of the *Inventory of Italian Sanctuaries* (*Censimento dei santuari italiani*) and searching on the terms *acqua* (water), *fonte* (source), *fontana* (spring), *fiume* (river), *fosso* (gully), or *ponte* (bridge), brings up at least two hundred records, which in itself constitutes a significant collection. But a number of Italian sanctuaries associated with water do not include any explicit reference to this element in their names, and so to assess the full measure of the importance of the link between water and the sacred, it is necessary to broaden the search to include the terms *grotta* or *crypta* (grotto), *spelunca* (cavern), or *sasso* (a rocky hill), which are especially numerous from the Alps to the Apennines. In these limestone regions of central and northern Italy, the majority of sacred places combining grotto, stream, and mountain were initially dedicated to Saint Michael. The research of Mario Sensi and Giorgio Otranto has demonstrated the existence, all along the spine of the peninsula, of a chain of sanctuaries on the model of Monte Sant'Angelo in Gargano.[50] Their miraculous character was tied to the presence of water in the text *Apparitio sancti Michelis in monte Gargano* (Apparition of Saint Michael on Mount Gargano), composed at the end of the eighth or beginning of the ninth centuries:

> From the rock that encompasses the sacred edifice, is seen drop by drop, a sweet and especially clear water that the inhabitants call *stilla*. This is why a glass vase especially made for collecting [this water] is suspended from a silver chain, and the people usually have the custom, after the ceremony, of climbing the stairs, one

---

49. Froeschlé-Chopard, *Itinéraires pèlerins de l'ancienne Provence*.
50. Mario Sensi, "Santuari in grotto tra Umbria e Marche," in Mario Sensi, *Mulieres in ecclesia: Storie de monache e di bizzoche*, vol. 1 (Spoleto: CISAM, 2010), 137–78; Otranto, "Le rayonnement du sanctuaire de saint Michel."

by one, up to this small receptacle to taste the gift of the heavenly liquid. It is true that it is sweet to the taste and beneficial to the touch. And when they drink of this *stilla*, those who suffer from a lengthy fever very quickly attain the easing of the cure.[51]

From the fourteenth century, most of the sanctuaries of this type, in Italy as well as in France, were placed under the patronage of the Virgin Mary, under pressure from the clergy and with the full and complete adhesion of the faithful. This process reached its high point in Lourdes, where Bernadette Soubirous, on February 11, 1858, saw in the grotto of Massabielle a "beautiful lady" appear, later designated as "the Immaculate Conception" in conformity with the dogma that had just been promulgated in 1854 by Pope Pius IX. A few days later, at the time of the ninth apparition of this figure and upon her request, Bernadette knelt in penitence and kissed the ground, where a stream subsequently bubbled up under her hands, its water at first muddy before quickly becoming clear. The Virgin then said to her, "Go and drink from the spring and wash yourself there," leading her to undertake the ritual purification that is common in the sanctuaries of the medieval and modern era.[52] The spring's miraculous properties, especially curative, did not take long to manifest publicly and be recognized by the Church: the waters of Lourdes, in which the sick submerged themselves during their pilgrimages, would soon become famous and be distributed in little bottles around the world. But, as Alphonse Dupront has written:

> That which grabs the cosmic certitude in the reality of Lourdes the most is the whole complex of mountain, grotto and stream. Earth and water. The relationship is essential and posed with vibrant vitality: that of open ground, that of flowing water. . . . In this place where people and water pass through, with the intensity of moving waves, there is a prodigious balance in place, of land, water, and sky: it is evidence of the sacred.[53]

In the medieval period, the majority of these sanctuaries were of a modest size and comprised essentially of a chapel or a church adjacent

---

51. *Apparitio sancti Michaelis in Monte Gargano*, trans. François Bougard, in Bouet, Otranto, and Vauchez, *Culte et sanctuaires de Saint-Michel dans l'Europe médiévale*, 10.
52. Caulier, *L'eau et le sacré*, 141–47; and Ruth Harris, *Lourdes: Body and Spirit in the Secular Age* (London: Allen Lane, 1999).
53. Alphonse Dupront, *Du sacré: Croisades et pèlerinage. Images et langages* (Paris: Gallimard, 1987), 362.

to the miraculous well or spring. A certain number of them developed around streams or springs that possessed extraordinary characteristics: intermittent flows, periodic upsurges, or a peculiar appearance or smell to the water. In Voltri, near Genoa, a sanctuary dedicated to Nostra Signora dell'Acquasanta (Our Lady of the Holy Water) has existed since at least 1465, due to the presence of a spring of sulfurous water considered to be miraculous. In the Marches, the mountain sanctuary of Santa Maria dell'Acquanera (Saint Mary of the Black Water), in Frontone near Pesaro, owes its name to the water that flowed along the wall of a volcanic grotto, which gives it its dark color.

We can link this category of sanctuaries to ones that were sometimes established on bridges. These last, far from serving only as river crossings, also had a prophylactic function as, by their presence alone, they protected the faithful against the threat of dangerous waters. In certain cases, propitiatory rites had to be performed by those crossing the bridge, sometimes on their knees, and by throwing stones over their shoulders. Most of these were dedicated to the Virgin, like Notre-Dame du Pont in Saint-Junien, on the Vienne, rebuilt by the bishop of Limoges in 1394 and where, in 1464, Louis XI came on pilgrimage. After this royal visit, the nave and the choir of the structure were extended in 1475 with the help of the nobles of the area. In the same region, in Corrèze, on the river of the same name, various documents attest to the existence in the fifteenth century of a chapel dedicated to Notre-Dame du Pont du Salut where pilgrims came to venerate a statue of the Virgin Mary.[54]

Some sanctuaries associated with water developed after the fortuitous discovery, in the water of a river, of an *ymage* of the Virgin to which great power was attributed. Santa Maria di Rasiglia in Umbria, located on a little rivulet, the Fosso Terminario, was created in 1450 after a statue of the Virgin with Child was found in the streambed, and which was brought to the parish church of Verchiano. According to the founding legend, the statue then returned by itself to the waters where it had been discovered, and it proved impossible to bring it back to the church, even with an ox-drawn cart, because it had become so heavy. Finally, the authorities of Verchiano allowed the inhabitants of

---

54. Sophie Cassagnes-Brouquet, "La chapelle sur le pont: Fonctions et symbolique d'un edifice au Moyen Age," in *Faire la route (IIIe–XXe siècle)*, ed. Céline Perol (Clermont-Ferrand: Presses universitaires Blaise Pascal, 2007), 35–49.

Rasiglia to construct a chapel on the original site.[55] In the same period, there were also water sanctuaries connected to Marian apparitions. In Caravaggio, a village located near Bergamo, a female peasant saw the Madonna appear to her on May 26, 1432. On the site of the vision, a stream started to flow from a nearby grotto, and a structure housing a wooden statue of the Virgin, called Santa Maria del Fonte (Saint Mary of the Spring) was soon built there. Expanded and decorated with frescos in the sixteenth century, it went on to become one of the most visited places of pilgrimage in northern Italy.[56]

The distinctions between the different types of sanctuaries associated with water must not be overly rigid because a number of them cover several categories simultaneously. Santa Maria di Pietrarossa in Umbria, as an example, located on the border between Trevi and Foligno, first appears in the documentary sources in 1444, when representatives of the nearby cities of Spoleto and Foligno, which had been in conflict for a long time, came together under the influence of the preaching of the Franciscan Observants Francesco di Trevi and Jacob de Marchia (James of the Marches) to publicly celebrate their reconciliation.[57] But this holy site, placed from that time under the sign of penance and pardon, already had a long history. Next to the church dedicated to the Virgin was the Pozzo di San Giovanni (the Well of Saint John), a basin that periodically produced streams of bubbling water, *acqua santa* (holy water), that possessed curative properties. And before that, it had been the site of Roman baths, built on a large block of ancient masonry, *pietrarossa* (red stone), which gave the sanctuary its name. A Marian image there was deemed to be "ancient" (in fact, it was a fresco of the Virgin with Child from the fourteenth century), and the basin was visited by women who bathed there naked, on the eve of the feast of Saint John the Baptist, hoping to bear children. In the modern era, the ecclesiastical authorities took measures to prohibit these rites, which closely echoed pagan rites, but the annual feast and pilgrimage to the waters of San Giovanni have survived almost up to the present. According to a local tradition, Saint Francis of Assisi would send a leper there from a nearby leprosarium, who was healed after having drunk the waters.

---

55. Sensi, "Santuari terapeutici di frontiera nella montagna folignate," 96-113.
56. Giancarlo Andenna, "Santuari e difesa dei confini politici e religiosi: Il caso Lombardo tra Medioevo e prima Età moderna—Caravaggio e Tirano," in Vauchez, *I santuari cristiani d'Italia*, 269-97; Roberto Ziglioli, *L'apparizione e il santuario di Caravaggio* (Caravaggio: Lyasis, 1992).
57. Sensi, "Santuari del perdono e santuari eremitici 'à répit.'"

Purification, healing, remission of sin, and spiritual regeneration: all of these aspects come together in the context of a centuries-old devotion connected with water, one that the Church could not really oppose.

Folklorists in the nineteenth and twentieth centuries were eager to underline the cultic continuities between the Middle Ages and pagan antiquity or even prehistory with regard to water shrines. But even if the origins of certain ritual practices are lost in the mists of time, to consider them simply as surviving traces of a disappeared civilization would be to suppose an unchanging world, resistant to historical dynamics. As Roger Bastide has written about cults of African origin still practiced in present-day Brazil: "The ancient can only survive by being adapted to new conditions of existence. . . . One can only speak about an adaptive survival."[58] As Mario Sensi has pointed out, these holy places constitute sites that stitch together pagan remembrances and Christian beliefs: "The water that flows from the sacred stream adds meaning to human fertility; the image of Mary—be it an icon or statue—really corresponds to the iconography of the mother goddess, the *Virgo paritura*. But from the breast of this Virgin, like the water from the grotto, issued the Son of God, fruit of the earth; and in Mary, thanks to her maternity, is actualized that which had been prefigured in pre-Christian religions."[59]

Maritime Sanctuaries

The modern concept of the sea as a place of relaxation (the beach) and beauty, or even paradise (islands and capes), should not obscure the fact that, up until recently, humans primarily sought to protect themselves from elements of the sea. In classical antiquity, well-illustrated by certain verses in Horace, a negative picture of the sea prevails: unstable and full of dangers. The Middle Ages inherited this perspective and had recourse to the intercession of God and saints to confront the perils of the waves.[60] The Mediterranean world, where *terra firma* was never very

---

58. Roger Bastide, *Les Amériques noires* (Paris: L'Harmattan, 2002), 45.
59. Sensi, "Santuari terapeutici di frontiera nella montagna folignate," 96.
60. André Vauchez, "L'homme au péril de la mer dans les miracles médiévaux," in *L'homme face aux calamités naturelles dans l'Antiquité et au Moyen Age*, ed. Jacques Jouanna, Jean Leclant, and Michel Zink (Paris: De Boccard, 2006), 183–95; Luciano Fanin, ed., *Dio, il mare e gli uomini*, Quaderni di storia religiosa 15 (Caselle di Sommacampagna, Cierre Edizioni, 2008); Maria Stella Calò Mariani, ed., *I Santi venuti dal mare* (Bari: Adda, 2009); Immacolata Aulisa, ed., *I santuari e il mare (Santuario di Santa Maria di Monte Berico)* (Bari: Edipuglia, 2014).

far from the sea and where maritime trips were a necessity for journeys and commercial exchanges, has historically been a special place for the emergence and spread of sanctuaries. This fact confirms a certain continuity of cultic phenomena since Greek antiquity in particularly important or exposed sites, like those of Riace in Calabria or of Santa Maria di Leuca, in the extreme south of Apulia. Recent research has made clear the importance of sacred promontories and holy islands, like that of Lérins: physical and metaphysical places where the beauty of the landscape and the interaction with the natural elements have allowed human beings, across all civilizations and cultures, to access the sacred through the spectacle and experience of the sea, symbol of the infinite.[61]

But the sea does not play the same role as running waters in the genesis of sanctuaries. If certain religious sites located on its shores have been pilgrimage destinations, it is generally because of their geographic location rather than of an organic link to a natural element that, for thinkers of the age, had a negative, if not diabolical, connotation. Among the miracles that were produced at Mont-Saint-Michel at the time, few had any relation with fishing or navigation; the sea is hardly present, in fact, except in the story of a pregnant woman surprised by the rise of the waters while she was crossing the bay to get to the Mont; saved by the archangel, she was able to give birth on a small island that had miraculously appeared. Even in Brittany, oriented toward the sea and swept by it, medieval miracles prior to the end of the fourteenth century hardly concern maritime activities, even if one attributed to the pious Duke Charles of Blois († 1364), venerated after his death as a saint, the power to hold back the rising tide while he was laying siege to the town of Quimper in 1344. Along the French Atlantic coast, from Normandy to Flanders, there was only one sanctuary where miracles relating to maritime life were preponderant: that of Notre-Dame de Boulogne in Boulogne-sur-Mer, which witnessed a great expansion between the thirteenth and fifteenth centuries. According to its founding legend, which developed the theme of "marvelous navigation," the Virgin Mary was said to have arrived there one day on a ship, without her veil, and asked to be venerated in the chapel located on a bluff overlooking the port; it was soon adorned with a statue of the Virgin with

---

61. Yann Codou and Michel Lauwers, eds., *Lérins: Une île sainte de l'Antiquité au Moyen Age* (Turnhout: Brepols, 2010).

Child, which became the principal recourse of sailors both in the region and far beyond it.

In fact, it is especially in the Mediterranean world that the reference to maritime sanctuaries seems to have had a particular importance (figure 28). As the work of Henri Bresc has shown, sailors never failed to salute the sanctuaries, great and small, that they noticed along their sea lanes, or to say prayers when they went around a cape that was deemed dangerous and that was surmounted by a chapel, like that of San Vito in Sicily near the Madonna Nunziata (Our Lady of the Annunciation) of Trapani.[62] On the portolan charts—the first detailed maritime charts that proliferated between the thirteenth and fifteenth centuries—numerous sanctuaries and several hundred sites that testify to the presence of intercessors that one finds within litanies are identified. These prayers, recited by the crew at departure, were intended to protect the boat and its passengers in times of storms and other perils. The text of these litanies can be found in a fifteenth-century manuscript of Venetian origin, but preserved in Florence, *Le Sancte Parole* (The Holy Words). A Genoese version of it also exists, which Christopher Columbus had recourse to on his ship when he was approaching the island of Domenica in 1492.[63] In it are the names of around forty saints whose intercession was solicited, along with a list of 163 coastal sanctuaries visible from the ships or particularly important (including the Holy Sepulcher); the majority of these belonged to the Mediterranean world, but others, fewer in number, were located on the shores of the Atlantic, the English Channel, and the North Sea.

These lists include both ancient sanctuaries, like Saint Sabas of Alexandria or Monte Sant'Angelo in the Gargano, as well as more recent ones like the Basilica of the Holy Blood in Bruges. And there is special veneration for sanctuaries that marked out the routes of the high seas: Mount Carmel in Palestine, Saint George in Beirut, the Church of the Holy Cross or the Madonna de la Cava in Cyprus near Famagusta,

---

62. Henri Bresc, "Mediterrâneo medieval: A geografia da graças," in *O Mediterrâneo medieval reconsiderado*, ed. Niéri De Barros Almeida and Robson Della Torre (San Paolo: Editora da Unicamp, 2019), 241–78.

63. Michele Bacci, *The Holy Portulan: The Sacred Geography of Navigation in the Middle Ages* (Berlin: De Gruyter, 2014); Aulisa, *I santuari e il mare*; Amalia Galdi, "Navigazione e devozione nel XV secolo: Il Mar Tirreno nel Portolano dei santi," in Aulisa, *I santuari e il mare*, 149–66. On the efficacy of prayer to the saints, see Patrick Henriet, ed., "'*Invocatio sanctificatorum nominum*': Efficacité de la prière et société chrétienne (IXe–XIIe siècle)," in *La prière en latin de l'Antiquité au XVIe siècle*, ed. Jean-François Cottier (Turnhout: Brepols, 2006), 229–44.

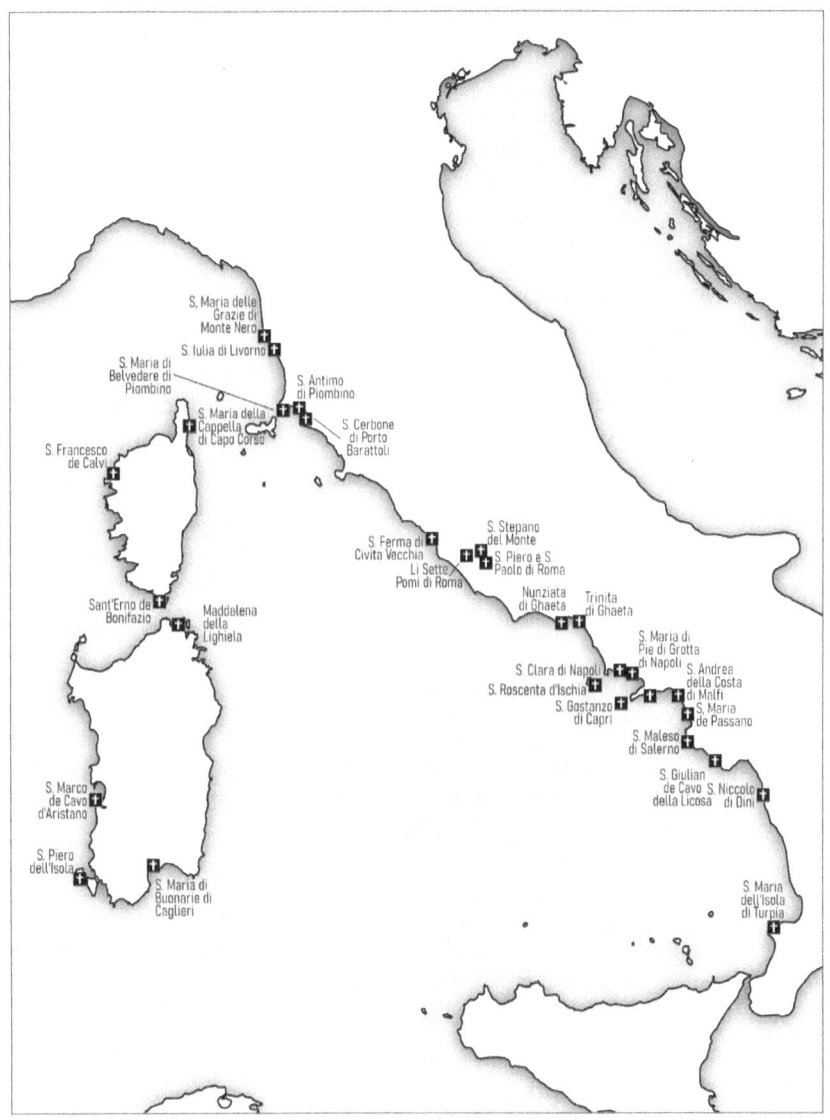

FIGURE 28. The principal maritime sanctuaries on the coasts of the Tyrrhenian Sea. Credit: A. Christesen.

the Abbey of Lérins, the Chapel of Cape Leucat, and the Chapel of La Pointe Saint-Mathieu in western Brittany, to name just a few. In general, these entries associate the name of an important saint, a particularly evocative site, a church or chapel, with the presence of relics or an *ymage* famous for their miraculous power. The cult rendered to Mary was preponderant here, in connection with the recitation of the prayer *Ave maris stella*—as accounts of voyages during storms attest. Sailors' invocations addressed saints by name, as well as the sacred places where they were venerated, which often began as simple oratories and evolved into true sanctuaries. These constituted points of reference for navigation, earning them a mention in the portolan charts. Notre-Dame de la Garde in Marseilles, for example, was first a simple chapel frequented by fishermen and became, in the fourteenth century, a major sanctuary for the whole city and the surrounding region. At Santa Maria de Bonaria in Sardinia, a church located a few dozen meters from the coast near Cagliari, prayers were recited by sailors to obtain *bonancia* (fair winds) in the uncertain sea that they were preparing to confront.

A text from the thirteenth century takes into account the existential dimension of humanity's relationship to the sea; in a passage from the *Life of Saint Louis*, Jean de Joinville recounts that the ship bringing Louis IX and his wife Marguerite de Provence back to France in 1248 after the crusade was hit by a violent storm that threatened to sink it off the coast of Cyprus.[64] The queen asked Louis to pray to God or his saints so that they might escape this peril when she ran into the seneschal on the bridge, who counseled her to entrust herself to Saint Nicolas de Varangéville and to offer him an ornamental silver jar in the form of a ship, filled with five marks, that he promised to carry to the Lorraine sanctuary from his castle in Joinville, if the royal couple and their three children survived. The queen accepted, and a little later the winds diminished and the seas calmed. On their return to France, she kept her word, and Joinville himself carried the ex-voto to the sanctuary as promised. This testimony is doubly interesting. First, it shows that those facing danger on the sea made a vow not only to a saint but also to a sanctuary where the saint was venerated. Second, it is of note that this maritime miracle was not commemorated by an ex-voto placed in a coastal sanctuary after the ship arrived in Provence but in one where the prestigious relics of Saint Nicolas, so important to the kingdom of

---

64. Jean de Joinville, *Vie de saint Louis*, ed. Jacques Monfrin (Paris: Classiques Garnier, 2010), 315.

France were found: Saint-Nicolas-de-Port in Varangéville, near Nancy. This is a convenient reminder that a sanctuary, from the medieval perspective, was above all a place where the power of the saint incarnated in their remains, their *virtus*, is manifested in the most concrete and effective manner.

From the twelfth and thirteenth centuries, the intercessory power of saints extended to all of the dangerous aspects of life, especially the perils of the sea. During the inquiry carried out in Marseilles in 1376–78 into the miracles attributed to Pope Urban V, who had died in the "odor of sanctity" in 1370 and was being canonized, witnesses attributed to him the merit of having saved through his intercession twenty-eight ships from being shipwrecked and of the thirty-two miracles concerning a mastery over the elements.[65] However, Urban V had no particular connection to the sea except that his body had been buried in the Abbey of Saint-Victor in Marseilles where he had been a monk, with the result that many sailors and fishermen of Marseilles had heard about his reputation of holiness and thus resorted to calling on him. In similar fashion, at sanctuaries like Rocamadour or Santiago de Compostela, although distant from the sea, numerous pilgrims testified to having benefited from miracles tied to the sea and its turbulences. This explains how the scallop shell, a symbol of Saint James at Compostela, came to be worn by pilgrims throughout Europe during the last centuries of the Middle Ages and why the pilgrims often extended their journey on the Camino de Santiago to Santa Maria das Areas in Finistre, on the most westerly cape on the Atlantic coast.

At the end of the Middle Ages, specific forms of piety appeared among seafaring people—sailors, fishermen, merchants, shipbuilders, and the like—as Michel Mollat's research has demonstrated.[66] In the sanctuaries they visited, they offered ex-votos connected to maritime life, among which were paintings depicting storms and shipwrecks that they had survived. This development is tied to the rise of exchanges through maritime journeys in this era, as in the example of Brittany—a region that was profoundly affected by the sea on all sides but lacked sailor sanctuaries during the early Middle Ages. When in the fourteenth and fifteenth centuries the region became integrated into the

---

65. Paul Amargier, "Gens de mer en Méditerrannée dans les années, 1375–1390," in *Navigation et gens de mer en Méditerrannée* (Paris: CNRS, 1980), 68–83.
66. Michel Mollat, *La vie quotidienne des gens de mer en Atlantique, IXe–XVIe siècle* (Paris: Le Grand Livre du mois, 2001).

naval networks of the Atlantic, new Breton sanctuaries associated with the cults of Saint Yves († 1303) at Tréguier, Charles of Blois († 1364) at Guingamp, and Saint Vincent Ferrer († 1419) at Vannes witnessed an inrush of pilgrims and those who came to thank the saints for having escaped certain death on the sea. In Sardinia, too, maritime sanctuaries only appeared at the end of the Middle Ages, when the large island became economically and politically dependent on Catalonia and the Kingdom of Aragon, which contributed to the development of commercial navigation there.[67] Among the new forms of maritime piety was the practice of baptizing boats, which received on this occasion the name of a saint or, more often, that of the Virgin Mary.

---

67. Meloni, "Il fenomeno santuariale in Sardegna."

CHAPTER 4

The Life of Sanctuaries

Founding Legends

All sanctuaries have a life—that is to say, a beginning, a history, and sometimes an end. Most often, there is sufficient documentation about them only for the period during which they witnessed their greatest influence, attested to by memorials, physical depictions, and miracle collections. Yet their beginnings remain generally obscure or mysterious; often there are only the founding legends drawn up after the fact. Thus, it is important to interpret them prudently. These texts are, for the most part, the work of clerics who experienced the need to justify the existence of the sanctuary by emphasizing the supernatural character of its origins and the thaumaturgical power manifested there.[1] In the case of sanctuaries of eremitical or monastic origin, it was especially a matter of underscoring the role of the founder, emphasizing his merits and charisms within a hagiographical perspective. But the most interesting legends concern the hierophanic sanctuaries, associated with the appearance of Saint Michael or the Virgin Mary, like the *Apparitio sancti Michaelis in monte Gargano* (Apparition of Saint Michael on

---

1. Giorgio Cracco, "Le leggende di fondazione dal Medioevo all'età moderna," *Annali dell'Istituto storico italo-germanico di Trento* 26 (2000): 393–413.

Mount Gargano), which dates from the end of the eighth or beginning of the ninth century.[2] Its anonymous author juxtaposes two accounts of the origins of the sanctuary. The first describes the discovery by a certain Garganus of an immense grotto before which a bull was standing and that did not want to leave the site. Astonished by its behavior, the man went to warn the bishop of Siponto, who sent emissaries to the place. Up on the mountain, the men found within the grotto an altar prepared by the archangel and a purple-colored coat—which was a way of saying that the sanctuary had not yet been consecrated by the bishop, who only arrived later—placed there by Saint Michael himself. At a later moment, another account tells of a battle fought by the Christians of Siponto and Gargano against the pagan Neapolitans. The Christians won the day thanks to the intervention of the archangel who, having caused an earthquake, put their enemies to flight. Returning to the grotto to give thanks to him for his help, the victors discovered the imprint of his foot in the rock.

This mythical account probably refers back to an episode in the wars around 650 that pitted the Lombards of southern Italy against "Roman armies"—those coming from the Byzantine Empire. But the Lombards, recently converted to Christianity, had adopted Saint Michael as their patron saint, and in fact, his cult then developed in northern Italy and in particular at Pavia, their capital, where one of their kings had built a great chapel dedicated to the archangel and had coinage struck with his likeness. In this latter text, the archangel appeared as an especially powerful protector, procuring victory to those who rendered him worship and to whom he had given a sign of their election. This legend was widely diffused, and from the eighth century the sanctuary welcomed numerous pilgrims from northern Europe and the British Isles, who inscribed graffiti on the wall of the grotto with their names; certain ones still visible today were written in runic characters.

Around the middle of the ninth century, a similar legend titled the *Revelatio ecclesiae sancti Michaelis* (Revelation of the Church of Mont-Saint-Michel) was composed in France about the origins of the Norman sanctuary.[3] It recounts the three visions of Aubert, the bishop of Avranches, in which an angel asked him to consecrate to him Mont Tombe, a small island located in his diocese. As the prelate dragged his feet, the angel struck him forcefully, leaving a hole in Aubert's

---

2. *Apparitio sancti Michaelis in Monte Gargano*, in *Culte et pèlerinages à saint Michel en Occident*.
3. *Revelatio ecclesiae sancti Michaelis*, in *Cultes et pèlerinages à Saint Michel en Occident*.

skull that was visible when he awoke and remained until his death (figure 29). Aubert went to the Mont, and as the angel had foretold, he found a bull there that had marked out a circular space on the ground, inside of which there was no dew from the previous night. On this site, at the foot of a rocky cliff, the bishop had a church built, which was consecrated on October 16, 709, and a grotto constructed on the model of Gargano, where he sent his messengers to look for relics. According to the tradition, they returned with a fragment of the archangel's coat and a piece of the rock on which he had placed his foot. Then, still on orders from the archangel, Aubert caused a spring of drinkable water to burst forth with his staff, allowing for the installation of a community of twelve clerics to whom he gave a plot of land adequate for their livelihood.

The *Revelatio* apparently drew its inspiration from the Gargano *Apparitio* and, at first glance, seems to imply a connection of affiliation

FIGURE 29. The third apparition of Saint Michael to the bishop of Avranches, Aubert, in which the archangel struck him in the head because he had not yet built the sanctuary in his honor on the island of Mont Tombe. Cartulaire du Mont-Saint-Michel, twelfth century, Bibliothèque municipale d'Avranches, MS 210, fol. 4v.

between the new, still modest holy site and the famous sanctuary in Apulia. But, as recent studies have shown, an attentive reading of the text shows that its redactors did not consider the Mont as a simple satellite of the Monte Sant'Angelo.[4] Whereas in the *Apparitio*, the archangel is presented as a holy warrior giving victory to those who claimed to be his followers, the accent in the *Revelatio* is put on his functions as a psychopomp—a conductor of souls—and guardian of paradise. His role is more eschatological, as the title of the legend attests: *Revelatio* is the name of the Apocalypse in Latin. Indeed, the foundation of Mont-Saint-Michel fits into the penitential perspective of the Carolingian Church, and the text presents it as a place where it was possible to achieve salvation through the practice of a contemplative asceticism, aided by the beauty of the site and the presence of the surrounding sea, making the Mont a holy island comparable to that of Lérins on the Mediterranean coast. Moreover, the author of the *Revelatio* presents the creation of the Mont-Saint-Michel as a kind of translation from the East to the West of the charism and power of the archangel, who had finally found in the Frankish Empire a people marked by the grace of Christ and a sanctuary destined to play a crucial role in the history of salvation.

In certain cases, the founding legend also opens up new insights for the historian. For example, Giorgio Cracco has analyzed the various aspects of the foundation of the great sanctuary of Santa Maria on Monte Berico, a wooded hill overlooking the town of Vicenza in northern Italy.[5] The text was drawn up, most likely by notaries, in 1431, to support and legitimize the expansion of the sanctuary that the commune had just built there. According to the account, Mary appeared twice in 1428 to an old woman from a very humble background while she was carrying food for her husband who was working up the hill. The Virgin had entrusted her with a message, according to which the plague that was then afflicting Vicenza would only cease after its inhabitants had constructed a church in her honor on the same site as the apparition. The woman went to the bishop to speak to him about her vision, but he scornfully sent her away. Her story, however, quickly resonated with the people, and the communal authorities built a small shrine on the site, which they entrusted to a community of Brigittines—females

---

4. George N. Gandy, "*Revelatio* on the Origins of Mont-Saint-Michel (Fifth–Ninth Centuries)," *Speculum* 95 (2020): 132–66.

5. Cracco, "Le leggende di fondazione dal Medioevo all'età moderna."

religious who, like their founder, Saint Birgitta of Sweden, emphasized Mary's omnipotence and her power of intercession on behalf of sinners. The plague ceased at once. There were numerous miracles, and above all, the people of Vicenza, previously divided into antagonistic clans, recovered their unity and were reconciled to God under the auspices of the Virgin. The bishop eventually supported the community's initiative, and the sanctuary of Monte Berico became (and remains so to the present) one of the most important of the Veneto mainland, along with that of Saint Anthony in Padua. It is worth noting in passing the importance of the Virgin Mary's request for a cult, which allowed the faithful to justify their undertaking and made it difficult for the local ecclesiastical authorities to refuse their support.

This example illustrates two fundamental aspects of the life of shrines: on the one hand, that the initiative for their creation was often taken by laity, either lords or communal authorities; on the other hand, it required the necessary collaboration of laity and clergy, for only the latter could celebrate the cult there and welcome pilgrims on a daily basis. Still, it is necessary to specify that it was most often members of the religious clergy—monks, mendicant friars, and later the Olivetans, Brigittines, Carmelites, and Jesuits—since the secular clergy, fearing the loss of precious donations, rarely looked favorably on the appearance of a new sanctuary in their parish or town. The founding legends are, moreover, full of stories of conflicts between the laity who wanted to venerate a holy image or the memory of an apparition in a given place, and the pastor or bishop who was trying to bring, willingly or by force, the object of veneration into the parish church or cathedral. In spite of their efforts, they were generally not successful, and the statue or painting would return itself "miraculously" to the place of its discovery. This hagiographical commonplace reflected the underlying conflict between the faithful—attached to the place of the miraculous apparition or of the "invention" (or discovery) of the relic—and a clergy worried, above all, about integrating this unexpected event into the territorial structures of the Church from a pastoral perspective.

Relics, Reliquaries, and Holy Images

A relic is an inanimate object presented and recognized as being of divine origin to which people attributed a supernatural power. It is a fragment of eternity offered for the veneration of the living that attests to the presence of the Absolute in the midst of the vicissitudes of life.[6] In the sensory code of late antiquity and the Middle Ages, saints' relics possessed certain gifts that differentiated them from common bones. In particular, when one opened the tomb or the reliquary that contained them upon translation, it gave off (giving credence to the hagiographers of the period) "the odor of sanctity," which immediately demonstrated the blessedness they had attained and the power that resided in them. But they were also the guarantors of divine protection, and their presence or collection in a place was a pledge of prosperity and fecundity for their holders, as well as for those who traveled to venerate them.[7]

Sometimes Catholicism is defined as a "religion of things," in which certain objects—relics, in particular—play a mediating role between the profane and the sacred. This is particularly true in this period. Indeed, it is hard to imagine the considerable role played by the cult of saints and their bodily remains from the end of antiquity up through the Middle Ages. These sacred objects reconciled Christian faith with their deepest popular beliefs. Two human attitudes were at the root of this veneration: first, an innate need to admire and idealize exceptional persons, before and after their death, which was satisfied in an appropriate manner in each culture and each period, including today; second, in a society such as that of the medieval West, where religion occupied a considerable place, a need for the concrete and the tangible. The instinct to touch, to put one's hands on the sacred: relics provided a solution to these aspirations.

The cult of relics is founded on the principle that contact, ingestion, use, or veneration of a thing that had been a part of, belonged to, or was in proximity to a person rich in virtue allowed one to participate in the qualities of that person. They provide the physical closeness sought by people struggling with life's difficulties who look to the saints as protectors and intermediaries with God.[8]

---

6. Luigi Canetti, *Frammenti di eternità: Corpi e reliquie tra Antichità e Medioevo* (Rome: Viella, 2002).

7. Edith Bozoky and Anne-Marie Helvétius, eds., *Les reliques: Objets, culte, symboles* (Turnhout: Brepols, 1999); Martin Roch, *L'intelligence d'un sens: Odeurs miraculeuses et odorat dans l'Occident du Moyen Age* (Turnhout: Brepols, 2009).

8. Nicole Herrmann-Masquard, *Les reliques des saints: Formation coutumière d'un droit* (Paris: Klincksieck, 1975); Sofia Boesch Gajano, "Gli oggetti di culto: Produzione, gestione, fruizione," in *Lo spazio del santuario: Un osservatorio per la storia di Roma e del Lazio*, ed. Sofia Boesch Gajano and Francesco Scorza Barcellona (Rome: Viella, 2008), 129-60.

The presence of relics ensured the continuity of sanctuaries, while their loss generally led to their decline or disappearance. A single example will suffice. In 1297, a young Franciscan died in Brignoles in Provence, a man with a passion for perfection. He was called Saint Louis of Anjou (or of Toulouse), so named because, against his wishes, he had been made bishop of this city for a few months in 1295. He was the son of the king of Naples, Charles II, and he renounced the throne to enter religious life, earning him great renown. His body was brought back to Marseilles, where he was buried in the church of the Friars Minor. Miracles soon began taking place at his tomb, and after due process, he was canonized in 1317 by Pope John XXII. His tomb became a popular place of pilgrimage until, in 1423, the city of Marseilles was conquered by the Aragonese, who pillaged it and took the port chains and the relics of Saint Louis of Anjou to Barcelona. These were placed in a church in Valence, but his cult failed to take root in this foreign land, while the sanctuary of Marseilles quickly fell into disrepair because his relics were no longer to be found there.[9]

Pilgrims aspired to touch relics in order to benefit from their marvelous vitality, at least for a moment. This tactile piety has nothing to do with any kind of "popular religiosity": from the earliest centuries in Jerusalem, it was customary to kiss the ground of the places where Christ had been physically present during his lifetime, and at Compostela, the pilgrims' first gesture was to kiss the feet of the statue of Saint James, the apostle who had touched God when he was physically present at his side. But outside the Holy Land, their hope was almost always disappointed, as the clergy who administered the sanctuaries feared that their precious treasure might be stolen and thus they multiplied the protections and obstacles to accessing them. The most extreme case is that of Saint Francis of Assisi. In 1230, the Friars Minor decided to transfer his remains into the basilica that Pope Gregory IX and Brother Elias (minister general of the friars) were building just outside of the city walls. But the translation took place in such confusion that the faithful, having come in great numbers, were not able to view them.[10] Indeed, under pretext that the relics of the "Poverello" risked being stolen, Elias had them buried beneath the basilica in a location

---

9. Jacques Paul, *Louis d'Anjou, prince et franciscain* (Padua: Centro Studi Antoniani, 2018), 315.
10. André Vauchez, *Francis of Assisi: The Life and Afterlife of a Medieval Saint*, trans. Michael F. Cusato (New Haven: Yale University Press, 2012), 152–55.

so inaccessible that the memory of the precise spot where they had been placed was soon lost, and they were only rediscovered at the beginning of the nineteenth century!

The faithful often had to content themselves with looking at relics in their reliquaries or behind glass, separated by grates and barriers of stone or marble. The clergy, who only exhibited them on the occasion of the great feasts, was led to develop, over the course of the thirteenth century, a pastoral practice for viewing them. This was inaugurated by Pope Innocent III when he instituted in Rome an annual procession of the Veil of Veronica, considered to be the "true image" of Christ, as it had been imprinted on the cloth with which a Jerusalem woman had wiped the Holy Face, awash in sweat and blood, during the ascent to Calvary. As Roland Recht has shown, the aim of this practice was to arouse and maintain the desire—almost always frustrated—of the faithful to see the relic through a series of periodic ostensions, followed by long periods of occlusion, as illustrated by the spread in this period of the rite of elevation of the consecrated Host and chalice during Mass.[11] The "real" presence of Christ in the species, the Eucharistic bread and wine, was manifested, outside of Mass, through the display of the monstrance containing a consecrated Host, carried in procession on the occasion of the Corpus Christi, instituted in 1264 by Pope Urban IV and extended to the whole of Christianity at the beginning of the fourteenth century. From that time, the Eucharist was considered a relic of Christ's bloody sacrifice and venerated as such. It was said that those who gazed upon it in a spirit of piety could benefit from both the healing of their ills and the absolution of their sins.[12]

The relics held in sanctuaries were not immobile. In times of peace, they were taken out in procession on certain feast days, in particular the Rogations during the spring, when they were taken around the countryside to obtain bountiful harvests in lands sanctified by their *virtus*, at the end of a theatrical action that had both symbolic and performative value. They were also brought out in broad daylight when crowds

---

11. Roland Recht, *La croire et le voir: L'art des cathédrales (XIIe–XVe siècle)* (Paris: Gallimard, 1999); Dominique Rigaux, "Miracle, reliques et images dans la chapelle du Corporal à Orvieto (1357-1364)," in *Pratiques de l'eucharistie dans les Églises d'Orient et d'Occident (Antiquité et Moyen Age)*, ed. Béatrice Caseau-Chevallier, Nicole Bériou, and Dominique Rigaux (Turnhout: Brepols, 2009), 201–45; Anton Legner, *Reliquien in Kunst und Kult, zwischen Antike und Aufklärung* (Darmstadt: Wissenschaftliche Buchgesellschaft, 1995).

12. Godefridus J. C. Snoek, *Medieval Piety from Relics to Eucharist* (Leiden: Brill, 1995).

gathered, and it was upon these relics that the great and the good swore oaths to respect the commitments they had made before the people. Physically present through their relics, saints thus strengthened the Peace of God movement, born in Aquitaine around 980–90, and the assemblies in the eleventh century. At the time of the first Peace council held in Limoges in 994, the statue-reliquary of Saint Martial was carried in procession and his body raised, in the presence of the relics of other saints solemnly brought there. Martial thus became the apostle of the Peace in Aquitaine.[13] After the great council of 1031, the fame of the hermit Saint Leonard, buried in Noblat (ten kilometers from Limoges), where "any imprisoned person who invokes his name will see his chains broken," was affirmed. In 1048, Duke William established the Peace in Normandy by gathering relics and swearing an oath—"Sor li cors sainz lor fist jurer / Paiz à tenir, paiz à garder"—as reported in the thirteenth-century *Roman de Rou*.[14]

The spontaneous tendency of institutions in possession of relics was to seek to increase their number. In the sixteenth century, as previously discussed, the collegiate church of Saint-Sernin in Toulouse claimed twenty-seven "holy bodies" in its collection, some of which, like the body of Saint James, had been given to it by Charlemagne upon his return from Spain.[15] It was the same with holy images, as demonstrated by the role that the icon of the Virgin known as *Salus Populi Romani* (Salvation of the Roman People), conserved at Santa Maria Maggiore, played in the life of Rome during the Middle Ages. Its archaic character, from a stylistic point of view, allowed it to be considered particularly venerable, and it was brought out in procession when a serious threat weighed on the city and its populace, especially during times of plague. It is interesting to note that, during Holy Week in 2020, when Rome had been struck as elsewhere by the COVID-19 epidemic, this icon was brought out to the piazza of Saint Peter's for the Good Friday prayer and placed next to Pope Francis, alongside the Crucifix of San Marcello, also known for its intercessory powers. The pope later offered

---

13. Richard Landes, *The Peace of God: Social Violence and Religious Response in France around the Year 1000* (Ithaca, NY: Cornell University Press, 1992).

14. Wace, *Le Roman de Rou*, vol. 2 (Rouen: Édouard Frère Éditeur, 1828), 97-98.

15. Sophie Brouquet and Michelle Fournié, "Le saint des saints: Le trésor de Saint-Sernin de Toulouse," in *Corps saints et reliques dans le Midi*, ed. Michelle Fournié, Daniel Le Blévec, and Catherine Vincent, Cahiers de Fanjeaux 53 (Toulouse: Privat, 2018), 205-64.

them for veneration by Romans for several days in the Church of San Marcello al Corso.[16]

Nothing better illustrates the fact that relics and holy images were situated at the heart of the two-way relationship between the saint and the community that venerated their mortal remains or their effigy and were thus considered an instrument of mediation between members of the community and the Invisible. In particular, the Virgin Mary and the saints were said to have control over the natural elements: When rain failed for too long a time, the relic or the image was brought out from its sanctuary, and a solemn procession was organized across the territory of the village community. It was the same in periods of scarcity or famine, as numerous accounts of miracles show, especially those of Saint Nicholas, whose relics had been venerated in Bari since 1087.[17]

Relics were generally kept in reliquaries that served both to ensure their protection and to emphasize their sacred character.[18] In the treasuries of churches or abbeys, they were often wrapped in precious fabrics of Eastern origin—Byzantine or Islamic—and provided with authentications, parchment strips by which an ecclesiastical authority, sometimes very old, had indicated the name of the saint and certified their legitimacy. There were obviously many fakes, which ended up prompting a certain mistrust among those who acquired relics: "If I do not see the tomb yet intact and if a writing does not tell me whose body is enclosed here, know that no one will get my money," said Abbot Nantère of Saint-Mihiel (1020–44) to his Roman host, who wished to sell him a few bones from the Catacombs.[19]

Sovereigns and world leaders paid homage to holy bodies with sumptuous offerings, as can be seen at the Church of Saint Maurice in Vienna, which held the head of the leader of the Martyrs of the Theban Legion, to whom a number of kings of Burgundy and Italy presented

---

16. Gerhard Wolf, *Salus populi romani: Die Geschichte römischer Kultbilder im Mittelalter* (Weinheim: Wiley-VCH Verlag, 1990).

17. Giorgio Cioffari and Angela Laghezza, eds., *Alle origini dell'Europa: Il culto di San Nicola tra Oriente e Occidente, Italia-Francia* (Bari: Nicolaus Studi Storici, 2011); Véronique Gazeau, Catherine Guyon, and Catherine Vincent, eds., *En Orient et en Occident: Le culte de saint Nicolas en Europe, X^e–XXIe siècle* (Paris: Éditions du Cerf, 2015).

18. Marie-Madeleine Gauthier, *Les routes de la foi: Reliques et reliquaires de Jérusalem à Compostelle* (Fribourg im Breisgau: Bibliothèque des arts, 1983).

19. *Chronique de Saint-Mihiel*, trans. Michèle Gaillard, Monique Goullet, and Anne Wagner, cited by Philippe George, *Reliques: Se connecter à l'au-delà* (Paris: CNRS Éditions, 2018), 116.

THE LIFE OF SANCTUARIES   167

FIGURE 30. Reliquary bust of Saint Baudime, twelfth century. Church of Saint-Nectaire, Puy-de-Dôme. Photo: © Raimond Spekking via Wikimedia Commons (CC BY-SA 4.0).

golden crowns in the ninth and tenth centuries.[20] In the same period, reliquary busts like those of Saint Gerald of Aurillac and Saint Baudime in the Auvergne first appeared and proliferated over the next centuries (figure 30). In 1215, the Fourth Lateran Council prohibited (in canon 62) the display of fragments of holy bodies outside the container in which they were housed. The intended purpose was to assure their protection but also to guarantee their status; for "outside of its reliquary, a relic risked being considered as simple organic remains."[21] The reliquary had to be composed of noble materials—gold or silver, to which were attributed extraordinary properties—and richly decorated with precious stones, the *virtus* of which was activated through the rite

---

20. Anne Baud, ed., *Organiser l'espace sacré au Moyen Age: Topographie, architecture et liturgie (Rhône-Alpes, Auvergne)* (Lyons: Alphara, 2014).

21. Philippe Cordez, *Trésor, mémoire, merveilles: Les objets des églises au Moyen Age* (Paris: EHESS, 2016).

of consecration. The goldsmith's decoration and the inlay of gems on the precious, leather-lined wooden case that contained the relics were also intended to evoke the heavenly Jerusalem and enable the faithful to imagine the splendor of the kingdom of heaven where the chosen ones would find themselves. Beginning in the twelfth century, the decoration was often enriched with depictions of the saint or scenes from their life on champlevé enameling or blackened enamel plates: thus "to the apotropaic and thaumaturgical dynamic of relics, the reliquary added the teaching power of images."[22]

The holy images themselves were not immutable, and over the years and centuries, they could be enriched by new, nonincidental elements, such as a coating of precious stones, a gilded wood or silver frame, or rays emanating from them. The clothing worn by statues of the saints in modern times concealed their bodies, often consisting of a core of wood and plaster, revealing only their faces and hands. This process of "over-sacralization" was sometimes accentuated by the use of curtains, which were only opened on certain feast days, thus contributing to the desire to see the holy image. In some cases, sacredness was intensified by the clergy adding precious metal crowns to the statues' heads, as part of solemn ceremonies that ensured the periodic revival of devotion.

Pilgrims and Pilgrimages: The Clientele of the Sanctuaries

This is not the place to draw up an inventory of the places of pilgrimage in the West during the medieval and modern eras, nor to study their place in the religious life of the faithful. There are already a number of excellent studies on these subjects.[23] However, the attitude and behavior of pilgrims, both on their journey and once they have reached their destination, merit greater attention here.

The Christian pilgrimage appears to be a self-evident practice that does not require much consideration, since it can be found today in almost all religions and so is seemingly well understood. In fact, this tradition has not always existed, and it results historically from

---

22. Gauthier, *Les routes de la foi*, 18.
23. Edmond-René Labande, *Pauper et peregrinus: Problèmes, comportements et mentalités du pèlerin chrétien* (Turnhout: Brepols, 2004); Luciano Vaccaro, ed., *L'Europa dei pellegrini* (Gazzada: Centro Ambrosiano, 2004).

the intersection of the ideal of leaving one's homeland and ascetic wandering—put into practice on the continent by the Celtic monks and Saint Columbanus in the seventh century—and of the search for a place sanctified by the story of Christ and the Virgin, or by the tombs of the saints and servants of God. The time it might take to make the journey could range from one day to several years; but the distance of travel was the price for the efficacy of the ritual. The pilgrimage was also an experience—temporary but impactful—of a flight from the world. Although often referred to as a "voyage" in medieval texts, it was not limited to travel, but implied, at least ideally, a way of moving around in poverty and without baggage, free from earthly ties, in pursuit of a goal. When there was a sea to cross on the way to the Holy Land, people spoke of a "passage" (*passagium*), a term that came to be applied to the journey of crusaders and pilgrims to the Holy Land. Originally, the Latin word *peregrinus* referred to a foreigner or anyone making a long journey. During the Middle Ages, it would come to take on its current meaning, but special status was attributed to pilgrims insofar as their true homeland was considered heaven, which they were striving to reach by way of the visiting of sanctuaries. To go to a shrine was, in effect, to leave the world of daily habits in order to enter a different dimension of existence, marked by an encounter with the sacred. For the pilgrim, what was fundamental was the attainment of that which they were longing to see or touch, which would then become the patrimony of their memory.

Why go to a sanctuary? Pilgrims' motives are rarely known, but one of the principal reasons seems to have been the desire to fulfill a commitment made in a vow that had not yet been kept. If someone could not go on pilgrimage themselves, they might accomplish the vow through a proxy: testaments from the fourteenth and fifteenth centuries often include clauses obliging a son, under pain of being disinherited, to make the pilgrimage or pilgrimages that the testator had promised to make. If there were no children, a replacement could be hired by the family, hence the term "vicarious pilgrimage" given to this practice, which would become commonplace. The distance to be covered varied by case and era: In Provence in the fifteenth century, the portion of regional sanctuaries (the tombs of Saint Peter of Luxembourg among the Celestins of Avignon, of Saint Elzéar in Apt or of the Blessed Louis Aleman in Arles) listed in testaments was comparatively minimal (sixteen of seventy cases); more often, the laity preferred to go to a renowned

FIGURE 31. Pilgrims climbing Mount Gargano to reach the Sanctuary of Monte Sant' Angelo. Fresco in the Church of the Madonna del Parto, Sutri, Italy. Photo by André Vauchez.

and distant sanctuary, like Santiago de Compostela (thirty-four of seventy cases), Saint Peter's in Rome, or Monte Sant'Angelo on Mount Gargano (figure 31).[24]

But these statistics are probably misleading because the nearby pilgrimages—the distance of a canton or a valley—have barely left any traces in the written documentation, whereas they were, undoubtedly, the most frequent. The presence of relics or the memory of a heavenly appearance were necessary for such a place to be considered sacred, but that alone did not suffice; it was the ritual behavior of pilgrims that, in the final analysis, made it a sanctuary and determined its creation and fortune. What did these rituals consist of? The first element was the journey, which was imperative to make (if possible) on the feast day of the saint—that is, on the anniversary of their death and their birth into heaven (*dies natalis*)—according to the liturgical calendar.[25]

---

24. Noël Coulet, "L'ermitage de Notre-Dame-de-Anges de sa fondation (XIIIe siècle?) à l'installation des oratoriens," *Provence historique* 68 (2018): 401–20; Olivier Thuaudet, "La pratique du pèlerinage en Provence à la fin du Moyen Age et au début de l'époque moderne," *Archéologie médiévale* 47 (2017): 90–129; for Italy, see Giovanni Cherubini, "Le mete del pellegrinaggio medievale," in *Itinerari medievali e identità europea*, ed. Roberto Greci (Bologna: CLUEB, 1999), 136–46.

25. Raymond Oursel, *Sanctuaires et chemins de pèlerinage* (Paris: Éditions du Cerf, 1997).

Different types of pilgrimages can be distinguished, the most spectacular of which was the expiatory pilgrimage, made after committing murder or a serious and notorious sin: People went to a sanctuary to be delivered from a personal fault that had a social impact, insofar as it involved a human community. For example, Fulk III the Black, count of Anjou (ca. 970–1040), went to Jerusalem three times (in 1003–5, 1009–11, and again in 1039) to seek pardon for his crimes, which included burning alive his wife, whom he suspected of adultery; setting fire to the city of Angers, as well as the monastery in Sens; and trespassing the cloister of the Abbey of Saint-Martin de Châteauneuf, which he then pillaged while roughing up the monks. Censured by the Church, he went on pilgrimage to Saint-Martin of Tours, but that was not considered adequate expiation, so he had to go to the Holy Land three times. To be absolved of such grave sins, it was not enough to simply be repentant and confess to a priest: In the penitential discipline of the time, a grave crime of a public character necessarily called for public reparation. These penances were imposed by an ecclesiastical juridical authority, but in certain regions, beginning in the thirteenth century, lay authorities could also levy lengthy pilgrimages as sanctions against certain criminals. Thus, in 1370, the aldermen of Bruges sent problematic individuals from the city to expiate their sins in Jerusalem on Mount Sinai (at Saint Catherine's Monastery), Rome, Compostela, or Rocamadour. The presence in these sanctuaries of a particular sacred power made them places of pardon and reconciliation, where offenders could both unburden themselves of the weight of their sins and get a glimpse of the promise of a blessed life in eternity. Penitents often arrived at the sanctuary in chains or handcuffs—as is seen at Rocamadour, Saint-Leonard of Noblat in Limoges, or Saint Leonard de Siponto in Apulia—and there offered up their shackles as an ex-voto, after having benefited from a grace or a miracle.[26]

Even when the sins committed were not extremely serious, there was always an expiatory dimension to pilgrimage given that the pilgrim hoped to be absolved by way of direct contact with a holy place. It is this desire that the Latin inscription found at the entrance to the sanctuary

---

26. The author of *Le Guide de pèlerin de Saint-Jacques de Compostelle* offers lively praise for Saint Leonard and his popular sanctuary. See *Le Guide de pèlerin de Saint-Jacques de Compostelle*, ed. Jeanne Vielliard (Mâcon: Protat Frères, 1963), 55–57, and also Maria Stella Calò Mariani, "Icone e statue lignee medievali nei santuari mariani della Puglia," in *Santuari cristiani d'Italia*, ed. Mario Tosti (Rome: École Française de Rome, 2003), 3–44, regarding the sanctuary of Saint Leonard near Siponto in Apulia.

of Mount Gargano echoes: "Here where the rocks are split open, the sins of men are pardoned; here is a particular dwelling where every bad act is wiped away." If the sanctuary was distant from where the pilgrims lived, they went in procession while singing canticles on the eve or vigil of the feast day, and often slept on the floor of the church or a nearby building. The evening was marked by songs and conviviality between the various groups who had come together in one place. We can interpret these actions as a typical moment of liminality—that is, of a transition from the everyday to the extraordinary, from work time to feasting, celebrated the following day. Pilgrims who went to Compostela, for their part, gathered stones from a quarry on the descent down Mount Cebreiro in Galicia and transported them to the kilns of La Castañeda, where the lime was sent to the cathedral building site. After taking a purifying bath in the cold waters of the Lavacolla River, they made the journey up Mount Gozo, and the first to catch sight of Compostela was proclaimed the "king of the pilgrimage."

In addition to these well-established forms of pilgrimage, there existed others that Alphonse Dupront has characterized as "panicked pilgrimages."[27] This term describes collective movements toward certain sanctuaries that occurred many times during the medieval period. The term can also refer to "popular emotions" such as those that, on several occasions during the fourteenth century, sent squads of the faithful on the road to Rome, imploring the divine mercy, under the supervision of confraternities and guided by charismatic leaders. This was the case in Italy in 1334/35 under the impetus of the Dominican preacher Venturino of Bergamo, and again in 1399/1400, in Tuscany and the Veneto, with the Flagellants (*Battuti* or *Disciplinati* in Italian) who went from one sanctuary to another spreading devotion to the Madonna dell'Ulivo (Our Lady of the Olive Tree), who is said to have appeared in Umbria to a group of devotees and performed miracles there.[28]

Even more curious are the children's pilgrimages that proliferated throughout Christendom between the middle of the fourteenth and end of the fifteenth centuries. For example, in the years 1366–71, contemporary sources mention the departures of groups of young people, coming from Anjou and the countryside of the Loire, following the

---

27. Alphonse Dupront, *Du sacré: Croisades et pèlerinages. Images et langages* (Paris: Gallimard, 1987), especially 462.

28. Amleto Spicciani, ed., *La devozione dei Bianchi nel 1399: Il miracolo del Crocifisso di Borgo a Buggiano* (Pisa: ETS, 1998).

death of the duke of Brittany, Charles of Blois, at the battle of Auray in 1364. Devout and generous, Charles of Blois had enjoyed a great reputation of holiness, orchestrated by his son-in-law, Louis of Anjou, brother of King Charles V. According to many witnesses during Charles's canonization process held in Angers in 1371: "God, having revealed to men and women his sanctity, afterward people of the region took to the road to his tomb *en masse*," located in Guingamp in Brittany, where numerous miracles were being produced. "The children had shown the path to those who came after them, by piling up at the intersections mounds of stones bearing the French name 'Montjoies' to indicate the road to those who were going there."[29] As the hoped-for canonization did not take place and the new duke, John IV de Montfort, staunchly opposed the nascent cult, the movement ended up collapsing, and the church of Guingamp where the remains of Charles of Blois reposed did not become a sanctuary, even though numerous miracles had been produced there.

But it is at Mont-Saint-Michel that the connection between children's pilgrimages and a holy place intersected most closely.[30] In 1333, the French chroniclers recorded the appearance of groups of shepherds who left their flocks and departed for Mont-Saint-Michel without saying goodbye to anyone. Rather than children per se, these were young people between the ages of ten and fifteen who, according to the testimony of the Florentine banker Francesco Datini, had crossed paths with them in Avignon, justified their spontaneous departure by declaring that "great miracles were being produced there and that fathers and mothers who had not allowed their children to leave were going to see them die."[31] The pilgrimage seems to then have become a kind of initiation trial, a rite of separation between the young people and their families, at the end of which they could be considered adults. The fifteenth century witnessed a vigorous resumption of these collective journeys, which strongly struck their contemporaries. In 1441/42, Pierre Soybert, bishop of Saint-Papoul, counseled parents of his diocese to not block the departure of their children unless they were leaving in order

---

29. Process of canonization of Charles de Blois (Angers, 1371), cited by André Vauchez, *La sainteté en Occident aux derniers siècles du Moyen Age: D'après les procès de canonisation et les documents hagiographiques* (Rome: École Française de Rome, 1981), 269–70.

30. Ilona Hans-Collas, "Le Mont-Saint-Michel et les pèlerinages d'enfants aux XIVe et XVe siècles: Sources françaises et germaniques," in *Pellegrinaggi e santuari di San Michele nell'Occidente medievale*, ed. Giampietro Casiraghi and Giuseppe Sergi (Bari: Edipuglia, 2009), 207–39.

31. *Datini Archives*, cited in Hans-Collas, "Le Mont-Saint-Michel," 209.

to shirk their family chores.³² But other prelates and clergy reacted in a negative—if not overtly hostile—manner in response to these spontaneous initiatives; the Dominican Felix Fabri, for example, denounced the "infants" as impostors. In the years 1455–58, the departure of hundreds if not thousands of young people for the Mont while singing songs in honor of the archangel were observed in the Rhine Valley, southern Germany, and Switzerland. (It is notable that, in certain chronicles from the German world reporting on these doings, the French sanctuary is referred to as "Mount Gargano in Normandy.")

Historians have wondered about the motives that would push these young people to leave their families to try and reach such a distant sanctuary together. Perhaps it was an anguished reaction to the incursion of the Turks into central Europe on the part of these "children" who, unable to go to war, would have sought to fight them rather by prayer and physical effort. But what can also not be neglected is the extraordinary and fascinating nature of the Mont itself, located "at the peril of the sea," for young people, most of whom had never seen the maritime elements up close. This explanation is even more likely since it is consonant with the comment made by the monk Benedict, who had gone to Mont-Saint-Michel around 860 on his way back from a pilgrimage in the Holy Land. He had noted that "on the feast day of Saint Michael, the sea does not rise, so as to permit the influx of pilgrims"—something that in turn reminded him of the miraculous dry-footed crossing of the Red Sea by the Hebrew people, pursued by the Egyptians.³³ Similarly, the author of the *Chronicle of Strasburg* wrote, in a passage about the pilgrimage of children in 1457:

> While some left, others returned and said that one church, Saint-Michel, was located in the sea and, when the waters receded every six hours, one went there dry-shod, another remained there for six hours, another still heard the Mass there and one made offerings; there, to each one was given a memento of Saint Michel, and, after six hours, one hurried outside and departed once again. The pilgrimage was thus made; it was claimed that miracles were produced there and that old fools even went there.³⁴

---

32. Vital Chomel, "Pèlerins languedociens au Mont-Saint-Michel à la fin du Moyen Age," *Annales du Midi* 70 (1958): 230–39.

33. *Der "Itinerarium Bernardi monachi": Edition, Übersetzung, Kommentar*, ed. Josef Ackermann (Hannover: Verlag Hahnsche Buchhandlung, 2010), 154. See also Bouet, Otranto, and Vauchez, *Culte et pèlerinages à Saint-Michel en Occident*.

34. Cited by Hans-Collas, "Le Mont-Saint-Michel," 230.

The pilgrimages of young people to Mont-Saint-Michel continued into the modern era, even if these took on other forms within an institutional framework—that of the trade guilds—that did not originally exist.[35]

But if the phenomenon of children's pilgrimages gained importance in the thirteenth century, most people who visited sanctuaries were adults. Many went there to ask God and the saints to heal their children, especially in the fourteenth century, if contemporary miracle collections and acts of canonization are any guide. Most were men, but women appear, too, in large numbers, although it is difficult to provide more precise statistics given the insufficiency of the data. In principle, at least since the reform of the monasteries by Benedict of Aniane in the ninth century, women could not enter monasteries because their presence would sully those places due to the impurity attributed to their gender.[36] But this prohibition began to be contested in the twelfth century. The *Life* of Robert of Arbrissel, rediscovered and edited by Jacques Dalarun, describes a violent conflict on this subject.[37] At the end of his itinerant preaching tours, in 1114, the founder of Fontevraud arrived in Menat, a village of the Auvergne, site of the sanctuary of Saint Ménelé, a locally venerated hermit. When Robert wanted to enter the monastery with his female followers, the guards objected, saying that access to the sanctuary was forbidden to women; should one of their number gain entry, she would die immediately. The holy man protested violently against these assertions and, with his group, forced his way into the church, after which the porter—no doubt a monk—petitioned Saint Ménelé to avenge this violation of his sanctuary. Seized with indignation, Robert began to speak and, in a magnificent sermon of evangelical inspiration and feminist in nature, he asserted that women had the same rights as men in their relationship with the sacred, concluding with the following: "If a woman takes and eats the body and blood of Jesus Christ, what folly to believe that she should not enter the church!"[38]

---

35. Dominique Julia, *Le voyage des saints: Les pèlerinages dans l'Occident moderne (XVe–XVIIIe siècle)* (Paris: Seuil, 2016), 259–302.

36. Julia Mary Howard Smith, "L'accès des femmes aux reliques durant le Haut Moyen Age," *Médiévales*, no. 40 (2001): 83–100; Mary Douglas, *Purity and Danger: An Analysis of the Concepts of Pollution and Taboo* (London: Routledge & Keegan Paul, 1966).

37. Jacques Dalarun, *L'impossible sainteté: La vie retrouvée de Robert d'Arbrissel* (Paris: Éditions du Cerf, 1987).

38. Dalarun, *L'impossible sainteté*, 297–98.

This case of a prohibition levied against women to access sanctuaries is not an isolated example: it echoes in other hagiographical texts, like the *Life* of Saint Calais, a hermit of the Perche. Was it simply a matter of a rigid application of the Rule of Saint Benedict, based on the fear that the sight of women might turn monks away from their ascetical life? Or was it a taboo as found in many other religious contexts, based on the idea of a fundamental impurity in women tied to her menstrual flow, which could elicit divine chastisement upon the sanctuary and its residents?[39] In fact, beginning in the second half of the twelfth century, a middle way seems to have prevailed in many cases. At the Cathedral of Durham in northern England, for example, where the relics of Saint Cuthbert were venerated, a chapel reserved for women was built so that they might be able to worship, without being seen by the monks who ministered in the church. And in the last centuries of the Middle Ages, papal dispensations granted to abbeys and priories in possession of precious relics multiplied, allowing "the daughters of Eve" to enter most sanctuaries, even those of a monastic type, without too much difficulty.

According to studies by Pierre-André Sigal on miracles in France during the twelfth and thirteenth centuries, around 60 percent of pilgrims belonged to the lower classes (a statistic that rises to more than 70 percent for English sanctuaries in the fourteenth and fifteenth centuries). These sociological realities are even more difficult to grasp as they evolve over time. The sanctuary of Rocamadour, for example, seems to have been visited in the twelfth century mostly by aristocrats and only later attracted more common classes, among them numerous women.[40] At Malmedy in the sixteenth century, in a small book of the miracles performed by its patron, Saint Quirin, society appears in all its diversity. The miracles involve artisans—a tanner, a stonecutter working on the church tower, a blacksmith, a carpenter building a new granary—as well as laborers: a digger and a craftsman. Priests, too, were among those healed, as well as many from the bourgeoisie in Malmedy or elsewhere (Maastricht, Liège, Tongres, and Namur). Equally involved, too, was the *familia* of the monastery itself. Although it might be impossible to identify them in a more precise fashion, the given names of pilgrims do not seem to have been made up; on the contrary, these references

---

39. Jacques Dalarun, *Dieu changea de sexe, pour ainsi dire: La Religion faite femme, XIe–XVe siècle* (Paris: Fayard, 1985).

40. Pierre-André Sigal, *L'homme et le miracle dans la France médiévale (XIe–XIIe siècle)* (Paris: Éditions du Cerf, 1985).

are, for the hagiographer, an additional mark of the authenticity of the miracles, to which the "little people," some from the countryside, could testify.[41]

The Route

In the eleventh and twelfth centuries, the primary holy places in Christianity—Jerusalem, Rome, or Compostela—were far from where most pilgrims lived. The distance in time and space was thus an essential aspect of the access to sanctuaries, and in the course of their journeys, pilgrims were led to discover peoples whose customs often seemed strange to them, and to connect to a sacred past that impressed them all the more because they saw it through the eyes of faith. Before going to Rome in 1349, Birgitta of Sweden dreamed of discovering this city "where the streets and places are red with the blood of the martyrs," which helps to explain her disappointment when she subsequently stayed there for a long time. But the length of the voyage and the difficulties of the journey did not seem to have discouraged them, since there are numerous examples of repeat pilgrimages. As previously noted, the count of Anjou, Fulk III the Black, went to Jerusalem three times in the eleventh century; in the thirteenth century, the lay saint Bona of Pisa († 1207) and the Blessed Facio of Cremona († 1272) traveled, respectively, nine and eighteen times to Compostela over the course of their lives. The importance of the road in the eyes of the pilgrim lay in the fact that it marked their passage from a profane space to a sacred one, by means of an initiatory journey often marked by privations, dangers, and suffering, enabling them to cover the distance separating them from their goal in the quickest way possible. Numerous testimonies relating to Santiago de Compostela emphasize the joy experienced by pilgrims when they arrived at Mount Gozo, from which they could make out the sanctuary henceforth, now so close, and the disappointment of some among them when they realized, upon arriving at the basilica, that the apostle's relics were inaccessible.

For a long time, in the wake of scholarship by Joseph Bédier and Elias Lambert, historians believed that pilgrimage "routes" existed in the Middle Ages, along which *chansons de geste* and Romanesque art were born, from oral traditions and stylistic influences transmitted by

---

41. George, *Reliques*.

pilgrims who traveled them, especially between France and Compostela: "In the beginning was the road. . . ." The formula is lovely but largely inaccurate. In fact, historians of literature and art were deceived by a twelfth-century text that became famous thanks to its being frequently cited: *Iter pro peregrinis ad Compostellam* (*Guide for the Pilgrim to Compostela*). It constitutes the last part of the *Liber sancti Jacobi* or *Codex Calixtinus*, attributed (falsely) to Pope Calixtus II († 1124), whereas it was actually from the years 1140/50.[42] The author of this "guide"—probably a French cleric from Parthenay, in the Poitou, named Aymeric Picaud—describes four possible itineraries for traveling from northern France and the Midi, across the Pyrenees, and toward Galicia: (1) from Toulouse through Arles, Saint-Gilles in the Gard, and Saint-Guilhelm-le-Desert; (2) from Le Puy through Sainte-Foy de Conques; (3) from Vézelay to Limoges, Saint-Léonard-de-Noblat, and Périgueux; and (4) from Tours—the most detailed route in the book—through Poitiers, Saintes, Blayes (where the remains of Roland, considered as a martyr, could be venerated), Bordeaux, and Belin (where the bodies of Olivier, Ogier, and a few of their companions—"dead for the faith of Christ"—were buried in the "Field of Charlemagne"). This description gave birth to a map, similar to present-day road maps, that has often been reproduced in historical works, contributing to the widely disseminated idea that there had been paths to Santiago de Compostela, "routes of faith" that believers would have faithfully followed along their journey. This assertion is all the more questionable given that the *Guide* is preserved in only a small number of manuscripts, and therefore seems to have been little used in the Middle Ages.

Closely studying surviving accounts of pilgrims shows that, in fact, most followed itineraries that were rather different from those described in the *Guide* and that only partially align with the four routes it describes (figure 32).[43] Many of those who came from northern Europe avoided Tours and Bordeaux, preferring to pass through Blois, Berry, and Périgueux, or to reach the Midi via the Regordane Way, which cuts across the Auvergne and Languedoc. Further, these accounts do not

---

42. Latin text in *Liber Sancti Jacobi Codex Calixtinus*, ed. Klaus Herbers and Manuel Santos Noia (Santiago de Compostela: Xunta de Galicia, 1998), 235–58. Available in French as *Le Guide de pèlerin de Saint-Jacques de Compostelle*.

43. Humbert Jacomet, *Les Chemins de Saint-Jacques de Compostelle* (Vic-en-Bigoree: MSM, 1999); Marcel Girault and Pierre-Gilles Girault, *Visages de pèlerins au Moyen Age: Les pèlerinages européens dans l'art et l'épopée* (La-Pire-qui-Vire: Zodiaque, 2001); Denis Péricard-Méa, *Compostelle et cultes de saint Jacques au Moyen Age* (Paris: Presses universitaires de France, 2000), 395.

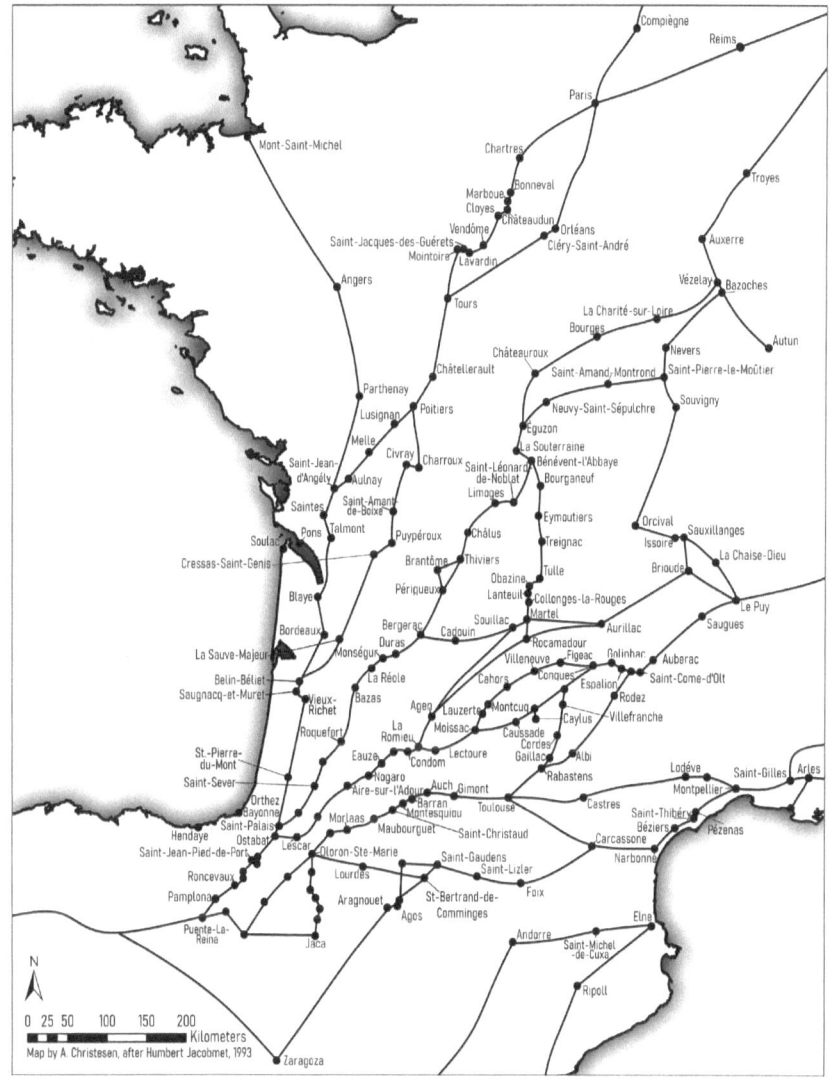

FIGURE 32. Main routes followed by French pilgrims to Santiago de Compostela in the Middle Ages. Credit: A. Christesen.

include certain great sanctuaries, like Rocamadour, and in travels from Le Puy, Conques is the only such shrine to be mentioned. While the author of the *Guide* devotes long sections to the road from Arles to Toulouse, passing through Saint-Gilles, the majority of pilgrims seem to have taken the more direct route though Nîmes and Montpellier, or chosen alternative routes like the one that, in passing through Auch and Tarbes, ends up at Col du Somport, a pass through the Pyrenees. Finally, the only cathedral-sanctuaries that are named in the pilgrims' accounts are those of Orléans, Périgueux, and Arles; but the author of the *Guide*, when he describes the relics found there, does not mention their names nor even indicate that they are cathedrals!

Taking these anomalies and inexactitudes into account, it seems more appropriate to see the *Guide* as an attempt to capture preexisting pilgrim flows and clientele networks for the benefit of Santiago de Compostela, in particular those that gravitated around the Abbey of Saint-Gilles. This abbey was at the time one of the most visited sanctuaries by pilgrims from northern Europe, which would explain the abundance of details the narrator provides about its golden reliquary, its founder, and the miracles that occurred there. By integrating the Via Egidiana with the routes to Compostela, the *Guide*'s author elevates the prestige of Santiago de Compostela by conferring on it a centrality that it did not yet have in Europe at that time. Finally, it is a polemical work that aims to eliminate competing sanctuaries in favor of those it recommends: the monks of Corbigny in the Nièvre are accused of deception because they claimed to possess the body of Saint Leonard, which then risked to do harm to Saint-Léonard-de-Noblat in the Limousin, as well as to Chamalières in the Upper Loire; or again the canons of Saint-Gilles in the Cotentin, who prided themselves on having the relics of Saint Gilles, whereas the remains of the holy hermit reposed intact in the great abbey in the Gard that bore his name.[44]

Beyond this particular case, important as it is, it is worth considering the notion of the road in the Middle Ages. As Giuseppe Sergi has shown, it was less a well-defined and signposted route than a zone of mobility within which different routes were possible to reach a given town or direction.[45] To get from one point to another, there existed numerous,

---

44. *Le Guide du pèlerin de Saint-Jacques de Compostelle*, 53–55.

45. Giuseppe Sergi, "Il pellegrinaggi altomedievali e lo spaesamento della communicazione," in *Communicare e significare nell'alto Medioevo* (Spoleto: CISAM, 2007), 1165-88; Céline Perol, ed., *Faire la route (IIIe–XXe siècle)* (Clermont-Ferrand: Presses universitaires Blaise Pascal,

interchangeable itineraries depending on the season, the weather, and the political situation in the territories to be crossed, except for the Spanish part of the Camino de Santiago, which was marked out by a network of monastic, canonical, or municipal hospitality establishments, spaced out according to the distance a pilgrim could travel in a day. This remark also applies to the Via Francigena or Via Romea—as it was called from the ninth century—that led travelers from the north of France to Rome, and was extended southward by way of the Via dell'Angelo (Way of the Angel) that went through Montecassino to reach the great sanctuary of Monte Sant'Angelo on Mount Gargano.[46] This was the route followed by the archbishop of Canterbury, Sigeric, when he went to Rome in 989, where he arrived after marking out eighty stops. The itinerary followed by pilgrims changed over the years: the coastal road, the Via Aurelia, was abandoned in the sixth century, after the Gothic Wars, and so the north-south route was switched to one in the interior of Italy (figure 33). Crossing the Alps in the Frankish period, the most frequented passes were Mont-Cenis, for those coming from Gaul, and Grand-Saint-Bernard for the faithful coming from Germany. The two routes converged in Piacenza, site of the only bridge over the Po River, after which pilgrims went either by Monte Bardone or over the Cisa pass to Lucca in Tuscany, in order to venerate the aforementioned Volto Santo (Holy Face); they then crossed the Arno at Altopascio, which had a large hospice for pilgrims dedicated to Saint James, went on to Siena, where one took the Via Cassia down to Rome, while passing through Bolsena and Monte Mario, a kind of Montjoie from which pilgrims could contemplate the city of Rome before descending toward it. This is essentially the route that Nicholas of Munkathvera, the abbot of Thigor in Iceland, followed, when he went to Rome in 1153, after passing through Utrecht and the Rhine Valley. Having arrived in the Eternal City, he went to venerate the Blood of Christ at Saint John Lateran and his foreskin, the clothing and a few drops of milk from the Virgin Mary, as well as the bones of Saint John the Baptist. He then got back on the road toward Monte Sant'Angelo and reached the port of Brindisi, where he embarked on a ship for Jerusalem.

2007); Ludwig Schmugge, "Die Anfänge des organisierten Pilgerverkehrs im Mittelalter," *Quellen und Forschungen aus italienischen Archiven und Bibliotheken* 64 (1984): 1–83.

46. Paolo Caucci von Saucken, ed., *Il mondo dei pellegrinaggi: Roma, Santiago, Gerusalemme* (Milan: Jaca Book, 1996), 137–86.

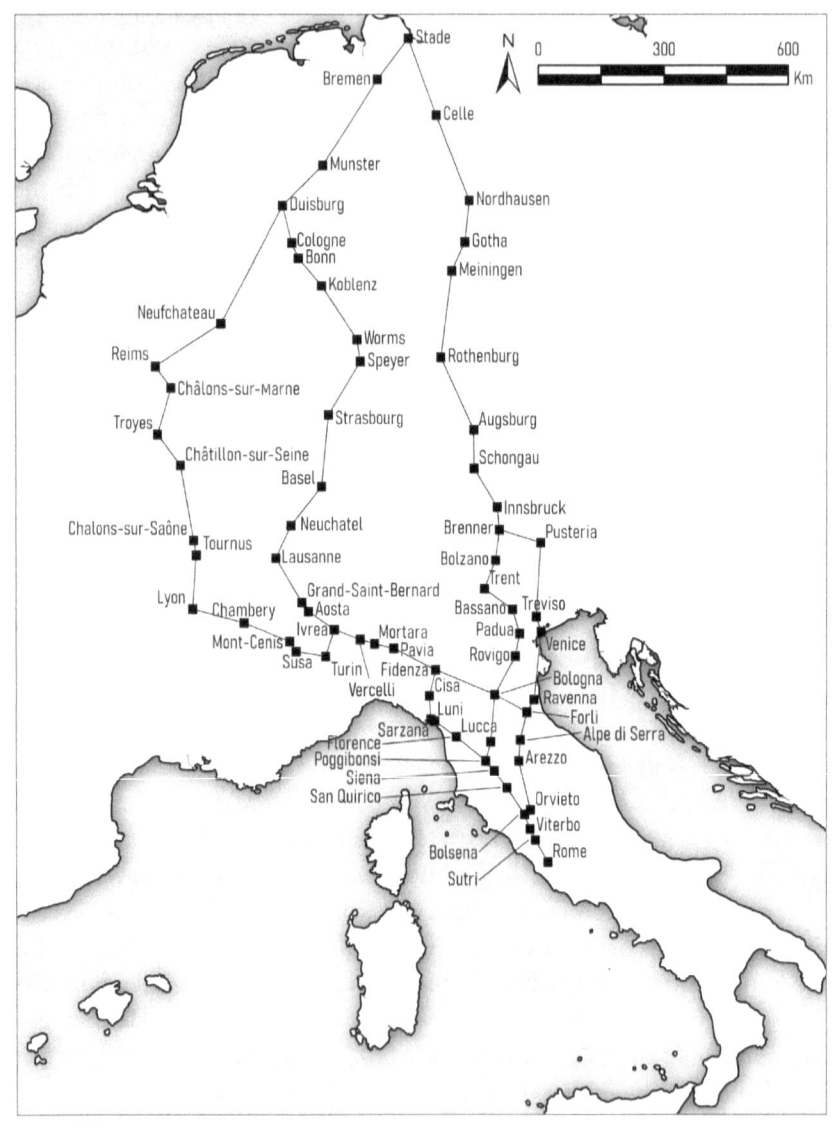

FIGURE 33. Pilgrimage routes from German cities to Rome in the thirteenth century. Credit: A. Christesen.

In the thirteenth century, however, as the testimony of the English monk Matthew Paris and the itinerary of Eudes Rigaud, archbishop of Rouen and a Franciscan, both show, numerous pilgrims from northern Europe preferred to leave the Via Francigena above Fidenza to take the Via Emilia, which led them through Parma, Bologna, and Florence. Then they reached Arezzo and from there, Assisi, where they venerated the tomb of Saint Francis, before going on to Rome through Spoleto on the Via Flaminia.[47] But soon the Roman routes became so diverse that it was no longer possible to fit them into preexisting frameworks. In 1254, Eudes Rigaud crossed over the Alps through the Simplon pass, by which he reached Milan; pilgrims from German-speaking lands, though, increasingly took the Saint Gothard pass or the Brenner pass to the city of Verona. During the last centuries of the Middle Ages, Umbria—along with Assisi, Perugia, and Foligno—played a strategic role in the pilgrimage to Rome or Loreto, as well as for the southern Italians traveling to Santiago de Compostela. Finally, the importance of maritime routes should not be overlooked, especially those that connected Pisa to Saint-Gilles, and then to Catalonia, which allowed pilgrims to avoid the fatigue and dangers of the overland route.

Moreover, the roads to Rome weren't just for pilgrims; they were also frequented by travelers from one city to another, merchants, and, above all, clerics—increasingly numerous after the Gregorian Reform—who went to the Roman Curia to settle the affairs of their monastery or diocese, or to obtain a benefice. In addition, during some periods, they were joined by crusaders seeking to reach the ports of Apulia (Barletta, Bari, Otranto, Brindisi) and ship out for the East. After 1250, with the loss of the Holy Land by Latin Christians, this last part of the route was increasingly less traveled, and in the fourteenth century, the sanctuary of Gargano lost the international profile that it had enjoyed since the early Middle Ages to become a regional sanctuary, devoted to penance and to prayers for the dead. All in all, the only itineraries in Italy that could be reasonably called established "pilgrimage routes" were the paths used by shepherds to move their flocks from the plains to the mountains and back, according to the seasons, but also by pilgrims from Tuscany or Umbria who were journeying to Apulia to visit Monte

---

47. Renato Stopani, *La via Francigena: Una strada europea nell'Italia del Medioevo* (Florence: Le Lettere, 1988).

Sant'Angelo.⁴⁸ The same can be said about the roads that took pilgrims from the region around Paris to Mont-Saint-Michel. In the modern era, it is well known that young people and their companions seem to have followed routes marked out by hospices and small towns where they could be easily welcomed. In the medieval period, however, pilgrims arrived at the Mont by very different roads, according to their point of departure, and it does not appear that there was a preferred route used only by them.

The Sanctuary: The Place and the Memorial

A sanctuary can be defined both as a natural space, enriched by the objects that made it sacred, and as a religious monument. Most of them included a chapel or church, even if some were simple caves in which an altar had been installed.

Cosmic Places and Historical Places

There was not always a direct relationship between the sacred character of a sanctuary and the landscape into which it was inserted. Some of these sites—down in a valley or out on a plain—had nothing particularly special about them. Many of them, however, were distinguished by a remarkable environment that contributed to their power of attraction. As Alphonse Dupront has underscored about the pilgrimage to Rocamadour, "It is the site that imposes its law, and it is already a cosmic certitude to which everything here contributes": the layering of the sanctuary on several levels, the ascent to the grotto along a dark valley, set between two rocks, by a 216-step *scala santa*, "which favors the ascent to heaven while remaining on earth, the vertical of salvation experienced in depth or in the bowels of the earth but under the light of heaven"; then, beneath a twelve-meter overhang, the sacred place where the Black Madonna stands, "at once a chthonic consecration and a physical manifestation of the link to the East" (figure 34).⁴⁹ Added to this was the presence of a fountain dedicated to Our Lady (Notre Dame), from which the pilgrim always collected water, and a visit to the tomb of Saint Amadour, considered by local tradition to be a servant

---

48. Mario Sensi, *Santuari e pellegrini lungo le "vie dell'angelo": Storie sommerse del culto micaelico* (Rome: Istituto Storico Italiano per il Medioevo, 2014).

49. Dupront, *Du sacré*, 315–39.

FIGURE 34. A view of the village of Rocamadour in France. Dynamosquito via Wikimedia Commons (CC BY-SA 2.0).

of the Holy Family, whose body, found intact in 1166, represented for them a promise of integrity and eternity.

A comparable analysis could be made, mutatis mutandis, of the grotto of Saint Michael on Mount Gargano, of Notre-Dame of Montserrat in Catalonia, or of the Franciscan sanctuary of La Verna in Tuscany, at the top of a stark mountain where scattered blocks of stone seem to have been thrown around by an earthquake, which medieval authors compared to the one that, according to the Gospels, accompanied the death of Christ on Golgotha. The importance of the mineral element here is notable, a sign of the presence in these sites of a supernatural power expressed through the grandeur, durability, and appearance—the shape and color—of the rocks. These sanctuaries, characterized by Dupront as "cosmic," differ from both "historical" places connected to apparitions of the Virgin Mary or "ancient" ones where holy statues were "discovered" or that were rendered sacred long ago by the presence of the tomb of a saint or relics.[50] But these differences remain secondary, insofar as

---

50. Dupront, *Du sacré*, 432–60.

pilgrims were not driven in their quest by the location of the shrine to which they went, but by their desire to reach a place of intercession and there experience an encounter, accompanied or followed by an "improvement," which could affect the body as well as the soul, the world here below as well as the hereafter.

The Memorial

Most of the time, sanctuaries took the form of human-built memorials, usually churches. During the early Middle Ages, the centerpiece of these buildings was the main altar, where the Eucharistic sacrifice was celebrated as a priority during the community Mass. At Saint-Michel de Cuxa, around the year 1000, Abbot Oliba had a baldachin built above the high altar, similar to the one that protected the Ark of the Covenant in Solomon's Temple. In the liturgical rituals of the time, the altar is said to refer to Jerusalem, from where Christ's message had spread.[51] From the sixth century onward, however, altars and relics began to converge more and more frequently. Gregory the Great recommended placing the main altar above the tomb of a saint, in the choir of the church, but this practice took hold only slowly, and certain holy bodies were sometimes buried under the portico, as at the Chapel of Saint-Symphorian in the abbatial church of Saint-Germain-des-Prés. Beginning in the seventh century and continuing into the Carolingian period, we see circular crypts appearing in sanctuaries, on the model of Saint Peter's in Rome (*more romano*), with separate access for those allowed to enter the choir. In this way, pilgrims could give free rein to their devotion in the church basement or at the far end of its choir, without disrupting the liturgical life of the canons or monks.[52] But this evolution was more marked in northern France than in the Mediterranean region; in Italy, for example, the adoption of elevated choirs maintained the use of crypts that were level with the nave.

Over the centuries, relics increasingly proliferated within churches: at the Abbey of Saint-Riquier, in Picardy, in the time of Abbot Angilbert († 814), there were twelve altars served by monks. Architectural evolution accompanied the development of relics within buildings and

---

51. Éric Palazzo, *L'espace rituel et le sacré dans le christianisme: La liturgie de l'autel portatif dans l'Antiquité et au Moyen Age* (Turnhout: Brepols, 2008).

52. Pierre Gillon and Christian Sapin, eds., *Cryptes médiévales et culte des saints en Île-de-France et en Picardie* (Villeneuve d'Ascq: Septentrion, 2019).

the monumentalization of sanctuaries. The famous plan of Saint-Gall (ca. 830), which presents a kind of ideal model of the Benedictine monastery, reflects the presence and hierarchical organization of the saints, whose remains were inserted in nineteen altars inside the church. From the tenth century, with the Norman invasion of the northern half of France and the "Saracen" incursions in the Mediterranean regions, holy bodies and remains were often enclosed within wooden or precious-metal reliquaries that could be easily transported to avoid being pillaged or destroyed; this ended up multiplying the sites where they could be venerated. In the eleventh and twelfth centuries, crypts became widespread in France and Italy, and their plans took on a variety of forms, with the construction of vast hall-crypts containing three vessels designed to showcase the relics and allow people to see the tombs of the saints. This evolution became even more pronounced in the last centuries of the Middle Ages, when a whole network of chapels linked to aristocratic families or to devout or professional brotherhoods developed, especially in the churches of the mendicant orders. These were reserved for members of the group that exercised a right of patronage and gathered there on certain dates to celebrate the memory of its celestial protector and affirm its collective identity. In the countryside, the development was not the same, and sanctuaries often took the form of chapels scattered throughout rural areas.

From the thirteenth century onward, sanctuaries began to elevate the sarcophagus or tomb in which the relics of the saint venerated there had been deposited.[53] The new sepulcher housing them was often supported by four columns, as if to signify the condition of the soul of God's servant in the afterlife (figure 35). To explain this elevation, the most frequent biblical reference was the passage from Saint Matthew's Gospel, which speaks of "a lamp burning on a lampstand to give light to all who see it" (Matt. 5:15–16).

The clerics who served at the sanctuary had to find the means to reconcile two contradictory demands: to assure the protection of the relics against theft with a whole set of barriers and grills, while at the same time allowing pilgrims to get as close to them as possible, and sometimes to even touch them, in such a way as to assure the transmission of the *virtus* from the saint to the devout through a process not too dissimilar from contagion.

---

53. Michele Tomasi, *Le arche dei santi: Scultura, religione e politica* (Rome: Viella, 2012).

FIGURE 35. The reliquary shrine of Saint Thibault, thirteenth or fourteenth century, Saint-Thibault-en-Auxois, Côte-d'Or. Photo: MOSSOT via Wikimedia Commons (CC BY 3.0).

Generally speaking, the purpose of the monument was to highlight the celestial nature of the body resting there. But whatever its shape and size, the sanctuary endured above all in the sense that it was the repository of a communal history made up of stones, paintings, inscriptions, rites, and oral traditions. Through the objects and images found there, which reflected the building's cult stratigraphy and devotion, it served as a collective memory for the human and social groups associated with it.

Lights and Scents

One of the aspects of the sanctuary that is most often mentioned in pilgrims' accounts is the presence of abundant sources of light inside the edifice, especially close to the reliquary being venerated. The church was a space "seen" more than "heard," even if Bernard d'Angers, in the *Book of the Miracles of Sainte-Foy*, evokes the "rustic cantilenas" of the pilgrims who came to disturb the quiet of the monks. Numerous accounts and documents mention the presence of candelabras and crowns of gold covered with candles suspended from the ceiling: upon arriving, the pilgrim lit a candle before the reliquary of the saint whom they had come to implore and, in some places, votive candles offered by the sovereigns or municipal authorities burned day and night near the tomb. But the purpose of all this lighting went beyond its utilitarian function. Catherine Vincent has clearly demonstrated the importance of lighting in the Middle Ages, an era in which the saints were considered to be and depicted as beings of light.[54] To have a candle burning—a sign of gratitude—in their honor was both a rite of participation and a testimony to their celestial glory, with which the pilgrim endeavored to be associated in order to benefit from their propitiatory power. Some of these candles were scent-bearing and released a fragrance along with its flame. The floor of the sanctuary—clay in the most modest of structures—was strewn with flowers on the occasion of feasts and ceremonies, and their scent, mingling with the whiff of incense administered by the clergy, contributed to make of the sacred space a garden of delights.

The Devotional Practices

Enter, See, and Touch: A Tactile Piety

To enter a space considered sacred was not a pedestrian activity. According to numerous testimonies that have come down to us, visitors to sanctuaries seem to have experienced a wonderment that was not merely sensory; the moment they crossed over the threshold, it gave them access to a place where it was possible to come into contact with relics or other traces of a saintly person and, through their mediation, with God. This threshold was a transitional space that allowed the faithful to pass from the secular world to the spiritual plane. Significantly, the pilgrim did not travel to Rome or Compostela but, rather, "to the threshold of Saint Peter" (*ad limina beati Petri*) or Saint James, as if, in entering their "places," they were crossing a frontier. Engraved inscriptions, moreover, sometimes reminded visitors of the conditions required to ensure that their visit to the sanctuary was not considered sacrilegious: "If you do not refrain from repeating your sinful deed," stated one of those at the entrance of a French Marian shrine in the twelfth century, "refrain from

---

54. Catherine Vincent, *Fiat Lux: Lumière et luminaires dans la vie religieuse du XIIIe au XVIe siècle* (Paris: Éditions du Cerf, 2004), 692.

crossing over this threshold, for the Queen of Heaven desires a worship without stain!"[55]

Most of the faithful hoped to appropriate, at least for a moment, the power of the saint whose relics were venerated. Hence the importance of touching, of having a physical contact with, the holy place and, to the extent possible, with the relic or image, the sight of which marked the end of the pilgrimage. They would kiss the threshold of the sanctuary or the statue of the saint, as witness in the ritual of *abrazo* at Santiago de Compostela, thus associating the use of the senses with the ritual and the sanctity of the place. Such practices were not exceptional, as the example of three small sanctuaries in Umbria demonstrates.[56] At San Paterniano, near Sellano on the mountain of Spoleto, on the right-hand side of the chapel there is a huge stone with an incision and a small cavity attributed, respectively, to the staff and the elbow of a holy bishop of Fano, Paterniano (who, in the fourth century, had stopped there on the way to Rome to rest and to pray). Pilgrims who were suffering from back or joint pain kneeled, placed themselves on the slab of stone in the same position as had the holy bishop, and then arose relieved of their ills. They then went into the small neighboring church to venerate his statue and to place ex-votos in thanksgiving. Upon leaving, they stopped by the enormous beech tree, reputed to be as old as the sanctuary itself, and the clear stream from which they drank the water, by way of devotion, before returning home or celebrating with other pilgrims. Not far from there, at the Abbey of Sant Eutizio, the tomb of the founding saint of the monastery, which was reputed to heal migraines, was venerated. Visitors had to put on an iron helmet that belonged to the saint, before passing under his tomb in the hope of being healed. Finally, at Pale, near Foligno, the sick came on pilgrimage to the hermitage of Santa Maria Giacobbe to place their diseased or crippled feet within the imprint that the saint—the mother of the Apostles James the Lesser and James the Greater, who according to local tradition, retired here at the end of her life—left in the wall of the mountain, and to place their fingers into the holes that she had carved there with her own hands. After this, they rubbed the suffering parts of their bodies against

---

55. *Corpus des inscriptions de la France médiévale*, vol. 18, *Allier, Cantal, Loire, Haute-Loire, Puy-de-Dôme*, ed. Robert Favreau, Jean Michaud, and Bernadette Mora (Paris: CNRS, 1995), 110.

56. Mario Sensi, "Santuari terapeutici di frontiera nella montagna folignate," in Sensi, *Vita di pietà e vita civile di un altopiano tra Umbria e Marche (secc. XI–XVI)* (Rome: Edizioni di storia e letteratura, 1984), 239–74.

the rock. As the author of *Le Guide de pèlerin de Saint-Jacques* has written regarding the sanctuary of Saint-Gilles: "Who will embrace more fully his tomb? Who will kiss his venerable altar or tell the story of his pious life?" (Quis amplius amplexabitur sarcophagum? Quis osculabitur eius altare venerandum aut quis vitam suam piisimam enarrabit?)[57]

In the great sanctuaries, pilgrims crowded around the tombs or reliquaries. This pious jostling is described by Abbot Suger († 1151) in his account of the consecration of the Basilica of Saint-Denis:

> At times you could see, a marvel to behold, that the crowded multitude offered so much resistance to those who strove to enter in to worship and kiss the holy relics, the Nail and Crown of the Lord, so that no one among the countless thousands of people because of their very density could move a foot; that no one, because of their very congestion, could [do] anything but stand like a marble statue, stay benumbed or, as a last resort, scream.[58]

Other practices of this type are attested elsewhere. At Déols, in Berry, where a certain Saint Greluchon was venerated, women slept on his tomb so that he might help them conceive a child or, at the Cathedral of Embrun—with the same aim—swallowed wine mixed with a little powder scraped from the statue of the saint that was called "holy vinegar." The practice of *vinage*, which consisted of spreading wine, water, or oil on a saint's tomb and then collecting the precious liquid into vials or ampules, was widely practiced. At Reading Abbey in England, the hand of Saint James was periodically dipped in a vat of water, which was then distributed to pilgrims. In Sancerre, the arm of Saint Maurice was plunged into wine, whereas in Pisa, the whole body of Saint Rainier was soaked on the occasion of his feast day. These therapeutic drinks were highly prized and often became the object of a lively trade.

To Implore and to Threaten

In some cases—unfortunately all too rare—certain practices of supplication that took place in the sanctuaries are noticeable. According to the

---

57. *Le Guide de pèlerin de Saint-Jacques de Compostelle*, 38–39.
58. *Abbot Suger on the Abbey Church of St.-Denis and Its Art Treasures*, ed. Erwin Panofsky (Princeton, NJ: Princeton University Press, 1946), 87–89. See also Suger, *De consecratione ecclesiae S. Dionysii*, ed. Françoise Gasparri (Paris: Les Belles Lettres, 1996); Françoise Autrand, Claude Gauvard, and Jean-Marie Moeglin, eds., *Saint-Denis et la royauté: Études offertes à Bernard Guenée* (Paris: Publications de la Sorbonne, 1999).

miracles reported by the abbot of Saint-Pierre-sur-Dives in Normandy, for example, the reconstruction of his monastery, where a statue of the Virgin Mary was venerated, was accompanied by a wave of fervor among the faithful, who volunteered to drag carts filled with materials and foodstuffs intended for the workers. On this occasion, "children" (more likely young people) joined the adults who performed flagellations in the church to obtain from the Virgin Mary the healing of five people who had been brought because they were ill.[59] Four of them immediately recovered their health, but as the health of the fifth lagged behind, they threw themselves on the ground naked and crawled up to the altar in tears; there, they shouted at the image of the Virgin, reproaching her for her inaction, as well as at the Holy Innocents, imploring them to not despise children of their own age. Returning to the main altar, they ended up obtaining satisfaction.

In fact, faith in the power of relics was so great that it sometimes pushed the clergy and laity to defy them—indeed to humiliate them—if their requests were not heard. For there was a kind of moral contract between the faithful and the saints they venerated, based on the idea that the petitioner should obtain the help of the celestial figure whom they had addressed, as soon as their obligations had been fulfilled. If the supplicant was not then answered in return, it was permissible for that individual to force the saint to act, publicly mocking their impotence and sometimes even assaulting their iconographic representations. Caesarius of Heisterbach, for example, a Cistercian, recounts in his *Dialogus miraculorum* (around 1230) the story of a woman named Jutta whose daughter, three years old, had been snatched by a wolf near the castle of Valdenz. After searches in the nearby forest failed to find the child, who had been vowed to Mary, the mother attacked an ancient statue of the Virgin with Child, "endowed with great power" according to the chronicler, snatched the infant Jesus from his mother's breast, and told her: "You will never have your child back until you give me back mine safe and sound!"[60] A little later, the little girl was found unharmed, although the story does not say whether the mother apologized after her assault on the Virgin Mary.

---

59. *Chronique de Saint-Pierre-sur-Dives*, cited by Jean-Marie Sansterre, "Sacralité et pouvoir thaumaturgique des statues mariales (X^e-première moitié du XIIIe siècle)," *Revue Mabillon*, n.s. 2 (2011): 53–77.

60. Jean-Marie Sansterre, "Quand les textes parlent des images: Croyances et pratiques," in *Les images dans l'Occident médiéval*, ed. Jérôme Baschet and Pierre-Olivier Dittmar (Turnhout: Brepols, 2015), 169–78.

As Lester K. Little and Patrick Geary have shown, such attitudes were not at all exceptional, and there is evidence, in the eleventh and twelfth centuries, of similar practices in various religious communities. When the latter were involved in a conflict with a local lord over the ownership of certain landed domains, the monks might petition the saints whose relics they held in their abbey to strike down the usurper with a punishment that would force him to give up his claims.[61] If the miracles they were awaiting did not occur, the monks did not hesitate to remove the relics from their altars and place them on the ground to shame them for their lack of action and invite them to avenge themselves. This ritual was known as "the humiliation of the saints."

The Feasts

Going on pilgrimage did not merely consist of reaching and visiting a holy place. It also meant entering a "suspended time," the rhythm of which was not the same as that of ordinary life. For local sanctuaries, a community's collective pilgrimage generally took place on the saint's feast day, once a year, although this did not prevent individuals or families from going there on other occasions. In the great sanctuaries, there were generally several feast days each year when the faithful flocked there in droves. Each had its own purpose and often its particular audience. The Sanctuary of Monte Sant'Angelo had no fewer than three. On May 8, the Apparition of the Archangel, which had allowed the Lombards to win the day over their pagan adversaries, was celebrated, and Saint Michael was venerated as prince of the heavenly armies coming to the aid of Christians in their struggle against demons and other forces of evil. On September 29, Michael's feast day, the accent was put on his role as "guardian of paradise," and pilgrims especially sought his intercession for the dead and for the souls in purgatory. And finally, October 16, the anniversary of the dedication of Mount Gargano's underground basilica in 1021 was commemorated, marked by a number of liturgical ceremonies that attracted the clergy in particular.

In the last centuries of the Middle Ages, the influx of pilgrims to holy places was mainly determined by the indulgences they could obtain by going on pilgrimage on the day of a saint's feast, the night before (the

---

61. Patrick Geary, *Furta sacra: Thefts of Relics in the Central Middle Ages* (Princeton, NJ: Princeton University Press, 1978); Lester K. Little, *Benedictine Malediction: Liturgical Cursing in Romanesque France* (Ithaca, NY: Cornell University Press, 1993).

vigil), or during the octave (the week following the feast). In Marian sanctuaries, for example, the faithful were granted indulgences on the feasts of the Virgin Mary, the number of which grew steadily over time, from the Annunciation (March 25) to the Assumption (August 15), via the Purification of Mary or Candlemas (February 2), and the Visitation (May 31), which was added to the calendar at the end of the fourteenth century.

In local sanctuaries, the saint's feast usually began with a Mass and was followed by a procession. Sometimes there were two feasts. In the Argonne, for example, villagers in the region went each year on September 17 to Saint Rouin, an isolated hermitage belonging to an abbey, which had become a sanctuary with the construction of a chapel dedicated to this local hermit. But the more popular feast was the "Rapport," which took place on Whit Monday. People enjoyed a meal on the grass, drank water from the fountain, then danced, boys and girls alike. As Serge Bonnet has noted, this is not to say that there was no religious fervor, but "this festival, with such deep human roots, was the expression of a certain attachment to the Christian hermitage . . . and the young people served as the clergy of this popular festival."[62]

The same was true in Provence where *romérages* (processions of relics) in honor of a village's patron saint were the occasion for a procession to his sanctuary—a genuine memorial site for the community. This was marked by the presence of young people who gave themselves over, on this occasion, to extravagances and noisy demonstrations known as *bravades*, the goal of which was to publicly extol the glory of their saint, more powerful than the one in a neighboring village, and to reach "a level of self-transcendence where the distinction between the sacred and the profane was abolished."[63]

Pilgrims' expressions of hope did not take such violent forms everywhere. In Montevergine, a great abbey located not far from Naples, a miraculous icon of the Virgin Mary was venerated, known locally as Mamma Schiavona, because its Byzantine hieratic style suggested it had come from the Balkan regions, then known as Sclavonia. Pilgrims, mostly young girls, would go there barefoot and, after having honored the image of the Madonna, sang and danced, as if the fact of being in a

---

62. Serge Bonnet, *Entre Champagne et Lorraine: Histoire de l'ermitage et du pèlerinage de Saint Rouin* (Nîmes: Éditions Lacour-Ollé, 1996), 184.

63. Marie-Hélène Froeschlé-Chopard, *Espace et sacré en Provence (XVIe–XXe siècle): Cultes, images, confréries* (Paris: Éditions du Cerf, 1994).

sacred space allowed them to manifest a very free and festive religiosity, different from the ordinary expressions of faith in the parish setting.[64] In the Meuse region, pilgrimages were oriented toward the famous centers where treasuries were displayed according to a schedule that varied from sanctuary to sanctuary. These ostentations were particularly important in the context of devotional events. In the region around Maastricht, a Pilgrimage of the Relics took place every seven years to honor the relics held by sanctuaries in Maastricht, Tongeren, Aix-la-Chapelle, and Kornelimünster. During this septennial event, pilgrimage was encouraged with indulgences and festivities of all kinds that accompanied the holy *kermesse* (church festival). In Maastricht, the relics were shown to the pilgrims from the top of the gallery of the apse of the Basilica of Saint Servatius, facing the city's main plaza, the Vrijthof. To mark this occasion, pious images were brought out and displayed, and stories about the life of the saint and pilgrimage badges were made available.[65]

Miracles

A miracle can be defined as a historical event in which humanity's primary needs with regard to bodily integrity, pain, and death are manifested.[66] During the period addressed in this book, a sanctuary was, above all else, a place—church, chapel, or grotto—where miracles occurred. Most often, these miracles were connected to the presence of relics or holy images, but this was not always the case. For example, in Sainte-Catherine-de-Fierbois in Touraine, there was a chapel that enjoyed its heyday for about a century after 1375, and in 1429 was visited by Joan of Arc, who had come to pray to the saint to give her the strength to drive the English out of France.[67] However, this edifice possessed no relics or effigies of the Alexandrian saint (Catherine). In

---

64. Genoveffa Palumbo, *Giubileo, giubilei: Pellegrini e pellegrine, riti, santi, immagini per una storia dei sacri itinerari* (Rome: Rai Eri, 1999).
65. George, *Reliques*, 218.
66. Benedicta Ward, *Miracles and the Medieval Mind: Theory, Record and Events, 1000–1215* (Philadelphia: University of Pennsylvania Press, 1987); André Vauchez, *Saints, prophètes et visionnaires: Le pouvoir surnaturel au Moyen Age* (Paris: Albin Michel, 1999), 79–98; Sofia Boesch Gajano and Marilena Modica, eds., *Miracoli: Dai segni alla storia* (Rome: Viella, 2015); Nicolas Balzamo, *Les miracles dans la France du XVIᵉ siècle* (Paris: Les Belles Lettres, 2014).
67. *Le Livre des miracles de Sainte Catherine de Fierbois*, ed. Yves Chauvin, Archives historiques de Poitou 60 (Poitiers: Société des archives historiques du Poitou, 1976); Christiane Deluz, "Un pèlerinage en Touraine au XVᵉ siècle: *Le Livre des miracles* de Sainte Catherine de Fierbois," in *Auctoritas: Mélanges offerts à Olivier Guyot*, ed. Giles Constable and Michel Rouche (Paris: Presses universitaires Paris-Sorbonne, 2006), 635–45. On the cult of Saint Catherine in the

fact, it had only become famous when a citizen of Fierbois, paralyzed and blind, remembered an abandoned chapel he had glimpsed one day, deep in the forest, and decided to go there in the hopes of being delivered from ills that were afflicting him. His servants cut a path through the forest with hatchets and took him to the chapel where he prayed a novena, at the end of which he was fully healed. News of the event spread rapidly throughout the region, and a blind woman from Angers, having invoked Saint Catherine, recovered her sight there as well. Subsequently, the sanctuary's reputation only grew, as evidenced by the *Livre des miracles de Fierbois*, which lists no fewer than 237 cases of miraculous deliverance, most of which (69 percent) involved the release of prisoners during the Hundred Years' War. The sanctuary of "Madame Saint Catherine" then became a reference point for supplicants who solicited her intercession "in remembrance of her beautiful miracles," and then went on pilgrimage to Fierbois to give thanks. This case is not exceptional. In Rocamadour, too, there were originally no relics: the statue of the Virgin Mary dates back to the beginnings of the cult, and it was only in 1166 that the intact body of Saint Amadour was discovered there, identified as a servant of the Holy Family. Everything seems to have happened as if the Virgin had chosen to manifest herself directly through miracles, as Saint Catherine would do at Fierbois two centuries later.

Traditional Miraculous Happenings at the Sanctuaries

Up to the thirteenth century, many of the men and women who went to sanctuaries were *contracti*—people afflicted with paraplegia and partial or total paralysis. According to Pierre-André Sigal's study of five thousand miracle accounts recorded in France in the eleventh and twelfth centuries, those afflicted with mobility problems represented around a third of the total.[68] Next came cases of blindness and deafness, and finally nervous or mental disorders, quite clearly differentiated from madness, which was attributed to demonic possession. At the conclusion of a novena, some pilgrims, having made a vow to the saint whose relics they were venerating, saw a brilliant light, followed by a

---

Middle Ages, see Jacqueline Jenkins and Katherine J. Lewis, eds., *St Katherine of Alexandria: Texts and Contexts in Western Medieval Europe* (Turnhout: Brepols, 2013).

68. Sigal, *L'homme et le miracle*; Luigi Canetti, "'*Olea sanctorum*': Reliquie e miracoli tra Tardoantico e Medioevo," in *Olio e vino nell'Alto Medioevo* (Spoleto: CISAM, 2007), 1335–1415.

cure: bones reset in place with a loud noise and contracted nerves were loosened, and they would emerge, even though everyone had seen them enter the sanctuary on a stretcher, standing on their own, having left their crutches behind as ex-votos.

These different categories of miracles figure prominently in a text from the end of the twelfth century about the miracles produced in Cremona, in Lombardy, on the day after the death of Saint Homobonus († 1197), a pious laymen canonized by Innocent III two years later:

> The Lord who opens the eyes of the blind and raises up the lame, who has opened the eyes of the one born blind, made straight the legs of the paralytic and promised to his disciples that they would be able to do the same, has given back sight to numerous visually impaired and blind and has made the lame to stand up again through the intercession of Saint Homobonus. . . . By his merits, he has untied the tongue of the mute and blocked that of those who uttered iniquity. Indeed, the tongues of those who had spoken ill of his miracles swelled up to the point that they rightfully became mute. But just as a bad conscience gnaws at him, he formulated a vow in his heart and his tongue then became loosened, so that he might be able to express his shame and his repentance. Another one, injured in the neck during combat in Jerusalem [at the time of Jerusalem's conquest by Saladin in 1187], had lost his voice for ten years, and many others of both genders who had suddenly lost it and fully came to know him, believed in him and recovered the use of their voices. What more is there to say? . . . Another—a child of ten years who was blind and mute since birth—thanks to the desires of his parents, received the use of his sight and tongue and began to give praise to God. Even among those who were possessed by unclean spirits, many were freed.[69]

This is, of course, a hagiographical text, the author of which was undoubtedly Bishop Sicard of Cremona, a well-educated man; and one should not see in this description a realistic snapshot of miracles accomplished through the intercession of Saint Homobonus. This is clearly demonstrated in the section devoted to the healing of the mute, in which the author describes another wonder that can be found in almost all medieval collections of miracles: the punishment of the

---

69. André Vauchez, *Saint Homebon de Crémone, "père des pauvres" et patron des tailleurs: Vies médiévales et histoire du culte* (Brussels: Subsidia Hagiographica, 2018), 78–83.

unbeliever who doubted a saint's thaumaturgical power. It is obvious here that Sicard has a tendency to interpret the phenomena he witnessed in terms of Christ's miracles as described in the Gospels, which are all about the blind, the deaf, the mute, paralytics, and demoniacs, and to classify them according to the infirmities concerning the different senses. But, as this text is close to the event that he is describing, it must reflect to some extent the specific pathology of the sanctuaries and the climate of exaltation that prevailed there. Some paintings of the fifteenth century and the beginning of the sixteenth century take account of this particular atmosphere and the desires of the pilgrims who gathered around the tombs or images of saints (figure 36).[70]

Among the miraculous healing practices mentioned in the sources is "incubation," which took place while the pilgrim slept, following the appearance of the saint to whom they had appealed. It often occurred at the end of a long journey that signified, for the sick person, a physical, moral, and emotional rupture with their usual life. Having entered the sanctuary, they would immediately find themselves in an extraordinary and spectacular setting, whether a grotto or a crypt, which must have made a profound impression. This was heightened by the contrast between the darkness of the site itself and the light diffused by the candles, as well as by the whiffs of incense and melting wax that one breathed in. Being able to stay there for long periods, surrounded by sympathetic people, helped to pacify their soul and relax their muscular and nervous tensions, paving the way for the pilgrim's return to normality. Many of the healed spoke about a dream or celestial vision that inspired a cathartic phenomenon, after which the saint's intervention allowed the supplicant to be liberated from the clutches of the dark forces at the root of their illness.[71]

According to Gregory of Tours, around 15 percent of miraculous healings followed a vision of the saint by the pilgrim during sleep, in close proximity to the saint's tomb. Pierre-André Sigal found the same percentage in the miracles in the eleventh and twelfth centuries. This

---

70. This is the case especially with the painters Gentile da Fabriano (concerning the relics of Saint Nicholas of Bari), of Josse Lieferinxe (for those of Saint Sebastian in Rome in 1497), and of the Master of Saint Agilof (on the predellas of the altar of this saint at the Cathedral of Cologne in 1521). See also Henri-Jacques Stiker and Alain Blanc, *Le handicap en images: Les representations de la déficience dans les oeuvres d'art* (Toulouse: Erès, 2005).

71. François-Olivier Touati, "Guérisons et apparitions en Orient et en Occident: Réflexions sur l'incubation," in *Purifier, soigner ou guérir*, ed. Cécile Chapelain de Serville-Niel, Christine Delaplace, Damien Jeanne, and Pierre Sineux (Rennes: Presses universitaires des Rennes, 2020), 153–58; Luigi Canetti, "L'incubazione cristiana tra Antichità e Medioevo," *Rivista di storia del cristianesimo* 7 (2010): 149–80.

FIGURE 36. Gentile da Fabriano, *The Crippled and Sick Cured at the Tomb of Saint Nicholas*, 1425. National Gallery of Art, Samuel H. Kress Collection.

type of healing seems to have had to do, in particular, with those afflicted with fevers or neurological and vascular pathologies, and to have been more frequent in the small local sanctuaries, like the tomb of the holy priest Thomas Hélye († 1257) in Biville, in Normandy, where this category accounts for 20 percent of the miracles reported in the second half of the thirteenth century. Later, healings of this type are much less frequently attested. That does not mean that recourse to incubation might have disappeared, but it became suspect in the eyes of the higher clergy, who were inclined to see in it the surviving traces of paganism and probably avoided mentioning incubation in order not to harm the cause of the saint and his sanctuary.

The Evolution of the Typology of Miracles

Between the thirteenth and fourteenth centuries, the clientele of sanctuaries and the typology of the miracles produced in them evolved. Whereas until then the petitioner's presence near the tomb of the saint was required for their wish to be granted, afterward a growing number of healings were obtained at a distance, in which case the pilgrimage to the holy place was instead a manifestation of gratitude.[72] Also, as time moves forward, the percentage of healing miracles declined. According to the surviving documentary evidence, they comprised an average of 90 percent of the total number of miracles in the eleventh and twelfth centuries, and almost 80 percent in the thirteenth century, as witnessed in Provençal sanctuaries (550 of 700).[73] From the middle of the fourteenth and fifteenth centuries, however, they constituted no more than half of all miracles, as attested by the miracles at Saint-Martial de Limoges in 1388, and at Sainte-Catherine-de-Fierbois, as well as those that occurred in Scandinavia at the same time.[74] The thaumaturgical function of the saints thus lost some importance at the expense of their protective function—in the broader meaning of the term—from successful births and the release from prison of men-of-arms and those condemned to be hanged, to shipwrecks avoided and finding lost objects. Another feature was the growing importance of children and the illnesses and misfortunes that could befall them. Increasingly, there are examples of miracles concerning stillborn children or those smothered by their parents in the conjugal bed or drowned in the moats of castles and windmills, which were previously quite rare. Likewise, miracles concerning women and their specific illnesses were recorded in greater numbers. Generally speaking, from the end of the Middle Ages, saints were invoked in all of the difficult or tragic circumstances of life.[75] They were the figures to whom people turned when they were lost in the woods or at sea, if a fire broke out in their house or they were snatched by robbers or soldiers in time of war.

---

72. Vauchez, *La sainteté en Occident*, 530–58.

73. Gérard Veyssière, "Miracles et merveilles en Provence aux XIIIe et XIVe siècles," in *Miracles, prodiges et merveilles au Moyen Age* (Paris: Publications de la Sorbonne, 1995), 91–114; Thuaudet, "La pratique du pèlerinage en Provence."

74. Jean-Loup Lemaître, "Les miracles de saint Martial accomplis lors de l'ostension de 1388," *Bulletin de la Société archéologique et historique du Limousin* 102 (1975): 66–139; Anne Carion, "Miracles de saint Martial," in *Les miracles, miroirs des corps*, ed. Jacques Gélis and Odile Redon (Saint-Denis: Presses de l'université de Paris VIII, 1983), 87–124; Christian Krötzl, "Miracles au tombeau—miracles à distance: Approches typologiques," in *Miracle et Karama: Hagiographies médiévales comparées*, ed. Denise Aigle (Turnhout: Brepols, 2000), 557–76.

75. Vauchez, *La sainteté en Occident*, 540–58; and Vauchez, *Saints, prophètes et visionnaires*.

Petitions and Prayers

In late medieval accounts of miracles, petitions and accompanying prayers are often explicitly mentioned and seem to have played an important role. Faced with imminent danger or a humanly insoluble problem, the man or woman would address a brief invocation to God, asking him to intervene in their favor through the merits of a saint to whom they referred spontaneously or on another's counsel. Then they made a vow, which was a real commitment, as evidenced by the fact that monastics could not make it without the authorization of their superior. The questioning of witnesses during canonization proceedings has preserved many such formulas. The conviction expressed was almost always the same: The petitioner "renders" to the saint whom he or she invokes by name or whom they invoke on behalf of another, entrusting to that saint in some way the ownership and responsibility for it. In the case of a miracle, the supplicant commits to go to the sanctuary, barefoot and in shirt and undergarments, and place there a waxen image, as well as an offering of food or money, symbolized in England by a coin that was bent for that purpose. They would plead with the saint to use the "credit" they had earned from God through their merits and sufferings in order to restore them (or their loved ones) to health or to rescue them from a precarious situation. In practical terms, this "donation" meant that those making such hopeful petitions would bring to the sanctuary a candle that was the same height or weight as the petitioner. It was the same for communities: towns offered to their heavenly protector a thread coated with wax that was equal in length to the circumference of their walls, as was the case at Valenciennes from the eleventh century right up to the COVID-19 epidemic. As Catherine Vincent has aptly stated: "The vertical flame rising to the sky is matched by the more horizontal measure of the body's gravity or the extent of the dwellings, in a synthesis successfully achieved by the wax candle that combines materiality and immateriality."[76]

The use—in this time quite common—of the "circling" of a saint's tomb or of a city with a wax-coated thread has sometimes been interpreted as a "magic" rite, without further explanation. The reality is more complicated. These requests were often accompanied by other types of ascetical commitments (like the promise to fast each year on a saint's feast day) or charitable promises (like feeding a certain number

---

76. Vincent, *Fiat lux*, 448.

of poor people on that day). In fact, through the ritual of measuring, the supplicant sought to circumscribe the sacred while being inserted within it, in such a way as to create a particular link between oneself, the saint, and the place where the latter's power was being demonstrated. These practices do not appear to have become objects of criticisms or reservation on the part of the clergy, and they were presented in canonization processes as the "external manifestation of an interior devotion." The clerics who were in charge of sanctuaries could, for their part, only rejoice to see the cured confirm, through their healing or deliverance, the reputation of the power of their patron saint.[77] The sixteenth century, however, witnessed the beginning of attempts to regulate these practices; in 1563, the thirty-fifth session of the Council of Trent defined conduct when observing a miraculous event: A miracle should not be made public or be made into an object of devotion until the local bishop had recognized its supernatural character and approved its circulation. This reduced by a considerable amount the number of miracles that were recorded.

Offerings and Ex-Votos

Once cured or delivered from an evil that was weighing them down, pilgrims were sure to offer thanks to the Virgin or the saints for the favor that they had been granted and, if they had the means, to show their gratitude through gifts to the poor and to the sanctuary. The offering made by the faithful on this occasion was more than a simple act of thanksgiving. It had to be seen as the symbolic restitution of the gift received and the establishment of an implicit pact between the supplicant and his or her heavenly protector in the form of a vow. This ritual, which consisted of "untying the vow," allowed the blessed to be freed from their commitment to the saint by being released from their promise.[78] To refuse to do so was considered a unilateral rupture of the contract that bound them. In the miracle collections and hagiographical texts, the negligence of the ungrateful pilgrim led to a recurrence of the evil that had disappeared, until they came to their senses and undertook to keep their commitments as soon as possible. On the other hand, if the petition had not produced its anticipated effect, the

---

77. Vauchez, *La sainteté en Occident*, 636.

78. Christian Krötzl, *Pilger, Mirakel und Alltag: Formen des Verhaltens im skandinavischen Mittelalter* (Helsinki: Suomen Historiallinen Seura, 1994), 307–38.

petitioner maintained the right to turn to a more effective intercessor than the one they first solicited and thus to go to another sanctuary. Before leaving the holy place, pilgrims often left behind graffiti, especially in grottos or crypts, with their name and a short note of thanksgiving.

Then, as now, one of the chief characteristics of sanctuaries is the presence of ex-votos draped around the reliquary or the image of a saint or the Virgin, hanging on the walls of the edifice or gathered in a special room.[79] Ex-votos were objects in wax, wood, or metal offered to the shrine by the healed as a sign of gratitude. They could be either anatomical ex-votos, which reproduced the part of the body that was injured and healed, or historical ex-votos, which depict the accident or illness that gave rise to the miraculous intervention. This practice is as old as human civilization, and archaeologists have discovered quantities of ex-votos during excavations of shrines from the Greek and Roman periods, and even from prehistoric times. In the Middle Ages, as in antiquity, a good number of them represented parts of the body or organs. Thus, when the commission appointed by Pope Clement V to investigate the life and miracles of Saint Thomas de Cantilupe († 1282), visited his tomb in Hereford Cathedral in 1310, they found the following objects: 170 silver boats, 41 waxen boats, 129 images of men, women, or body parts in silver, 1,424 images of the same kind in wax, 77 representations of animals, 108 crutches, and a wooden cart for a paralytic.[80] The numerous boats offered as ex-votos obviously corresponded to shipwrecks that had been averted by sailors or merchants thanks to the intercession of the saint. Wealthy recipients of his intercession did not hesitate to offer objects made of silver or even gold. The collection of ex-votos placed around the reliquary or the holy *ymage* reaffirmed the sacredness of the place for those who had obtained graces there.

From the fourteenth century, more and more ex-votos were painted on a wooden frame or canvas, in the form of small tableaux representing both the donor, the danger they had escaped, and the supernatural patronage that had saved or healed them, and in a corner of the sky there would appear the figure of the Virgin Mary or of the saint they

---

79. Elisabeth Antoine, "Images de miracles: Le témoignage des ex-voto peints en Italie centrale (XIVᵉ–XVIᵉ siècle)," in Aigle, *Miracle et Karama*, 353–74; Michele Bacci, "Italian ex-votos and *Pro anima* Images in the Late Middle Ages," in *Ex-voto: Votive Giving across Cultures*, ed. Ittai Weinryb (Chicago: University of Chicago Press, 2016), 76–105; Ulrika Ehmig, Pierre-André Sigal, and Marie-Anne Polo de Beaulieu, eds., *Les ex-voto: Objets, usages, traditions. Un regard croisé franco-allemand* (Gutenberg: Computus Druck Sata & Verlag, 2019).

80. Vauchez, *La sainteté en Occident*, 530–36.

had petitioned. The focus of the composition is on the body and its preservation in the most diverse of situations. These paintings are often naïve and lacking in artistic merit, but they do testify to the gratitude of the believer toward one's heavenly protector and the search for salvation amid life's difficulties: illness and misfortune, but also accidents and natural catastrophes. They hint at the sufferings and pains of the supplicant but also the joy they and their loved ones would have felt after obtaining the requested favor. Above all, the ex-voto illustrates the power of prayer, which brings the unbearable or the deadly of the here-below into contact with the hereafter. Through the grace of the miracle, these two separate worlds share the same space for a moment, and it is this unforgettable encounter that the donor endeavored to clumsily celebrate in an image.

Souvenirs and Insignias

When leaving a sanctuary, pilgrims sought to carry away a token that they might bring home in order to hold onto their memory of the pilgrimage and to show to others their new identity as a devotee to one or another saint. Sometimes, a pilgrim brought back small stones or fragments found near the sacred place. In 1025, Fulk III the Black brought back from Jerusalem a small piece of the wall of the Holy Sepulcher, which he had pulled out with his teeth after softening the rock with his tears. Ampoules of glass or lead containing either waters from a sacred fountain or the liquid that sometimes flowed from a saint's tomb were also piously collected,[81] as were drops of the miraculous water or wine in which a saint's relics had been bathed, as at Canterbury, where water tinged with a few drops of the saint's blood was distributed to pilgrims, leading them to say, "Saint Thomas is the best physician."

The pilgrim's major mark of distinction was a metal badge (*signum*, in Latin) that he or she wore on their clothes or hats, notably the Saint James scallop shell attesting that they had indeed been to Compostela.[82] Each of the great sanctuaries had their own badge; thousands of them have been discovered, all very different from each other, in urban archaeological sites. The pilgrim's badge was not only a pious souvenir:

---

81. Canetti, "'*Olea sanctorum*.'"
82. Denis Bruna, *Enseignes de pèlerinage et enseignes profanes* (Paris: Réunion des musées nationaux, 1996); and Denis Bruna, *Saints et diables au chapeau: Bijoux oubliés du Moyen Age* (Paris: Seuil, 2007).

FIGURE 37. Pilgrim's badge with Saint Leonard, fifteenth century, lead and tin alloy. The Metropolitan Museum of Art, The Cloisters Collection, 1986.

it was "the saint in its own right" and a sign of the bearer's pilgrim identity, as was immediately clear from the appearance of the seal on which was depicted, sometimes very picturesquely, the intercessor venerated at the shrine just visited. These little objects, lightweight and fragile, made of lead or from an alloy of lead and tin, are exceptional historical testimonies of worship and devotion. They often show a representation of the saint who had been invoked and were intended to be worn, like a brooch, by means of a fastening device. The fabrication of these artifacts was doubtless incumbent on goldsmiths or engravers (figure 37).

It has often been asserted that sanctuaries went into decline during the final centuries of the Middle Ages, paving the way for their suppression by Protestant reformers in the sixteenth century. In fact, the reality is more complex and difficult to measure. This decline is well attested in England, where one sees a drop in visits, leading to a decline in offerings in the fifteenth century—with the exceptions of the tomb of Saint

Thomas à Becket in Canterbury and that of King Henry VI, venerated as a saint at Windsor Castle.[83] However, this did not seem to happen in France and Italy, and the number of pilgrimage sites grew appreciably in the Germanic and Scandinavian world in this period. Where crowds and miracles declined, however, the cause was not necessarily a sign of disaffection but rather a change in the way saints were worshiped. With the multiplication of their images in churches and chapels, the faithful tended to invoke the saints through these "intermediaries" or petition them, in cases of a vital urgency, where they happened to be found, while the visit to a sanctuary became simply the occasion for them to show their gratitude for the grace or miracle they had received through their intercession.

---

83. Ronald Finucane, *Miracles and Pilgrims: Popular Beliefs in Medieval England* (New York: Palgrave Macmillan, 1977).

Chapter 5

Capitalizing on the Sacred

Lay Authorities

The origins of sanctuaries often lie in the hands of the laity, either sovereigns or great lords—anxious to assert or sacralize their power by building a religious edifice designed to ensure the survival of their memory and that of their families—or members of the lower classes: shepherds, peasants, or even children who had benefited from an apparition or celestial vision. In the eyes of the faithful, sanctuaries were indeed places chosen by God to manifest himself to humanity. But they could not be developed without the support of the authorities, both secular and ecclesiastical, who often played a fundamental role in their birth and survival.

To Own and Consolidate the Sacred: The Treasuries of Relics

Elites were not slow to recognize the considerable prestige that the possession of relics could bring them, and in the West, a number of rulers, on the model of the Byzantine emperors, sought to create treasuries containing great numbers of relics. A function of kings in the ecclesiology of the early Middle Ages was, in effect, to be the guardians not only of churches but also of the sacred treasuries that constituted a guarantee of salvation for both them and their people.[1] One of the first rulers in the West to thus establish a collection of precious religious objects was Alfonso II the Chaste, king of Asturias, who in 802 created, in his palace in Oviedo, a chapel dedicated to the Holy Savior in which he placed objects that had been rescued from the Muslims during their conquest of Spain.[2] Charlemagne did the same in his residence of Aix-la-Chapelle, enriching the church dedicated to Saint Mary, built according to a central octagonal plan surrounded by an ambulatory, and the imperial chapel with relics and works of art. Visitors came here to venerate the robe of the Virgin Mary, the swaddling clothes of the Child Jesus, the cloth in which the head of John the Baptist had been wrapped, and the linen that had covered the face of Jesus after his death.[3] From the eleventh century, because of a whole literary corpus that attributed to Charlemagne the deed—all purely mythical—of having gone on pilgrimage to Jerusalem, it was believed in the Middle Ages that he had brought back these precious relics from the Holy Land, to which were added those of numerous saints, in particular Saint Boniface, who had played a decisive role in converting the Germanic peoples to Christianity. Through this concentration of sacred objects, an exchange with the Invisible was supposed to occur: the guarantee of salvation for the ruler whose power was strengthened by this contact.

Subsequently, many kings and princes took their turn in appropriating the sacred. According to a story circulating in the twelfth century, the Holy Roman Emperor Henry II († 1024), having heard during a visit to Monte Sant'Angelo in 1022 that the angels celebrated Mass in the grotto once a week at midnight, wanted to witness the event for himself, despite the ban on human beings entering the grotto on this occasion. After recommending himself to Saint Michael, he ducked into a corner and saw the angels enter. One of them detached himself from the procession and, after handing him a gospel, touched his leg to chastise him for his temerity, as a result of which the emperor remained lame for the rest of his life, like Jacob at the end of his fight

---

1. Jean-Pierre Caillet, *Les trésors des sanctuaires, de l'Antiquité à l'époque romane* (Paris: Picard, 1996).

2. Philippe George, *Reliques: Se connecter à l'au-delà* (Paris: CNRS, 2018), 308–9.

3. Philippe Cordez, *Les trésors au Moyen Age: Discours, pratiques et objets* (Florence: SISMEL, 2010); Philippe Cordez, *Charlemagne et les objets: Des thésaurisations carolingiennes aux constructions mémorielles* (Bern: Peter Lang, 2012); Philippe Cordez, *Trésor, mémoire et merveilles: Les objets des églises au Moyen Age* (Paris: EHESS, 2016); Krzystof Pomian, *Des saintes reliques à l'art moderne: Venise-Chicago, XIIIe–XXe siècle* (Paris: Gallimard, 2003).

with the angel.⁴ His successor, Conrad II († 1039), had the Holy Lance inserted, along with pieces of the True Cross, within the *Reichskreuz* (the Imperial Cross), which was used for imperial coronations. In the middle of the fourteenth century, Charles IV († 1378), who had been raised in Paris and was impressed by the Sainte-Chapelle, brought back with him from France a thorn from the Crown of Thorns that had been preserved there. After his election as Holy Roman Emperor, he gathered together all of the imperial relics into the castle he built in Karlstein, close to Prague, placing them in the Chapel of the Holy Cross, where they became the object of a liturgical cult.⁵ The precious treasury was only opened to the public once a year, and those who witnessed it were graced on this occasion with an indulgence granted by Pope Innocent VI in 1354. This practice was maintained by the Emperor Sigismund († 1437) who, in 1424, transferred the relics and the regalia of the imperial treasury to Nuremburg. Various princes of the Holy Roman Empire followed this example. In the sixteenth century again, the duke of Saxony and protector of Luther, Frederick the Wise († 1546) established a collection of more than seventeen thousand relics—which had to be worth to him tens of thousands of years of indulgences! Later still, King Philip II of Spain († 1598) did the same in the palace he built at the Escorial, the architectural plan of which was inspired by the shape of the stake of Saint Lawrence.⁶ For all of these rulers, the fact of possessing relics was a guarantee of their prestige in this world and a talisman for the afterlife.

Generally speaking, the majority of those who held power in the Middle Ages and in the early modern era showed a lively interest in relics and sanctuaries, and this devotion has been at the foundation

---

4. According to the *Vita sancti Heinrici imperatoris (additamentum)*, ed. G. H. Waitz, Monumenta Germaniae Historica, Scriptores 6 (Hannover: Hahn, 1841), 818-20. On the policy of the relics of the dukes of Normandy in the tenth and eleventh centuries, see Lucile Trân-Duc, "Les princes normands et les reliques (X^e-XIe siècles): Contribution du culte des saints à la formation territoriale et identitaire d'une principauté," in *Reliques et saintetés dans l'espace médiéval*, ed. Jean-Luc Deuffic (Saint-Denis: PECIA, 2006), 525-61.

5. David Mengel, "Bohemia's Treasury of Saints: Relics and Indulgences in Emperor Charles IV's Prague," in *Les saints et leur culte en Europe centrale au Moyen Age (XIe–début du XVIe siècle)*, ed. Marie-Madeleine de Cevins and Olivier Marin (Turnhout: Brepols, 2017), 57-86; and Pierre Monnet, *Charles IV, un empereur en Europe* (Paris: Fayard, 2020). See also Iva Rosario, *Art and Propaganda: Charles IV of Bohemia, 1346–1378* (Woodbridge: Boydell, 2000).

6. Guy Lazure, "Posséder le sacré: Monarchie et identité dans la collection de reliques de Philippe II à l'Escorial," in *Reliques modernes: Cultes et usages chrétiens des corps saints, des Réformes aux Révolutions*, ed. Philippe Boutry, Pierre-Antoine Fabre, and Dominique Julia (Paris: Éditions de l'EHESS, 2009), 372-404.

of important collections of relics. According to the testimony of the monk Helgaud de Fleury, Robert the Pious († 1031) spent a good part of his reign going from one sanctuary to another to venerate relics: those of Saint Stephen in Bourges, Saint Maieul in Savigny, Saint Julien in Brioude, among many others—and this practice was unexceptional. In accordance with his coronation vow, the Capetian king was merely fulfilling his oath by praying to God, the Virgin Mary, and the saints for the prosperity of his kingdom. Indeed, the presence of the king at one or another sanctuary is frequently attested to in the chronicles of the period.

The Dynastic "Pantheons"

In line with this trend, lay rulers sought to ensure the continuity of their memories and of their dynasties by founding churches and especially monasteries laden with prestigious relics, a practice that dates to the sixth century in western Europe. It is sufficient to mention two great French abbeys. Saint-Médard in Soissons was built around 557 by King Chlothar I to house the relics of the bishop of Noyon to whom the church was dedicated and where some Merovingian rulers had themselves buried. It was rebuilt and considerably enlarged during the reigns of the Carolingian emperors Louis the Pious and Charles I the Bald before being redone once again in the eleventh century.[7] But the most striking example is that of the Abbey of Saint-Denis.[8] From the seventh century, Denis—considered the first bishop of Paris, martyred in the third century—was one of the privileged patron saints of the dynasties that governed France, beginning with Charles the Bald who was buried in the abbey in 877. The Robertians carried on this same tradition, and Eudes, lay abbot of Saint-Denis, was buried there as well in 888. The first mention of the *vexillum* or oriflamme (the royal sacred banner) that was kept in the abbey dates to 923. Suger rebuilt and widened the shrine around 1130, and the king came there to pray to the saint before going off to meet Emperor Henry IV in battle, who was preparing to

---

7. Abbé Delanchy, "Étude historique," in *Saint-Médard: Trésors d'une abbaye royale*, ed. Denis Defente (Paris; Somogy, 1997), 53–69.

8. Colette Beaune, *Naissance de la nation France* (Paris: Gallimard, 1985); English trans: *The Birth of an Ideology: Myths and Symbols of Nation in Late Medieval France*, trans. Frederic L. Cheyette (Berkeley, CA: University of California Press, 1991); and Françoise Autrand, Claude Gauvrard, and Jean-Marie Moeglin, eds., *Saint-Denis et la royauté: Études offertes à Bernard Guenée* (Paris: Publications de la Sorbonne, 1999).

invade the kingdom. Philip II Augustus would do the same in 1214 to thank Saint Denis after his victory at Bouvines. Around the middle of the thirteenth century, Saint Louis had the tombs of all the kings of France consolidated at Saint-Denis. It was the same in other countries of Christendom. For example, in 1063, Ferdinand I, king of Castile, and his spouse, Sancha of León, founded a royal pantheon in the Church of Saint Isidore in Oviedo, after Abbad II al-Mu'tadid, emir of Seville, authorized the transfer of the relics of Saint Isidore—one of the principal figures of the Spanish Church—there. The earliest structure had been destroyed, and the new, much larger church was consecrated in 1146 by the archbishop of Toledo, in the presence of King Alfonso VII, who had imperial aspirations.[9] In general, the kings and princes who founded or expanded these sanctuaries entrusted their administration to monks or canons belonging to communities or religious orders known for their great spirituality. This did not always suffice to make these sites into active sanctuaries, but the acquisition of precious relics, like those of Saint Sebastian, brought back from Rome to Saint-Medard in 826 by the Abbot Hilduin or, especially, those of Saint Louis placed at Saint-Denis in 1270, with the miracles that accompanied them, did not fail to attract crowds.

Imitating these rulers, whose political prerogatives they wanted to latch onto, their principal vassals, in their turn, sought, after the tenth century, to procure prestigious relics for themselves and to develop cults around them through processions. The first counts of Flanders multiplied their holdings of holy bodies, the principal beneficiaries of which were the abbeys of Saint-Bertin and Saint-Pierre on Mont Blandin in Ghent, which was the preferred place of burial for members of the count's family from 918 to the middle of the eleventh century.[10] Once they consolidated their power in the territorial area they controlled, these feudal lords chose a prestigious monastery as the dynastic pantheon for the deceased of their lineage. The count of Flanders, Arnulf of Ghent († 964), when he had conquered Ponthieu, confiscated the relics of Saint Riquier and Saint Valery and transferred them to the

---

9. Patrick Henriet, "Oviedo, Jérusalem hispanique au XIIe siècle," in *Pèlerinages et lieux saints dans l'Antiquité et le Moyen Age: Mélanges Pierre Maraval*, ed. Béatrice Caseau, Jean-Claude Cheynet, and Vincent Déroche (Paris: Association des amis du Centre d'histoire byzantine, 2006), 245–60.

10. Edina Bozoky, "La politique des reliques des premiers comtes de Flandres (fin du IXe siècle–fin du XIe siècle)," in Edina Bozoky, *Le Moyen Age miraculeux: Études sur les légendes et les croyances médiévales* (Paris: Riveneuve, 2010), 42–61.

Abbey of Saint Bertin. He also acquired the treasury of relics from the Abbey of Saint-Wandrille (Fontenelle), which he placed at the Abbey of Saint-Pierre on Mont Blandin. But in 980, Arnulf's grandson, Arnulf II, had to hand over Saint Riquier's relics to his sovereign lord, Hugh Capet, who was seeking to increase his own dynastic legitimacy. Baldwin V, one of Arnulf's successors, fortified Lille in the middle of the tenth century, where he established the collegiate church of Saint-Pierre; on the occasion of its dedication in 1065, he gathered all of the relics held in the churches of Flanders there.

An Italian example—that of Sardinia—illustrates the close collaboration between the clergy and the ruling classes regarding sanctuaries.[11] In the eleventh and twelfth centuries, the island's judges—the leaders of its four districts—all committed themselves to the construction of important churches, like that of San Gavino in Torres (which later became the Cathedral of Logudoro). Around 1100, the judge of this region, Constantine I († 1127), and his wife Marcusa—who had gone to Torres to implore the saint to give them an heir after the deaths of their children—stopped at a place called Saccargia, which had been a sacred site in antiquity; an angel appeared and announced that their prayer would be answered if they built a sanctuary dedicated to the Holy Trinity there. Having taken this vow, and with the approval of the archbishop of Torres, they built a splendid church there in 1112, which still stands today, and they soon had the son they wanted. Constantine I was buried there, and it soon became a place of pilgrimage for the inhabitants of the region and, in particular, for couples unable to have children. After a period of neglect in the fourteenth century, the Basilica of the Holy Trinity of Saccargia (Santissima Trinità di Saccargia) was restored by the Spanish rulers who had conquered the island (figure 38). But from then on, it was a wooden statue of the Virgin Mary, to whom miraculous powers were attributed, that in particular attracted pilgrims.

This investment in religious architecture was motivated not only by political prestige, but also for economic and social reasons: the island's beautiful Romanesque churches, built by Pisan master craftsmen, exerted a strong attraction on the inhabitants of these regions, encouraging their settlement and the development of new lands around them. Often entrusted to the Camaldolese, an austere and prestigious monastic order, they became penitential sanctuaries where the inhabitants

---

11. Maria Giuseppina Meloni, "Il fenomeno santuariale in Sardegna," in *I santuari cristiani d'Italia*, ed. André Vauchez (Rome: École Française de Rome, 2007), 203–15.

FIGURE 38. The Basilica of the Holy Trinity of Saccargia, Sardinia. Photo: Wojtek Piotrowski via Wikimedia Commons (CC BY-SA 4.0).

of the area came on pilgrimage to seek pardon for their sins, in the absence of a sufficient and trained secular clergy. We find the same process at work at San Giorgio de Suelli, in the judiciary of Cagliari; this place commemorated Saint George, appointed bishop of Barbagia around the year 1000, and one of the most popular saints of the region. The sanctuary, where pilgrims came to venerate his relics, to which numerous miracles were attributed, was supported from its founding by the ruling family, which had made donations up to the beginning of the thirteenth century.[12] Later, in Sardinia as throughout the rest of Christianity, bishops played a growing role in the creation or appropriation of new sanctuaries These latter places could not, however, welcome the local populations and pilgrims until they had been approved by the local ordinary (bishop), either through a dedication ceremony

---

12. Maria Giuseppina Meloni and Olivetta Schena, eds., *Santuari d'Italia: Sardegna* (Rome: De Luca, 2020), especially 238–41 and 291–94.

(if it was a matter of a new church) or the translation of relics (if the church predated their recognition).

The Political and Religious Role of Sanctuaries in the Last Years of the Middle Ages: Holy Chapels

The most remarkable of these sanctuaries that were established by lay powers is undoubtedly the Sainte-Chapelle, built by Louis IX on the Île de la Cité in Paris after 1239 to house the Crown of Thorns that he had just purchased from the Venetians. Commemorative Masses for the dead of the royal family were celebrated here in front of the holy relics. A feast day for the Crown of Thorns was instituted on August 11, while the feast of the dedication of the Sainte-Chapelle took place on April 26.[13] On major occasions, the church was open to the public, in particular on Good Friday, for showcasing the Crown of Thorns, performed by the sovereign in person, dressed in his royal vestments. On this occasion, the king of France was actually the officiant of the rite, and the Sainte-Chapelle a sanctuary of the royal religion. In subsequent years, twenty-one Byzantine relics were added to the collection, along with various sacred objects, most of which were connected to the Passion of Christ. Only the king had access to this precious treasury and could thus fully play his role as mediator between heaven and earth.

For a long time, there existed a particularly close link between the relics of the Passion of Christ and the imperial or royal reputation, which thus explains the value that sovereigns attached to them in the Middle Ages. Already in the fourth century, Saint Ambrose had mentioned to Emperor Theodosius that one of the nails of the Cross had been inserted into the diadem of Constantine to inspire in him true wisdom; later Frankish and then Germanic emperors endeavored to procure pieces of the Holy Cross and later generously distributed fragments of it to bishoprics and abbeys that lay within their jurisdiction. After the acquisition of the Crown of Thorns and other relics of the Passion, the treasury of the Sainte-Chapelle became the palladium of France. With Saint Louis, the Capetian dynasty claimed a divine investiture that placed the king of France above all other sovereigns of Christendom.

---

13. Chiara Mercuri, *Saint Louis et la couronne d'épines: Histoire d'une relique à la Sainte-Chapelle* (Paris: Riveneuve, 2011); M. Cecilia Gaposchkin, "Between Historical Narration and Liturgical Celebrations: Gautier Cornut and the Reception of the Crown of Thorns in France," *Revue Mabillon*, n.s., 30 (2019): 91–145.

The transfer to Paris of the relics of the Passion sanctioned the *translatio imperii* that had occurred in the Christian world, after the fall of Constantinople in 1204, to the benefit of the French monarchy and in the person of Louis IX, the "new Solomon" and restorer of the Law of Christ in the West.[14] The erection of the Sainte-Chapelle, temple of the New Covenant and housing the relics of the Passion, made this supremacy visible. It was in turn manifested by sending thorns from the Crown to certain sovereigns, like the kings of Norway and Scotland, as well as to various cathedrals or sanctuaries of Christendom, from the abbey of Saint-Maurice of Agaune in the Valais, up to Vicenza in northern Italy, where the Dominicans, engaged in the struggle against heretics, dedicated their conventual church to the Holy Crown (Santa Corona) following a gift made by Saint Louis. After the death of Frederick II in 1250, no other ruler except the king of France could consider themselves as the temporal and spiritual leader of Christianity.

Later, in 1298, Philip the Fair sought to bring back to the Sainte-Chapelle the relics of Saint Louis, which had been placed in Saint-Denis upon their return from Tunis. But the monks firmly opposed this, and the king had to make do with his grandfather's head, which was transferred to Paris and placed in the Sainte-Chapelle in 1306. In the fourteenth and fifteenth centuries, the kings of France built other holy chapels, such as that in Vincennes under Charles V, and the blood relatives imitated them by creating their own, based on the Parisian model: in Viviers-en-Brie, Bourbon-l'Archambault, Bourges, Dijon, Champigny-sur Veude, and Aigueperse in the Auvergne.[15] Each was given a thorn from the Crown of Thorns and a fragment of the True Cross so as to radiate out into the provinces the charisma of Saint Louis and his descendants.

As Bernard Guenée has shown, the devotion of the kings of France in the fourteenth and fifteenth centuries was divided between three sacred poles: Saint-Denis, where Charles VI went to retrieve the fleur-de-lis oriflamme each time he left on a military campaign and where he had the relics of Saint Louis placed within a luxurious reliquary in 1392; the Sainte-Chapelle, where the king showed the relics of the True Cross to the people every Good Friday; and especially Notre-Dame

---

14. Beaune, *Naissance de la nation France*. See also Daniel Weiss, "Architectural Symbolism and the Decoration of the Ste.-Chapelle," *Art Bulletin* 77 (1995): 308–20.

15. Claudine Billot, "Les saintes-chapelles (XIIIe–XVe siècle): Approche comparée de fondations dynastiques," *Revue d'histoire de l'Église de France* 72 (1987): 229–48.

in Paris.[16] The piety of the kings of France effectively evolved along the same rhythm as that of their subjects, and the Virgin Mary held an increasingly important place, as illustrated by the interest that they brought to the church of Boulogne-sur-Seine (a satellite sanctuary of Boulogne-sur-Mer), particularly dear to Parisians after 1320. Philip VI offered Notre-Dame a silver statue of the king on his horse and a silver *ymage* of the future John the Good, who had miraculously survived a serious illness. Charles V went to Notre-Dame at least twenty-five times during his reign, and each time he set up a provisional altar in front of the statue of the Virgin, which was located next to the rood screen entrance on the right side of the church. During his visits, he offered the cathedral chapter a precious relic or a valuable example of a silversmith's handiwork. These were not simply works of prestige or expressions of a particular devotion, but rather a temporal use of the sacred treasures accumulated by the Capetian dynasty. As Yann Potin sees it, from Saint Louis to Charles V, "the political rhetoric of the Valois came to forge in the fourteenth century a legitimate and autonomous form of sacred treasure-building, integrated into and set within the domestic space of power."[17]

The last Capetians were not content simply to ascribe an increasingly important role to the great Parisian sanctuaries. During the Hundred Years' War, in a period of crisis, they sought to mobilize a number of other sanctuaries to their advantage and that of their kingdom, as become clear at the moment when the insanity of Charles VI began to manifest itself: the sovereign went in person, of course, to Saint-Denis, but also to Mont-Saint-Michel in 1393 and to Notre-Dame du Puy in 1395, in the hopes of recovering his health. He also ordered a squire, furnished with the title of "the king's pilgrim" to visit various holy places and make offerings in his stead and to pray for his health. Charles VI journeyed throughout France on horseback and successively visited Saint-Thibaut in Burgundy, Saint-Nicolas de Port, the Mont-Saint-Michel, Saint-Martin de Tours, Saint-Fiacre in the Brie, Notre-Dame de Chartres, Rocamadour, and Notre-Dame du Puy. Finally, in 1399, the

---

16. Bernard Guenée, "Le voeu de Charles VI: Essai sur la dévotion des rois de France aux XIIIe et XIVe siècles," *Journal des Savants*, 1996, no. 1: 67–135; Humbert Jacomet, "Jehan le Chapelain, écuyer-pèlerin du roi Charles VI (1394–1396), simulateur ou loyal serviteur?," in *Les pèlerinages de l'Antiquité à nos jours*, ed. André Vauchez (Paris: Éditions du CTHS, 2012), 79–119.

17. Yann Potin, *Trésors, écrits, pouvoirs: Archives et bibliothèques d'État en France à la fin du Moyen Age* (Paris: Éditions du CNRS, 2020), 35.

king had the Holy Shroud of Cadouin, for which he had a great devotion, brought to him from Toulouse.[18] From the fourteenth century, the list was enriched by the addition of several Marian shrines: Liesse-Notre-Dame in Champagne, Basilique Notre-Dame-de-l'Immaculée-Conception in Boulogne-sur-Mer, Notre-Dame de Béhuard in Touraine, and Notre-Dame-de-la-Treille in Lille, as well as Notre-Dame de Cléry, where Philip VI had gone three times during his reign and that was so dear to Louis XI that he had it entirely rebuilt and was buried there. Even the great sanctuaries located outside of the borders of France received gifts from French kings: Santiago de Compostela, of course, and also Saint-Claude Cathedral in the Jura, and Notre-Dame of Loreto, where Louis XI set up a benefice intended for a French chaplain. Louis XI likewise went three times to Mont-Saint-Michel to ask the intercession of the archangel, and he created a knightly order—the Order of Saint Michael—that he placed under his patronage.

This alliance between the throne and altar around certain sanctuaries was not a specifically French phenomenon: it can also be found in the realms of the House of Savoy. In the second half of the fourteenth century, the dukes there got ahold of the Holy Shroud that had been discovered in Champagne, at Lirey, and in 1532, they placed it in the chapel of their palace in Chambéry, before it was transferred to Turin in 1578 when this city became the capital of the duchies.[19] It is interesting to note that the veneration of this depiction of the Christ after his Passion—which has maintained such importance up to the present in Catholic devotion—was, in the beginning, forbidden by the bishops of Troyes, before being authorized by the Avignon pope, the antipope Clement VII, at the time of the Great Schism. In the bull that he promulgated on this subject, however, he stressed that the sanctity of this image rested only upon popular belief (*ut pie creditur*). His successor, Benedict XIII, promoted devotion toward the Holy Shroud of Cadouin by granting indulgences to those who went to venerate it in Toulouse, where it had many followers. In the modern era, the little sanctuary of Notre-Dame du Laghet, located in the maritime Alps, on the border between Provence and Piedmont, has likewise enjoyed the favor of the dukes of Savoy, who entrusted it to the Discalced Carmelites and gave

---

18. Beaune, *Naissance de la nation France*.
19. Laurent Ripart, "Le Saint Suaire, les Savoie et Chambéry (1453-1515)," in *The Shroud at Court: History, Usages, Places and Images of a Dynastic Relic*, ed. Paolo Cozzo, Andrea Merlotti, and Andrea Nicolotti (Leiden: Brill, 2019), 57-74.

it their steadfast support, both to affirm their own sovereignty over these peripheral regions and to protect their duchies from conflicts and crises.[20]

The dukes of Milan, for their part, supported the Marian sanctuary of Caravaggio, which became within a few decades one of the most important in northern Italy.[21] In 1432, after five years of war, the Virgin appeared to a young peasant woman, not far from the walls of a village on the border between Milan and Venice, delivering a message that Christ would soon destroy mankind for its countless sins. Mary is said to have added that she opposed this with all her might through her prayers, but that in return the inhabitants of Caravaggio were to fast on bread and water on Fridays and devote half of their Saturdays to celebrating and praying to her. As proof of her presence, she caused a spring to bubble up in a meadow, and its waters were soon revealed to be miraculous, hence the name Santa Maria del Fonte ("of the spring") given to the sanctuary built there. The woman recounted all that had happened to her to Brother Cristoforo de Fano, of the Order of the Humiliati, who in turn communicated these facts to the chancellor of Milan. Not knowing whether it was an authentic Marian apparition or a diabolical illusion, the chancellor waffled. But the bishop of Cremona authorized the creation of a church at the site of the miracle, to be served by a cleric, appointed by the commune, and a *consorzio* to welcome the pilgrims who were beginning to flock there in large numbers. In 1433, Filippo Visconti, the duke of Milan, established a perpetual annuity for the nascent sanctuary and entrusted its administration in 1457 to a Franciscan Observant, Amedeo Menez da Silva, a great reforming figure within his order. This friar, of Spanish origin, dedicated the church to the Virgin of Guadalupe. King Louis XII of France went there on pilgrimage in 1509, after his conquest of Milan, and the king of Spain, Philip IV, instituted a nine-day fair here, helping to make the town an important economic and commercial center.

---

20. Marie-Hélène Froeschlé-Chopard, *Itinéraires pèlerins de l'ancienne Provence* (Marseilles: La Thune, 2002).

21. Giancarlo Andenna, "Santuari e difesa dei confini politici e religiosi: Il caso Lombardo tra Medioevo e prima Età moderna—Caravaggio e Tirano," in Vauchez, *I santuari cristiani d'Italia*, 269–97; Dieter Bauer, Klaus Herbers, and Gabrielle Signori, eds., *Patriotische Heilige: Beitrage zur Konstruktion religiöser und politischer Identitäten in der Vormoderne* (Stuttgart: Steiner, 2007); and Federica Cengarle, "I Visconti e il culto della Vergine (XIV secolo): Qualche osservazione," in *Images, cultes, liturgies: Les connotations politiques du message religieux*, ed. Paola Ventrone and Laura Gaffuri (Paris: Éditions de la Sorbonne; Rome: École Française de Rome, 2014), 105–24.

The papacy itself sought to create a "modern" sanctuary by granting privileges to Notre-Dame of Loreto, and by subjugating the church and its territory to the authority of the bishop of Recanati, thus attaching them directly to the Holy See. One of the reasons for this particular favor on the part of the Renaissance popes was their desire to endow the Papal States with a common spiritual reference point, likely to strengthen their unity and the obedience of their inhabitants to the Roman Church. During the Wars of Religion, Notre-Dame of Loreto became an emblem of Catholicism and of its main supporters, the Habsburgs of Austria, as demonstrated by the great monumental complex built in Prague modeled on it after the defeat of the Protestants and Hussites at White Mountain in 1620.

The Sanctuaries of Civic Religion

In regions such as northern and central Italy, where there was no royal power, public initiatives in favor of local sanctuaries came mainly from the local communities. As noted by Mario Sensi for Umbria and Charles de La Roncière for Tuscany, in the fourteenth century, villagers often showed a particular attachment to the old baptismal church (*pieve* in Italian), long abandoned and sometimes in ruins, as well as to the surrounding cemetery, where their ancestors were buried.[22] If a fresco or a damaged statue of the Madonna or of a saint was found there by chance, the people cried out that it was a miracle and the place now sacred, and an oratory or a chapel was then built. Afterward, the newly created sanctuary would often be taken over by a lay confraternity, which managed it with the help of a cleric and organized the site to make it available for the visitation of pilgrims and the sick.

This joint administration of holy places by the laity and clergy—of which there are many examples—gave rise in central Italy to an institution known as the *santesato*, which endured into the nineteenth century and sometimes even well beyond it. Village communities were the owners of the sanctuaries located in their territories, and they entrusted their service to a hermit or a Tertiary Franciscan.[23] To do this,

---

22. Mario Sensi, *Santuari e pellegrini lungo le "vie dell'angelo": Storie sommerse del culto micaelico* (Rome: Istituto Storico Italiano per il Medio Evo, 2014); Charles de La Roncière, *Religion paysanne et religion urbaine en Toscane (c. 1280–c. 1450)* (Aldershot: Variorum, 1994).

23. Mario Sensi, "Santuari terapeutici di frontiera nella montagna folignate," in Mario Sensi, *Vita di pietà e vita civile di un altopiano tra Umbria e Marche (secc. XI–XVI)* (Rome: Edizioni di storia e letteratura, 1984), 207–38; de La Roncière, *Religion paysanne et religion urbaine*.

they would present one or several candidates to the diocesan bishop, who chose the one he assessed most capable of exercising these functions. This rector, who received his subsistence from the local villagers, maintained the edifice—in general, a small church, flanked by a small house and a well—with the revenues from pilgrimages and from adjacent fields. But their administration often became points of conflicts between the clergy and laity. At Notre-Dame des Anges, near Aix-en-Provence, the priors of the confraternity (or the *luminaire* attached to the sanctuary) fought several times at the end of the Middle Ages with the pastor of the nearby parish, who reproached them for keeping the profits derived from offerings for themselves, as well as the revenues of the hermitage, which he claimed to possess. It was then necessary to turn to the local bishop or lord to put an end to the dispute, which would flare up again at the slightest opportunity.[24]

In the Italian world of the communes, some sanctuaries often became, after the thirteenth century, temples of civic religion as part of a process aimed at uniting the civic community around a privileged intercessor.[25] In 1145, at Pistoia in Tuscany, Bishop Atto brought an important relic of Saint James—a fragment of his skull—that he placed in the cathedral and for which he built a chapel to which the faithful flocked. As numerous miracles occurred, the clergy had them recorded into a collection that has survived up to the present. The popular success of this devotion prompted the fledgling commune to take an interest in it and establish the office of the Opera di San Jacopo (Works of Saint James)—mentioned in 1181 in the city's oldest statutes—that was charged by the commune to watch over this treasury and to manage the offerings made by visitors and pilgrims.[26] The bishop took umbrage at this, and fierce conflicts arose between him and the commune until the early thirteenth century. Eventually, however, the commune gained the upper hand and increased its control over the sanctuary. In the 1240s, the cathedral became one of the city's most important

---

24. Noël Coulet, "L'ermitage de Notre-Dame des Anges de sa fondation (XIIIe siècle?) à l'installation des oratoriens," *Provence historique* 68 (2018): 401–20.

25. Anna Benvenuti and Pierantonio Piatti, eds., *Beata civitas: Pubblica pietà e devozioni private nella Siena del' 300* (Florence: SISMEL, 2016).

26. Diana Webb, "Saint James in Tuscany: The Opera di San Jacopo of Pistoia and Pilgrimage to Compostela," *Journal of Ecclesiastical History* 50 (1999): 207–34; Giampaolo Francesconi, "Il Comune e i santi: Il culto iacobeo e l'"acclamazione' del potere a Pistoia (secoli XII–XIV)," in *Culto dei santi e culto dei luoghi nel Medioevo pistoiese*, ed. Anna Benvenuti and Renzo Nelli (Pistoia: Società Pistoiese, 2010), 159–72.

landmarks, and the city took over responsibility for organizing the feast of Saint James on July 25. From 1272, the apostle's effigy appeared on the seal of the city of Pistoia in the guise of a pilgrim holding a bumblebee, and a lamp in the chapel, maintained by the municipality throughout the year, attested to the city's veneration of its patron saint and protector. In addition, the municipal authorities felt obliged to offer a *pallio*—a piece of precious cloth—every year on the occasion of his feast day, which was soon accompanied by a horse race. The participation of all Pistoia's citizens in these events became compulsory and regulated: they had to fast the day before, and on July 25, the whole city marched, each according to rank, in a procession through the city streets. Thus, within at least a century, the chapel dedicated to Saint James within the cathedral became a sanctuary of civic religion. But make no mistake! The control of communal power was not intended to attenuate the religious character of devotion or to secularize the festival, but to allow the city to gather around the "spiritual common good" and to set itself up as a model "holy city," or "New Jerusalem," by celebrating the memory of its patron saint.[27]

In Siena, which from the thirteenth century has proclaimed itself the "City of the Virgin" and has no other official patron saint, the same process was at work during the August 15 celebrations, where since 1260 a ritual offering of the city's keys to the Mother of God has been commemorated every year. In the cathedral, the commune built an altar dedicated to the Madonna del Voto (Our Lady of the Vow), and in 1359, it purchased a collection of Byzantine relics, for which a chapel of relics was built.[28] Sometimes a city went a step further by constructing, at its own cost, a sanctuary dedicated to the saint on whose feast day an important victory had been won. This was the case in Siena, for Saint George, after the Ghibillines defeated the Guelfs at Montaperti on April 23, 1266. The Florentines did the same in 1289 by dedicating a church to Saint Barnabas, after conquering the army of the bishop of

---

27. Anna Benvenuti, "Il bene comune spirituale," in Benvenuti and Piatti, *Beata civitas*, 559-85. On the title of "New Jerusalem" attributed to the Italian communal cities, see Anna Imelde Galletti, "Gerusalemme o la città desiderata," *Mélanges de l'École Française de Rome–Moyen Âge* 96 (1984): 459-87; Franco Cardini, ed., *La città e il sacro* (Milan: Libri Scheiwiller, 1994); Anna Benvenuti and Pierantonio Piatti, eds., *Come a Gerusalemme: Evocazioni, riproduzioni, imitazioni dei Luoghi Santi tra Medioevo ed Età Moderna* (Florence: SISMEL, 2014).

28. Wolfgang Loseries, "Presentation of Relics in Late Medieval Siena: The 'Cappella delle reliquie' in Siena Cathedral," in *Matter of Faith: An Interdisciplinary Study of Relics and Relic Veneration in the Medieval Period*, ed. James Robinson, Lloyd De Beer and Anna Harnden (London: British Museum, 2015), 56-65.

Arezzo and the Ghibillines at the Battle of Campaldino, on the day of his feast. Municipal sanctuaries consecrated to the "saints of victory" could be found in almost all the important cities of central and northern Italy.[29] But the theme of supernatural intervention by the saints on the battlefield or a God-given military victory is not confined to the Middle Ages—and is still very popular today.

Similar trends can be found in many other Italian cities and in German-speaking countries. In Venice, the great Basilica of Saint Mark's was the personal chapel of the doge, whose palace adjoined the sanctuary, while the bishop was exiled to the outlying district of Castello, where he had to make do with a very modest cathedral. In Strasburg, the Foundation of the Work of Our Lady, which oversaw the construction site of the city's cathedral, passed under the control of the municipality in the second half of the thirteenth century, and Ellenhard the Great († 1304), a patrician who had led the communal troops against those of the bishop in 1262, commissioned Gottfried of Ensingen to write up a collection of miracles of the Virgin, who had become the protector of the interests of the commune. This illustrates the elasticity of the figure of Mary as defender of the city and all of its inhabitants.

In the last centuries of the Middle Ages, this appropriation of the cult of saints and shrines by political powers took on new forms, linked to rising tensions within cities and a number of catastrophic events, in particular the recurrent attacks of the plague from 1348 onward. In Umbria and Tuscany, votive shrines were erected on the initiative of local authorities to commemorate the end of an epidemic, attributed to the intercession of the Virgin Mary, sometimes associated with Saint Roch or Saint Sebastian, reputed as "anti-plague" saints. In general, this was a church with a central plan, often located outside the city walls, near a gate, like the Santa Maria della Consolazione in Todi or the Madonna del Popolo in Assisi, a kind of collective ex-voto resulting from a vow made by the city in times of serious crisis.[30] These buildings also had an apotropaic function, insofar as they were intended to prevent the return of the epidemic. They were generally served by religious

---

29. Philippe Desmette and Philippe Martin, eds., *Le miracle de guerre dans la chrétienté occidentale* (Paris: Coédition Hémisphères / Maisonneuve & Larose, 2018).

30. Mario Sensi, "Santuari, culti e riti *'ad repellendam pestem'* tra Medioevo e Età Moderna," in *Luoghi sacri e spazi della santità*, ed. Sofia Boesch Gajano and Lucetta Scaraffia (Turin: Rosenberg & Sellier, 1987), 381–96. On the sanctuaries of Saint Roch, see Antonio Rigon and André Vauchez, eds., *San Rocco: Genesi e prime espansione di un culto* (Brussels: Société des Bollandistes, 2006).

priests, not by the parish clergy; they attracted all strata of the population, but their construction had been financed by the commune, with the support of the great families of the local aristocracy, who often reserved funeral chapels for themselves.

In general, the major Italian cities were concerned with collecting as many holy bodies as possible, and the loss of communal autonomy was often accompanied by the loss of relics from small towns in the surrounding area. Perugia, for example, after forcing the town of Bettona into its *contado* (the region surrounding the city) in 1265, transferred the relics of Saint Crispol to within its own walls. The same was later true for those of Saint Ercolano (Herculanus), who became the patron saint of the town of Perugia in the fourteenth century, at the expense of Saint Costanzo, who was favored by the local clergy. The tendency to concentrate relics in a few large urban sanctuaries was not confined to Italy. It can also be found in southwestern France, particularly in Toulouse: according to a 1661 inventory, the collegiate church of Saint-Sernin held twenty-seven "holy bodies," some of which had been donated by Charlemagne from other churches; Notre-Dame du Taur had acquired the Holy Shroud from Cadouin in the Dordogne, and since 1369, the Convent of the Jacobins housed the relics of Saint Thomas Aquinas, taken from the Cistercian monks of Fossanova in Campania, and transferred to France on the orders of Pope Urban V.

The Church and the Sanctuaries

From the fourth century onward, as Peter Brown has shown, the places made sacred by the relics of martyrs and saints played a fundamental role in the development of ecclesiastical structures. The example of Saint Ambrose in Milan is a good illustration of the link established between bishops' power in society and their management of relics and shrines. The cult of local saints, or those considered as such, could only create or reinforce the unity of the city around the bishops. But bishops found themselves in competition with monks, whose prestige grew after the tenth century, and who often strove to turn their abbeys into sanctuaries that would attract large numbers of faithful and their donations.

Monks and Bishops in Competition

From the tenth century onward, the dynamics at work in the sanctuarization process become highly complex, but the available documentation rarely allows for a detailed reconstruction. One of the few exceptions is Rouen, the largest city in the duchy of Normandy, which has been the subject of a remarkable study by Jacques Le Maho.[31] In the tenth century, the principal sanctuary of the city was the Abbey of Saint-Ouen († 684), located in the eastern part of the *suburbium*. Placed in a tomb by his successor, the relics of the holy bishop were transported far from the town during the Norman invasions, then returned to Rouen in 918, inspiring a wave of popular fervor. The Emperor Otto II went on pilgrimage to the sanctuary in 946, and in 980, Duke Richard II offered him a reliquary in gold, studded with precious stones. Between 1056 and 1110, the abbey, which had by then become independent of the archbishop, was rebuilt, and after 1050, a compendium of Saint Ouen's miracles was written by the monk Fulbert, in which he recalled "the battalions of sick people from many corners of the earth" who flocked to the saint's tomb every day to regain their health. In this text, the author seeks—not without exaggeration—to portray his monastery as a sanctuary of international renown, comparable to Saint-Martin de Tours or Monte Sant'Angelo on Mount Gargano.

But, from the end of the eleventh century, the prestige of Saint Ouen began to decline, in conjunction with the rise of the cult of Saint Romain († 636), whose relics lay in an ancient sarcophagus of red marble. During the reign of Charles the Bald, around 840, the head of Saint Romain had been transferred to the Abbey of Saint-Médard in Soissons, but the rest of the body remained in the collegial church of Saint-Romain (today, Saint-Godard), which had close ties to Rouen Cathedral. In 1036, Archbishop Robert recognized his relics, and a new *Life* of Saint Romain, followed by a collection of miracles, was written up for the occasion. His relics were often taken out in procession through the streets of the city, since they supposedly protected the city from the flooding of the Seine, and a fair—which continues until today—was held around the church on October 23, his feast day. Around 1110, the saint's reliquary was transferred to Notre-Dame Cathedral by Archbishop Guillaume Bonne-Ame, who had a sumptuous reliquary constructed for it. The Pardon of Saint Romain ended up becoming the greatest religious feast of the city, and Romain soon superseded Ouen as the city's patron saint. Later, the arrangement of the city's holy

---

31. Jacques Le Maho, "Le lieux de pèlerinage rouennais au temps des ducs (X^e–XIIe siècles)," in *Identités pèlerines*, ed. Catherine Vincent (Rouen: Publications de l'Université de Rouen, 2004), 93–106.

sites was complemented, outside the walls, by a sanctuary dedicated to Monte Sant'Angelo, and especially, to the north, by the abbey of Sainte-Catherine-au-Mont, where, since the 1050s, a relic of the saint brought back from the Holy Land by a Norman had been kept. It emanated a liquid called "St. Catherine's oil," which possessed thaumaturgical powers and was much sought-after by the faithful and pilgrims alike. In sum, it is clear that a leading monastic shrine—Saint-Ouen—was succeeded in popular favor by a cult more closely linked to the cathedral and the life of the city in the precommunal era, that of Saint Romain, whose memory took root in the collective imagination through festivals and processions. Such an evolution reflects the balance of power between the various clerical groups within the city, where episcopal power took precedence over that of the monks at the beginning of the twelfth century. But this interclerical rivalry was not the only factor determining the popularity of the sanctuaries. It was also linked to changes in devotion, as demonstrated by the rise of Sainte-Catherine-du-Mont, linked to the renewed interest of the faithful in the Holy Land.

The Papacy, the Jubilee, and the Pastoral Use of Indulgences

From a pastoral point of view, shrines were of major interest to the Church, insofar as the faithful flocked to them in large numbers in search of a special relationship with the supernatural, and their approach had to be supervised to avoid possible deviations.

Around the year 1000, the evolution of the penitential system led the clergy to impose on repentant sinners a whole series of weighty expiatory practices, intended to erase their most serious sins. Beginning at the end of the eleventh century, popes and bishops began granting collective reprieves to the faithful who performed works recommended by the Church. These are known as indulgences.[32] Urban II († 1099) was the first to link particular indulgences to a specific place: in 1095, at the Council of Clermont, he promised those who left on crusade to the Holy Land "the remission of all their sins." This privilege was

---

32. Philippe Cordez, "Les usages du trésor des graces: L'économie idéelle et matérielle des indulgences au Moyen Age," in *Le trésor au Moyen Age: Questions et perspectives de recherche*, ed. Lucas Burkart, Philippe Cordez, Pierre-Alain Mariaux, and Yann Potin (Neuchâtel: Institut d'histoire de l'Art et de Musicologie, 2005), 55–88; Esther Dehoux, Caroline Galland, and Catherine Vincent, eds., *Des usages de la grâce: Pratiques des indulgences du Moyen Age à l'époque contemporaine* (Lille: Presses universitaires du Septentrion, 2021); Robert N. Swanson, ed., *Promissory Notes on the Treasury of Merits: Indulgences in Late Medieval Europe* (Leiden: Brill, 2006).

founded on the notion of a treasury of merits accumulated by Christ and the saints through their sufferings; this was placed at the disposal of the faithful by the hierarchy of the Church, which could draw from it absolutions, in compensation for certain acts of devotion or charity. Later, bishops granted partial indulgences for visiting any given sanctuary; this reinforced among the faithful the conviction that there existed places where divine graces were more easily obtained than at others. At Neufmoustier, near Huy, visiting the local sanctuary founded by Peter the Hermit meant that those who had vowed to go on crusade were exempted from making the journey to the Holy Land. These practices gave rise to numerous abuses.[33] In the twelfth century, for example, false papal bulls appeared to enhance the value of a particular shrine, such as Einsiedeln in Switzerland, where monks claimed that their abbey had been consecrated by Christ himself in 948, and that Pope John VIII had granted a plenary indulgence to pilgrims who went there. The duration of these indulgences was measured in days, months, and years, and from the thirteenth century onward, these figures were applied to the time sinners would have to spend in purgatory before gaining access to a blissful eternity.

At the beginning of the thirteenth century, the papal bulls granting indulgences to sanctuaries became increasingly numerous in connection with the development of canonization procedures. In 1220, Stephen Langton obtained from Honorius III an indulgence of one year and forty days for the Cathedral of Canterbury on the occasion of the fiftieth anniversary of the martyrdom of Saint Thomas à Becket, and the pope granted others for new saints he had just raised to the altars. The faithful who on the occasion of their feast days went to the place where their relics now rested were granted indulgences of between forty days and one year, depending on the case. These modest numbers are connected to the fact that, in 1215, the Fourth Lateran Council had forbidden bishops from granting more sweeping indulgences. But in 1234, the Decretals of Gregory IX authorized the pope to go even further. On the occasion of the translation of the relics of Saint Francis of Assisi in 1230, he granted a year's indulgence to Italian pilgrims who came to Assisi for the event and subsequently on its anniversary—but two years to those who came over the mountains and three to those who came from overseas. The same was true for Saint Anthony of Padua in 1231,

---

33. George, *Reliques*, 329 and 377.

while pilgrims who came to Marburg in large numbers in 1235 for the transfer of the relics of Saint Elisabeth of Hungary were granted indulgences for a year and forty days. From then on, indulgences continued to be an instrument for promoting the cults and devotions that the Church wanted to encourage.

Gregory's successors expanded the movement and began to grant favor and indulgences to various sanctuaries with special bulls that began with the words *Loca sanctorum omnium* or *In sanctorum festivitatibus*.[34] Pontigny Abbey in Burgundy—where the body of Saint Edmund of Abingdon was buried; he had died here in 1240 and was canonized in 1247—was the subject of several bulls from Innocent IV. These authorized the monks to welcome pilgrims, including women, and to use—in spite of Cistercian norms—gold and silver, as well as precious stones, in the fabrication of the reliquary of the saint. In visiting the basilicas of Rome in a spirit of piety, pilgrims benefited, in the thirteenth century, from an indulgence of a year and forty days—a number that in 1450 was lengthened to seven years and seven forty-day periods by Pope Nicholas V. The trend toward progressively higher indulgences can be seen at Mont-Saint-Michel in Normandy. It was granted an indulgence of one hundred days in 1255, renewed in 1332, then another of one year and forty days by Popes Urban V and Gregory XI, on the occasion of the three annual feasts of the archangel and the Virgin Mary. The quantitative importance of indulgences granted by the papacy, which varied from case to case, enables the historian to establish a hierarchy between the holy places of Christendom that benefited from them.

But other indulgences, known as *collective indulgences* (because they were granted by groups of cardinals or prelates residing in the Curia), sometimes muddied the waters by granting indulgences to shrines that had none. In 1340, for example, five bishops granted an indulgence to those who went to the Church of Saint-Vorles in Châtillon-sur-Seine, in memory of the "Lactation of Saint Bernard" (his vision of being nursed by the Virgin Mary), which never received pontifical approval. Bishops, for their part, retained the right to grant up to forty days of indulgences to any place of worship or shrine in their diocese. If the French example is anything to go by, they seem to have done so mainly to help restore

---

34. Roberto Paciocco, *Canonizzazioni e culto dei santi nella christianitas, 1198–1302* (Assisi: Edizioni Porziuncola, 2006).

religious buildings damaged by war or fire.[35] But research remains to be done that could perhaps uncover the existence of sanctuaries that are not otherwise documented, such as the collegiate church of Marigny-sur-Ouche, to which the bishop of Autun granted an indulgence in 1306 following a Eucharistic miracle about which nothing is known.

An important change came with the institution of the jubilee by Boniface VIII in 1300.[36] The approach of this event raised great expectations and hopes of renewal in the West; according to Boniface's counselor, Cardinal Stefaneschi, crowds had already started to make their way to Rome in 1299. The arrival of so many pilgrims led the pope to promulgate, on February 22, 1300, a bull in which he announced the intention to extend a plenary indulgence for pilgrimages to Rome, on the occasion of this Holy Year, a privilege that had up until that point been reserved for crusaders and pilgrims who went to Palestine to worship at the Holy Sepulcher. Having announced this, he noted—without saying so explicitly—that the Holy Land was now definitively lost and proposed to substitute Rome for Jerusalem as the holy city for the pious of Western Christendom. His call echoed widely through all levels of society, and the faithful streamed into Rome in great numbers. Subsequently, Boniface VIII even granted the exceptional privilege of a plenary indulgence to pilgrims who had died on the way.

In 1350, at the request of the Roman people, the Avignon Pope Clement VI proclaimed a new jubilee that was highly successful; it was followed by further jubilees of 1390, 1400, and 1425, which attracted fewer people because of the existence of two (and then three) rival popes then in dispute with each other over the See of Peter.[37] Later, the time between jubilees was reduced from fifty to twenty-five years, in such a way that each generation might be able to benefit. That said, at the time of the Avignon papacy and during the Great Schism (1378–1415), the papacy contributed to the diminishing importance of the Roman jubilee by granting indulgences "on the model of the jubilee" to a large number of Italian sanctuaries. The "Roman" pope, Boniface IX († 1404), responded to the expectation of his Italian partisans by granting a plenary indulgence to pilgrims who went to Monte Sant'Angelo on Mount

---

35. Vincent Tabbagh, "Les évêques et les indulgences de la France des XIVe et XVe siècles," in Dehoux, Galland, and Vincent, *Des usages de la grâce*, 107–18.

36. Agostino Paravicini Bagliani, *Boniface VIII: Un pape hérétique* (Paris: Payot, 2003).

37. André Vauchez, "Les jubilés romains des XIVe et XVe siècles," in *Le Grand Pardon de Chaumont et les Pardons dans la vie religieuse (XIVe–XXIe siècles)*, ed. Patrick Corbet, François Petrazoller, and Vincent Tabbagh (Dijon: Le Pythagore, 2011), 47–53.

Gargano, Saint Mark's in Venice, Santa Maria degli Angeli in Assisi, or the Basilica di Santa Maria di Collemaggio in L'Aquila in the Abruzzi, where the remains of Pope Celestine V, canonized in 1313, rested. But Boniface IX's generosity prompted protest even among his own entourage, and so in 1402, he finally cancelled some of the privileges he had previously granted and reduced these overly generous indulgences to the level of those that could be acquired by visiting Roman basilicas.

In 1446, upon the entreaties of the cardinal of Estouteville in Normandy, Pope Eugenius IV granted a plenary indulgence to the pilgrims who went to Mont-Saint-Michel, which Nicholas V renewed in 1451; this allowed pilgrims to benefit in their turn from the indulgence of the Roman jubilee of 1450.[38] Finally, in 1520, Leo X extended a plenary indulgence to Notre-Dame of Loreto for a limited length of time; this put this Marian shrine on equal footing with the most prestigious holy sites in Christianity. In the modern era, the Catholic Church encouraged, through the granting of indulgences, the multiplication of "bridge-sanctuaries" or satellites dedicated to Notre-Dame of Loreto, with three goals in mind: to limit the movement of the faithful, which could cause disorder; to unify religious practices and devotions within the confraternities placed under their patronage by having them conform to the Roman model; and to spiritualize the pilgrimage by refocusing it on the figure of the Virgin Mary. The laity, for their part, appreciated the fact that the papacy recommended these nearby sanctuaries, and that miracles were produced in them in great numbers assured them that God's grace was not lacking.[39] In the great sanctuaries, we also find temporary penitentiaries (a clerical position) named by the pope who were authorized to absolve all sins and in particular those whose remission had been reserved to bishops. The faithful streamed to them in force, attracted also by the prospect of going to confession to an unknown priest rather than to their own pastor, or of not having to report to their diocese in order to be in good standing with the Church.

In the final years of the Middle Ages and into the sixteenth century, indulgences were gradually integrated into the general system of penance. At the request of bishops, the papacy decentralized the Roman

---

38. Catherine Vincent, "Les indulgences romaines à la fin du Moyen Age," in *Du bon usage de la grâce: Pratiques des indulgences du Moyen Age à l'époque contemporaine*, ed. Esther Dehoux, Caroline Galland, and Catherine Vincent (Lille: Presses universitaires du Septentrion, 2021), 177–86.

39. Philippe Martin, "Sanctuaires-mères et pèlerinages-relais," in Vincent, *Identités pèlerines*, 107–11.

jubilee by instituting various "pardons"—that is, opportunities for grace—to sanctuaries where one could acquire important indulgences on specific dates and well-defined periods of time.[40] Thus, John XXII granted a pardon to the collegiate church of Saint-Sernin in Toulouse, which possessed an impressive treasury of relics; and the Avignon pope, Clement VII, instituted one in favor of Saint-Hillary in Poitiers, which the faithful could enjoy by visiting between June 24 and 27, 1381. In other cases, a fixed timeframe was established—from seven to ten years—between two "great pardons," which was intended to enhance the high point of the pilgrimage: thus, at Notre-Dame de Liesse in Annecy, the pardon took place every seven years. At the collegial church of Saint-Jean de Chaumont, from 1476 forward, one obtained a "general pardon from sin and guilt" by visiting the edifice and by going to confession on the feast day of Saint John the Baptist (June 24) each time it fell on a Sunday.[41] It was the same for Notre-Dame du Puy, where one could gain a plenary indulgence when Good Friday coincided with the feast of the Annunciation (March 25); and also at Compostela where pilgrims enjoyed a plenary indulgence on years that Saint James's feast day (July 25) fell on a Sunday.[42] Parallel to this, the papacy accorded to various cities of Christendom—Milan in 1390, Lyons in 1393, Lausanne in 1450—for a limited amount of time, indulgences equivalent to those earned by pilgrims going to Saint Mark's in Venice. The motivations for these pardons seem to have often been financial, as their concession was accompanied by the Holy See's levy of a higher tax.

The relaxation of ecclesiastical discipline that followed the Great Schism was also translated into a number of initiatives, local or national, taken by bishops to attract the faithful to a given sanctuary. Once the unity of the Church was reestablished, the papacy took matters in hand. In 1420, Pope Martin V strongly condemned the archbishop and chapter of Canterbury, which had accorded, without the consent of the Holy See, a plenary indulgence to the faithful who visited the tomb of Saint Thomas à Becket on the 250th anniversary of his assassination, thus organizing, on their own initiative, a kind of jubilee.[43] In favor

---

40. Francis Rapp, "Indulgences, jubilé, pardons," in Corbet, Patrazoller, and Tabbagh, *Le Grand Pardon de Chaumont*, 17–26.

41. Rapp, "Indulgences, jubilé, pardons."

42. Bruno Maes, Daniel Moulinet, and Catherine Vincent, eds., *Jubilé et culte marial (Moyen Age–époque contemporarine)* (Saint-Étienne: Presses universitaires de Saint-Étienne, 2009).

43. Raymonde Foreville, *Le Jubilé de saint Thomas Becket, du XIIIe au XVe siècle (1220–1470): Études et documents* (Paris: SEVPEN, 1958).

of this development, the jubilee came to meet the expectations of laity who were happy to be able to benefit from the exceptional pardons accorded by the Roman Church. Moreover, indulgences of this type, when they were accompanied by a fixed timetable, aligned the calendar of local shrine churches with that of the universal church. Time thus came to prevail over place in the faithful's perception of the sacred character of those sanctuaries.

The question for the historian is whether or not these generous indulgences increased the attractiveness of the shrines that benefited from them. It is difficult to give a comprehensive answer to this question, since accounts from the period are contradictory. On the one hand, some pilgrims scarcely mention indulgences in their travel accounts: the German Jérôme Münzer, who toured Europe at the end of the fifteenth century, only mentions those that could be acquired at Sainte-Baume, which were by no means the most important. At the same time, Jean de Tournai, a merchant from Valenciennes who visited Rome in 1488, mentions 193 indulgences in his travel diary, distributed among thirty of the city's sanctuaries, the main ones being those of Saint Peter and Saint John Lateran.[44] As most accounts of other sanctuaries point in the same direction, it seems that the faithful were attentive to the amount of indulgences they could obtain by visiting one or another, and they were inclined to favor those where attendance could be most useful to them and their deceased. Indeed, they considered that indulgences could be applied to souls in purgatory, whose suffering would be shortened accordingly. As is often the case in the history of the Church, practice had long preceded theory. In the second half of the fifteenth century, the papacy, ratifying this widely held Christian belief, officially authorized the application to the dead of indulgences obtained by the living.

In the case of newer sanctuaries, the ecclesiastical hierarchy generally ended up approving these new foundations and granting them indulgences if they contributed to the "increase of the divine cult," as the pontifical bulls and letters of approval from the period attest. But these decisions lacked coherence and often only increased confusion, at the risk of perturbing the faithful. In the middle of the sixteenth century, the Council of Trent, which dealt with the question briefly at the end of its final session, took barely any measures to strengthen control over

---

44. Jean de Tournai, *Le récit des voyages et pèlerinages de Jean de Tournai (1488–1489)*, ed. Béatrice Dansette and Marie-Adélaïde Nielen (Paris: Éditions du CNRS, 2017).

indulgences, and the situation began to stabilize only with the creation of the Roman Congregation of Relics and Indulgences by Pope Clement IX in 1667.

The Religious Orders: Promoters and Guardians of the Sanctuaries

We have the tendency to believe that sanctuaries in the Middle Ages were tied to religious orders, as is frequently the case today. In fact, this was not true until the twelfth century in as much as religious orders—properly speaking—did not exist at that time, and monastic and canonical establishments enjoyed a high degree of autonomy in this domain. Thus Cluny, in the eleventh century, did not constitute, strictly speaking, a religious order but rather an abbey whose influence extended throughout a large part of Christendom by way of the practice of a common liturgical *ordo* at a certain number of monasteries and priories. It is only with Cîteaux that one can begin to speak about a religious order in the canonical meaning of the term; this implied a certain degree of centralization and common institutions, the principal one being the general chapter. But Saint Bernard strongly discouraged his spiritual sons from leaving on pilgrimage to the Holy Land, and he certainly did not want to take charge of the administration of such sanctuaries.

The role of religious orders in the management of sanctuaries increased from the end of the twelfth century. The monks of Pulsano—an abbey founded by John of Matera († 1139) near Monte Sant'Angelo—developed the cult of Saint Michael of Apulia in Tuscany and contributed to orienting pilgrims coming from northern Europe to the sanctuary on Mount Gargano and Italians going to Santiago de Compostela.[45] The Franciscans, for their part, worked to make Assisi a city-sanctuary after the death of their founder. Francis had asked to be interred at Santa Maria degli Angeli, in the tiny church called the Portiuncula, where his spiritual journey had begun. But his wishes were not honored, and his relics were finally placed in the great basilica that was constructed between 1230 and 1250, more or less at the initiative of the minister general of the order, Elias of Cortona, and Pope Gregory IX, on a hill near the entrance to the city. But a faction among the Friars

---

45. André Vauchez, "Du Gargano à Compostelle: La sainte pèlerine Bona de Pise († 1207)," in *Puer Apuliae: Mélanges Jean-Marie Martin* (Paris: Publications de la Sorbonne, 2008), 737–43.

Minor—especially those called the "Spiritual Franciscans"—claimed the benefit of the plenary indulgence for Santa Maria degli Angeli, which was finally recognized in the fourteenth century.[46] Another Franciscan shrine-church was that of Saint Anthony of Padua († 1231), a highly popular miracle worker, which became one of the Veneto's main religious centers; they were later responsible for La Verna in Tuscany, at the top of a forested mountain where the Poor Man of Assisi had received the stigmata. But it is especially in the fifteenth and sixteenth centuries that the Franciscan Observants, reformed by Bernardino of Siena († 1444) and his like-minded brothers, settled in the territory by creating or developing sanctuaries in the countryside—still close to towns or roads—which soon became alternative religious poles to the parish churches and convents of the older orders. Within a half century, the Observants thus acquired the principal holy places of the Franciscan movement: San Damiano in Assisi in 1380, Santa Maria degli Angeli (the cradle of the order) in 1415, Eremo delle Carceri (near Assisi) in 1426, and notably La Verna in 1431. Some Franciscan authors compared this mystical site to Mount Sinai, where Moses received the Tablets of the Law. A major pilgrimage developed there, and one chronicler wrote that "there is no mountain in the world more holy" (altro monte non ha più santo il mondo).[47] The friars then proceeded to undertake improvements at all of these sanctuaries, with the intent of making of them attractive places of pilgrimage for the faithful and obtaining generous indulgences from the papacy. In 1475, Sixtus IV conferred on La Verna the plenary indulgence—until then only Santa Maria degli Angeli among the Franciscan sanctuaries had benefited from one—and reversed, even for women, the interdiction on visitors from spending the night on the Holy Mountain. Finally, the Observants built a great church in L'Aquila where Saint Bernardino had died and had laid his relics to rest there in 1472. Numerous miracles were produced there, and it became one of the most popular sanctuaries of central Italy. But the role of the Observants as creators of sanctuaries was not limited to the

---

46. Stefano Brufani and Enrico Menestò, eds., *Il Perdono di Assisi e le indulgenze plenarie* (Assisi: CISAM, 2017).

47. Mauro Mussolin, "Deserti e crudi sassi: Mito, vita religiosa e architetture dalle origini al primo Quattrocento," in *"Altro monte non ha più santo il mondo": Storia, architettura ed arte alla Verna dalle origini al Quattrocento*, ed. Nicoletta Baldini (Florence: Edizioni Studi Francescani, 2012), 117–36; and Gábor Klaniczay, "Da Verna a San Giovanni Rotondo: La ierofania nelle esperienze dei stigmatizzati," in *Ierofanie e luoghi di culto*, ed. Luca Avellis (Bari: Edipuglia, 2016), 197–215.

Italian peninsula. In 1458, the friars of Savoy established a sanctuary in Myans, in the foothills of Mont Granier, not far from Chambéry.[48] When a massive section of Mont Granier collapsed in 1248, crushing the surrounding villages and killing thousands, a chapel dedicated to Notre-Dame de la Nativité atop a small hill was discovered unscathed amid the cascade of rocks and gravel. The friars eventually set up a convent there and, in cooperation with members of the ducal family of Savoy, made Notre-Dame de Myans, where a statue of the Black Madonna had been venerated, into a sanctuary. Numerous miracles were produced there after 1471, as attested to by numerous ex-votos, and thousands of pilgrims rushed there from all regions every year for the annual festival on September 8.

The intervention of these religious orders, whose austerity of life and piety were renowned, was often solicited by the local communities, who appreciated these new sanctuaries where they could easily go to ask for graces. Their most original aspect was undoubtedly the absence, in many of them, of prestigious relics, replaced by *ymages*—paintings, crucifixes, or statues of the Virgin or a saint—to which healings and various miracles were attributed. During the Renaissance, which overturned the accepted conceptions of art and of the world itself, these sanctuaries became covered with frescos and filled with statues of fired clay from the workshop of the Della Robbia, appearing as places more heavenly than earthly—a kind of anticipation of paradise, where the faithful could come into contact with God in a harmoniously natural and artistic environment, and ascend to God by the way of beauty (*via pulchritudinis*) rather than contemplation, which for the laity was difficult to access.[49]

The more intellectual Dominicans were less inclined than the Franciscans to mobilize on behalf of sanctuaries they held dear, with the exception of Saint-Maximin, where a sarcophagus containing the relics of Saint Mary Magdalene had been discovered in 1279. On this occasion, Charles I of Anjou sent a royal crown to the friars so that they might place it on the reliquary of the saint's head. Over the next few years, several of the order's general chapters took legislative steps to ensure

---

48. Jacques Berlioz, *Le monde Granier: La chute d'un géant* (Veurey: Le Dauphiné, 2020).

49. Mauro Mussolin, *"Decus magnificentia, sumptus*: Loci e santuari dell'Osservanza francescana in Umbria e Toscana fra Quattrocento e primo Cinquecento," in *"Altro monte non ha più santo il mondo": Storia, architettura ed arte alla Verna fra il XV ed il XVI secolo*, ed. Nicoletta Baldini (Florence: Edizioni Studi Francescani, 2014), 89–133.

that her feast day be solemnly celebrated in all Dominican convents in a manner equal to that of the Nativity of John the Baptist, although one of the chapters decided to remove the final part of the matins office for Mary Magdalene that mentioned the abbey of Vézelay, which also claimed her relics. Relics of the saint had indeed been distributed to certain convents, especially to the one in Lausanne where various miracles had occurred.[50] But the Dominicans—perhaps due to the major role they were playing in the Inquisition, which did not make them very popular—did not succeed in creating sanctuaries out of San Domenico in Bologna (which since 1267 housed the magnificent *arca* of marble that contained the remains of their founder), Sant'Eustorgio in Milan (where the relics of Saint Peter Martyr were located), or the convent of the Jacobins of Toulouse (where those of Saint Thomas Aquinas had rested since 1370).

The order of the Hermits of Saint Augustine—the Augustinians— which had expanded throughout Christendom from the end of the thirteenth century, was confronted with a different problem because it did not have a clearly identifiable founder. Thus, it endeavored—without success—to nourish devotion to Saint Augustine, to the rule bearing his name that it followed, and whose tomb and relics were, according to the legendary biography lacking any anchoring in historical truth, venerated in Pavia. In the fourteenth century, the Augustinians finally succeeded in creating a great sanctuary, covered in frescos and ex-votos, in Tolentino in the Marches, in honor of one of their own—Saint Nicholas of Tolentino († 1305)—endowed with a reputation for performing miracles and who had been the object of a process of canonization.[51] They also established, in the fifteenth century, the shrine of Cascia, in Umbria, where the relics and memory of Saint Rita († 1457)—a laywoman called "the saint of the impossible"—were venerated. Her popularity was—and still is—immense, due to her ability to help her devotees out of the most inextricable situations.[52]

At the end of the Middle Ages, bishops sometimes called on religious orders to take over a sanctuary that, in their eyes, was being poorly managed or not especially edifying. To cite one example, the archbishop

---

50. Froeschlé-Chopard, *Itinéraires pèlerins de l'ancienne Provence*, 65-118.
51. *Il processo di canonizzazione di S. Nicola da Tolentino*, ed. Nicola Occhioni (Rome: Padri Agostiniani di Tolentino / École Française de Rome, 1984); *San Nicola, Tolentino, le Marche: Contributi e ricerche sul Processo (a. 1325) per la canonizzazione di san Nicola da Tolentino* (Tolentino: Biblioteca Egidiana, 1985).
52. Andrea Turchini, *Uomo e spazio nell'alto Medioevo* (Spoleto: CISAM, 2003).

of Pisa, in 1442, asked the Congregation of Jesuati—a small eremitical congregation founded in the fourteenth century by a pious layman from Siena, Giovanni Colombini, who owned the important convent in the diocese of Santa Maria alla Sambuca—to take over the sanctuary of Santa Maria delle Grazie in Montenero.[53] A miraculous image of the Virgin and Child discovered by a shepherd had been venerated there since the middle of the fourteenth century. Numerous pilgrims from the region between Pisa and Livorno came to see it, and their donations assured the sanctuary an important patrimony. It was administered, rather poorly it seems, by Franciscan Tertiaries, who had come into conflict with the local parish priest. The archbishop put an end to this situation by granting the superior of La Sambuca the right to choose the minister of the sanctuary, from which the Tertiaries were expelled.

The creation and administration of numerous sanctuaries by religious orders during the later Middle Ages constitute an important phenomenon, overcoming local particularities and prompting a certain unification of devotional practices across Europe. In every town, there were one or more convents with images to which people could devote themselves: the stigmatization of Saint Francis, the Virgin Mary handing on the rosary to Saint Dominic (and sometimes to Saint Catherine of Siena), the marvelous preaching of Saint Bernardino of Siena, or the miracles of Saint Anthony of Padua. Of course, the secular clergy did not always approve of the preponderance of religious orders in the administration of sanctuaries on behalf of the faithful. In Italy, some cathedral chapters tried, in the fifteenth century, to challenge and even compete with the supremacy of the mendicant orders. At the cathedral in Vicenza, in the fifteenth century, the canons endeavored to reinvigorate the cult of a saintly bishop, Giovanni Cacciafronte († 1184), that had existed since the end of the twelfth century, as well as several others whose relics the church possessed. On several occasions, they recorded miracles that occurred at his tomb, but these attempts were unsuccessful, and the cathedral failed to become a shrine.[54] The very failure of these attempts only serves to illustrate—by way of counterexample—the

---

53. Isabella Gagliardi, "*Ave maris stella*: Il santuario mariano di Montenero presso Livorno," in *Dio, il mare e gli uomini*, ed. Luciano Fanin, Quaderni di storia religiosa 15 (Caselle dei Sommacampagna: Cierre Edizioni, 2008), 185–214.

54. Laura Gaffuri, "Scritture e riscritture di uno spazio sacro: La cattedrale di Vicenza nel XV secolo," in *Ottanti'anni da maestro: Saggi degli allievi offerti a Giorgio Cracco*, ed. Daniela Rando, Paolo Cozzo, and Davide Scotto (Rome: Viella, 2014), 87–100.

influence of certain mendicant saints and the sanctuaries where their relics were found during the Renaissance.

It is difficult to proceed much further on this topic because detailed research is still lacking outside of a few regions. But to understand the relation between the religious orders and sanctuaries, the official documentation of the various congregations is not always helpful.[55] In the sixteenth century, for example, there is little mention about sanctuaries in the normative sources of the Society of Jesus, but it would be wrong to think that they did not take any interest in sanctuaries. On the contrary, there existed among the Jesuits a whole body of literature that sought to encourage the participation of the laity, in particular its social elites, in certain sanctuaries and pilgrimages by means of devotional confraternities. The same could be said about other religious orders created in the modern era, like the Congregation of the Feuillants (Reformed Cistercians) or the Discalced Carmelites (*Scalzi*, in Italian), which often took over and developed Marian sanctuaries, without them being mentioned in their constitutions. Notre-Dame of Loreto, which began as a simple local sanctuary dependent upon the commune and bishop of Recanati, became, from the end of the fifteenth century, the sanctuary par excellence of the modern papacy, which entrusted its administration first to the Carmelites, then to the Jesuits, to make of it a high point of repentance through the practice of confession and spiritual direction. It became an obligatory extension of pilgrimage to Rome, as illustrated by the detour that Montaigne made in 1581—well worth it, since he was in the Marian basilica when he witnessed the miracle he described in his *Journal de voyage en Italie*.[56]

At the same time, sanctuaries became a major issue during the Wars of Religion. Wherever it could, Protestantism suppressed them, destroying their *ymages* and forbidding their followers to visit them.[57] Within Catholicism, on the contrary, the ecclesiastical hierarchy sought to make these holy places key points of resistance to the penetration of the new ideas. From the Piedmont to Lombardy, the *sacri monti* flourished near the zones of contact between Catholics and Protestants, with the creation of the sanctuaries of Belmonte, Crea, Varese, and Oropa

---

55. Laura M. Olivieri, ed., *Ordini religiosi e santuari in età medievale e moderna* (Bari: Edipuglia, 2013).

56. Michel de Montaigne, *Journal de voyage en Italie*, ed. Charles Dédéyan (Paris: Les Belles Lettres, 1946), 261.

57. Olivier Christin, *Une révolution symbolique: L'iconoclasme huguenot et la reconstruction catholique* (Paris: Les Éditions de Minuit, 1991).

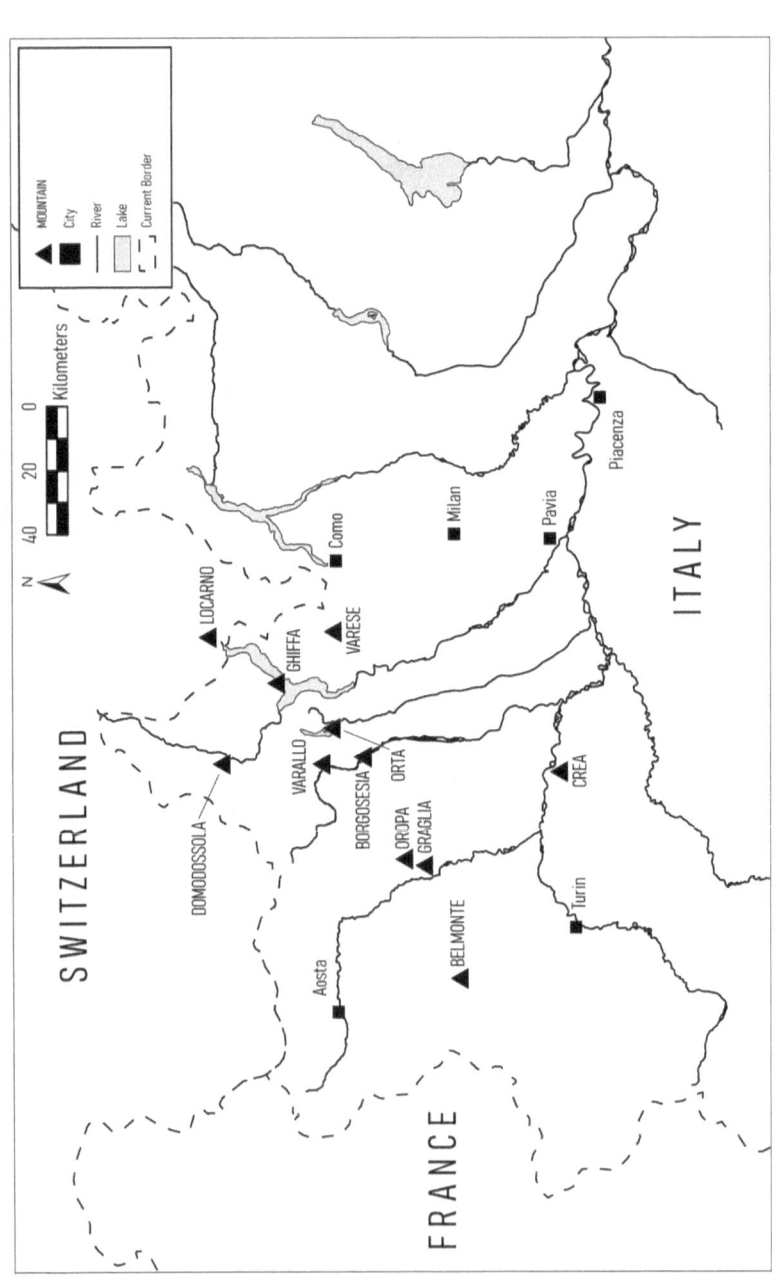

FIGURE 39. Sacred mountains in North Italy (fifteenth and sixteenth centuries). Credit: A. Christesen.

in the Italian Alps, through the inspiration of a few great reforming prelates like Saint Charles Borromeo, archbishop of Milan, or Carlo Bescapè, bishop of Novara (figure 39).[58] Each one of them then became a kind of spiritual citadel, integrated into an increasingly dense network that aimed to protect Catholic identity against the dangers of the Reformation.

The Transformation of Sanctuaries from the End of the Middle Ages to the Modern Period: Toward an Organization of Popular Sacrality

Sanctuaries are neither eternal nor immutable. Certain ones disappear after being destroyed due to war or natural catastrophe or, more rarely, through authoritarian suppression by ecclesiastical authorities. They could also be transformed, and the medieval and modern periods offer different examples of this evolution. The history of numerous smaller local sanctuaries placed under the patronage of Saint Michael in central Italy demonstrates this. Thus, the grottos of the Apennines visited by Saint Francis of Assisi and his companions were almost all, in the beginning, micro-sanctuaries dedicated to the archangel, whether at the Carceri outside Assisi, La Verna, the Sacro Speco near Narni, or Sant'Angelo del Pennino in Bagnara near Nocera Umbra, where the Poor Man of Assisi, gravely ill, was taken during the summer of 1226. Over the course of the thirteenth century, these were transformed into Franciscan places of pilgrimage, and the memory of the "Poverello" erased the traces of any previous cult.[59] But the principal beneficiary of this transformation was the Virgin Mary. In 1216, at Ninfa, in the southern part of Latium (Lazio), Cardinal Hugolino (the future Pope Gregory IX) blocked the rocky sanctuary of San Michele Arcangelo, dedicated to Saint Michael and well attested to at the end of the twelfth century. He had a new sanctuary built on the heights of Mount Mirteto, overlooking the village, called Santa-Maria de Monte Mirteto, and entrusted it to the Cistercians. In Umbria, another Michael-themed sanctuary, located near Trevi, became the Madonna dell'Arcangelo, while that of Sant'Angelo de Gructis (Saint Michael of the Grottos) was later dedicated to the

---

58. Dominique Julia, *Le voyage aux saints: Les pèlerinages dans l'Occident moderne (XVe–XVIIIe siècle)* (Paris: Seuil, 2016).
59. Mario Sensi, "Santuari in grotto tra Umbria e Marche," in Mario Sensi, *Mulieres in ecclesia: Storie de monache e di bizzoche*, vol. 1 (Spoleto: CISAM, 2010), 137–78.

Madonna del Riparo (Our Lady of the Shelter). In Latium, an underground church in Sutri changed its dedication from the archangel to the Madonna del Parto (Our Lady of Childbirth). It seems that the principal purpose of these changes of attribution was to allow the clergy to put an end to suspect or illicit practices, especially the nocturnal rituals of incubation and purification that were taking place in some of the cavernous sanctuaries dedicated to Saint Michael. In 1642, for example, the bishop of Marsico Nuovo in the Basilicata forbade the celebration of Masses and processions in honor of the archangel in the grottos of the surrounding area, due to their "indecent and rustic" character, and transferred his cult to a nearby abbey.[60]

Beginning in the thirteenth century, the clergy—especially the bishops and religious orders—took coercive measures against the visitation of certain sites considered holy by the local population and forbade them to do so. The earliest case about which we have specific information is that of Saint-Guinefort in the Dombes, north of Lyons, well known through the research of Jean-Claude Schmitt. According to the account of Stephen of Bourbon, a Dominican preacher and inquisitor, who traveled through the region in the 1240s and 1250s, peasants brought their sick or disabled children into a forest located between several neighboring villages, to venerate the tomb of a greyhound unjustly killed by its master, even though the dog had saved the master's son from a snake bite while the master had been away. The fortified house where these events happened had been razed over the course of the twelfth century, but the memory of it remained alive, and in the eyes of the villagers, "the murder of the greyhound that saved the child authorized its veneration as a martyr who saved children."[61] Thus, they continued to go there and to complete various rites in the hope of the healing of disabled or sickly children, so-called changelings whom the demons of the forest had switched out for their own healthy children. This was not, strictly speaking, a sanctuary, but a wooded area and a pit where the dog had been buried. The inquisitor had the trees cut down, unearthed the remains of the "holy greyhound," and burned everything before gathering the laity to enjoin on them to put an end to their "superstitious" practices. Archaeological excavations on the site

---

60. Sensi, *Santuari e pellegrini lungo le "via dell'angelo,"* 247.

61. Jean-Claude Schmitt, *Le saint Lévrier: Guinefort, guérisseur d'enfants depuis le XIIIe siècle* (Paris: Flammarion, 1993); Jean-Claude Schmitt, "Les 'superstitions,'" in *Histoire de la France religieuse*, ed. Jacques Le Goff and René Rémond, vol. 1 (Paris: Seuil, 1988), 520–21.

have recently illuminated the traces of pilgrimage that, after a phase of neglect, resumed in the sixteenth century and survived up to the end of the nineteenth century, as illustrated by the discovery of numerous shoes of infants most likely afflicted with deformed legs. A hermit seems to have watched over the place, henceforth dedicated to "Saint Guy le Fort," an orthodox cover that allowed a cult to be maintained.[62]

In the fifteenth century, some bishops took authoritarian measures in order to establish some control over the sanctuaries and to stop new ones being created without their permission. Thus, in 1443, Pierre Soybert, bishop of Saint-Papoul, in the ecclesiastical province of Toulouse, from 1426 to 1451—a prelate moved by a great reforming zeal—undertook to put an end to a pilgrimage that was developing around a spring in Plaigne.[63] There was a chapel dedicated to Saints Julien and Basilisse, but the laity instead venerated the tomb of an unknown person, as well as a spring, whose water was reputed to be miraculous ever since a herdsman had wanted his oxen to drink from it and one of them had knelt before the fountain. The place attracted many visitors, and its reputation spread throughout the region. Informed of these facts, and even though Plaigne was not located in his diocese, but in the diocese of Mirepoix, which adjoined it, Soybert decided to intervene to prevent the development of a shrine with no link to ecclesiastical authority. After an on-site inquiry and consultation with a Dominican inquisitor in Toulouse, the bishop forbade the faithful from going to the spring at Plaigne under pain of excommunication, and with the accord of the bishop of Mirepoix, he had the spring filled in and took measures to impede the laity's access to it. On the other hand, and probably to compensate for the effects of this sanction, he promoted visitation of another spring, which had also become the object of local pilgrimage, at a place called "the Hermitage." According to legend, it was here that the martyr Papulus († ca. 300), the patron saint of the diocese, placed his own head on the ground after being decapitated. A spring then bubbled up on this site, and each year on his feast day (November 3), the faithful, surrounded by their priests, went there on pilgrimage. As we see with the case of the spring in Plaigne, it is

---

62. Jean-Michel Poisson, *Châteaux médiévaux dans l'espace rhodanien* (Lyons: Coédition Alpara–CIHAM, 2018).

63. Schmitt, "Les 'superstitions'"; and André Vauchez, "Pèlerinages posthumes et purgation des péchés: La vision de Narni (milieu du XIe siècle)," in *Mediterraneo, Mezzogiorno, Europa: Studi in onore di Cosimo Damiano Fonseca*, ed. Giancarlo Andenna and Hubert Houben, 2 (Bari: Adda, 2004), 1081–90.

not the fact that a sanctuary was tied to miraculous waters that posed a problem for the bishop, but rather the absence of any reference to a saint recognized by the Church, and the fact that the initiative for a cult probably originated with the laity. Such a reaction was not unique to this period. In 1479, the synodal statutes of the diocese of Langres condemned "respite shrines" and forbade the faithful from visiting them; and the synodal statutes in Sweden in the fifteenth century mention the suppression of several unauthorized popular cults dedicated to figures whose holiness was judged to be dubious by the clergy.

One of the most astonishing manifestations of such popular religious movements took place in Niklashausen, near Würzburg.[64] In 1475, a shepherd named Hans Böhm, referred to in the chronicles as "the Drummer of Niklashausen," called on his contemporaries to visit his village; he claimed that the Virgin Mary had appeared to him in the parish church and promised a plenary indulgence to those who went to the statue as penitents. At his call, crowds flocked—one report claimed fifty thousand visitors in a single day!—and listened as the shepherd told them that the widespread scarcity in the region was punishment inflicted on humanity by Mary and her Son for its evil conduct. But the clergy were disturbed by this message, tinged with both anticlericalism and social protest, and the authorities looked unfavorably on his attacks against the rich and powerful, whom he urged to undertake manual labor instead of exploiting the poor. When the visionary began to say that one could dispense from paying the rents demanded by the local lord (in this case the bishop of Würzburg), he was quickly arrested and burned as a heretic. The church of Niklashausen, which in the past had become a center of contestation, was razed, but the memory of this episode remained alive for a long time in the Germanic world.

The repression of popular sacralities intensified after the Council of Trent but generally took on subtler forms. In 1636, the bishop of Gubbio had the eremitical grotto sanctuary of Sainte-Cécile de Montelovesco, mentioned for the first time in 1237, enclosed. It was a cavity dug into the rock, where parents would put their sick children to sleep in a ceremony that, according to the prelate, "resembled the incubation of the pagans."[65] Another way for the clergy to diminish the influence

---

64. Klaus Arnold, *Niklashausen 1476: Quellen und Untersuchungen zur sozialreligiösen Bewegung des Hans Behem und zur Agrarstruktur eines spätmittelalterlichen Dorfes* (Baden-Baden: Verlag Valentin Koemer, 1980).

65. Sensi, "Santuari in grotto tra Umbria e Marche."

of these local sanctuaries consisted of transporting the relics or holy images found there to the parish church or the cathedral of the nearby city. This happened in Assisi for Saint Vital († 1370), a former brigand who converted to a better life and had ended his days in the "odor of sanctity" in a hermitage located on the slopes of Mount Subasio.⁶⁶ A chapel was created near the place where his body had been buried, and the town's inhabitants often climbed up here to drink from the nearby spring. Its waters, called "the water of violets" due to its taste, was in fact famous for its miraculous powers, especially for healing fractures. In 1586, the canons of San Rufino decided to create a treasury of relics for the diocese of Assisi by gathering together, in a chapel in the cathedral at Assisi, the relics of Saint Vital, Saint Rufino d'Arce (a monk martyred in the area in 1281), and Saint Facondino, all of which could be previously found in various little sanctuaries out in the *contado*. Apparently, this represented a kind of promotion for these obscure figures. After the translation of these relics, the small sanctuary that had been established on the hill at the tomb of Saint Vital declined, even if the inhabitants of the town still continued to come for some time seeking the spring with the "water of violets." The same thing took place in Città di Castello, where the bishop had the relics of Blessed Ventura—a priest killed by a woodcutter in the thirteenth century who was venerated in the region—transported into the cathedral in 1684.⁶⁷

The "normalizing" of the life of the sanctuaries by the clergy sometimes took more spectacular forms. This is the case in Palermo, whose patron saint, Saint Rosalia, had been venerated since the middle of the seventeenth century in the cathedral but also on the slopes of a nearby mountain, Monte Pellegrino, where she is said to have lived in a grotto, though precisely when is difficult to nail down.⁶⁸ The custom was to pass the night from June 2 to June 3—the day of her feast—near the grotto, which had been transformed into a chapel, while giving oneself over to poorly understood dreamlike and thaumaturgical rituals. "Stones of Saint Rosalia"—broken off from the mountain—were bought and sold here, and to which were attributed curative powers. The pilgrims recited or chanted episodes of her *Life*, which presented her as a princess,

---

66. Clara Amandoli, "Santuari scomparsi, santuari in disuso nell'area di Assisi," in *Santuari cristiani d'Italia: Committenze e fruizione tra Medioevo e età moderna*, ed. Mario Tosti (Rome: École Française de Rome, 2003), 279–306.
67. Clara Amandoli, "Santuari cristiani in Umbria," in Vauchez, *I santuari cristiani d'Italia*, 145–64.
68. Sara Cabibbo, *Santa Rosalia tra terra e cielo* (Palermo: Sellerio Editore, 2004).

a descendant of either Charlemagne or King Roger. According to the legend, her father had wanted her to marry a prince, but having decided to be a "Bride of Christ," she ran away to the grotto where she led an ascetical life, receiving visits from the Virgin during great liturgical feasts. Upon her death, her remains were said to be buried by angels under a pile of rocks and her name fell into oblivion. But four centuries later, on the occasion of a major epidemic, she was remembered in Palermo, and a search began for her relics, which were miraculously recovered on the mountain in 1624—an event that ended the epidemic. A cult developed on the site, and the grotto where she was said to have lived became a sanctuary, managed by a community of eremitical Franciscans. In 1647, the relics of Saint Rosalia were brought to the Cathedral of Palermo and, in 1651, a Jesuit composed and published an official *Life* in which the author endeavored to find Christian justification for what might have been considered "pagan" practices among the pilgrims, while at the same time preserving the lyrical and sentimental character of the legend so as to not undercut the cult from its popular base. As the anthropologist Valerio Petrarca has emphasized in this case—which is far from unique—"numerous rituals and practices were witnessed here that shed light on their meaning."[69] Thus the ecclesiastical hierarchy felt itself obligated, beginning in the seventeenth century, to more closely control those devotions where the religious dimension seemed to be limited to ritual actions that the Church considered, if not deviant, then aberrant. But it would be somewhat of an exaggeration to speak of this as a generalized suppression, given that some prelates in this period were themselves not too estranged from such popular beliefs and practices. For example, in 1656, as the plague raged throughout the kingdom of Naples, the bishop of Siponto, Giovanni Alfonso Puccinelli, implored Saint Michael for help. A few days later, the prelate said that the archangel appeared to him in a dream and suggested that he use stones from the grotto on Mount Gargano to combat the epidemic, after which he sent a stone to each one of his colleagues whose dioceses were also in the grip of the plague.

---

69. Valerio Petrarca, "Dinamiche simboliche di un santuario tra storia e antropologia," in Vauchez, *I santuari cristiani d'Italia*, 329–46.

Conclusion

The sixteenth and seventeenth centuries marked an important turning point in the history of Christian sanctuaries. With the success of humanist ideas and the Protestant Reformation, the cult of the saints was, in effect, considered a collection of superstitious practices in much of western Europe. Luther denounced the selling of indulgences in the *Theses* he posted in Wittenberg in 1517, and Calvin condemned the cult of relics and pilgrimages as manifestations of a "papist idolatry" founded on the exploitation of the credulity and ignorance of the popular masses. During the Wars of Religion that followed, reformers burned relics and destroyed the statues of the Virgin and the saints in churches in what historians have called the "Protestant iconoclasm." In France, they attacked with a particular violence important places of pilgrimage, such as Saint-Martin of Tours, Rocamadour, and Saint-Gilles, some of which never recovered from the shock.[1] In Protestant countries, the visiting of sanctuaries was prohibited by pastors; even if these measures were not immediately followed,

---

1. Olivier Christin, *Une révolution symbolique: L'iconoclasme huguenot et la reconstruction catholique* (Paris: Les Éditions de Minuit, 1991); Dominique Julia, "Sanctuaires et lieux sacrés à l'époque moderne," in *Lieux sacrés, lieux de culte, sanctuaires*, ed. André Vauchez (Rome: École Française de Rome, 2000), 252–57.

especially in rural regions, they ultimately resulted in the disappearance of sanctuaries from the whole upper part of Europe that had joined the Reformation, as well as in England and Scotland. There is something staggering in the brutal and rapid collapse of the cult of the saints and its manifestations across a large part of the West, and it is not sufficient to simply explain it away because of the advent of modernity. How could Christians, accustomed to venerating relics and visiting sanctuaries for a millennium, so suddenly reject what they had once worshiped?

However astonishing this assertion appears, the Church itself, which was still undivided at the end of the Middle Ages, contributed in some measure to this turn. Since 1400, an English cleric (for a long time confused with Jean Gerson) had proposed to lay worshipers who were tempted to go to Rome on the occasion of the jubilee that they replace this journey with a visit to their local churches over a course of fifty days for the "going" and as many for the "return," while reciting prayers for the unity of the Church, at that time torn apart by the Great Schism. A few decades later, the author of the *Imitatio Christi* called into question the spiritual value of pilgrimages, while invitations to the inner pilgrimage multiplied in the second half of the fifteenth century. In 1487, Pope Innocent VIII granted to the Dominicans of Saint Catherine in Augsburg indulgences each time that they followed a kind of *via sacra* around the altars and various chapels in their convent, as substitutes for the Holy Places of Jerusalem, while at the same time contemplating paintings of the principal churches of Rome, which served as the visual media for their meditation.[2] The expanding role assigned by the Church to works of art—paintings and soon engravings light enough to carry—contributed, moreover, to detaching pilgrimages from the tombs of the saints and to reinforcing their own spiritual responsibilities. This transformation took on different forms according to geographical and spiritual contexts. Thus, among the Italian Franciscan Observants who attached great importance to space and nature, this process of substitution was translated, as previously discussed, into the creation, within the context of *sacri monti*, of a Jerusalem both

---

2. Katheryne Beebe, "The Jerusalem of the Mind's Eye: Imagined Pilgrimage in the Late Fifteenth Century," in *Visual Constructs of Jerusalem*, ed. Bianca Kühnel, Galit Noga-Banai, and Hanna Vorholt (Turnhout: Brepols, 2014), 409–20; Jean Wirth, "Théorie et pratique de l'image sainte à la veille de la Réforme," *Bibliothèque d'humanisme et renaissance* 48 (1986): 319–59. Indulgences were granted to certain holy images. See Flora Lewis, "Rewarding Devotion: Indulgences and the Promotion of Images," in *The Church and the Arts*, ed. Diana Wood, Studies in Church History 28 (Oxford: Ecclesiastical History Society, 1997), 179–94.

CONCLUSION 247

monumental and fictional, located in mountainous regions.[3] Without having to exert great physical effort or put their lives in danger, the laity could, through sight and imagination, experience the principal steps of the life and Passion of Christ. Elsewhere, as in Brittany, popular devotion was focused on the Crucifixion, and memorial calvaries multiplied close to certain churches.

Parallel to this evolution were the efforts of the clergy to displace the laity's devotion toward the saints and sensitize the faithful to the universal dimension of the Church. In this lengthy process, the creation of the Roman jubilee by Boniface VIII constituted a point of departure by placing Rome—and no longer Jerusalem—at the center of Christian piety. Later on, and especially in the fifteenth century, his successors granted to a certain number of sanctuaries the benefit of the plenary indulgence, "following the model of the jubilee," which allowed the faithful to acquire spiritual privileges tied to the Roman pilgrimage without having to take part in it physically. Besides, by privileging certain moments of the year and different feasts in which the faithful could receive forgiveness, the papacy helped shift the emphasis from holy places to sacred time and from individual initiative to liturgical and collective piety.

Another way that the ecclesiastical hierarchy tried to reshape popular faith expressed in the sanctuaries was to favor those dedicated to the Virgin Mary. The extraordinary influence of the Marian cult in the fourteenth and fifteenth centuries was certainly not only due to the actions of the papacy but was the result of several profound and intersecting trends in Christian piety. For the religious orders enamored with reform, the preference given to the Virgin over other saints was a way of reorienting themselves toward the beginnings of the Church, for Mary connotes its origins, and she was readily depicted at this time as praying in the Cenacle with the twelve apostles. For the laity, the Mother of God was both the most perfect human creature—this is when the Council of Basel was already elaborating the foundations of the dogma of the Immaculate Conception—and the most powerful and merciful saint toward those who invoked her. After emerging as victor in its struggles against conciliarism, the Roman Church took over the responsibilities for the aspirations of the faithful in this domain. Beginning with Nicholas V and Sixtus IV, the papacy lent all of its power to favor the Marian

---

3. Dorino Tuniz, ed., *I Sacri Monti: Itinerari ascetici cristiani*, Archivio italiano per la storia della pietà 28 (Rome: Edizioni di storia e letteratura, 2015).

sanctuary of the Basilica della Santa Casa in Loreto and endeavored to attract the pilgrims of Europe there by granting to the shrine the privilege of the plenary indulgence. Archetype of the Church, the house of God in the midst of humanity, the Santa Casa—brought from Nazareth to Italy by the angels—became a kind of Ark of the New Covenant around which clergy and laity, the powerful and the poor, gathered under the leadership of the successor of Peter.

This new interest by ecclesiastical institutions in such sanctuaries was, however, too late and too limited to be effective beyond the Mediterranean basin. Besides, even if the principal centers of pilgrimage evolved in the direction desired by the Church, local sanctuaries were barely affected by the spiritualizing process that marked the end of the Middle Ages. In the countryside, the cult of the saints responded to the concrete and permanent needs of rural peoples: protection from epidemics, assurance of plentiful harvests, curing people and their animals of certain maladies. Numerous small sanctuaries, therefore, seem to have survived unnoticed and without any great changes, sometimes into the nineteenth or even the beginning of the twentieth centuries, insofar as the rather spotty documentary record indicates.

Whether dedicated to obscure local saints or to the Mother of God, the dual nature of spaces where believers came to request the intervention of supernatural forces for themselves or for their loved ones would persist until the present: on the one hand, as a parish—the place of sacramental practice where priestly mediation is exercised by the secular clergy; on the other, as a sanctuary, managed by laity or religious orders, with the possibility of a direct rapport between the human and the divine. Although not a historian, Maurice Barrès in his 1913 novel, *La Colline inspirée* (*The Sacred Hill*), centered on Notre-Dame de Sion-Vaudémont in Lorraine, draws a distinction (without opposing them) between "the religion of the chapel" and "the religion of the prairie," and he recalls with joy that alongside the churches, "there are places where the spirit breathes."[4] Even if some of these formulations seem outmoded today, they reveal a permanent reality and tension. Historians owe it to themselves to recognize that the life of the sanctuaries does not only result from a history of piety or popular devotion. Inserted into landscapes that were often constructed around them and for them, they have contributed to forging both well-defined territorial

---

4. Maurice Barrès, *La Colline inspirée* (Paris: Du Rocher, 2005).

identities and feelings of belonging to shared spaces—to a Christianity where the local converges with the universal. In this sense, it would not be anachronistic to see sanctuaries in the same way as the crusades and the medieval universities as being at the origin of a European consciousness.

Bibliography

Primary Sources

Alfonso X "El Sabio." *Cantigas de Santa Maria*. Edited by Walter Mettmann, vol. 2. Coimbra [Madrid]: Por ordem da Universidade, 1961.
Apparitio sancti Michaelis in Monte Gargano. Translated by François Bougard. In *Culte et pèlerinages à saint Michel en Occident: Les trois monts dédiés à l'archange*, edited by Pierre Bouet, Giorgio Otranto, and André Vauchez, 7–10. Rome: Ecole française de Rome, 2003.
Augustine, "Sermon CCLXV," § 5. In *Patrologiae Cursus Completus, Series Latina*, edited by J.-P. Migne, 39, cols. 39–40. Paris: Migne, 1863.
Basil of Caesarea. "Treatise on the Holy Spirit." In *Patrologiae Cursus Completus, Series Graeca*, edited by J.-P. Migne, 32, cols. 129–30. Paris: Migne, 1857.
Bede (the Venerable). *Liber de locis sanctis*. Edited by J. Fraipont. Corpus Christianorum Series Latina 175. Turnhout: Brepols, 1965.
Caesarius of Arles. "Sermon CCLXXVII." In *Sermons au people*, edited by Marie-José Delage, 2:178–79. Paris: Éditions du Cerf, 1978.
Campi, Pietro Maria. *Dell'historia ecclesiastica di Piacenza*. Edited by Pietro Maria Campi [the younger], vol. 1. Piacenza, 1651.
Catherine of Siena. "Lettera 201." In *Le Lettere di Santa Caterina da Siena*, edited by Niccolò Tommaseo, 76–77. Florence: Giunti Barbera, 1866.
Codice di Diritto canonico. Rome: Unione editori cattolici italiani, 1983.
Corpus des inscriptions de la France médiévale, vol. 18, *Allier, Cantal, Loire, Haute-Loire, Puy-de-Dôme*. Edited by Robert Favreau, Jean Michaud, and Bernadette Mora. Paris: CNRS, 1995.
Cyril of Jerusalem. *Catéchèses*. Edited by J. Bouvet. Namur: Éditions du Soleil Levant, 1962.
Decretorum Ecclesiae Gallicanae Libri, VII. Edited by Laurent Bouchel. Paris: Mural, 1609.
Gregory the Great. *Dialogues*. Edited by Adalbert De Vogüé. Paris: Éditions du Cerf, 1980.
Le Guide de pèlerin de Saint-Jacques de Compostelle. Edited by Jeanne Vielliard. Mâcon: Protat Frères, 1963.
Historia translationis Sanctae Coronae Spineae. Edited by M. Cecilia Gaposchkin. In "Between Historical Narration and Liturgical Celebrations: Gautier Cornut and the Reception of the Crown of Thorns in France," 121–39. *Revue Mabillon*, n.s. 30 (2019): 125.
Der "Itinerarium Bernardi monachi": Edition, Übersetzung, Kommentar. Edited by Josef Ackermann. Hannover: Verlag Hahnsche Buchhandlung, 2010.

Jean d'Outremeuse. *Ly Myreur des histors*. 7 vols. Brussels: M. Hayez, 1864–87.
Jean de Joinville. *Vie de saint Louis*. Edited by Jacques Monfrin. Paris: Classiques Garnier, 2010.
Jean de Tournai. *Le récit des voyages et pèlerinages de Jean de Tournai (1488–1489)*. Edited by Béatrice Dansette and Marie-Adélaïde Nielen. Paris: Éditions du CNRS, 2017.
Kempe, Margery. *Le Livre de Margery Kempe: Une aventurière de la foi au Moyen Age*. Translated by Louise Madignier. Paris: Éditions du Cerf, 1989.
Lamberto de Etcheverria. *Code de droit canonique annoté*. Paris: Éditions du Cerf; Bourges: Tardy, 1989.
Leggenda di Santo Galgano confessore. Edited by Franco Cardini. Siena: Cantagalli, 1982.
Liber Sancti Jacobi Codex Calixtinus. Edited by Klaus Herbers and Manuel Santos Noia. Santiago de Compostela: Xunta de Galicia, 1998.
Le Livre des miracles de Sainte Catherine de Fierbois. Edited by Yves Chauvin. Archives historiques de Poitou 60. Poitiers: Société des archives historiques du Poitou, 1976.
Montaigne, Michel de. *Journal de voyage en Italie*. Edited by Charles Dédéyan. Paris: Les Belles Lettres, 1946.
Paulinus of Nola. *Epistulae*. Edited by Wilhelm von Hartel. Vienna: Tempsky, 1894.
Il processo di canonizzazione di S. Nicola da Tolentino. Edited by Nicola Occhioni. Rome: Padri Agostiniani di Tolentino / École Française de Rome, 1984.
Revelatio ecclesiae sancti Michaelis. Transcription by Pierre Bouet and Olivier Desbordes of ms. Avranches, Bibliothèque municipal, 211, fol. 180v–189. In *Culte et pèlerinages à Saint-Michel en Occident: Les trois monts dédiés à l'archange*, edited by Pierre Bouet, Giorgio Otranto, and André Vauchez. Rome: École Française de Rome, 2003.
Suger. *De consecratione ecclesiae S. Dionysii*. Edited by Françoise Gasparri. Paris: Les Belles Lettres, 1996.
Victrix of Rouen. *De laude sanctorum*. Edited by J. Mulders. In *Liber contra Arrianos; De laude sanctorum; Libellus emendationis; Epistulae; Commonitorium. Excerpta ex operibus s. Augustini; Altercatio legis inter Simonem Iudaeum et Theophilum christianum*. Corpus Christianorum Series Latina 64. Turnhout: Brepols, 1985.
Vita sancti Heinrici imperatoris (additamentum). Edited by G. H. Waitz. In Monumenta Germaniae Historica, Scriptores 6, 818–20. Hannover: Hahn, 1841.
Wace. *Le Roman de Rou*. 2 vols. Rouen: Édouard Frère Éditeur, 1828.

Secondary Sources

Agusta-Boularot, Sandrine, Sandrine Huber, and William van Andringa, eds. *Quand naissent les dieux: Fondation des sanctuaires antiques; motivations, agents, lieux*. Rome: École Française de Rome; Athens: École Française d'Athènes, 2017.
Albe, Edmond, and Jean Rocacher, eds. *Les miracles de Notre-Dame de Rocamadour au XIIe siècle*. Toulouse: Le Pérégrinateur, 2007.

Alvino, Giovanna, and Terenzio Leggio. "Acque e culti salutari in Sabina." In *Usus veneratioque fontium: Fruizione e culto delle acque salutari nell'Italia romana*, edited by Lidio Gasparini, 17–54. Tivoli: Tipigraf, 2006.
Amandoli, Clara. "Santuari cristiani in Umbria." In *I santuari cristiani d'Italia*, edited by André Vauchez, 145–64. Rome: École Française de Rome, 2007.
Amandoli, Clara. "Santuari scomparsi, santuari in disuso nell'area di Assisi." In *Santuari cristiani d'Italia: Committenze e fruizione tra Medioevo e età moderna*, edited by Mario Tosti, 279–306. Rome: École Française de Rome, 2003.
Amargier, Paul. "Gens de mer en Méditerrannée dans les années, 1375–1390." In *Navigation et gens de mer en Méditerrannée*, 68–83. Paris: CNRS, 1980.
Andenna, Giancarlo. "Santuari e difesa dei confine politici e religiosi: Il caso Lombardo tra Medioevo e prima Età moderna—Caravaggio e Tirano." In *I santuari cristiani d'Italia*, edited by André Vauchez, 269–97. Rome: École Française de Rome, 2007.
Andreani, Laura, and Agostino Paravicini Bagliani, eds. *Il "Corpus Domini": Teologia, antropologia e politica*. Florence: SISMEL / Edizioni del Galluzzo, 2015.
Angenendt, Arnold. *Heilige und Reliquien: Die Geschichte ihres Kulturs vom frühen Christentum bis zur Gegenwart*. Munich: Beck, 1994.
Antoine, Elisabeth. "Images de miracles: Le témoignage des ex-voto peints en Italie centrale (XIVe–XVIe siècle)." In *Miracle et Karama: Hagiographies médiévales comparées*, edited by Denise Aigle, 353–74. Turnhout: Brepols, 2000.
Arnold, Klaus. *Niklashausen 1476: Quellen und Untersuchungen zur sozialreligiöse Bewegung des Hans Behem und zur Agrarstruktur eines spätmittelalterlichen Dorfes*. Baden-Baden: Verlag Valentin Koemer, 1980.
Atkinson, Clarissa. *Mystic and Pilgrim: The Book and the World of Margery Kempe*. Ithaca, NY: Cornell University Press, 1985.
Aulisa, Immacolata, ed. *I santuari e il mare (Santuario di Santa Maria di Monte Berico)*. Bari: Edipuglia, 2014.
Autrand, Françoise, Claude Gauvard, and Jean-Marie Moeglin, eds. *Saint-Denis et la royauté: Études offertes à Bernard Guenée*. Paris: Publications de la Sorbonne, 1999.
Auzépy, Marie-France. "Les Isauriens et l'espace sacré: L'Église et les reliques." In *Le sacré et son inscription dans l'espace à Byzance et en Occident*, edited by Michel Kaplan, 13–24. Paris: Publications de la Sorbonne, 2001.
Avellis, Luca, ed. *Ierofanie e luoghi di culto*. Bari: Edipuglia, 2016.
Bacci, Michele. *The Holy Portulan: The Sacred Geography of Navigation in the Middle Ages*. Berlin: De Gruyter, 2014.
Bacci, Michele. "Italian ex-votos and *Pro anima* Images in the Late Middle Ages." In *Ex-voto: Votive Giving across Cultures*, edited by Ittai Weinryb, 76–105. Chicago: University of Chicago Press, 2016.
Bacci, Michele. *Il pennello dell'evangelista: Storia delle immagini sacre attribuite a S. Luca*. Pisa: ETS, 1998.

Bacci, Michele. *"Pro remedio animae": Immagini e pratiche devozionali in Italia centrale (secoli XIII–XIV)*. Pisa: ETS, 2000.
Bacci, Michele. *Lo spazio dell'anima: Vita di una Chiesa medievale*. Bari: Laterza, 2005.
Bachelard, Gaston. *L'eau et les rêves: Essai sur l'imagination de la matière*. Paris: Jose Corti, 1942.
Baciocchi, Stéphane, and Christophe Duhamelle, eds. *Reliques romaines: Invention et circulation des corps saints des catacombes à l'époque moderne*. Paris: École Française de Rome, 2016.
Baiocco, Simone, Marie-Claude Morand, and Sylvie Aballéa, eds. *Des saints et des hommes: L'image des saints dans les Alpes occidentales au Moyen Age. Catalogue*. Milan: Officina Libraria, 2013.
Balzamo, Nicolas. "Image miraculeuse: Le mot, le concept et la chose." In *L'image miraculeuse dans le christianisme occidental: Moyen Age – Temps modernes*, edited by Nicolas Balzamo and Estelle Leutrat, 15–41. Tours: Presses universitaires François Rabelais, 2020.
Balzamo, Nicolas. *Les miracles dans la France du XVIᵉ siècle*. Paris: Les Belles Lettres, 2014.
Balzamo, Nicolas, and Olivier Christin, eds. *L'Atlas Marianus de Wilhelm Gumppenberg: Édition et traduction*. Neuchâtel: Éditions Alphil / Presses universitaires suisses, 2015.
Barnay, Sylvie. *Le ciel sur la terre: Les apparitions de la Vierge au Moyen Age*. Paris: Éditions du Cerf, 1999.
Barral i Altet, Xavier. *Compostelle: Le grand chemin*. Paris: Gallimard, 1999.
Barreiro-Rivas, Xosé Luís. "Mille anni di pellegrinaggio a Santiago." In *Del visibile credere*, edited by Davide Scotto, 573–90. Florence: Olschki, 2011.
Barrès, Maurice. *La Colline inspirée*. Paris: Du Rocher, 2005.
Barthélemy, Dominique. *Chevaliers et miracles: La violence et le sacré dans la société*. Paris: Armand Colin, 2004.
Baschet, Jérôme. *Lieux sacrés, lieux d'images: Les fresques de Bominaco (Abruzzes, 1263). Thèmes, parcours, fonctions*. Rome: École Française de Rome, 1992.
Baschet, Jérôme, and Pierre-Olivier Dittmar, eds. *Les images dans l'Occident médiéval*. Turnhout: Brepols, 2015.
Bastide, Roger. *Les Amériques noires*. Paris: L'Harmattan, 2002.
Baud, Anne, ed. *Organiser l'espace sacré au Moyen Age: Topographie, architecture et liturgie (Rhône-Alpes, Auvergne)*. Lyons: Alphara, 2014.
Bauer, Dieter, Klaus Herbers, and Gabrielle Signori, eds. *Patriotische Heilige: Beitrage zur Konstruktion religiöser und politischer Identitäten in der Vormoderne*. Stuttgart: Steiner, 2007.
Beaune, Colette. *Naissance de la nation France*. Paris: Gallimard, 1985.
Beebe, Katheryne. "The Jerusalem of the Mind's Eye: Imagined Pilgrimage in the Late Fifteenth Century." In *Visual Constructs of Jerusalem*, edited by Bianca Kühnel, Galit Noga-Banai, and Hanna Vorholt, 409–20. Turnhout: Brepols, 2014.
Bensa, Alban. *Les Saints guérisseurs du Perche-Gouët: Espace symbolique du bocage*. Paris: Institut d'ethnologie, 1978.

Benvenuti, Anna. "Il bene comune spirituale." In *Beata civitas: Pubblica pietà e devozioni private nella Siena del' 300*, edited by Anna Benvenuti and Pierantonio Piatti, 559–85. Florence: SISMEL, 2016.

Benvenuti, Anna. "Il santuario: Definizioni, metodo di studio, significato storico." In *Andare per santuari*, edited by Giorgio Cracco and Paolo Cozzo. Aosta: Bertoncello, 2006.

Benvenuti, Anna, and Pierantonio Piatti, eds. *Beata civitas: Pubblica pietà e devozioni private nella Siena del' 300*. Florence: SISMEL, 2016.

Benvenuti, Anna, and Pierantonio Piatti, eds. *Come a Gerusalemme: Evocazioni, riproduzioni, imitazioni dei Luoghi Santi tra Medioevo ed Età Moderna*. Florence: SISMEL, 2014.

Bercé, Yves-Marie. *Lorette aux XVIᵉ et XVIIᵉ siècles*. Paris: Presses universitaires Paris-Sorbonne, 2011.

Bianco, Rosanna. *La conchiglia e il bordone: I viaggi di San Giacomo nella Puglia medievale*. Perugia: Edizioni Compostellane, 2017.

Billot, Claudine. "Les saintes-chapelles (XIIIᵉ–XVᵉ siècle): Approche comparée de fondations dynastiques." *Revue d'histoire de l'Église de France* 72 (1987): 229–48.

Birch, Debra J. *Pilgrimage to Rome in the Middle Ages: Continuity and Change*. Woodbridge: Boydell, 1998.

Boeckl, Christine M. *Images of Plague and Pestilence: Iconography and Iconology*. Kirksville, MO: Truman State University Press, 2000.

Boesch Gajano, Sofia. "Gli oggetti di culto: Produzione, gestione, fruizione." In *Lo spazio del santuario: Un osservatorio per la storia di Roma e del Lazio*, edited by Sofia Boesch Gajano and Francesco Scorza Barcellona, 129–60. Rome: Viella, 2008.

Boesch Gajano, Sofia. *Res sacrae: Strumenti della devozione nella società medievale*. Rome: Viella, 2022.

Boesch Gajano, Sofia, and Marilena Modica, eds. *Miracoli: Dai segni alla storia*. Rome: Viella, 2015.

Boespflug, François, and Nicolas Lossky, eds. *Nicée II (787–1987)*. Paris: Éditions du Cerf, 1987.

Bonnet, Charles. "Les églises du haut Moyen Age d'après les recherches archéologiques." In *Grégoire de Tours et l'espace gaulois*, edited by Nancy Gauthier and Henri Galinié, supplement to the *Revue archéologique du Centre de la France* 13, 217–36. Tours: Association Grégoire 94, 1997.

Bonnet, Serge. *Entre Champagne et Lorraine: Histoire de l'ermitage et du pèlerinage de Saint Rouin*. Nîmes: Éditions Lacour-Ollé, 1996.

Bouet, Pierre, Giorgio Otranto, and André Vauchez, eds. *Culte et pèlerinages à Saint-Michel en Occident: Les trois monts dédiés à l'archange*. Rome: École Française de Rome, 2003.

Bousquet-Labouérie, Christine, and Yossi Maurey, eds. *Espace sacré, mémoire sacrée: Le culte des évêques dans leurs villes (IVᵉ–XXᵉ siècle)*. Turnhout: Brepols, 2015.

Boutry, Philippe, ed. *Reine au Mont-Auxois: Le culte et le pèlerinage de sainte Reine, des origines à nos jours*. Paris: Éditions du Cerf, 1997.

Boutry, Philippe, and Dominique Julia, eds. *Pèlerins et pèlerinages dans l'Europe moderne (XVIe–XVIIIe siècle)*. Rome: École Française de Rome, 2000.
Bozoky, Edina. *Miracle! Récits merveilleux des martyrs et des saints*. Paris: Vuibert, 2013.
Bozoky, Edina. "La politique des reliques des premiers comtes de Flandres (fin du IXe siècle–fin du XIe siècle)." In Edina Bozoky, *Le Moyen Age miraculeux: Études sur les légendes et les croyances médiévales*, 42–61. Paris: Riveneuve, 2010.
Bozoky, Edith, and Anne-Marie Helvétius, eds. *Les reliques: Objets, culte, symboles*. Turnhout: Brepols, 1999.
Bresc, Henri. "Mediterrâneo medieval: A geografia da graças." In *O Mediterrâneo medieval reconsiderado*, edited by Niéri De Barros Almeida and Robson Della Torre, 241–78. San Paolo: Editora da Unicamp, 2019.
Bresc-Bautier, Geneviève. "Les imitations du Saint-Sépulcre de Jérusalem (IXe–XVe siècle): Archéologie d'une dévotion." *Revue d'histoire de la spiritualité* 50 (1974): 319–42.
Bresc-Bautier, Geneviève. "Partir, prier, donner: Les églises fondées en souvenir du pèlerinage en Terre Sainte (Xe–XIe siècle)." In *Il Cammino di Gerusalemme*, edited by Maria Stella Calò Mariani, 565–89. Bari: Adda, 2002.
Brouillet, Louis, ed. *Liber miraculorum Sanctae fidis*. Paris: Alphonse Picard et Fils, 1897.
Brouquet, Sophie, and Michelle Fournié. "Le saint des saints: Le trésor de Saint-Sernin de Toulouse." In *Corps saints et reliques dans le Midi*, edited by Michelle Fournié, Daniel Le Blévec, and Catherine Vincent, Cahiers de Fanjeaux 53, 205–64. Toulouse: Privat, 2018.
Brufani, Stefano, and Enrico Menestò, eds. *Il Perdono di Assisi e le indulgenze plenarie*. Assisi: CISAM, 2017.
Bruna, Denis. *Enseignes de pèlerinage et enseignes profanes*. Paris: Réunion des musées nationaux, 1996.
Bruna, Denis. *Saints et diables au chapeau: Bijoux oubliés du Moyen Age*. Paris: Seuil, 2007.
Bynum, Caroline Walker. *Wonderful Blood: Theology and Practice in Late Medieval Northern Germany and Beyond*. Philadelphia: University of Pennsylvania Press, 2007.
Cabibbo, Sara. *Santa Rosalia tra terra e cielo*. Palermo: Sellerio Editore, 2004.
Caillet, Jean-Pierre. *Les trésors des sanctuaires, de l'Antiquité à l'époque romane*. Paris: Picard, 1996.
Caillet, Jean-Pierre, Sylvain Destephen, Bruno Dumézil, and Hervé Inglebert. *Des dieux civiques aux saints patrons (IVe–VIIe siècles)*. Paris: Picard, 2015.
Calò Mariani, Maria Stella. "Icone e statue lignee medievali nei santuari mariani della Puglia." In *Santuari cristiani d'Italia: Committenze e fruizione tra Medioevo e età moderna*, edited by Mario Tosti, 3–44. Rome: École Française de Rome, 2003.
Calò Mariani, Maria Stella, ed. *I Santi venuti dal mare*. Bari: Adda, 2009.
Campione, Ada. "Il Censimento dei santuari cristiani d'Italia: Ierofanie e luoghi di culto." In *Ierofanie e luoghi di culto*, edited by Luca Avellis, 115–42. Bari: Edipuglia, 2016.

Canetti, Luigi. *Frammenti di eternità: Corpi e reliquie tra Antichità e Medioevo*. Rome: Viella, 2002.
Canetti, Luigi. "'*Olea sanctorum*': Reliquie e miracoli tra Tardoantico e Medioevo." In *Olio e vino nell'Alto Medioevo*, 1335–1415. Spoleto: CISAM, 2007.
Cannella, Tessa. *Storia e leggenda del santuario di S. Michele al Monte Tancia*. Bari: Edipuglia, 2020.
Cannon, Joanna, and Beth Williamson, eds. *Art, Politics and Civic Religion in Central Italy, 1261–1352*. Aldershot: Ashgate, 2007.
Cardini, Franco, ed. *La città e il sacro*. Milan: Libri Scheiwiller, 1994.
Cardini, Franco. *Gerusalemme d'oro, di rame, di luce: Pellegrini, crociati, sognatori d'Oriente fra XI e XV secolo*. Milan: Il Saggiatore, 1991.
Carion, Anne. "Miracles de saint Martial." In *Les miracles, miroirs des corps*, edited by Jacques Gélis and Odile Redon, 87–124. Saint-Denis: Presses de l'université de Paris VIII, 1983.
Caroli, Martina. "Tipologia di santuari in Emilia Romagna." In *Santuari locali e religiosità popolare nelle diocesi di "Ravennatensia,"* edited by Maurizio Tagliaferri, 33–60. Imola: Bologna University Press, 2003.
Carosi, Attilio, and Gianfranco Ciprini. *Gli ex-voto del santuario della Madonna della Quercia di Viterbo: Immagini e testimonianze di fede*. Rome: Cassa di Risparmio di Viterbo, 1993.
Carrier, Michel. *Penser le sacré: Les sciences humaines et l'invention du sacré*. Montreal: Liber, 2005.
Casiraghi, Giampiero, and Giuseppe Sergi, eds. *Pellegrinaggi e santuari di S. Michele nell'Occidente medievale*. Bari: Edipuglia 2009.
Cassagnes-Brouquet, Sophie. "La chapelle sur le pont: Fonctions et symbolique d'un edifice au Moyen Age." In *Faire la route (IIIe–XXe siècle)*, edited by Céline Perol, 35–49. Clermont-Ferrand: Presses universitaires Blaise Pascal, 2007.
Caucci von Saucken, Paolo, ed. *Il mondo dei pellegrinaggi: Roma, Santiago, Gerusalemme*. Milan: Jaca Book, 1996.
Caulier, Brigitte. *L'eau et le sacré: Les cultes thérapeutiques autour des fontaines en France du Moyen Age à nos jours*. Paris: Beauchesne, 1990.
Cengarle, Federica. "I Visconti e il culto della Vergine (XIV secolo): Qualche osservazione." In *Images, cultes, liturgies: Les connotations politiques du message religieux*, edited by Paola Ventrone and Laura Gaffuri, 105–24. Paris: Éditions de la Sorbonne; Rome: École Française de Rome, 2014.
Charrier, René. *L'ermite de Saint-Sorlin, Joseph-Élie Simonin (1792–1856): Contribution à l'histoire religieuse du Jura et de la Congrégation du Saint-Esprit*. Langres: Éditions Dominique Guéniot, 2000.
Cherubini, Giovanni. "Le mete del pellegrinaggio medievale." In *Itinerari medievali e identità europea*, edited by Roberto Greci, 136–46. Bologna: CLUEB, 1999.
Chomel, Vital. "Pèlerins languedociens au Mont-Saint-Michel à la fin du Moyen Age." *Annales du Midi* 70 (1958): 230–39.
Christin, Olivier. *Une révolution symbolique: L'iconoclasme huguenot et la reconstruction catholique*. Paris: Les Éditions de Minuit, 1991.

Cioffari, Giorgio, and Angela Laghezza, eds. *Alle origini dell'Europa: Il culto di San Nicola tra Oriente e Occidente, Italia-Francia*. Bari: Nicolaus Studi Storici, 2011.
Citterio, Ferdinando, and Lucciano Vaccaro, eds. *Loreto crocevia religioso tra Italia, Europa e Oriente*. Brescia: Morcelliana, 1997.
Cocchini, Francesca. "Eau." In *Dictionnaire encyclopédique du christianisme ancien*, 1:735–37. Paris: Éditions du Cerf, 1990.
Codou, Yann, and Michel Lauwers, eds. *Lérins: Une île sainte de l'Antiquité au Moyen Age*. Turnhout: Brepols, 2010.
Congourdeau, Marie-Hélène. "Jérusalem et Constantinople dans la littérature apocalyptique." In *Le sacré et son inscription dans l'espace à Byzance et en Occident*, edited by Michel Kaplan, 125–36. Paris: Éditions de la Sorbonne, 2001.
Constable, Giles. "Monachisme et pèlerinage." *Revue historique* 101 (1977): 3–27.
Construction de l'espace au Moyen Age: Pratiques et représentations. Actes du 37e Congrès de la SHMES, 2006. Paris: Publications de la Sorbonne, 2007.
Cordez, Philippe. *Charlemagne et les objets: Des thésaurisations carolingiennes aux constructions mémorielles*. Bern: Peter Lang, 2012.
Cordez, Philippe. *Trésor, mémoire, merveilles: Les objets des églises au Moyen Age*. Paris: EHESS, 2016.
Cordez, Philippe. *Les trésors au Moyen Age: Discours, pratiques et objets*. Florence: SISMEL, 2010.
Cordez, Philippe. "Les usages du trésor des graces: L'économie idéelle et matérielle des indulgences au Moyen Age." In *Le trésor au Moyen Age: Questions et perspectives de recherche*, edited by Lucas Burkart, Philippe Cordez, Pierre-Alain Mariaux, and Yann Potin, 55–88. Neuchâtel: Institut d'histoire de l'Art et de Musicologie, 2005.
Cornini, Guido. "'Non est in toto sanctior orbe locus': Collecting Relics in Early Medieval Rome." In *Saints, Relics and Devotion in Medieval Europe*, edited by Martina Bagnoli, Holger A. Klein, C. Griffith Mann, and James Robinson, 69–78. Cleveland: The Cleveland Museum of Art, 2011.
Corvisier, André. *Les saints militaires*. Paris: H. Champion, 2006.
Coulet, Noël. "L'ermitage de Notre-Dame des Anges de sa fondation (XIIIe siècle?) à l'installation des oratoriens." *Provence historique* 68 (2018): 401–20.
Cracco, Giorgio. "La grande stagione dei santuari mariani (XIVe–XVIe siècle)." In *I santuari d'Italia: Bilancio del censimento e proposte interpretative*, edited by André Vauchez, 17–44. Rome: École Française de Rome, 2007.
Cracco, Giorgio. "Le leggende di fondazione dal Medioevo all'età moderna." *Annali dell'Istituto storico italo-germanico di Trento* 26 (2000): 393–413.
Crook, John. *The Architectural Setting of the Cult of Saints in the Early Christian West, ca. 300–1200*. Oxford: Clarendon Press, 2000.
Dagron, Gilbert. "Vérité du miracle." In *Del visibile credere*, edited by Davide Scotto, 139–58. Florence: Olschki, 2011.
Dalarun, Jacques. *L'impossible sainteté: La vie retrouvée de Robert d'Arbrissel*. Paris: Éditions du Cerf, 1987.

De Certeau, Michel. *L'invention du quotidien*. Vol. 1, *Arts de faire*. Paris: Gallimard, 1990.
De La Roncière, Charles. *Religion paysanne et religion urbaine en Toscane (c. 1280–c. 1450)*. Aldershot: Variorum, 1994.
De Martino, Ernesto. "Angoscia territoriale e riscatto culturale nel mito Achilpa delle origini." *Studi e materiali di storia e storia delle religioni* 23 (1951/52): 52–66.
Dehoux, Esther, Caroline Galland, and Catherine Vincent, eds. *Des usages de la grâce: Pratiques des indulgences du Moyen Age à l'époque contemporaine*. Lille: Presses universitaires du Septentrion, 2021.
Delehaye, Hippolyte. "Loca sanctorum." *Analecta Bollandiana* 48 (1930): 5–64.
Deluz, Christiane. "Un pèlerinage en Touraine au XVe siècle: Le *Livre des miracles* de Sainte Catherine de Fierbois." In *Auctoritas: Mélanges offerts à Olivier Guyot*, edited by Giles Constable and Michel Rouche, 635–45. Paris: Presses universitaires Paris-Sorbonne, 2006.
Desmette, Philippe, and Philippe Martin, eds. *Le miracle de guerre dans la chrétienté occidentale*. Paris: Coédition Hémisphères / Maisonneuve & Larose, 2018.
Dierkens, Alain, and Anne Morelli, eds. *Topographie du sacré: L'emprise religieuse sur l'espace*. Brussels: Université de Bruxelles, 2008.
Dolbeau, François. *Prophètes, apôtres et disciples dans la tradition chrétienne d'Occident*. Brussels: Société des Bollandistes, 2012.
Douglas, Mary. *Purity and Danger: An Analysis of the Concepts of Pollution and Taboo*. London: Routledge & Keegan Paul, 1966.
Duby, Georges. *L'art cistercien*. Paris: Flammarion, 2017.
Ducellier, Alain. "Une mythologie urbaine: Constantinople vue d'Occident au Moyen Age." *Mélanges de l'École Française de Rome–Moyen Âge* 96 (1984): 495–524.
Dupré Theseider, Eugenio. "La grande rapina dei corpi santi dell'Italia al tempo di Ottone." In *Festschrift Percy Ernst Schramm: Zu Seinem Siebzigsten Geburtstag von Schülern und Freunden Zugeeignet*, edited by Peter Classen, Percy Ernst Schramm, and Peter Scheibert, 1:420–32. Wiesbaden: Franz Steiner, 1964.
Dupront, Alphonse. *Du sacré: Croisades et pèlerinage. Images et langages*. Paris: Gallimard, 1987.
Dupront, Alphonse. *L'image de religion dans l'Occident chrétien*. Paris: Gallimard, 2015.
Durkheim, Émile. *The Elementary Forms of the Religious Life: A Study in Religious Sociology*. Translated by Joseph Ward Swain. London: G. Allen & Unwin, 1915.
Durnecker, Laurent. 'Tête de l'Église diocésaine et chef du saint patron: Le pèlerinage à Saint-Mammès de Langres à la fin du Moyen Age." In *Cathédrale et pèlerinage aux époques médiévales et modernes*, edited by Catherine Vincent and Jacques Pycke, 145–59. Louvain-la-Neuve: Collège Érasme / Universiteitsbibliotheek, 2010.

Édouard, Sylvène, ed. *Saintetés politiques du IXe au XVIIIe siècle: Autour de la Lotharingie—Dorsale catholique.* Paris: Classiques Garnier, 2020.

Ehmig, Ulrika, Pierre-André Sigal, and Marie-Anne Polo de Beaulieu, eds. *Les ex-voto: Objets, usages, traditions. Un regard croisé franco-allemand.* Gutenberg: Computus Druck Sata & Verlag, 2019.

Eliade, Mircea. *The Sacred and the Profane: The Nature of Religion.* Translated by Willard R. Trask. New York: Harcourt, Brace & World, 1959.

Fanin, Luciano, ed. *Dio, il mare e gli uomini.* Quaderni di storia religiosa 15. Caselle di Sommacampagna: Cierre Edizioni, 2008.

Faure, Philippe. *Les Anges.* Paris: Éditions du Cerf, 1988.

Finucane, Ronald. *Miracles and Pilgrims: Popular Beliefs in Medieval England.* New York: Palgrave Macmillan, 1977.

Foreville, Raymonde. *Le Jubilé de saint Thomas Becket, du XIIIe au XVe siècle (1220–1470): Études et documents.* Paris: SEVPEN, 1958.

Foscati, Alessandra. *"Ignis sacer": Una storia culturale del fuoco sacro dell'Antichità al Settecento.* Florence: SISMEL, 2013.

Fournié, Michelle, Daniel Le Blévec, and Catherine Vincent, eds. *Corps saints et reliques dans le Midi.* Cahiers de Fanjeaux 53. Toulouse: Privat, 2018.

Francesconi, Giampaolo. "Il Comune e i santi: Il culto iacobeo e l''acclamazione' del potere a Pistoia (secoli XII–XIV)." In *Culto dei santi e culto dei luoghi nel Medioevo pistoiese,* edited by Anna Benvenuti and Renzo Nelli, 157–72. Pistoia: Società Pistoiese, 2010.

Freedberg, David. *The Power of Images.* Chicago: University of Chicago Press, 1991.

Froeschlé-Chopard, Marie-Hélène. *Espace et sacré en Provence (XVIe–XIXe siècle): Cultes, images, confréries.* Paris: Éditions du Cerf, 1994.

Froeschlé-Chopard, Marie-Hélène. *Itinéraires pèlerins de l'ancienne Provence.* Marseilles: La Thune, 2004.

Frolow, Anatole. *La relique de la Vraie Croix: Recherches sur le développement d'un culte.* Paris: Institut des études byzantines, 1961.

Frugoni, Arsenio. *Il Giubileo de Bonifacio VIII.* Bari: Laterza, 1999.

Fustel de Coulanges. *The Ancient City: A Study on the Religions, Laws and Institutions of Ancient Greece and Rome.* Translated by Numa Denis. Garden City, NY: Doubleday, 1956.

Gaborit, Jean-René, and François Avril. "L'*Itinerarium Bernardi monachi*' et les pèlerinages d'Italie du Sud pendant le Haut Moyen Age." *Mélanges de l'École Française de Rome* 79 (1967): 259–98.

Gaffuri, Laura. "Luoghi di culto e santuari del Medioevo occidentale: Bibliografia ragionata." In *Lieux sacrés, lieux de culte, sanctuaires,* edited by André Vauchez, 176–86. Rome: École Française de Rome, 2000.

Gaffuri, Laura. "Scritture e riscritture di uno spazio sacro: La cattedrale di Vicenza nel XV secolo." In *Ottant'anni da maestro: Saggi degli allievi offerti a Giorgio Cracco,* edited by Daniela Rando, Paolo Cozzo, and Davide Scotto, 87–100. Rome: Viella, 2014.

Gagliardi, Isabella. "*Ave maris stella*: Il santuario mariano di Montenero presso Livorno." In *Dio, il mare e gli uomini,* edited by Luciano Fanin. Quaderni

di storia religiosa 15, 185-214. Caselle dei Sommacampagna: Cierre Edizioni, 2008.
Galdi, Amalia. "Navigazione e devozione nel XV secolo: Il Mar Tirreno nel Portolano dei santi." In *I santuari e il mare (Santuario di Santa Maria di Monte Berico)*, edited by Immacolata Aulisa, 149-66. Bari: Edipuglia, 2014.
Galland, Bruno. *Les authentiques de reliques du Sancta Sanctorum*. Vatican City: Bibliotheca Apostolica Vaticana, 2004.
Galletti, Anna Imelde. "Gerusalemme o la città desiderata." *Mélanges de l'École Française de Rome–Moyen Âge* 96 (1984): 459-87.
Gandolfo, Francesco. "Luoghi dei santi e luoghi dei demoni: Il riuso dei templi nel Medioevo." In *Santi e demoni nell'Alto Medioevo occidentale*, 883-923. Spoleto: CISAM, 1989.
Gandy, George N. "*Revelatio* on the Origins of Mont-Saint-Michel (Fifth–Ninth Centuries)." *Speculum* 95 (2020): 132-66.
Gaposchkin, M. Cecilia. "Between Historical Narration and Liturgical Celebrations: Gautier Cornut and the Reception of the Crown of Thorns in France." *Revue Mabillon*, n.s., 30 (2019): 91-145.
Gaposchkin, M. Cecilia. "Nivelon of Quierzy, the Cathedral of Soissons and the Relics of 1205: Liturgy and Devotion in the Aftermath of the Fourth Crusade." *Speculum* 95 (2020): 1087-1129.
Gauthier, Marie-Madeleine. *Les routes de la foi: Reliques et reliquaires de Jérusalem à Compostelle*. Fribourg im Breisgau: Bibliothèque des arts, 1983.
Gazeau, Véronique, Catherine Guyon, and Catherine Vincent, eds. *En Orient et en Occident: Le culte de saint Nicolas en Europe, X^e–XXIe siècle*. Paris: Éditions du Cerf, 2015.
Geary, Patrick J. *Furta sacra: Thefts of Relics in the Central Middle Ages*. Princeton, NJ: Princeton University Press, 1978.
Gélis, Jacques. *Les enfants des limbes: Mort-nés et parents dans l'Europe chrétienne*. Paris: Louis Audibert Éditions, 2006.
Gensini, Sergio, ed. *La "Gerusalemme" di San Vivaldo e i Sacri Monti in Europa*. Pisa: Pacini, 1989.
George, Philippe. "*Maledictio adversus ecclesiae Dei persecutores*: À propos d'un ouvrage récent." *Revue belge de philologie et d'histoire* 73 (1995): 1011-17.
George, Philippe. *Reliques: Se connecter à l'au-delà*. Paris: CNRS, 2018.
George, Philippe. "Le trésor de reliques du Neufmoustier près de Huy (XIIe–XVIIIe siècle): Une part de Terre Sainte en pays mosan." *Bulletin de la Commission royale d'Histoire* 169 (2003): 17-36.
Gillon, Pierre, and Christian Sapin, eds. *Cryptes médiévales et culte des saints en Île-de-France et en Picardie*. Villeneuve d'Ascq: Septentrion, 2019.
Girault, Marcel, and Pierre-Gilles Girault. *Visages du pèlerins au Moyen Age: Les pèlerinages européens dans l'art et l'épopée*. La-Pire-qui-Vire: Zodiaque, 2001.
Golsenne, Thomas. "Les images qui marchent: Performance et anthropologie des objets figuratifs." In *Les images dans l'Occident médiéval*, edited by Jérôme Baschet and Pierre-Olivier Dittmar, 79-136. Turnhout: Brepols, 2015.

Grabar, André. *Martyrium: Recherches sur le culte des reliques et l'art chrétien antique.* Paris: Collège de France, 1948.
Groppo, Lalla, and Oliviero Gerardi, eds. *Nigra sum: Culti, santuari e immagini delle Madonne nere d'Europa.* Turin: Atlas, 2012.
Gros, Pierre, and John Scheid. "Sanctuaire, Grèce hellénistique et Rome antique." In *Encyclopedia universalis*, 20:491–501. Paris: Encyclopedia Universalis, 1986.
Guenée, Bernard. "Le voeu de Charles VI: Essai sur la dévotion des rois de France aux XIIIe et XIVe siècles." *Journal des Savants*, 1996, no. 1: 67–135.
Guerreau, Alain. "Les pèlerinages du Mâconnais: Une structure d'organisation symbolique de l'espace." *Ethnologie française* 12 (1982): 7–30.
Guerreau, Alain. "Structure et évolution: Les représentations de l'espace dans le haut Moyen Age occidental." In *Uomo e spazio nell'Alto Medioevo*, 91–115. Spoleto: CISAM, 2003.
Guilaine, Jean. "Des pèlerinages dans la Préhistoire?" In *Les pèlerinages dans le monde: À travers le temps et l'espace*, edited by Jean Chélini and Henri Branthomme, 13–20. Paris: Hachette Littératures, 2004.
Guyon, Jean. "Le pèlerinage à Rome et dans l'Occident chrétien pendant l'Antiquité Tardive (IVe–VIIe siècle)." In *Les pèlerinages dans le monde: À travers le temps et l'espace*, edited by Jean Chelini and Henri Branthomme, 21–42. Paris: Hachette Littératures, 2004.
Hadas-Lebel, Mireille. "Jérusalem cité terrestre et céleste." In *Solitudes sacrées et villes saintes*, edited by Catherine Marin and Anne-Marie Reijnen, 211–28. Paris: Bayard, 2019.
Hahn, Cynthia. "Seeing and Believing: The Construction of Sanctity in Early-Medieval Saints' Shrines." *Speculum* 72 (1997): 1079–1106.
Hahn, Johannes, Stephen Emmel, and Ulrich Gotter, eds. *From Temple to Church: Destruction and Renewal of Local Cultic Topography in Late Antiquity.* Leiden: Brill, 2008.
Hans-Collas, Ilona. "Le Mont-Saint-Michel et les pèlerinages d'enfants aux XIVe et XVe siècles: Sources françaises et germaniques." In *Pellegrinaggi e santuari di S. Michele nell'Occidente medievale*, edited by Giampiero Casiraghi and Giuseppe Sergi, 207–39. Bari: Edipuglia, 2009.
Harris, Ruth. *Lourdes: Body and Spirit in the Secular Age.* London: Allen Lane, 1999.
Hazebrouck-Souche, Véronique. *Spiritualité, sainteté et patriotisme: Glorification du Brabant dans l'oeuvre hagiographique de Jean Gielemans (1427–1487).* Turnhout: Brepols, 2007.
Heck, Christian. *L'échelle celeste dans l'art du Moyen Age.* Paris: Flammarion, 1997.
Hediger, Christine, ed. *La Sainte-Chapelle de Paris: Royaume de France ou Jérusalem celeste?* Turnhout: Brepols, 2007.
Heers, Jacques. "Bourgs et faubourgs en Occident: Pèlerinages et dévotion au Saint-Sépulcre." In *Jérusalem, Rome, Constantinople: L'image et le mythe de la ville au Moyen Age*, edited by Daniel Poirrion, 205–15. Paris: Presses universitaires de Paris-Sorbonne, 1986.

Heinzelmann, Martin. *Translationsberichte und andere Quellen des Reliquienkultes.* Turnhout: Brepols, 1979.
Henriet, Patrick, ed. "'*Invocatio sanctificatorum nominum*': Efficacité de la prière et société chrétienne (IXe–XIIe siècle)." In *La prière en latin de l'Antiquité au XVIe siècle*, edited by Jean-François Cottier, 229-44. Turnhout: Brepols, 2006.
Henriet, Patrick. "Oviedo, Jérusalem hispanique au XIIe siècle." In *Pèlerinages et lieux saints dans l'Antiquité et le Moyen Age: Mélanges Pierre Maraval*, edited by Béatrice Caseau, Jean-Claude Cheynet, and Vincent Déroche, 245-60. Paris: Association des amis du Centre d'histoire byzantine, 2006.
Herrmann-Masquard, Nicole. *Les reliques des saints: Formation coutumière d'un droit.* Paris: Klincksieck, 1975.
Housley, Norman. "Holy Land or Holy Lands? Palestine and the Catholic West in the Late Middle Ages and Renaissance." In *The Holy Land, Holy Lands and Christian History*, edited by R. N. Swanson, 228-49. Oxford: Ecclesiastical History Society, 2000.
Hubert, Étienne, and Odile Redon, eds. "Rome des Jubilés." Special issue, *Médiévales*, no. 40 (2001).
Hubert, Jean. "Le miracle de Déols et la trêve conclue en 1187 entre les rois de France et d'Angleterre." *Bibliothèque de l'Ecole des Chartes* 96 (1935): 285-300.
Hubert, Jean. "Sources sacrées et sources saintes." *Comptes rendus des séances de l'Académie des Inscriptions et Belles-Lettres* 111 (1967): 567-73.
Inglebert, Hervé, Sylvain Destephen, and Bruno Dumézil, eds. *Le problème de la christianisation du monde Antique.* Paris: Picard, 2010.
Iogna-Prat, Dominique. *La Maison-Dieu: Une histoire monumentale de l'Église au Moyen Age (v. 800–v. 1200).* Paris: Seuil, 2006.
Jacomet, Humbert. *Les Chemins de Saint-Jacques de Compostelle.* Vic-en-Bigoree: MSM, 1999.
Jacomet, Humbert. "Jehan le Chapelain, écuyer-pèlerin du roi Charles VI (1394-1396), simulateur ou loyal serviteur?" In *Les pèlerinages de l'Antiquité à nos jours*, edited by André Vauchez, 79-119. Paris: Éditions du CTHS, 2012.
Janes, Dominic, and Gary Waller, eds. *Walsingham in Literature and Culture from the Middle Ages to Modernity.* Aldershot: Routledge, 2010.
Jansen, Katherine L. *The Making of the Magdalen: Preaching and Popular Devotion in the Later Middle Ages.* Princeton, NJ: Princeton University Press, 2000.
Jenkins, Jacqueline, and Katherine J. Lewis, eds. *St. Katherine of Alexandria: Texts and Contexts in Western Medieval Europe.* Turnhout: Brepols, 2013.
Joas, Hans. *Les pouvoirs du sacré.* Paris: Seuil, 2020.
Johnston, James H., and Paul A. Hayward, eds. *The Cult of Saints in Late Antiquity and the Early Middle Ages: Essays on the Contribution of Peter Brown.* Oxford: Oxford University Press, 2002.
Judic, Bruno. "Le pèlerinage à Saint-Martin de Tours du VIIe au Xe siècle." In *Les pèlerinages dans le monde: À travers le temps et l'espace*, edited by Jean Chélini and Henri Branthomme, 55-72. Paris: Hachette Littératures, 2004.

Judic, Bruno, Robert Beck, Christine Bousquet-Labouérie, and Elisabeth Lorans, eds. *Un nouveau Martin: Essor et renouveau de la figure de S. Martin, IVe–XXIe siècle*. Tours: Presses universitaires François-Rabelais, 2019.

Julia, Dominique. "Continuités et ruptures dans la vie des pèlerinages, de la Réforme à la Révolution française." In *Del visibile credere*, edited by Davide Scotto, 3-39. Florence: Olschki, 2011.

Julia, Dominique. "Sanctuaires et lieux sacrés à l'époque moderne." In *Lieux sacrés, lieux de culte, sanctuaires*, edited by André Vauchez, 241-95. Rome: École Française de Rome, 2000.

Julia, Dominique. *Le voyage aux saints: Les pèlerinages dans l'Occident moderne (XVe–XVIIIe siècle)*. Paris: Seuil, 2016.

Kaplan, Michel, ed. *Le sacré et son inscription dans l'espace à Byzance et en Occident*. Paris: Publications de la Sorbonne, 2001.

Kedar, Benjamin Z. "Le miracle du feu de Jérusalem: Des origines à la suppression papale." In *De la Bourgogne à l'Orient: Mélanges offerts à Monsieur le Doyen Jean Richard*, edited by Jacques Meissonnier, 519-25. Dijon: Jacques Meissonnier, 2020.

Klaniczay, Gábor. "Da Verna a San Giovanni Rotondo: La ierofania nelle esperienze dei stigmatizzati." In *Ierofanie e luoghi di culto*, edited by Luca Avellis, 197-215. Bari: Edipuglia, 2016.

Kötting, Bernhard. *Peregrinatio religiosa: Wallfahrt und Pilgerwesen in Antike und alter Kirche*. Münster: Verlag Regensberg, 1950.

Krautheimer, Richard. *Rome: Profile of a City, 312–1308*. Princeton, NJ: Princeton University Press, 2000.

Krötzl, Christian. "Miracles au tombeau—miracles à distance: Approches typologiques." In *Miracle et Karama: Hagiographies médiévales comparées*, edited by Denise Aigle, 557-76. Turnhout: Brepols, 2000.

Krötzl, Christian. *Pilger, Mirakel und Alltag: Formen des Verhaltens im skandinavischen Mittelalter*. Helsinki: Suomen Historiallinen Seura, 1994.

Kühnel, Bianca. *From the Earthly to the Heavenly Jerusalem: Representations of the Holy City in Christian Art of the First Millenium*. Freiburg: Herder, 1987.

Kühnel, Bianca, Galit Noga-Banai, and Hanna Vorholt, eds. *Visual Constructs of Jerusalem*. Turnhout: Brepols, 2014.

Kuryluk, Ewa. *Veronica and Her Cloth: History, Symbolism and Structure of a True Image*. Oxford: Blackwell, 1991.

Kuzmova, Stanislava, Anna Marinkovic, and Trpimir Vedris, eds. *Cuius Patrocinio Tota Gaudet Regio: Saints' Cults and the Dynamics of Regional Cohesion*. Zagreb: Hagiotheca, 2014.

Labande, Edmond-René. *Pauper et peregrinus: Problèmes, comportements et mentalités du pèlerin chrétien*. Turnhout: Brepols, 2004.

Lauwers, Michel. *Monastères et espace social: Genèse et transformation d'un système de lieux dans l'Occident médiéval*. Turnhout: Brepols, 2014.

Lauwers, Michel. *Naissance des cimetières: Lieux sacrés et terre des morts dans l'Occident médiéval*. Paris: Aubier, 2005.

Lauwers, Michel. "Sanctuaires, liturgie et rayonnement du sacré dans le bassin occidental de la Méditerranée." In *Les sanctuaires et leur rayonnement dans le monde méditerranéen, de l'antiquité à l'époque moderne*, edited by Juliette de la Genière, André Vauchez, and Jean Leclant, 359-72. Paris: De Boccard, 2010.

Lauwers, Michel, and Laurent Ripart. "Représentations et gestions de l'espace dans l'Occident médiéval (Ve-XIIIe siècle)." In *Rome et l'État moderne européen*, edited by Jean-Philippe Genet, 115-71. Rome: École Française de Rome, 2007.

Lazure, Guy. "Posséder le sacré: Monarchie et identité dans la collection de reliques de Philippe II à l'Escorial." In *Reliques modernes: Cultes et usages chrétiens des corps saints, des Réformes aux Révolutions*, edited by Philippe Boutry, Pierre-Antoine Fabre, and Dominique Julia, 372-404. Paris: Éditions de l'EHESS, 2009.

Le Maho, Jacques. "Le lieux de pèlerinage rouennais au temps des ducs (X^e-XIIe siècles)." In *Identités pèlerines*, edited by Catherine Vincent, 93-106. Rouen: Publications de l'Université de Rouen, 2004.

Legner, Anton. *Reliquien in Kunst und Kult, zwischen Antike und Aufklärung.* Darmstadt: Wissenschaftliche Buchgesellschaft, 1995.

Lemaître, Jean-Loup. "Les miracles de saint Martial accomplis lors de l'ostension de 1388." *Bulletin de la Société archéologique et historique du Limousin* 102 (1975): 66-139.

Lemaître, Nicole. "Rome, cité de l'éternel pardon." In *Solitudes sacrées et villes saintes*, edited by Catherine Marin and Anne Marie Reijnen, 229-49. Paris: Bayard, 2019.

Leniaud, Jean-Michel, and Françoise Perrot. *La Sainte-Chapelle*. Paris: Éditions du Patrimoine, 2016.

Lewis, Flora. "Rewarding Devotion: Indulgences and the Promotion of Images." In *The Church and the Arts*, edited by Diana Wood, Studies in Church History 28, 179-94. Oxford: Ecclesiastical History Society, 1997.

Little, Lester K. *Benedictine Malediction: Liturgical Cursing in Romanesque France.* Ithaca, NY: Cornell University Press, 1993.

Lombardi Satriani, Luigi Maria, and Mariano Meligrana. *Il Ponte di S. Giacomo: L'ideologia della morte nella società contadina del Sud*. Palermo: Rizzoli, 1982.

Loseries, Wolfgang. "Presentation of Relics in Late Medieval Siena: The 'Cappella delle reliquie' in Siena Cathedral." In *Matter of Faith: An Interdisciplinary Study of Relics and Relic Veneration in the Medieval Period*, edited by James Robinson, Lloyd De Beer, and Anna Harnden, 56-65. London: British Museum, 2015.

Madignier, Jacques. *Diocèse d'Autun*. Fasti Ecclesiae Gallicanae 12. Turnhout: Brepols, 2010.

Maes, Bruno, Daniel Moulinet, and Catherine Vincent, eds. *Jubilé et culte marial (Moyen Age–époque contemporarine)*. Saint-Étienne: Presses universitaires de Saint-Étienne, 2009.

Mâle, Émile. *Les saints compagnons du Christ*. Paris: Hartmann, 1959.

Malquori, Alessandra, Manuela De Giorgi, and Laura Fenelli, eds. *Atlante delle Tebaidi e dei temi figurativi*. Florence: Centre Di, 2014.

Maraval, Pierre. *Lieux saints et pèlerinages d'Orient: Histoire et géographie, des origines à la conquête arabe.* 1985; reprinted Paris: CNRS, 2011.

Marignan, Albert. *Études sur la civilisation française*, vol. 2, *Le culte des saints sous les Mérovingiens.* Paris: Librairie Émile Bouillon, 1889.

Markus, Robert A. "How on Earth Could Places Become Holy? Origins of the Christian Ideas of Holy Places." *Journal of Early Christian Studies* 2 (1994): 257–70.

Martin, Philippe. *Les chemins du sacré: Paroisses, processions, pèlerinages en Lorraine du XVIe au XIXe siècle.* Metz: Éditions Serpenoise, 1995.

Martin, Philippe. "Sanctuaires-mères et pèlerinages-relais." In *Identités pèlerines*, edited by Catherine Vincent, 107–22. Rouen: Publications de l'Université de Rouen, 2004.

Matz, Jean-Michel. "Les miracles de l'évêque Jean Michel." In *Mirakel im Mittelalter*, edited by Martin Heinzelmann, Klaus Herbers, and Dieter Bauer, 377–98. Stuttgart: Steiner, 2002.

Matz, Jean-Michel. "Les miracles de le l'évêque Jean Michel et le culte des saints dans le Diocèse d'Angers, v. 1370–v.1560." PhD thesis, Université de Paris-Nanterre, 1993.

Mazel, Florian. *L'évêque et le territoire: L'invention médiévale de l'espace (V^e–XIIIe siècle).* Paris: Seuil, 2016.

Mazzei, Rita. "La Madonna degli Italiani: I santuari mariani d'Italia." In *Storia sociale e culturale d'Italia*, vol. 6, *La cultura folklorica*, edited by Franco Cardini, 161–233. Florence: Bramante, 1988.

McAvoy, Liz Herbert. *Anchoritic Traditions of Medieval Europe.* Woodbridge: Boydell, 2010.

Méhu, Didier. *Paix et communauté autour de l'abbaye de Cluny (X^e–XIe siècle).* Lyons: Presses universitaires de Lyon, 2001.

Meloni, Maria Giuseppina. "Il fenomeno santuariale in Sardegna." In *I santuari cristiani d'Italia*, edited by André Vauchez, 203–15. Rome: École Française de Rome, 2007.

Meloni, Maria Giuseppina, and Olivetta Schena, eds. *Santuari d'Italia: Sardegna.* Rome: De Luca, 2020.

Mengel, David. "Bohemia's Treasury of Saints: Relics and Indulgences in Emperor Charles IV's Prague." In *Les saints et leur culte en Europe centrale au Moyen Age (XIe–début du XVIe siècle)*, edited by Marie-Madeleine de Cevins and Olivier Marin, 57–86. Turnhout: Brepols, 2017.

Mercuri, Chiara. *Saint Louis et la couronne d'épines: Histoire d'une relique à la Sainte-Chapelle.* Paris: Riveneuve, 2011.

Mercuri, Chiara. *La Vera Croce: Storia e leggenda, dal Golgota a Roma.* Bari: Laterza, 2014.

Mériaux, Charles. *Gallia irradiata: Saints et sanctuaires dans le nord de la Gaule du Haut Moyen Age.* Stuttgart: Franz Steiner Verlag, 2006.

Meyer, Andreas, ed. *Il Volto Santo in Europa: Culto e immagini del Crocifisso nel Medioevo.* Lucca: Istituto Storico Lucchese, 2005.

Miedema, Nine Robijntje. *Die Römischen Kirchen im Spätmittelalter nach den "Indulgentiae Ecclesiarum Urbis Romae."* Tübingen: De Gruyter, 2001.

Migdal, Anna Maria. *Regina Coeli: Les images mariales et le culte des reliques. Entre Orient et Occident au Moyen Age.* Turnhout: Brepols, 2017.
Mollat, Michel. *La vie quotidienne des gens de mer en Atlantique, IXe–XVIe siècle.* Paris: Le Grand Livre du mois, 2001.
Monnet, Pierre. *Charles IV, un empereur en Europe.* Paris: Fayard, 2020.
Moore, Robert I. *Hérétiques: Résistances et répression dans l'Occident médiéval.* Paris: Belin, 2017. [Originally published in English as *The War on Heresy: Faith and Power in Medieval Europe* (Cambridge, MA: Harvard University Press, 2012).]
Morris, Colin. *The Sepulchre of Christ and the Medieval West: From the Beginning to 1600.* Oxford: Oxford University Press, 2005.
Mussolin, Mauro. "Deserti e crudi sassi: Mito, vita religiosa e architetture dalle origini al primo Quattrocento." In *"Altro monte non ha più santo il mondo": Storia, architettura ed arte alla Verna dalle origini al Quattrocento,* edited by Nicoletta Baldini, 117–36. Florence: Edizioni Studi Francescani, 2012.
Mussolin, Mauro. "*Decus, magnificentia, sumptus:* Loci e santuari dell'Osservanza francescana in Umbria e Toscana fra Quattrocento e primo Cinquecento." In *"Altro monte non ha più santo il mondo": Storia, architettura ed arte alla Verna fra il XV ed il XVI secolo,* edited by Nicoletta Baldini, 89–133. Florence: Edizioni Studi Francescani, 2014.
Muzzarelli, Maria Giusuppina. *Penitenze nel Medioevo: Uomini e modelli a confronto.* Bologna: Pàtron, 1994.
Oldoni, Massimo, ed. *Tra Roma e Gerusalemme nel Medioevo: Paesaggi, umani ed ambientali del pellegrinaggio meridionale.* 3 vols. Salerno: Laveglia, 2005.
Olivieri, Laura M., ed. *Ordini religiosi e santuari in età medievale e moderna.* Bari: Edipuglia, 2013.
Orselli, Alba Maria. *Basileousa polis, Regia civitas: Studi sul Tardoantico cristiano.* Spoleto: CISAM, 2015.
Orselli, Alba Maria. *L'immaginario religioso della città medievale.* Ravenna: Edizioni del girasole, 1985.
Otranto, Giorgio. "Le rayonnement du sanctuaire de saint Michel au Mont Gargan en Italie du Sud, à l'époque médiévale." In *Les sanctuaires et leur rayonnement dans le monde méditerranéen, de l'antiquité à l'époque moderne,* edited by Juliette de la Genière, André Vauchez, and Jean Leclant, 323–57. Paris: De Boccard, 2010.
Otranto, Giorgio, and Carlo Carletti. *Il santuario di S. Michele Arcangelo sul Gargano, dalle origini al X secolo.* Bari: Edipuglia, 1990.
Otto, Rudolf. *The Idea of the Holy: An Inquiry into the Non-Rational Factor in the Idea of the Divine and Its Relation to the Rational.* Translated by John W. Harvey. New York: Oxford University Press, 1958.
Oursel, Raymond. *Sanctuaires et chemins de pèlerinage.* Paris: Éditions du Cerf, 1997.
Pacciani, Riccardo, and Guido Vannini. *La Gerusalemme de San Vivaldo in Valdesa.* Montaione: Titivillus, 1998.
Paciocco, Roberto. *Canonizzazioni e culto dei santi nella christianitas, 1198–1302.* Assisi: Edizioni Porziuncola, 2006.

Palazzo, Éric. *L'espace rituel et le sacré dans le christianisme: La liturgie de l'autel portatif dans l'Antiquité et au Moyen Age*. Turnhout: Brepols, 2008.

Palumbo, Genoveffa. *Giubileo, giubilei: Pellegrini e pellegrine, riti, santi, immagini per una storia dei sacri itinerari*. Rome: Rai Eri, 1999.

Palumbo, Genoveffa. "Oggetti e devozioni nel Napoletano: Il sanctuario di Casaluce, le anfore, la Madonna, la scattola, il dragone." In *Santuari cristiani d'Italia: Committenze e fruizione tra Medioevo e età moderna*, edited by Mario Tosti, 109–24. Rome: École Française de Rome, 2003.

Papasidero, Marco. *Translatio sanctitatis: I furti di reliquie nell'Italia medievale*. Florence: Firenze University Press, 2019.

Paravicini Bagliani, Agostino. *Boniface VIII: Un pape hérétique*. Paris: Payot, 2003.

Paul, Jacques. *Louis d'Anjou, prince et franciscain*. Padua: Centro Studi Antoniani, 2018.

Paul-Lévy, Françoise, and Marion Segaud. *Anthropologie de l'espace*. Paris: Centre de création industrielle / Centre Georges Pompidou, 1984.

Péricard-Méa, Denis. *Compostelle et cultes de saint Jacques au Moyen Age*. Paris: Presses universitaires de France, 2000.

Perol, Céline, ed. *Faire la route (IIIe–XXe siècle)*. Clermont-Ferrand: Presses universitaires Blaise Pascal, 2007.

Petrarca, Valerio. "Dinamiche simboliche di un santuario tra storia e antropologia." In *I santuari cristiani d'Italia*, edited by André Vauchez, 329–46. Rome: École Française de Rome, 2007.

Petrucci, Armando. "Aspetti del culto e del pellegrinaggio di S. Michele Arcangelo sul Monte Gargano." In *Pellegrinaggi e culto dei santi in Europa fino all prima Crociata*, 145–80. Todi: Accademia tudertina, 1963.

Picard, Jean-Charles. *Évêques, saints et cités en Italie et en Gaule: Études d'archéologie et d'histoire*. Rome: École Française de Rome, 1998.

Picard, Jean-Charles. *Le souvenir des évêques: Sépultures, listes épiscopales et culte des évêques dans l'Italie du Nord, des origines au Xe siècle*. Rome: École Française de Rome, 1988.

Picard, Olivier. "Sanctuaire et prière dans la cité grecque classique." *Comptes rendus des séances de l'Académie des Inscriptions et Belles-Lettres* 160 (2016): 1529–37.

Pietri, Charles. *Roma christiana*. Rome: École Française de Rome, 1976.

Pietri, Luce. "Grégoire de Tours et la géographie du sacré." In *Grégoire de Tours et l'espace gaulois*, edited by Nancy Gauthier and Henri Galinié, supplement to the *Revue archéologique du Centre de la France* 13, 11–114. Tours: Association Grégoire 94, 1997.

Pietri, Luce. "*Loca sancta*: La géographie de la sainteté dans l'hagiographie gauloise (IVe–Ve siècle)." In *Luoghi sacri e spazi della santità*, edited by Sofia Boesch Gajano and Lucetta Scaraffia, 23–36. Turin: Rosenberg & Sellier, 1990.

Pietri, Luce. *La ville de Tours du IVe au VIe siècle: Naissance d'une cité chrétienne*. Rome: École Française de Rome, 1983.

Pomian, Krzystof. *Des saintes reliques à l'art moderne: Venise-Chicago, XIIIe–XXe siècle*. Paris: Gallimard, 2003.

Potin, Yann. *Trésors, écrits, pouvoirs: Archives et bibliothèques d'État en France à la fin du Moyen Age.* Paris: Éditions du CNRS, 2020.
Pouvreau, Florent. *Du poil et de la bête: Iconographie du corps sauvage en Occident à la fin du Moyen Age (XIIIe–XVIe siècle).* Paris: Éditions du CTHS, 2015.
Pycke, Jacques. "Les pèlerinages de dévotion dans la première moitié du XIVe siècle." In *Horae Tornacenses, 1171–2017: Recueil d'Études d'Histoire publiées à l'Occasion du VIIIe Centenaire de la Consécration de la Cathédrale de Tournai,* edited by Nicolas Huyghebaert, 110-30. Tournai: Archives de la Cathédrale, 1971.
Rapp, Francis. "Indulgences, jubilé, pardons." In *Le Grand Pardon de Chaumont et les Pardons dans la vie religieuse (XIVe–XXIe siècle),* edited by Patrick Corbet, François Petrazoller, and Vincent Tabbagh, 17-26. Paris: Le Pythagore, 2011.
Rapp, Francis, "Les pèlerinages dans la vie religieuse de l'Occident médiéval aux XIVe et XVe siècles." In F. Raphaël, et al., *Les pèlerinages de l'Antiquité biblique et classique à l'Occident médiéval,* 119-60. Paris: Paul Geuthner, 1973.
Rebillard, Éric. *Religion et sépulture: L'Église, les vivants et les morts dans l'Antiquité Tardive.* Paris: EHESS, 2003.
Recht, Roland. *Le croire et le voir: L'art des cathédrales (XIIe–XVe siècles).* Paris: Gallimard, 1999.
Ries, Julien. *Les Chemins du sacré dans l'histoire.* Paris: Éditions Aubier, 1992.
Rigaux, Dominique. "Miracle, reliques et images dans la chapelle du Corporal à Orvieto (1357-1364)." In *Pratiques de l'eucharistie dans les Églises d'Orient et d'Occident (Antiquité et Moyen Age),* edited by Béatrice Caseau-Chevallier, Nicole Bériou, and Dominique Rigaux, 201-45. Turnhout: Brepols, 2009.
Rigon, Antonio, and André Vauchez, eds. *San Rocco: Genesi e prime espansione di un culto.* Brussels: Société des Bollandistes, 2006.
Ripart, Laurent. "Le Saint Suaire, les Savoie et Chambéry (1453-1515)." In *The Shroud at Court: History, Usages, Places and Images of a Dynastic Relic,* edited by Paolo Cozzo, Andrea Merlotti, and Andrea Nicolotti, 57-74. Leiden: Brill, 2019.
Rocacher, Jean. *Rocamadour et son pèlerinage.* Vol. 1. Toulouse: Association les Amis de Rocamadour, 1979.
Roch, Martin. *L'intelligence d'un sens: Odeurs miraculeuses et odorat dans l'Occident du Moyen Age.* Turnhout: Brepols, 2009.
Rosenwein, Barbara. *Emotional Communities in the Early Middle Ages.* Ithaca, NY: Cornell University Press, 2006.
Rosenwein, Barbara. *Negotiating Space: Power, Restraint and Privileges of Immunity in Early Medieval Europe.* Ithaca, NY: Cornell University Press, 1999.
Rossetti, Gabriella. *Santa Croce e Santo Volto: Contributi allo studio dell'origine e della fortuna del culto del Salvatore (secoli IX–XV).* Pisa: ETS, 2003.
Rubin, Miri. *Corpus Christi: The Eucharist in Late Medieval Culture.* Cambridge: Cambridge University Press, 1991.
Rucquoi, Adeline. *Mille fois à Compostelle: Pèlerins au Moyen Age.* Paris: Les Belles Lettres, 2014.

Saint-Martin, Isabelle. "Les églises sont des lieux consacrés plus que des lieux sacrés." *Le Monde de la Bible*, no. 233 (2020): 72–76.
Saintyves, Pierre. *Le folklore des eaux dans la région des Pyrénées: Enquête religieuse*. Paris: Société d'ethnographie de Paris, 1935.
San Nicola, Tolentino, le Marche: Contributi e ricerche sul Processo (a. 1325) per la canonizzazione di san Nicola da Tolentino. Tolentino: Biblioteca Egidiana, 1985.
Sansterre, Jean-Marie. *Les images sacrées en Occident au Moyen Age: Histoire, attitudes, croyances. Recherches sur le témoignage des textes*. Madrid: AKAL, 2021.
Sansterre, Jean-Marie. "Quand les textes parlent des images: Croyances et pratiques." In *Les images dans l'Occident médiéval*, edited by Jérôme Baschet and Pierre-Olivier Dittmar, 169–78. Turnhout: Brepols, 2015.
Sansterre, Jean-Marie. "Sacralité et pouvoir thaumaturgique des statues mariales (X^e–première moitié du XIIIe siècle)." *Revue Mabillon*, n.s. 2 (2011): 53–77.
Sansterre, Jean-Marie. "La substitution des images aux reliques et des limites dans la diffusion de la *virtus* des saints (espace français, fin XIIIe–XVIe siècle)." *Analecta Bollandiana* 126 (2018): 61–106.
Saxer, Victor. *Le culte de Marie-Madeleine en Occident, des origines à la fin du Moyen Age*. 2 vols. Auxerre: Publications de la Société des Fouilles Archéologiques et des Monuments Historiques de l'Yonne; Paris: Clavreuil, 1959.
Saxer, Victor. *Le dossier vézelien de Marie-Madeleine: Invention et translation des reliques en 1265–1267*. Brussels: Société des Bollandistes, 1975.
Scaraffia, Lucetta. *Il Giubileo*. Bologna: Il Mulino, 1999.
Schmitt, Jean-Claude. *Le corps des images: Essai sur la culture visuelle du Moyen Age*. Paris: Gallimard, 2002.
Schmitt, Jean-Claude. *Le saint Lévrier: Guinefort, guérisseur d'enfants depuis le XIIIe siècle*. Paris: Flammarion, 1993.
Schmitt, Jean-Claude. "Les 'superstitions.'" In *Histoire de la France religieuse*, edited by Jacques Le Goff and René Rémond, 1:497–551. Paris: Seuil, 1988.
Schmugge, Ludwig. "Die Anfänge des organisierten Pilgerverkehrs im Mittelalter." *Quellen und Forschungen aus italienischen Archiven und Bibliotheken* 64 (1984): 1–83.
Schreiner, Klaus. *Maria Jungfrau, Mutter, Herrscherin*. Vienna: Hanser, 1994.
Sclafer, Jacqueline, ed. *Miracles de sainte Marie Madeleine*. Paris: CNRS, 1996.
Sensi, Mario. "Monti sacri, transfert di sacralità e santuari *ad instar*." In *Tra monti sacri, "sacri monti" e santuari: Il caso Veneto*, edited by Antonio Diano and Lionelli Puppi, 39–72. Monselice: Il Poligrafo, 2004.
Sensi, Mario. "Santuari, culti e riti *'ad repellendam pestem'* tra Medioevo e Età Moderna." In *Luoghi sacri e spazi della santità*, edited by Sofia Boesch-Gajano and Lucetta Scaraffia, 381–96. Turin: Rosenberg & Sellier, 1990.
Sensi, Mario. "Santuari del perdono e santuari eremitici *'à répit'*: Esempi umbro-marchigiani." In *Lieux sacrés, lieux de culte, sanctuaires*, edited by André Vauchez, 215–39. Rome: École Française de Rome, 2000.
Sensi, Mario. *Santuari e pellegrini lungo le "vie dell'angelo": Storie sommerse del culto micaelico*. Rome: Istituto Storico Italiano per il Medioevo, 2014.

Sensi, Mario. "Santuari in grotta tra Umbria e Marche." In Mario Sensi, *Mulieres in ecclesia: Storie de monache e di bizzoche*, 1:137–78. Spoleto: CISAM, 2010.

Sensi, Mario. "Santuari terapeutici di frontiera nella montagna folignate." *Bollettino storico della Città di Foligno* 4 (1980): 87–120.

Sergi, Giuseppe. *L'arcangelo sulli Alpi: Origini, cultura e caratteri dell'abbazia medievale di S. Michele della Chiusa*. Bari: Edipuglia, 2011.

Sergi, Giuseppe. "Il pellegrinaggi altomedievali e lo spaesamento della communicazione." In *Communicare e significare nell'alto Medioevo*, 1165–88. Spoleto: CISAM, 2007.

Sigal, Pierre-André. *L'homme et le miracle dans la France médiévale (XIe–XIIe siècle)*. Paris: Éditions du Cerf, 1985.

Sigal, Pierre-André. "Les miracles de saint Étienne de Muret († 1124) au XIIe siècle." *Études héraultaises* (1992): 43–51.

Signori, Gabriela. "La bienheureuse polysémie: Miracles et pèlerinages de la Vierge (X^e–XIIe siècle)." In *Marie: Le culte de la Vierge dans la société médiévale*, edited by Dominique Iogna-Prat, Daniel Russo, and Éric Palazzo, 591–617. Paris: Beauchesne, 1996.

Simeoni, Paola Elisabetta. "Santuari fra antropologia e storia: Il culto alla Santissima Trinità di Vallepietra." In *Lazio*, edited by Sofia Boesch Gajano, Santuari d'Italia 1, 104–17. Rome: De Luca, 2010.

Smith, Julia Mary Howard. "L'accès des femmes aux reliques durant le Haut Moyen Age." *Médiévales*, no. 40 (2001): 83–100.

Smith, Julia Mary Howard. "Care of Relics in Early Medieval Rome." In *Rome and Religion in the Medieval World: Studies in Honor of Thomas F. X. Noble*, edited by Valerie L. Garver and Owen Michael Phelan, 179–205. Farnham: Ashgate, 2014.

Snoek, Godefridus J. C. *Medieval Piety from Relics to Eucharist*. Leiden: Brill, 1995.

Sodini, Jean-Pierre. "Saint Syméon: L'influence de Saint-Syméon dans le culte et l'économie de l'Antiochène." In *Les sanctuaires et leur rayonnement dans le monde méditerranéen, de l'antiquité à l'époque moderne*, edited by Juliette de la Genière, André Vauchez, and Jean Leclant, 295–322. Paris: De Boccard, 2010.

Sotinel, Claire. "La disparition des lieux de culte païens en Occident: Enjeux et méthodes." In *Hellénisme et christianisation*, edited by Michel Nancy and Éric Rebillard, 35–60. Villeneuve d'Ascq: Septentrion, 2004.

Spicciani, Amleto, ed. *La devozione dei Bianchi nel 1399: Il miracolo del Crocifisso di Borgo a Buggiano*. Pisa: ETS, 1998.

Stahl, Gerlinde. "Die Wallfahrt zur 'Schönen Maria' in Regensburg." *Beiträge zur Geschichte des Bistums Regensburg* 2 (1968): 35–282.

Stiker, Henri-Jacques. *Religions et Handicap: Interdit, péché, symbole. Une analyse anthropologique*. Paris: Hermann, 2017.

Stopani, Renato. *La via Francigena: Una strada europea nell'Italia del Medioevo*. Florence: Le Lettere, 1988.

Swanson, Robert N., ed. *Promissory Notes on the Treasury of Merits: Indulgences in Late Medieval Europe*. Leiden: Brill, 2006.

Tabbagh, Vincent. "Les évêques et les indulgences de la France des XIVe et XVe siècles." In *Des usages de la grâce: Pratiques des indulgences du Moyen Age à l'époque contemporaine*, edited by Esther Dehoux, Caroline Galland, and Catherine Vincent, 107–18. Lille: Presses universitaires du Septentrion, 2021.

Thuaudet, Olivier. "La pratique du pèlerinage en Provence à la fin du Moyen Age et au début de l'époque moderne." *Archéologie médiévale* 47 (2017): 90–129.

Thunø, Erik. "The Miraculous Image and the Centralized Church: Santa Maria della Consolazione in Todi." In *The Miraculous Image in the Middle Ages and Renaissance*, edited by Erik Thunø and Gerhard Wolf, 29–56. Rome: L'Erma di Bretschneider, 2004.

Thunø, Erik, and Gerhard Wolf, eds. *The Miraculous Image in the Middle Ages and Renaissance*. Rome: L'Erma di Bretschneider, 2004.

Tilatti, Andrea, ed. *Santuari di confine: Una tipologia?* Gorizia: Edizioni della Laguna, 2008.

Tollet, Daniel, ed. *Études sur les Terres saintes et les pèlerinages dans les religions monothéistes*. Paris: H. Champion, 2012.

Tomasi, Michele. *Le arche dei santi: Scultura, religione e politica*. Rome: Viella, 2012.

Touati, François-Olivier. "Guérisons et apparitions en Orient et en Occident: Réflexions sur l'incubation." In *Purifier, soigner ou guérir*, edited by Cécile Chapelain de Serville-Niel, Christine Delaplace, Jeanne Damien, and Pierre Sineux, 153–58. Rennes: Presses universitaires de Rennes, 2020.

Trân-Duc, Lucille. "Les princes normands et les reliques (X^e–XIe siècles): Contribution du culte des saints à la formation territoriale et identitaire d'une principauté." In *Reliques et saintetés dans l'espace médiéval*, edited by Jean-Luc Deuffic, 525–61. Saint-Denis: PECIA, 2006.

Treffort, Cécile. "Consécrations de cimetières et contrôle épiscopal des lieux d'inhumation." In *Le sacré et son inscription dans l'espace à Byzance et en Occident*, edited by Michel Kaplan, 285–99. Paris: Publications de la Sorbonne, 2001.

Treffort, Cécile. *L'Église carolingienne et la mort: Christianisme, rites funéraires et pratiques commémoratives*. Lyons: Presses universitaires de Lyon, 1996.

Trexler, Richard. "Florentine Religious Experience: The Sacred Image." *Studies in the Renaissance* 19 (1972): 7–41.

Tuniz, Dorino, ed. *I Sacri Monti: Itinerari ascetici cristiani*. Archivio italiano per la storia della pietà 28. Rome: Edizioni di storia e letteratura, 2015.

Turchini, Andrea. *Uomo e spazio nell'alto Medioevo*. Spoleto: CISAM, 2003.

Vaccaro, Lucciano, ed. *L'Europa dei pellegrini*. Gazzada: Centro Ambrosiano, 2004.

Vauchez, André. "Les cathédrales." In *Les Lieux de mémoire*, vol. 3, *La France*, pt. 2, *Traditions*, edited by Pierre Nora, 94–127. Paris: Gallimard, 1993.

Vauchez, André. "Du Gargano à Compostelle: La sainte pèlerine Bona de Pise († 1207)." In *Puer Apuliae: Mélanges Jean-Marie Martin*, 737–43. Paris: Publications de la Sorbonne, 2008.

Vauchez, André. "Un eroe medievale: Il santo pellegrino nell'agiografia italiana." In *San Pellegrino tra mito e storia: I luoghi di culto in Europa*, edited by Adelaide Trezzini, 33-42. Rome: Gangemi, 2009.
Vauchez, André. "Faire voir Jérusalem: Des imitations du Saint-Sépulcre aux 'Sacri Monti' italiens." *Comptes rendus des séances de l'Académie des Inscriptions et Belles-Lettres* 160 (2016): 1559-72.
Vauchez, André. *Francis of Assisi: The Life and Afterlife of a Medieval Saint*. Translated by Michael F. Cusato. New Haven: Yale University Press, 2012.
Vauchez, André. "L'homme au péril de la mer dans les miracles médiévaux." In *L'homme face aux calamités naturelles dans l'Antiquité et au Moyen Age*, edited by Jacques Jouanna, Jean Leclant, and Michel Zink, 183-95. Paris: De Boccard, 2006.
Vauchez, André. "Les jubilés romains des XIVe et XVe siècles." In *Le Grand Pardon de Chaumont et les Pardons dans la vie religieuse (XIVe–XXIe siècles)*, edited by Patrick Corbet, François Petrazoller, and Vincent Tabbagh, 47-53. Dijon: Le Pythagore, 2011.
Vauchez, André. "Pèlerinages posthumes et purgation des péchés: La vision de Narni (milieu du XIe siècle)." In *Mediterraneo, Mezzogiorno, Europa: Studi in onore di Cosimo Damiano Fonseca*, edited by Giancarlo Andenna and Hubert Houben, 2:1081-90. Bari: Adda, 2004.
Vauchez, André. *Religion et société dans l'Occident mediéval*. Turin: Bottega d'Erasmo, 1980.
Vauchez, André. *La sainteté en Occident aux derniers siècles du Moyen Age: D'après les procès de canonisation et les documents hagiographiques*. Rome: École Française de Rome, 1981.
Vauchez, André. *Saint Homebon de Crémone, "père des pauvres" et patron des tailleurs: Vies médiévales et histoire du culte*. Brussels: Subsidia Hagiographica, 2018.
Vauchez, André. *Saints, prophètes et visionnaires: Le pouvoir surnaturel au Moyen Age*. Paris: Albin Michel, 1999.
Vauchez, André, and Andrea Giardina, eds. *Rome, l'idée et le mythe, des origines à nos jours*. Paris: Fayard, 1999.
Vergnolle, Éliane, ed. *Saint-Martial de Limoges: Millénaire de l'abbaye romane (1018–2018)*. Bulletin monumental 178 (1978). Paris: Société française d'archéologie, 2020.
Veyssière, Gérard. "Miracles et merveilles en Provence aux XIIIe et XIVe siècles." In *Miracles, prodiges et merveilles au Moyen Age*, 91-114. Paris: Publications de la Sorbonne, 1995.
Vincent, Catherine. *Fiat Lux: Lumière et luminaires dans la vie religieuse du XIIIe au XVIe siècle*. Paris: Éditions du Cerf, 2004.
Vincent, Catherine. "Les indulgences romaines à la fin du Moyen Age." In *Du bon usage de la grâce: Pratiques des indulgences du Moyen Age à l'époque contemporaine*, edited by Esther Dehoux, Caroline Galland, and Catherine Vincent, 177-86. Lille: Presses universitaires du Septentrion, 2021.
Vincent, Catherine. "Pour un inventaire des sanctuaires et lieux de pèlerinages français." In *Hagiographie et culte des saints dans la France méridionale*

(*XIIIᵉ–XVᵉ siècles*), Cahiers de Fanjeaux 37, 267–81. Toulouse: Privat, 2002.
Vincent, Catherine, and Jacques Pycke, eds. *Cathédrale et pèlerinage aux époques médiévales et modernes*. Louvain-la-Neuve: Collège Érasme / Universiteitsbibliotheek, 2010.
Vincent, Jeanne-Françoise, Daniel Dory, and Raymond Verdier, eds. *La construction religieuse du territoire*. Paris: L'Harmattan, 1995.
Vincent-Cassy, Mireille. "Pèlerinages et processions à la fin du Moyen Age: L'exemple parisien." in *Cathédrale et pèlerinage aux époques médiévales et modernes*, edited by Catherine Vincent and Jacques Pycke, 21–39. (Louvain-la-Neuve: Collège Érasme / Universiteitsbibliotheek, 2010.
Vocino, Giorgio. "Le traslazioni di reliquie in età carolingia: Uno studio comparativo." In *Del visibile credere*, edited by Davide Scotto, 217–64. Florence: Olschki, 2011.
Vogel, Cyrille. *Le pécheur et la pénitence au Moyen Age*. Paris: Éditions du Cerf, 1969.
Walker, Peter. *Holy City, Holy Places: Christian Attitudes to Jerusalem and the Holy Land in the Fourth Century*. Oxford: Clarendon Press, 1990.
Ward, Benedicta. *Miracles and the Medieval Mind: Theory, Record and Events, 1000–1215*. Philadelphia: University of Pennsylvania Press, 1987.
Webb, Diana. "Saint James in Tuscany: The Opera di San Jacopo of Pistoia and Pilgrimage to Compostela." *Journal of Ecclesiastical History* 50 (1999): 207–34.
Wipszycka, Ewa. "Les pèlerinages chrétiens dans l'Antiquité tardives: Problèmes de définitions et de repères temporels." *Byzantinoslavica* 56 (1995): 429–45.
Wirth, Jean. *L'image à la fin du Moyen Age*. Paris: Éditions du Cerf, 2011.
Wirth, Jean. "Théorie et pratique de l'image sainte à la veille de la Réforme." *Bibliothèque d'humanisme et renaissance* 48 (1986): 319–59.
Wolf, Gerhard. *Salus populi romani: Die Geschichte römischer Kultbilder im Mittelalter*. Weinheim: Wiley-VCH Verlag, 1990.
Zadora-Rio, Elisabeth. "Lieux d'inhumation et espaces consacrés: Le voyage d'Urbain II en France (août 1095–août 1096)." In *Lieux sacrés, lieux de culte, sanctuaires*, edited by André Vauchez, 197–213. Rome: École Française de Rome, 2000.
Zanzi, Luigi. *Sacri monti e dintorni: Studi sulla cultura religiosa e artistica della Controriforma*. Milan: Jaca Book, 2005.
Ziglioli, Roberto. *L'apparizione e il santuario di Caravaggio*. Caravaggio: Lyasis, 1992.
Zimmermann, Michel. "La consécration des églises de Cerdagne aux Xe et XIe siècle: Une territorialisation de la foi." *Études Roussillonnaises* 11 (2005): 65–85.

Index

Agaune, Abbey of Saint-Maurice, 46, 215
Alfonso VII, king of Castile, 211
Alphonso II, king of Asturais, 74, 208
Amadour, saint, 77, 184; relics of, 196
Ambrose, saint, 107, 214, 223; relics of, 46
Andrew, apostle and saint, relics of, 76
Anthony, saint (desert father), 54
Anthony of Padua, saint, 161, 226, 236; shrine church of, 97, 223
Assisi, 232; Basilica of Saint Francis, 3, 97, 164, 130, 183; Santa Maria degli Angeli, 130, 138–39, 229, 232–33; San Damiano, 233
Augustine of Hippo, saint, 18, 22, 142, 144; relics of, 235

Baldwin II, emperor of Latin Kingdom of Constantinople, 88
Bari, 68, 166
Bartholomew, apostle and saint, relics of, 77
Basel, Council of (1431–1449), 114, 120, 247
Benedict, saint, 20, 54; relics of, 67–68; rule of, 65, 176
Benedict XIII, pope, 217
Bernadino of Siena, 233, 236
Bernard d'Angers, 62, 188
Bernard of Clairvaux, saint, 66, 79, 103, 227, 232
Bethlehem, 35, 50, 88, 97, 115

Birgitta of Sweden, saint, 7, 161, 177,
Bologna, 183; San Domenico, 97, 235; Santo Stefano, 71, 131
Boniface IX, pope, 228–29
Boniface VIII, pope, 79, 139, 228, 247
Boulogne-sur-Mer, 216; Notre Dame de Boulogne, 151, 217
Brigittines, 160–61
Bruges, 92, 131, 171; Basilica of the Holy Blood, 152

Caesarius of Arles, 25, 144
Calvin, John, 99, 24. *See also* Protestant Reformation
Canterbury Cathedral, 91, 97, 204, 206, 226, 230. *See also* Thomas Becket of Canterbury
Canterbury Tales, 5, 84
Carmelites (including Discalced), 161, 217, 237
catacombs, 39, 60, 82, 119, 116
Catherine of Alexandria, saint, 196
Catherine of Siena, saint, 53, 236
Celestine V, pope and saint, 229
Charlemagne, 46, 56, 60, 75–76, 101, 165, 208, 223, 244; "Field of Charlemagne," 178
Charles I of Anjou, king of Sicily, 79, 234
Charles IV, Holy Roman Emperor, 209
Charles of Blois, duke, 151, 156, 172–73
Charles the Bald, 40, 60, 83, 210, 224

INDEX

Charles V, king of France, 86, 171, 173, 215–16
Charles VI, king of France, 215–16
Chartres, 83, 86, 100–101, 216
Cistercian Order, 69, 73, 91, 103, 227, 237, 239
Clement IX, pope, 232
Clement V, pope, 85, 92, 203
Clement VI, pope, 92, 140
Clement VII, pope, 217, 230
Cluny (Abbey and Cluniac Order), 55, 66, 67–68, 70, 74, 232
Conques, Church of Sainte-Foy, 63, 67, 178, 180. See also Foy of Conques
Conrad II, Holy Roman Emperor, 209
Constantine, emperor, 6, 19, 36, 40, 42, 70, 72, 86, 88, 214
Constantinople, 22, 41–45, 73, 84, 86, 88, 120, 215; Hagia Sophia, 43; Latin Patriarch of, 87
Corpus Christi (feast and procession of), 91–93, 164
Crusade (and crusaders), 70, 73, 88, 138, 169, 183, 228, 249; Albigensian, 130; First Crusade, 71, 225–26; Fourth Crusade, 44, 84, 86–88; Second Crusade, 79; Seventh Crusade (first crusade of Louis IX), 154
Cuthbert, saint, relics of, 176

Daniel the Stylite, saint, 41
Denis of Paris, saint, 33, 210
Devotio Moderna, 118
Dominicans (and Dominican Order), 79, 91–92, 215, 235

Edmund of Abingdon, saint, relics of, 227
Elisabeth of Hungary, saint, relics of, 227
Eucharistic relics and miracles, 91–96, 228. See also Holy Blood, cult, relics, and miracles of
Eugenius IV, pope, 93, 229
Eusebius of Caesarea, 19

Fécamp, 70, 92
Ferdinand I, king of Castille, 211
Fleury, Saint-Benoît-sur-Loire, 62, 67–68
Foy of Conques, saint, 62–63, 67, 127. See also Conques, Church of Sainte-Foy
Francis of Assisi, saint, 91, 97, 126, 129, 138, 149, 163, 183, 233, 236, 239; feast day of, 138; relics of, 163, 226
Franciscans (and Franciscan Order), vii, 91, 95, 103, 108, 115, 138, 163, 232–34, 244; Observants, 108, 149, 233, 246; Reformed, 135; Third Order, 138, 219, 236

Geneva, Saint Peter's Basilica, 81
George, saint, 152, 213, 221
Gilles, saint, 55–56; relics of, 55, 180. See also Saint-Gilles
Great Schism, the, 140, 217, 228, 230, 246
Gregorian Reforms, 55, 64, 138, 183,
Gregory IX, pope, 163, 226–27, 232, 239
Gregory of Tours, 25, 29, 33, 46, 198
Gregory the Great (d. 604), 7, 20, 22, 45, 50, 54, 78, 119, 186,
Gregory VII, pope, 64
Gregory XI, pope, 113, 227
Guinefort (the Holy Greyhound), saint, 240–41

Henry II, Holy Roman Emperor, 208
Henry II, king of England, 77, 101, 127
Henry IV, Holy Roman Emperor, 210
Henry VI, king of England, 206
Holy Blood, cult, relics, and miracles of, 70, 93–96. See also Bruges: Basilica of the Holy Blood
Holy Land, 55, 87–88, 95, 125, 163, 169, 171, 183, 226, 228; as holy site, 35–37, 87; relics from, 208,

225; travel and pilgrimage to, 5, 50, 66, 70–73, 117, 130–31, 138, 174, 232. *See also* Jerusalem; New Holy Land
Holy Shroud (including of Cadouin and of Turin), 73, 89–90, 119, 216–17, 223
Homobonus, saint, 85, 197–98
Honorius III, pope, 226

iconoclasm, 44–45, 245
icons and images, 96–99
indulgences, 54, 76, 85, 91–93, 95, 99, 104, 113–14, 117, 119, 131, 133, 193–95, 209, 217, 225–32, 245–46; plenary indulgence, 91, 114, 138–39, 226, 233, 242, 247–48. *See also* jubilee indulgence
Innocent III, pope, 88, 138, 164, 197
Innocent IV, pope, 97, 227
Innocent VI, pope, 209
Innocent VIII, pope, 246
Irenaeus of Lyon, saint, 33
Isidore, saint, relics of, 211

James the Greater, apostle and saint, 74–77, 86, 137, 181, 189–90; feast of, 221; images of, 96, 155; as *Matamoros,* 75; relics of, 76, 85, 165, 191, 220. *See also* Santiago de Compostela
James the Lesser, apostle and saint, 190; relics of, 38
Jerome, saint, 7, 35, 38
Jerusalem, 32, 35–37, 43–44, 70, 117, 171, 181, 246–47; Golgotha (Calvary), viii, 35–36, 59, 92, 116, 185; Holy Sepulcher, viii, 19, 22, 36–37, 50, 70–72, 130–31, 90–91, 110, 130–32, 136, 152; Holy Sepulcher relics from, 89, 204, 228; Mount of Olives, 71, 97, 116, 126; Mount Zion, 12, 37, 115; Temple, the (aka Temple of Solomon), 7, 11–13, 17, 35–36, 43, 59, 61, 119, 186. *See also* New Jerusalem
Jesuits (Society of Jesus), 161, 237
Jesus Christ: icons of, 7; relics of, 70–71, 119, 181, 208. *See also* Holy Blood, cult, relics, and miracles of; Holy Shroud; Passion relics; True Cross
Joan of Arc, 195
John the Baptist, saint, 20, 54, 71, 74, 149; feast of, 144, 149, 230; relics of, 87, 119, 181, 208
John VIII, pope, 226
John XXII, pope, 92, 99, 163, 230
jubilee indulgence, 119, 137–40, 225–32, 246–47. *See also* indulgences
Juliana of Liège (or of Mont-Cornillon), 91
Julien of Brioude, saint, 33

Kempe, Margery (d. ca. 1438), 5, 96

Lateran Council, Fourth (1215), 167, 226
Leo X, pope, 114, 117, 229
Leonard, saint, relics of, 165, 180. *See also* Noblat
Lérins island, 24–25, 151, 154, 160
Loreto, 183; Basilica della Santa Casa, 248; Notre-Dame of, 5, 113–15, 130, 217, 219, 229, 237; Virgin of, 129
Louis IX, king of France and saint, 77, 88–90, 154, 211, 214–16; relics of, 215
Louis XI, king of France, xi, 114, 148, 217
Louis XII, 218
Louis of Toulouse/Anjou, saint, relics of, 163
Lourdes, Basilica of Our Lady of, 1; grotto, 51, 147
Luther, Martin, 111, 121, 209, 245. *See also* Protestant Reformation

Mammes, saint, relic of, 88
Mark, saint, relic of, 87
Martial of Limoges, saint, 33, 68
Martin of Tours, saint, 20, 29, 47, 144–45; cloak/relic of, 45–46; *Vita Martini* of Sulpicius Severus, 30
Martin V, pope, 95, 230
Martyrium (*martyria*), 6, 21–22, 28, 36, 81
Mary Magdalene, saint, 77–80, 86; relics of, 234–35
Mary, the Blessed Virgin: Black Madonna, 83, 101, 128, 184, 234; cult and veneration of, 100–114, 117, 126, 136, 147–49, 151–54, 156, 157, 161, 166, 194, 210, 216, 218, 221–22, 229, 239, 247; feasts of, 227, 230; images, icons, or statues of, 43, 83, 95, 97, 99, 100, 105, 108–13, 119, 127–29, 148, 150, 165, 192, 194, 234, 236; miracles, apparitions, or visions of, 101, 103–7, 128, 133, 141, 147, 149, 160, 185, 218, 242, 244; relics of, 71, 87, 100, 208
Matthew, saint, relics of, 76
Maurice, saint (and the martyrs of the Theban Legion), 85; relics of, 46, 101, 166, 191
Maurice, saint, relics of, 101
Médard, saint, 60. *See also* Soissons: Saint-Médard
Michael, archangel and saint, 20, 48–52, 62, 126, 130, 144, 208, 244; apparition of, 7, 48, 133, 146, 157–59, 193; cult of, 50, 144, 232,; feast day of, 174, 193; Order of, 217; sanctuaries of, xiii, 132, 239–40. *See also* Mont-Saint-Michel; Mount Gargano
Milan, 32, 45–46, 86, 97, 183, 218, 223, 230, 235

Mithras, cult and sanctuaries of, 19, 49, 51
monasticism, 64–69
Montecassino, 20, 41, 54, 67–68, 181
Mont-Saint-Michel, 50, 52, 126, 132, 227, 229; miracles at, 151; pilgrimage to, 173–75, 184; the *Revelatio* (foundation story for), 158–60; royal visits to, 216–27
Mount Gargano (Apulia), 41, 126, 130, 132, 156–59, 172, 174, 193, 232; Grotto of Saint Michael, 7, 20, 48–52, 130, 132, 141, 146, 158, 185, 244; Monte Sant'Angelo, 41, 49, 146, 152, 160, 170, 181, 193, 208, 224–25, 228–29, 232

New Holy Land, 88–91, 113–15. *See also* New Jerusalem
New Jerusalem, 13, 90, 95–96, 116, 118–21, 221. *See also* New Holy Land
Nicholas V, pope, 95, 227, 229, 247
Nicholas, saint, relics of, 68, 154, 166
Noblat, 165; Saint-Léonard-de-Noblat, 171, 178, 180
novena (8-day prayer period), 47, 145, 196

Ouen, saint, relics of, 224–25

Paris, 46, 76, 83, 86, 89–90, 93, 101, 131, 184, 209–10; Notre Dame (cathedral), 83, 86, 215–16; Saint-Germain-des-Prés (monastery), 46, 74, 186; Sainte-Chapelle, 88–90, 209, 214–15. *See also* Saint-Denis, Abbey of
Passion relics (including Crown of Thorns), 60, 70, 88–90, 209, 214–15. *See also* Holy Blood, cult, relics, and miracles of; True Cross
Patrick, saint, Purgatory of, 51–53
Paul, apostle and saint, 18, 38; relic (head) of, 23

Peter Martyr, saint, 97; relics of, 235
Peter, apostle and saint, 38–39, 41, 51, 68, 70, 189; tomb or relics of, 22, 40, 120, 131, 137. *See also* Rome: Saint Peter's Basilica (including the Vatican)
Philip, saint, relics of, 28
Philip II Augustus, king of France, 83, 211
Philip II, king of Sapin, 209
Philip IV the Fair, King of France, 93, 215
Philip IV, king of Spain, 218
Philip VI, king of France, 216–17
Portiuncula, 91, 138, 232. *See also* Assisi: Santa Maria degli Angeli
processions, 9, 28, 37, 46, 80–81, 87, 95, 99, 105, 119, 172, 208, 221, 240; Corpus Christi, 92, 164; of images and statues, 119, 126–27, 165–66; intercessory, 50, 86; of relics, 31–32, 81, 164–66, 194, 21, 224–25
Protestant Reformation, 2, 95, 99, 121, 237, 239, 245–46
Puy-en-Velay, le, 83, 86, 132, 178, 180; Notre-Dame du Puy, 101, 216, 230

Rainier, saint, relics of, 191
Riquier, saint, relics of, 211–12
Robert of Arbrissel, 175
Rocamadour, 77, 101–2, 127, 155, 171, 176, 180, 184–85, 196, 216, 245
Romain, saint, relics of, 224
Rome, 10–12, 20, 23, 38–42, 44–46, 49, 51, 53, 55, 59–60, 65, 70, 74, 92, 98, 103, 114, 118–21, 125, 129–31, 164–65, 170–72, 177, 246; Church of the Holy Apostles, 38, 40; icon of the virgin, 129, 165; pilgrims and pilgrimage to Rome, 5, 137–40, 181–83, 189–90, 228, 237; Saint John the Lateran, basilica, 7, 40, 59, 67, 119, 140, 181, 231; Saint Paul Outside the Walls, basilica, 38, 119, 139; Saint Peter's Basilica (including the Vatican), 3, 38–40, 46, 67, 119–21, 130–31, 135, 137, 139–40, 165, 170, 186, 211, 227, 228, 231; Santa Croce in Gerusalemme, 59, 119, 131; Santa Maria in Trastevere, 100; Santa Maria Maggiore, 23, 38, 99–100, 119, 140; *Sancta Sanctorum*, 7, 59, 119
Rosalia, saint, relics of, 243–44
Rouen, Abbey of Saint Ouen, 224–25

Saint-Denis, Abbey of, 46, 60, 76, 86, 191, 210–11, 215–16; Hilduin of, 60, 211; Suger of, 191, 210; town of, 32
Saint-Gilles (abbey, town, shrine of), 55, 130, 141, 146, 178, 180, 183, 191, 245
Saint-Riquier (Centula), monastery of, 60, 186
Santiago de Compostela, 5, 55, 96, 114, 163, 170–72, 177–81, 189, 190, 204, 217, 230; *Liber Sancti Jacobi/Codex Calixtinus*, 75; pilgrimage to, 5, 137–38, 181, 183, 232; pilgrims' guide to, 56, 178–80, 191 sanctuary of, 74–77, 130, 155
Saturninus of Toulouse, saint, 33. *See also* Toulouse, Saint Sernin
Sebastian, saint, 110, 222; relics of, 60, 198n70, 211
Simeon the Stylite, saint, relics of, 41
Sinai, Saint-Catherine, Monastery, 42–43, 171
Sixtus IV, pope, 120, 233, 247
Soissons, 87, 101, 221; Saint-Médard, monastery, 60, 210–11, 221, 224

Spoleto, 131, 149, 183, 190
Stephen Protomartyr, saint and protomartyr, relic of, 87
Subiaco, 54, 141
Sutri, 51, 52, 170, 240

Theban Legion, martyrs of. *See* Maurice, saint
Thomas, apostle and saint, 7, 87
Thomas Aquinas, saint, 92; relics of, 223, 235
Thomas Becket of Canterbury, saint, 5, 84, 91, 97, 204–6, 226, 230. *See also* Canterbury Cathedral
Toulouse, Saint Sernin, 76, 85, 165, 223, 230
Tours, Basilica of Saint Martin, 32, 45–46, 130, 171, 216, 224, 245; Marmoutier, 29, 65
Trent, Council of, 2, 118, 143, 202, 231, 242
True Cross (cross relics), 22, 35–37, 43, 59, 70–73, 81, 85, 87, 89, 209, 215

Turin, Chapel of the Holy Shroud, 217. *See also* Holy Shroud

Urban II, pope, 225
Urban IV, pope, 92, 164
Urban V, pope, 155, 223, 227
Urban VI, pope, 93, 113

Vatican, the. *See* Rome: Saint Peter's Basilica
Vatican, Second Vatican Council, 4
Venice, 218; Basilica of Saint Mark, 222, 229–30
Veronica, the veil of, 98–99, 129, 164
Vézelay, 77–80, 178, 235. *See also* Mary Magdalene, saint
Victricius, bishop of Rouen, 22
Vincent Ferrier, saint, 156; relics of, 84
Volto Santo (Holy Face), 73, 98, 181

Walsingham (Norfolk), 101

Zachary, Pope, 31

www.ingramcontent.com/pod-product-compliance
Lightning Source LLC
Chambersburg PA
CBHW030527230426
43665CB00010B/798